Nights of the Dispossessed: Riots Unbound

Edited by Natasha Ginwala, Gal Kirn, and Niloufar Tajeri

Columbia Books on Architecture and the City

R

I Trouble with Riots: Alternative Definitions and Political Histories

O Mnemonic Spatiality of Violence

T Figuration/Disfiguration: Racial Logic and Representation

S

Shake the Ground: A Foreword
Keller Easterling

Nights of the Dispossessed: Riots Unbound travels around the world to assay a contemporary and historical spectrum of riots. Natasha Ginwala, Gal Kirn, and Niloufar Tajeri previously collaborated on *Riots: Slow Cancellation of the Future*—an exhibition at ifa Gallery (Berlin and Stuttgart). The editors have since expanded the project into book form and commissioned new pieces from scholars, artists, poets, and activists to reflect on the limits, misconceptions, and paradoxes that attend these traumatic episodes.

While often treated as the violent eruptions that stand in contrast to peaceful protests, riots might be regarded instead as an overdue form of self-defense from what Kirn and Tajeri call "riots from above (see pages 189–191)." This violence of disenfranchisement and segregation is enacted through demolished buildings, murderous policing, selective enforcement of laws, and the denial of security and welfare. Riots do not tip protest into the realm of crime, but rather represent the exposure of a violation of rights or a crime of dispossession. Riots may be uprisings among the dispossessed to "renew the demos", as contributor Dilip Gaonkar writes (see page 54). Or they are moments of "repossession," as Asef Bayat describes them (see page 277).

A riot may mark a breakthrough moment that fuels sustained creative dissensus, but this is not a book about those feints and parries that surprise and outwit power. Instead, it deliberately maintains focus on the open wound of the riot. Riots manifest not as a series of rare, fleeting eruptions, but rather as a constant presence. Each episode leads away into others in every part of the world and sends the story streaming back into deeper and deeper histories.

This anthology also returns to pogroms and genocidal massacres. Chandraguptha Thenuwara writes about the ongoing retaliatory ethnic clashes in Sri Lanka. Gauri Gill contributes a text about the 1984 Sikh genocide in the aftermath of Indira Gandhi's assassination. And again, beyond the uprising, some of these riots are often directed from the top of the hierarchy.

Over the course of the spectrum, riots begin to decouple from declarations or ideological platforms. The riot does not exist exclusively to counter the power of capital. Hatred of the other is not its sole fuel. Riots are initiated from both above and below. They are only *inflected* by ideology, racial discrimination, and the political sentiments of a particular regime.

By maintaining its focus, *Riots Unbound* makes palpable a default temperament—a potential or *necessity* for violence. The violent acts of a dominant power violate the rights of others and require the same threshold of aggression to redress that violation. Riots are often what it takes to finally shake the ground, even as they risk triggering retaliation or a symmetrical escalation of tension. These are the paradoxes that riots reproduce.

The default violent temperament often seems like a symptom of the residual modern Enlightenment mind that cobbles together false wholes and Manichaean binaries to replace a god. An ideational monotheism holds other cultural forms in its thrall. A rational order will control an irrational multitude. The new must kill the old, and any one anointed group must kill the other to maintain an exceptional purity—to be the one and only.

Temperament can be the chief carrier of information. With the sound turned down on lexical, legal, or ideological expressions, it is easier to see this underlying disposition. An ideology that almost comically declares a single enemy and oscillates between ultimate and binary—telos and dialectic—may have a radical label while being dispositionally conservative. Communicating through temperament also offers tricks and affordances to the demagogues of any era who scramble and confuse ideological positions, because their real targets are weaponized binaries that help them maintain power. These figures can easily stage a fake riot and use temperaments surrounding a diametrically opposed political ideology to tighten their own hold on power.

But by refusing to look away from the riot, this anthology perhaps even inspires an activist imagination beyond its subject. For the demos that regards itself to be *the many* rather than *the one and only*, there are moments to plunge into the vortex of the riot and inject the necessary force. But to avoid reproducing paradoxes or delivering the very violence that often nourishes power and releases pressure, the book prompts activist crafts for dancing on the lip of that vortex to keep the pressure on.

A Slow Cancellation of the Future and the Fires Next Time

Natasha Ginwala
Gal Kirn
Niloufar Tajeri

The editing of this volume started in 2019, in a year when the environmental consequences of protracted capitalist crisis reached new heights and a massive surge of uprisings and riots spread across the globe.[1] For many commentators, the fresh wave of upri ings, citizens' movements, and revolutionary struggles lasted an unexpectedly long time. And what they achieved in time they matched in breadth: protests stretched across the globe, from Chileand Haiti, to Iraq and Lebanon, to Algeria, Iran, India, Sudan, and Hong Kong; from yellow and black vests in France to struggles in Bolivia, in Gaza/Palestine, and elsewhere. Furthermore, environmental movements and Indigenous activism rose as a planetary front against the corporatization of land and water resources, against toxicity as well as the displacement of communities.

Even if these various political initiatives did not share political programs or grievances, they nevertheless assumed a radical political form: they were confrontational and leaderless, with youth and impoverished classes at the forefront. In a period of deep and systemic crises of capitalism, sharpened racial violence, and communal tensions, it seems that we have finally entered a new age/cycle of riots. These uprisings lead us to assert that the master fictions of the sovereign nation-state have imploded further, while failures in the hegemonic silencing of the dispossessed have revealed the cracks in their governability. Militarist and extremist forces have galvanized riots and pogroms in a zealous onslaught, particularly against ethnic, religious, and sexual minority communities. In historic and recent episodes, communal trauma lasts for generations as the politico-legal apparatus consistently violates the social contract to protect its body politic. The search for "truth" amid such riots can remain a blood-soaked, torturous, and highly dangerous inquiry—in many cases decades later, the wait for justice still continues.

One of the central aims of this book is to bring together artistic works, political analysis, and urban research from across the world in an endeavor to "sense," chronicle, and think through riots and uprisings from the 1980s and the aftermath of the long crisis of 2008. This edited volume draws from our collaborative work on exhibitions and conferences, as well as ongoing dialogues with many of the writers and artists published herein. Our approach could be considered a bit "wild" for foregrounding interdisciplinary threads that swell beyond the confines of scholarly division to invite artistic observations, discontent, overtones of poetry, and present-day activism to occupy a shared temporality in *Nights of the Dispossessed*. The three following sections of the book cover artwork and research, urban theory and activism, and political/theoretical/philosophical interventions. These sections all start with a more detailed introduction that surveys different angles and provides summaries of the contributions.

● 1.   This research on riots dates to 2015–2016, when Gal Kirn and Niloufar Tajeri produced a series of writings and events under the title "Thinking a Monument to (Sub)Urban Riots" at the Akademie Schloss Solitude. In 2018 Natasha Ginwala curated the exhibition *Riots: Slow Cancellation of the Future* (January–April) at ifa Gallery (Berlin and Stuttgart). The accompanying public program, "Riots: Dissent and Spectres, Control and Ruptures," at Acud Macht Neu in Berlin in January 2018 (http://untietotie. org/en/documentation/riots-dissent-andspectres-control-and-ruptures), was collaboratively organized by Ginwala, Kirn, and Tajeri with various artists, theorists, and activists, whose voices and dialogues demonstrated the urgency of assembling the shared positions into the present volume.

Now—well into 2020—as we arrive at the conclusion of our editorial process, daily reality has changed dramatically. The radical rupture that is the COVID-19 pandemic has crystallized and intensified the contradictions of capitalist organization and reproduction. All of a sudden we are witnessing a global strike on the side of capital: a suspension of production in the major loci of the global economy in China has generated a shock wave of planetary scale, and, the pandemic has arrested or slowed down the logistical circuits of fiscal resources and people. These events have already resulted in a dramatic contraction of the global economy, with GDPs and overinflated financial indexes collapsing and a dramatic reduction in oil production and demand. The effects of the pandemic and the intensification of this crisis will be felt for a long while by everyone; the most dramatic toll, however, is being taken on millions of dispossessed and disenfranchised workers, on the psycho-social, economic, and political levels—beyond resolution through current health measures. While the Global North struggles to cautiously reopen economies, the circuit of detrimental impact yields an increase in hunger and the onset of famine elsewhere on the planet.

With regard to recent and imminent riots, the wide-scale civilian actions that arose alongside the pandemic have been paired with a forced withdrawal from the streets. A militaristic tendency has emerged in the international calls for a "war" against the virus. In many parts of the globe, the belligerence of the police and armed forces has been demonstrated through months of curfews and lockdown. One does not need to go far to discern that many of the measures taken actively contribute to a "warlike situation" that either confines people to domestic spaces where there is existing violence or pushes vulnerable groups toward exploitative work environments and overburdened health-care facilities. Such are the failures of a late neoliberalism that unleashes a collapsing infrastructure upon millions of vulnerable people within weeks of this global pandemic.

Moreover, we have entered a new phase in digital surveillance and data mapping, the necropolitics of exacerbated policing, attacks on civil liberties by authoritarian leaders, censorship of the media and activists, and rule by decree within the temporal knot of disease. Various hard-fought rights—especially political freedoms and the right to assembly and protest—are now limited or suspended for an indefinite period. In this way, the political effects of the pandemic may be read as a temporary defeat of the worldwide people's movements and uprisings of 2019 and early 2020. However, the COVID-19 pandemic has also slowed down our hyperconnected social lives and given us time to reflect on and reconfigure modes of strategizing and organizing for solidarity and strikes, for practices of care and community building. While some argue that the possibility of alternative futures has been closed, others demand a reimagined society even more fiercely in the face of a pandemic that so painfully proves that the current system fails even to secure life and basic subsistence. Every lockdown has its limits, and authorities that impose longer periods of mass confinement and deep surveillance—with likely repetitions in the future and the continued danger of economic meltdown—risk triggering a new epoch of riots. Already, while composing this introduction, we can see that serious food shortages for an ever-increasing portion of the global population have already become a reality and, with these shortages, food riots—arguably the earliest historical form of riot—have returned. Simultaneously, we are witnessing the response to police violence and racialization in the fires and fury in Minneapolis, which have spread across the United States to Hong Kong and beyond.

If Mark Fisher's diagnosis of "the slow cancellation of the future" tackled the sense that culture lost its ability to articulate the present in neoliberal times, we could expand this diagnosis to other fields and take note of the slow cancellation of our social and economic life, natural resources, and environments in the vein of Rob Nixon's "slow violence." As the tentacles of extractivism spread unevenly at a planetary level, the ubiquitous effort to create an atmosphere of "there is no alternative" is, in fact, rapidly canceling the future. In the time of the COVID-19 pandemic, we should therefore ask if this abstract speculative and destructive logic is not reaching its own limits. If a systemic limit is not internal to the logic of capitalist expansion—since capital knows no border, it will always readapt—the answers to the current crisis might differ from the "non-solutions" to the crisis of 2008 and be much more fundamental. We believe that riots, riotous uprisings, and strikes will play an important role in the aftermath of the current crisis—and give a clear response to the increasingly authoritarian systems that are already practicing worrisome levels of violence.

This book deals especially with the riotous activities of the dispossessed, with the riots and riotous uprisings that have occurred around the world in recent decades. There are contributions that examine and inhabit riotous uprisings in the United Kingdom, France, Germany, Sweden, Australia, and the United States as well as in South Africa, Sri Lanka, India, Tunisia, and Egypt. The commentaries assembled here challenge the dominant view of riots that demonizes, moralizes, and criminalizes rioters. Rather, this book brings together a wide range of authors who advocate not only for a deeper understanding of riots but also for the necessity of recognizing the dialectics of riots, their violent and emancipatory core, and the traumatic fragments that inform future generations. This more antisystemic approach might run into the difficulty of "romanticizing" riotous immediacy that is not bound to any kind of party organization, or of seeing riots as merely the short-lived actualization of the Commune. However, we hope to escape this trap by looking closely and slicing open what the term "riot" actually means as a pluralist and recurring manifestation—how and why it is deployed and interpreted in so many different sociopolitical constellations. How do the image and the analysis of the political event change if we say "riot," "uprising," or "rebellion"? What happens if we compare the concept of "riot" with other forms of political and urban resistance and calls for collective action? How might the revolutionary potential of rioters' demands be otherwise read within the circuits of recent history and contemporary society? And how are we to understand the transgressive matrices of public rebellion when riots frequently grow into larger revolts, insurgencies, and systemic transformation? The difficulty in approaching the matter and energy that is the riot—as a certain limit concept of political theory—shall be investigated through different registers, enabling a spectrum of readings that have so far not been put together as an ensemble. Current critical research on riots and uprisings has offered a solid analysis of immiseration, racism, and capitalist dispossession and has contributed to a deeper understanding of riots, but the most fundamental "trouble" with riots persists. What is to be done, and how can we think about the highly paradoxical and negative epistemology of riots? Martin Luther King Jr. once remarked that "riots are the language of the unheard."[2] Communities rendered

● 2.   From Martin Luther King Jr.'s TV talk with Mike Wallace, *60 Minutes*, September 27, 1967, https://www.youtube.com/watch?v=_K0BWXjJv5s.

invisible and unheard become heard and visible in the uproar of riots. Their "opening scene" marks a peculiar space and temporality that already announces the tragic event of the riot: in the moment that communities and the systemic injustices they experience become visible, they are condemned as irrational, and their fury is denounced as a fundamental violation of civic life. Rioters become marked as unpolitical beings, harshly labeled as feral agents and a sick mob. This definitive negation has become a justification for the historical blind spot around riotous cycles throughout history (see Dilip Goankar's contribution to this volume).

The relegation of riots to the violent mob has justified an asymmetrical and brutal use of force by state authorities: the mob is molded by and visible only for the police baton, oppression, and the criminal (in)justice system, while their grievances continue to be ignored and invisible to the general public. The game of numbers has been played in a vile manner, while party-motivated demonstrations and pogroms fueled by extreme right-wing and militarist forces avoid the singular image of "rioter" and refuse responsibility for their devastation (see Gauri Gill's project and Chandraguptha Thenuwara's contribution to this volume). In 1960, Elias Canetti wrote "One of the most striking traits of the inner life of a crowd is its feeling of being persecuted." What happens when state forces provoke the crowd? Governments have repeatedly orchestrated mob violence, and the anti-Sikh genocide (1984) as well as the recent Delhi riots (2020) are a case in point: perpetrators affiliated with political parties and the policing system move freely, while the mainstream news media is at best blindsided by state regimes and at worst actively conceals their abuse; legal accountability goes "missing in action."

This brings us to the next assertion: riots as collective actions and events are themselves contradictory in orientation and outcome. Just like any group, the dispossessed are split and politically incoherent, as is demonstrated in the multiplicity of riotous events that are covered in this volume. On the side of the established order, there is an evident ideological investment in encouraging such splits and focusing only on the violence of riots and uprisings, which makes building solidarity a very challenging activity.

In this book, we want to articulate three major concerns: *first*, that riots with racial/ethnic roots are often instigated by authorities that orient the fears/prejudices of one dispossessed group against another, and result in lasting scars and traumas within society. *Second*, riots of the dispossessed have empowered the lower classes and generally are openly directed at untenable, subhuman living and social conditions. Here analyses contribute to thinking about "riots from above" (see Gal Kirn and Niloufar Tajeri's co-authored essay in this volume) in forms like urban destruction (Kirn and Tajeri), austerity unbound, excessive police violence, and controlled and uncontrolled politico-economic practices that destroy the social fabric of poorer neighborhoods. *Third*, the representation of riots is a major focus, since for far too long the visual and sonic corpus of riots has appeared before us only as a disjunction within normative society; it is given a brief moment before being moved into darkness and buried in archives. Through the work of poets, filmmakers, artists, and anthropologists, we can glean methods of call and response as well as lasting impressions that move beyond recycled tropes of the front lines of riots and rebellion.

The riot (practiced) "from above" can be seen as a trigger for riots from below. In other words, riots and uprisings can be seen as an intensification of the everyday life of those who live in poor urban and suburban neighborhoods. Structural conditions never sleep, while "riots from above" are also more pervasive at night. The nocturnal life of riots challenges the division of labor, the division between day and night, the regime of what is expected and accepted in our societies. Or as Frantz Fanon describes the liberation from colonial and racist repressions of the state:

> The first thing the colonial subject learns is to remain in his [or her] place and not overstep its limits. Hence the dreams of the colonial subject are muscular dreams, dreams of action, dreams of aggressive vitality. I dream I am jumping, swimming, running, and climbing. I dream I burst out laughing, I am leaping across a river and chased by a pack of cars that never catches up with me. During colonization the colonized subject frees himself [or herself] night after night between nine in the evening and six in the morning.[3]

Riots strike at the very core of the modern capitalist state—property, public order, and a monopoly on violence—by trespassing the limits imposed on Black bodies, on postcolonial subjects, and on discriminated against and racialized subjects. By trespassing the limits on action and movement, visibility and the occupation of space. By trespassing the limits on the power and strength of the colonized and racialized. Within the riot, power and strength are retrieved and exercised, and the unequal social contract is broken and reversed. Thus, the riot is a challenge to the property regime and to the monopoly over violence that has been a building block—part of an old, unequal social contract—of liberal and conservative ideology. Riots should be considered a vital part of a *counterhistory of violence* that brackets the only accepted state or market of violence, on the one hand, and generates the possibility for emancipatory changes, on the other.

The extractivist drives that have surged during pandemic capitalism are worsening the lives of increasingly larger segments of humanity. Throughout history, riots and epidemics have been testing grounds for surveillance and control measures. Combine this with the fact that, now, late neoliberal society has effectively dismantled liberal democracy as well as many of the technocratic beliefs that were supposed to sustain our ecosystems and the well-being of humanity in the future. This does not mean that we are about to see the final and catastrophic end of the world but that there have been many "ending worlds"—as feminist anti-racist scholar Kathryn Yusoff puts it, while "the Anthropocene might seem to offer a dystopic future that laments the end of the world... imperialism and ongoing (settler) colonialisms have been ending worlds for as long as they have been in existence."[4]

Riots, however, seem no longer to be only the domain of humanity. It seems more and more that we are entering an age where planetary forces act in rage, through ecological and pandemic riots against

3. Frantz Fanon, *The Wretched of the Earth* (New York: Grove Press, 1963), 15.
4. Kathryn Yusoff, preface to *A Billion Black Anthropocenes or None* (Minneapolis: University of Minnesota Press, 2018), https://manifold.umn.edu/read/untitled-5f0c83c1-5748-4091-8d8e-72bebca5b94b/section/b17181bd-c615-4a1b-8cb1-5c0fa03afd74.

humanity. This disruption against the capitalocene is not a "revenge narrative" of cinematic motifs or biblical times but rather an organic implosion in the earth's system: overheated oceans and solar radiation, bush and forest fires from Australia to the Amazon Basin, locust swarms across South Asia and parts of the African continent that decimate agrarian lands in the blink of an eye, the proliferation of diseases through wildlife, and mass extinctions that ravage biodiversity beyond its capacity to regenerate.

Frederick Douglass argued, "Those who profess to favor freedom yet deprecate agitation, are men who want crops without plowing up the ground; they want rain without thunder and lightning. They want the ocean without the awful roar of its many waters."[5] The question for our present is how to comprehend a thermodynamics that simultaneously governs burning cars and flaming forests. What kind of future comes after such violent scenarios?

A vital lesson from climate history is that ruling classes don't always survive climate transitions, or at least are slowed on their path into barbarity. Feudalism's class-enforced monocultures crumbled in the face of the Little Ice Age: famine and disease quickly followed. As a result, with the onset of the Black Death, webs of commerce and exchange didn't just transmit disease— they became vectors of mass insurrection. Almost overnight, peasant revolts stopped being local affairs and became large-scale threats to the feudal order.[6] Today we are entering into an age of bifurcation, where the declaration of a state of emergency is no longer exceptional and becomes a part of a longer temporality. This does not mean we are all affected in an identical way; rather, the continuous emergency intensifies existing asymmetries and with that can radicalize into an age of riots.

"Unlike the strike, it is hard to tell when and where the riot starts and ends," writes Joshua Clover. "This is part of what allows the riot to function both as a particular event and as a kind of holographic miniature of an entire situation, a world-picture."[7] Riots expose the antidisciplinary core of a society: traces of riots lurk and inhabit social relations, becoming the (un)even scars of a city or countryside. In the phenomenology of the multitude and "surplus life," there lies an emancipatory potential that may in part be unmanifest and unnameable, yet is easily resurrected in the restless flows of new generations—at times through demonstrations and strikes, at other times as riots or one of the many forms of uprising that refuse the "loophole of retreat."[8]

5.   From his "West India Emancipation" speech, delivered in Canandaigua, New York, on August 4, 1857. Frederick Douglass, *Two Speeches by Frederick Douglass* (Rochester, NY: C. P. Dewey, 1857), 22.

6.   Jason W. Moore and Raj Patel, "Unearthing the Capitalocene: Towards a Reparations Ecology," *ROAR Magazine 7* (Autumn 2017), https://roarmag.org/magazine/moore-patel-seven-cheap-things-capitalocene.

7.   Joshua Clover, *Riot. Strike. Riot: The New Era of Uprisings* (New York: Verso, 2016), 123.

8.   See Harriet A. Jacobs, *Incidents in the Life of a Slave Girl, Written by Herself*, ed. Jean Fagan Yellin (1861; repr., Cambridge, MA: Harvard University Press, 1987); and Saidiya Hartman, "Extended Notes on the Riot," *e-flux journal* 105 (December 2019), https://www.e-flux.com/journal/105/302565/extended-notes-on-the-riot.

The Manifesto Unwritten
Satch Hoyt

SATCH HOYT

R

The manifesto, dog eared, unwritten
The charter sadly still unread.
Yeah we been drowned in cold derision
Yeah we been classified as dead.
Too many centuries of revolutions
have been fought in dis ere head
Memory capacity done imploded
into confusion undefined.
Let's huddle close this morning breakfast,
count our limbs, pick scabs off sores,
Pay respect to the ancestors,
place offerings at secret shrines.
Know, little sister, little brother,
libations can open closed doors...

So stay real close, no, don't you wander,
tip toe round un-detonated mines
That various aggressors planted
in our yam fields, and in our minds.
See dread grim reaper back to harvest
all the death that he has sown.
Discarded, mangled metal corrosion
Unwanted war arms souvenirs
Scattered on strangled border landscapes
To de-marcate us from our soul keepsakes
and many venerated peers.

But, dude, it ain't so hip to speak of revolution
When all you want is a wage rise
From your exploitative corporation
Whose only goal is to capitalize.
The centuries of colonialism you inherited
in your diluted D N A
is rooted in sugar cane and cotton contusions.
He who stokes fire, must breathe smoke
So-li-d-arity, screamed out a comrade
In some mother tongue unspoke,
bring some water for this traitor
then we'll calmly watch him choke.
The distorted PA system's feedback
Hits a threshold way past pain,
to endure this ghostly frozen moment
one needs to be reborn again.
On future battlefields of new tomorrows
Boots on the ground will not exist
The power cyber cyborg maneuvers
Will be strategized from AI hit lists.

Satch Hoyt, *Riot*, 2014, wood, water hose, crystals, 33 × 24 × 7 cm,
Photograph courtesy of Trevor Lloyd Morgan.

Trouble with Riots: Alternative Definitions and Political Histories

Introduction
Gal Kirn

Riots and rioters have long been described in an array of extremely negative terms and moralistic tropes that disparage the supposedly irrational behavior of mobs or crowds. Within political history, riots have been seen as antipolitical and as outside the normative political realm, where rational political language and a set of respected rules define how to deal with public matters in prescribed political spaces. Thus, this section outlines the initial theoretical trouble with riots: What does the riot challenge as a word, as a political concept, and as a form of collective action? Also, should we not speak of a rebellion or an uprising rather than of a riot? Who is the political subject of the riot? Does the riot have a proper or stable form, or any precise political goal? Contributions to this section, "Trouble with Riots: Definitions and Alternative Political Histories," address these questions in their own ways to highlight the dissenting nature of riots.

To some, the riot can be defined as a "limit concept" that radically undermines the established horizons of political theory. Dilip Gaonkar considers the complexity of the study of riots:

> [Riots] are prompted by a submerged wrong or a fracture, an insult or an injury, an offense or an outrage that is gnawing and clawing its way to the surface. Or they might attest to the flailing of a cramped and besieged people "waiting to exhale" and find a voice. Be that as it may, most riots are collective, if not coordinated, acts of political protest. There are discernible patterns in these contentious moments and events. (See page 32 in this volume)

Gaonkar's essay retraces the two contentious approaches to riots in the history of political thought: the first views them in a revisionist and psychological way that operates around the term "crowd," and the second views them through the lens of social inequality and ethnic-religious differences. In short, riots point to the deep accumulation of contradictions and antagonisms in our societies, while at the same time they undermine the central pillars of capitalist liberal democracy: respect for public order, state monopoly over violence, and respect for property in its public or private form. One major thread through this section (and the book) is the chronicling of and thinking about how riots tell and contribute to a *counterhistory* of violence. Riots intervene in the dominant capitalist mode of production as well as the modes of domination that reinforce capitalism, such as urban exclusion and segregation, (post)colonialism, repression, and structural racism. This is precisely the point of Joshua Clover's contribution, which offers a rigorous dialectic of race and class categories, and which thinks about surplus population in a way that is pivotal to new "critical riot studies." Despite their negative nature, refusal, and violence, the counterhistory of riotous activities is also generative of new coalitions and emancipatory changes.

Riotous uprisings are thus not episodes of blind violence or mere self-righteous consumerism that can be defended as the "moral economy of the poor"; rather, they should be seen as political events in which political subjects are formed and transformative projects emerge.[1] And here another quandary arises: there is no consensus—even among our contributors—about who this political subject is. Are we speaking of the urban poor, tumultuous youth, Indigenous peoples, surplus populations, the *lumpenproletariat*, a rabble, mobs, or crowds? As editors of the book, we decided to highlight one unifying quality of riotous subjectivity: *the dispossessed*. The dispossessed are major agents of riots and are also the central and consistent targets of capital's enclosures with urban destruction and redevelopment projects, on the one hand, and criminalization and repression, on the other. The dispossessed are then all those made redundant by the structural force of capital and the exclusion of racialized bodies.

In a conversation with Natasha Ginwala, Vaginal Davis shares a personal testimony of riots in Los Angeles and the influences of Chicana culture, punk, feminism, and drag culture, which defy the heteronormative and masculine narrative of riots. To this underground history of rioting, we can add Elizabeth Povinelli's essay that maps how riots occur "inside a space of Indigenous refusal" and how riotous tensions play out amid group expressions of jealousy and reciprocity, forms of respect for ancestral beings, and the ever-invasive laws of settler governance.

Riots also carry an emancipatory potential worthy of further exploration, one that can detonate into real social changes. One such moment can be found in Ai Ogawa's poem on the riots that erupted in Los Angeles in 1992. Ogawa points to the riotous forms of poetry and to the sense and sound of riots. This expression of the riot—or of what comes in the aftermath of a riot, or perhaps even the promise of new riots—can be more powerful than brick walls and long, edited books. This riotous poem is complemented by an imagistic essay from Ala Younis that reflects on the bread riots in Egypt in 1977. The people's actions against World Bank and IMF policies spread new visions of popular leadership and martyrdom, which Younis analyzes in various Egyptian films.

Does the riot have a stable political form and expression? How can riots become revolutions, and must all revolutions start as riots? One vital characteristic of riots is that they do not follow plans, and we cannot prophesize future riotous formations and their results. Thomas Seibert's essay lucidly shows that riots uniquely perform an "excess." The riot is, as Seibert writes, "the communication of a resistance to communication itself" (see page 57 in this volume). Instead of giving a final definition of the term "riots," these contributions attempt the

- 1. E. P. Thompson, *Customs in Common* (New York: New Press, 1991).

difficult task of grasping riotous form, which escapes any formulaic definition. Nevertheless, the contributions do trace the unifying and uncontrollable force of riotous fury directed against the most blatant injustices of the past and the present. Riots will continue to occur until the structural reasons for their emergence are undone.

Demos Noir: Riot after Riot

Dilip Parameshwar Gaonkar

A riot is the language of the unheard.
—Martin Luther King Jr.

In recent decades, riots have been flaring up with increasing frequency across the globe. They are no longer confined to those poor countries in the Global South riddled with corruption, civil strife, and bad governance. Riots have come north to affluent countries where liberal democracy, bolstered by durable constitutions and mature public institutions, has long flourished.[1] As is evident from the George Floyd protests sweeping the United States today (May–June 2020) and the *mouvement des gilets jaunes* in Paris in October 2018, riots have arrived, as they always do, with tumultuous clamor and disruption. These are not isolated episodes. They are part of a larger political phenomenon of eruptive direct action that has spread across a distressed and listless Euro-America. They were preceded by the Milwaukee Riots (August 2016), the Ferguson Riots (August 2014–August 2015), the Baltimore Riots (April–May 2015), and Occupy Wall Street (September 2011) in the United States; and the Greek Riots (December 2008), the Stockholm Riots (May 2013), the London Riots (August 2011), the Belfast Riots (2011, 2012, 2013), the anti-austerity demonstrations led by *indignados* in Spain (May 2011), the Direct Democracy Now actions in Greece (May 2010), and many more events in Europe.

Wikipedia lists twenty-four well-documented riots or riot-like episodes in 2019 alone, of which ten occurred in Euro-America. This list is by no means comprehensive. These are only the better-known and more discussed riots, the demonstrations that have commanded significant national and international media attention. The vast majority of minor and local riot-like incidents don't get reported in national media outlets and, therefore, don't make it to the Wikipedia list. In India, which has refined and elevated the politics of direct action into a high public art (as if it were a sly tribute to Mahatma Gandhi), hardly a day passes without a riot occurring someplace in the country. Even in allegedly disciplined, orderly, and authoritarian China, riots abound and are increasing sharply. According to the Chinese Academy of Social Sciences, in 2010 alone there were an estimated ninety thousand "mass group incidents" (MGI), an ingenious characterization of disorderly protests and riot-like events.[2] These MGIs are quite different from the Umbrella Movement of 2014 in Hong Kong, for example, which keeps erupting in new incarnations—first in 2019 and now again in 2020—provoked as always by transgressive policies of the People's Republic of China

1. The distinction between the peaceful and well-governed Global North and the raucous and poorly governed Global South is, at best, a relative proposition. Riots have never left the shores of Euro-America since the onset of modernity. They have been a regular feature of political life in Europe, under monarchical as well as republican forms of government, since the early modern period, if not earlier. However, there is a tendency to view each period of disorder, of which riots are a distinct sign, as a mere prelude to a new and enduring social order. Hence, the historical memory and attention, both scholarly and popular, tends to gravitate toward the making of a new political and socioeconomic order and imaginary. The times of agitation and unrest are seen as a passing sideshow and quickly forgotten.

2. "Protest and Dissent in China," Wikipedia, https://en.wikipedia.org/wiki/Protest_and_dissent_in_China.

designed to undermine the island's autonomy. It is uncanny that the Hong Kong protests and the George Floyd protests in the United States are unfolding in tandem, simultaneously beleaguering the world's two largest economic and military powers.

Riots are a recurrent phenomenon, and they occur pretty much everywhere. They have multiple triggers. As I have written elsewhere:

> People riot over all sorts of things—price of bread, oil and onion, publication of a book, screening of a film, drawing of a cartoon. They riot on account of police brutality, political corruption, and desecration of the holy places. They riot when subjected to ethnic or racial slurs (real or imagined) and when continuously deprived of basic necessities—water, electricity, and sanitation. They riot for being ill-treated at health-care facilities, for being denied entrance to once public, now privatized, spaces of pleasure and recreation, and generally for justice denied and petitions ignored. They riot after soccer games, cricket games, music concerts, and also before, during, and after elections. The list of occasions and grievances that can precipitate riots can be extended indefinitely.[3]

Such an indefinitely extendable list suggests that there is something fundamentally rotten in the state of the body politic across the globe today. Too many accumulated injuries and continuing grievances are haunting and fracturing political solidarities and polarizing people everywhere. As the spread of riots attests to the declining legitimacy of the prevailing order, no nation appears to be immune to this hollowing from within. This is why Pankaj Mishra characterizes our time as an "age of anger" and Peter Sloterdijk titles his psychopolitical investigations of the present *Rage and Time*.[4]

Not all riots are politically motivated—such as those resulting from excessive exuberance at music concerts or bitter disappointments at sports events or those stemming from drunken brawls and sheer hooliganism. However, one might contend that there are always stirrings of a political unconscious waiting to be deciphered in these allegedly apolitical outbursts. Perhaps these eruptions are prompted by a submerged wrong or a fracture, an insult or an injury, an offense or an outrage that is gnawing and clawing its way to the surface. Or they might attest to the flailing of a cramped and besieged people "waiting to exhale" and find a voice. Be that as it may, most riots are collective, if not coordinated, acts of political protest. There are discernible patterns in these contentious moments and events. They do not occur randomly. The American

3. Dilip Parameshwar Gaonkar, "After the Fictions: Notes Towards a Phenomenology of Demos," *e-flux journal* 58 (October 2014), https://www.e-flux.com/journal/58/61187/after-the-fictions-notes-towards-a-phenomenology-of-the-multitude.

4. Pankaj Mishra, *Age of Anger: A History of the Present* (New York: Farrar, Straus, and Giroux, 2017); Peter Sloterdijk, *Rage and Time: A Psychopolitical Investigation*, trans. Mario Wenning (New York: Columbia University Press, 2010).

riots cited earlier—as well as many others—are mostly related to historically fraught race relations, especially between young Black men and the police. The recent riots in Europe have often been triggered by the tension between immigrants and their reluctant host communities. Riots in Belfast are usually sectarian. In India, where riots are frequently sectarian, often pitting Hindus and Muslims against each other, there are also a multitude of other nonreligious triggers that can and do ignite riots. "Prison riots" are common in highly carceral societies like the United States and its neighbors in the Southern Hemisphere, especially Brazil. Then there are the "food riots" (also known as the "IMF riots") that began in the mid-1970s and continued with noticeable frequency for two decades in debt-ridden Third World countries in response to the forcible imposition of austerity measures by national governments. These measures, which caused extreme and disproportionate hardship for the lower strata of society, were imposed to secure debt relief from international financial organizations under the now discredited "structural adjustment" programs that promised to spur growth by facilitating free markets.[5] Finally, there are genocidal riots targeting minorities, often instigated and orchestrated from above, as in Sri Lanka, the former Yugoslavia during its breakup, Rwanda, Myanmar, and elsewhere.

"Riot" is a hybrid and polysemous label. It does not have a stable referent. It ranges widely from brawls and rowdyism at one end of the spectrum to genocides and pogroms at the other. While the former is trivialized as juvenile and futile, the latter is justly condemned as irredeemably horrendous and ghastly. Squeezed and tarnished in the middle are various types of politically charged protest riots, often mischaracterized, maligned, and denounced on account of their apparent proximity and resemblance to brawls as well as genocidal eruptions. This essay is concerned with political riots as a *mode of collective agency* and as a *form of direct action* employed by those who feel substantively excluded from the two established routes for seeking a redress of grievances, the legislative and the judicial. Rioters are simply those forced by reasons of contextual necessity to resort, in Eric Hobsbawm's words, to "collective bargaining by rioting."[6] They have, as they see it, no other option. Whatever the necessity and its embedded rationality, the price of rioting is that inerasable stigma of illegitimacy it must always bear. The felt urgencies of a riot, in all their rich phenomenological resonances, are soon forgotten. What lingers in memory, in recall and remembrance, is the disruptive tear in the social fabric, an uncivil breach of the social contract. As a result, riots are almost always portrayed and remembered negatively. Take, for instance, the popular image of the riots surrounding the assassination of Julius Caesar (44 BC), one of the earliest documented riots. Unshakably fixed for generations of readers, the canonical literary portrait of that event is given to us by Shakespeare: a masterful depiction of the frenzied mob of Roman

5. John Walton and David Seddon, *Free Market and Food Riots: The Politics of Global Adjustment* (Oxford: Blackwell Publishers, 1994).
6. Eric J. Hobsbawm, "The Machine Breakers (1952)," *in Labouring Men: Studies in the History of Labour* (1964; repr., New York: Anchor Books, 1967), 9.

citizens, volatile and gullible, easily swayed hither and yon at Caesar's funeral by the fiery orations delivered successively by Brutus and Marc Antony.[7] This essay is a modest attempt to resist and dismantle the weight of the powerful and highly sedimented interpretive tradition regarding riots and to recuperate and resituate riots as a legible mode of direct action.

I. Two Explanations

There are two dominant explanations for the persistence of riots and riot-like events: the psychosocial explanation that links riots to the phenomenon of crowds and crowd behavior and the socioeconomic explanation that links them to the intolerable consequences of poverty and inequality—hunger, hardship, deprivation, and suffering. Propounded by Scipio Sighele, Gabriel Tarde, and Gustave Le Bon in the last quarter of the nineteenth century, the first explanation came to prominence following the tumultuous days of the Paris Commune in 1871.[8] In their theorizations of crowds and crowd behavior, each of these three thinkers was decisively influenced by Hippolyte Taine's revisionary historical interpretation of the revolutionary crowds and mobs of the French Revolution.[9]

First Explanation: The Psychosocial Crowd
Unlike Jules Michelet, who celebrates the people—embodied by the Third Estate—as the legitimate revolutionary agent, Taine describes how the Third Estate quickly lost control of the revolution and ceded power to crowds and mobs acting under the influence of various political clubs, especially the fanatical Jacobins.[10] For Taine, the mob rule that culminated in the Reign of Terror was neither a tragic accident, an unfortunate outcome of a sequence of contingent events that could have been otherwise, nor something that could have been avoided with a modicum of luck and prudence. The political tragedy was, instead, long in the making. In Taine's view, it was the calculable result of

7. The scenes of crowds, mobs, and riots are a recurrent and continuing theme in Western literature both before and after Shakespeare. These literary representations, even those composed by writers sympathetic to the plight of the poor and the exploited, tend generally to evoke fear, anxiety, and dread about crowds and crowd action by the popular classes.
8. For an excellent account of crowd theory from a psychosocial perspective, see Susanna Barrows, *Distorting Mirrors: Visions of the Crowd in Late Nineteenth-Century France* (New Haven, CT: Yale University Press, 1981). My interpretation of the work of the crowd theorists from this era is deeply indebted to this brilliant and pioneering book by Barrows. See also Jaap van Ginneken, *Crowds, Psychology, and Politics, 1871–1899* (Cambridge, UK: Cambridge University Press, 1992). Both Barrows and Ginneken discuss the contribution of a fourth crowd theorist from this period, Henri Fournial, who, after writing a seminal monograph, left academic research to serve as a medical doctor on a colonial expedition in Africa. Fournial's monograph is *Essai sur la psychologie des foules: Considérations médico-judiciaires sur les responsabilités collectives* (Lyon: A. Storck; Paris: G. Masson, 1892).
9. Hippolyte A. Taine, *The French Revolution*, vol. 1, is volume 2 in his *Les Origines de la France contemporaine* in 6 volumes (Paris: Hachette, 1876–1894), and was published in French in 1878 and translated into English by John Durand in 1880. The first book of this volume, titled "Spontaneous Anarchy," contains Taine's fearful and hyperbolic account of revolutionary crowds and rioting mobs.
10. Jules Michelet, *The People*, trans. John P. McKay (Urbana: University of Illinois Press, 1973).

a centralized and power-hungry monarchy faltering amid a prolonged crisis, a ruined economy, empty state coffers, and a vast number of people caught in the throes of hunger and starvation. Under these conditions, impractical republican political reforms concocted in the names of freedom and reason and in the shadow of the Enlightenment poisoned the vulnerable minds of the common people, unprepared as they were for the demands of self-rule. Driven by visions of emancipation and equality, and with their backs to the traditional wisdom that regulates desire, belief, and conduct in accordance with one's station within a stable hierarchical order, ordinary French people, once sensible and sober, became unhinged and reverted to the savage ways of a "state of nature." Individuality and individual responsibility were both set aside as hordes of people looted and pillaged. Basic instincts were let loose as licentiousness, alcoholism, and gratuitous violence prevailed. Such is the orgiastic and contagious nature of crowd behavior. While this atavistic reversion to savagery grips women more than men (and among men, the poor and ignorant more than the affluent and educated), once afflicted, no one is entirely free of the madness of the crowd. Motley or mighty, nothing threatens civilization more than a crowd, with its egalitarian ethos and leveling impulse. Civility and self-control simply evaporate. Hence, in Taine's account, the hollow republican promise of equality culminates in "spontaneous anarchy," followed by mob rule. Taine, who fashioned himself as the physician of French society, suggested that the same republican malady—an anarchist culture masquerading in the name of popular sovereignty— continued to haunt the nation, taking hold again in 1830, 1848, and 1871.[11]

In the wake of the massive carnage in the closing days of the Paris Commune, Taine's distorted account of the collective action and agency of the people during the French Revolution, as well as the unsettling political conclusions that he drew, had a receptive audience not only in France but all over Europe.[12] While Taine could bluntly reject claims of equality, popular sovereignty, and universal adult franchise as airy republican humbug, his social scientific followers—Sighele, Tarde, and Le Bon—couldn't afford to be so summarily dismissive. They lived and wrote under a different political climate, presciently anticipated by Alexis de Tocqueville: the drive for equality had been unleashed in all spheres of life, not just in politics, and it had gathered momentum, first in America and then in Europe.[13] To borrow a phrase from Pierre Rosanvallon, "the republic of universal franchise" was on its way.[14] Any

11. Wary of such a palpable incarnation of popular sovereignty and fearful of the material practices it invited, Taine wholly opposed granting universal adult suffrage, especially to women.
12. In the world of letters and scholarship, Taine's account instigated two strands of thought: the right-wing conservative historiography of the revolution and the psychosocial theories of the crowd and crowd behavior. While the former was immediately and ably challenged, the latter, clothed in social scientific garb, endures largely unscathed even today. Crowd theory, partly eclipsed by the "mass society thesis," is no longer as prominent as it was during the last quarter of the nineteenth century, but it has remained influential, often surreptitiously migrating to regions of opinion and belief aligned with the liberal political imaginary.
13. Alexis de Tocqueville, Democracy in America, trans. Gerald Bevan (1835 and 1840; repr., New York: Penguin, 2003), 583–587.
14. See Pierre Rosanvallon, "The Republic of Universal Suffrage," in Democracy:

liberal, whether progressive or conservative, had to either come to terms with republican politics and the republican polity, or risk being branded a reactionary.[15] All of a sudden, the fears that conservatively inclined parliamentary liberals had long harbored of collective agency, popular sovereignty, and universal franchise needed a new object. That object turned out to be the crowd, a necessary but not sufficient condition for various types of disorderly public conduct, including rioting. But where liberals had previously been able to quash republicanism through a strategy of outright refusal, crowds were quickly becoming an inescapable feature of modern life that could not be so simply contained.

One can refuse the republic but not the crowd. With rapid industrialization and urbanization, the crowd was no longer the exotic and menacing creature accompanying revolts and uprisings, but rather the mundane background of everyday life, especially in metropoles like Paris and London. The crowd cannot be made to disappear; it is a social fact, in the Durkheimian sense. Plato's (and also Taine's) *restricted* fear of the demos as a political agent had to be transfigured into a *generalized* fear of the crowd as a blind force, "a body without organs" in the Deleuzian sense. Two scholars, Sighele and Tarde, and a polymath, Le Bon, effectively carried out this transfiguration.[16] Sighele and Tarde began with a narrow criminological problematic. They wanted to figure out why, when perfectly normal people formed a crowd, they sometimes behaved in a wantonly destructive and barbaric fashion. Furthermore, they wanted to formulate guidelines for how to untangle the individual from the collective when a crowd crossed the line into lawlessness, and adjudicate whether such legal infractions deserved to be punished. From that narrow focus, Sighele and Tarde would cautiously develop a general theory of social action in crowds.

For Le Bon, who drew on the works of Sighele and Tarde (without always acknowledging his debt), the crowd posed both a greater challenge and a greater opportunity. He was distrustful of republican politics, especially of its docility and servility before the masses. He dismissed the republican promise of formal equality as a dysfunctional hoax, claiming that it discouraged disciplined leadership committed to honorable and prudent ends, and turned average politicians into toadies, habitually prone to the passing whims of a volatile people. As a young scholar, he had read Charles Darwin and Herbert Spencer closely and devised his own version of biological determinism explicitly devoted to a hierarchical view of races and sexes. His distaste for republicanism was also shaped by a decisive life experience. Unlike the older Taine, who was lecturing at Oxford University during the tumultuous days

Past and Future, ed. Samuel Moyn (New York: Columbia University Press, 2006), 98–116.

15. A liberal in this context means one who, while opposed to the restoration of monarchy, is anxious to varying degrees about the radical democratic and egalitarian possibilities inherent in the republican form of government.

16. As we shall see later, this transmuted fear of the demos would not go away; it would return, time and again, to be deferred and repressed in the name of liberal constitutionalism, the rule of law, public order, and good governance.

of the Paris Commune, a thirty-year-old Le Bon watched as retreating crowds of Communards burned down the Palais des Tuileries, the Louvre's Richelieu Library, the Palais de Justice, Hôtel de Ville, and many other priceless architectural wonders. The self-destructive rage of Communard crowds, even as they were being mercilessly butchered by an advancing army in a veritable dance of death, left an indelible imprint on Le Bon's political imagination. Thus, his distaste for republicanism and what he took to be its chief weakness—its reliance on and addiction to the leveling impulse of crowds—was formed early and only hardened with time. Ultimately, Le Bon's critique of republican politics was more psychosociological than it was normative. He simply equated republican/democratic politics with mass politics, and in that equation, he claimed to have discovered its fatal flaw, its Achilles' heel. Without an alternative form of government to recommend, Le Bon fell back on his conservatism, longing for an orderly tradition-bound society free from the egalitarian drive embodied in crowd politics.

However, there is no freedom from the crowd. In his extremely popular book *The Crowd*, Le Bon declared the crowd to be the "last surviving sovereign force of modern times" and warned that the coming age would be "the Era of Crowds": "While all our ancient beliefs are tottering and disappearing, while the old pillars of society are giving way one by one, the power of the crowd is the only force that nothing menaces, and of which the prestige is continually on the increase."[17] The defining political and cultural challenge of the modern era, as Le Bon and other proponents of the psychosociological explanation conceived it, was how to cope and live with the crowd, modernity's nefarious twin. In response, Sighele, Tarde, and Le Bon devised a crowd hermeneutics that they offered to an eager and unsettled reading public.

While these three scholars differ on the finer points of crowd psychology and behavior, they share three key tenets—deindividualization, suggestibility, and contagion—each of which points to the irrational and unconscious forces that motivate, shape, and direct the behavior of individuals in crowds. Each tenet also refers to a process, a temporal unfolding, that occurs when individuals are drawn into a crowd. First, deindividualization refers to the process by which individuals lose their mental and bodily autonomy as the distance and difference between self and other dissolves. To the extent that the individual is seen as the seat of reason, deindividualization yields a descent into the irrational. When people are drawn into a crowd, according to Le Bon, a new entity emerges that displays "characteristics very different from those of the individuals composing it." In a crowd, individuals' backgrounds—their education, profession, and social class—no longer matter, "their conscious personality vanishes," their sentiments and ideas coalesce with others, and the crowd moves in unison. Thus, "a collective mind is formed," and a "single being... subjected to the *law of mental unity of crowds*" emerges. Le Bon characterizes this emergent formation as

17. Gustave Le Bon, *The Crowd: A Study of the Popular Mind* (1895; repr., Mineola, NY: Dover Publications, 2002), x.

a steep, backward evolution. By the mere fact of becoming part of a crowd, the individual "descends several rungs on the ladder of civilization." In a crowd, a cultivated individual displays "the spontaneity, the ferocity... of primitive beings" and becomes a "barbarian... a creature of instinct."[18]

Sighele, Tarde, and Le Bon illustrate this process of atavistic regression with imagistic metaphors that repeatedly characterize the crowd as a child, a woman, a drunkard, a savage, and a beast. These metaphors accentuate the claim that the crowd is entirely bereft of reason, a creature of raw passions and impetuous actions. In terms of their prevalence and intensity, two of these images are particularly striking: the beast and the woman. For instance, these crowd psychologists often describe the individuals within a crowd as baboons while depicting the crowd itself as a headless "spinal creature."[19] As for the feminine imagery, even Tarde, the most scholarly of the three, succumbs to the deep and abiding misogyny that pervaded the crowd psychology of his time: "By its whimsy, its revolting docility, its credulity, its nervousness, its brusque psychological leaps from fury to tenderness, from exasperation to laughter, the crowd is feminine, even when it is composed, as is usually the case, of males."[20] This atavistic paradigm reaches a culmination in Le Bon's characterization of the crowd as a sphinx, half woman and half beast; volatility and alterity are combined to render the crowd enigmatic and dangerous, the mastering and bridling of which becomes the supreme challenge for modern mass politics, democratic or otherwise, and its leaders.[21]

To explain how a normal individual in a crowd loses all self-control and becomes a captive of primal instincts and affects, our authors resort to yet another paradigm, the doctrine of hypnotic suggestion. During this period, hypnotism was very much in vogue in medical circles. There were two competing schools: the Paris School, led by the famous neurologist Jean-Martin Charcot out of Salpêtrière Hospital, and the Nancy School, led by a country doctor, Ambroise-Auguste Liébeault, and his associate, Hippolyte Bernheim. While the former used hypnotic suggestion as a diagnostic technique to assess patients with specific psychopathological symptoms, the latter deployed it as a universal therapeutic strategy, not only to diagnose but also to treat a wide range of organic and psychic disorders. Thus, the Nancy School held that, under certain conditions, all human beings are highly susceptible to

18. Le Bon, *The Crowd*, 1–8.
19. According to Barrows, the image of the crowd as a "spinal creature" originated with Fournial and was also deployed by Tarde; see Barrows, *Distorting Mirrors*, 132 and 144, respectively.
20. Cited in Barrows, *Distorting Mirrors*, 149.
21. As a political realist, Le Bon didn't call for a restoration of monarchy. He was reconciled to the inevitability of a republican form of government and, to some degree, universal adult suffrage. Instead, he sought to develop a manual for authoritarian leaders to manipulate and control crowds. According to Barrows, Le Bon deserves to be seen not as the father of crowd psychology but rather as one of the architects of authoritarian right-wing politics. She writes: "He set out to teach the leader how to subvert democracy from within, how to silence demands for true social reform, how to forge a distinctly modern, wholly tyrannical state". Barrows, *Distorting Mirrors*, 188 and 196.

suggestion. The crowd psychologists, especially Tarde and Le Bon, subscribed to this maximalist thesis. It shared a strong affinity with Tarde's general theory of society and "the universal laws of imitation," which explain how the complex interplay of imitation, innovation, and repetition combine to initiate social change and development. It is precisely because the characters of human beings are formed by an endless series of repetitive imitations of sociocultural behaviors and habits that they are especially susceptible to hypnotic suggestion in a crowd. For Tarde, no sharp distinction existed between "normal" everyday interaction and "abnormal" crowd behavior: "Society is imitation, and imitation is a kind of somnambulism."[22]

Finally, contagion refers to the process of how ideas, sentiments, and affects circulate within a crowd. Once they surface, either contingently or through a nodal figure (leader), they spread with increasing speed and amplitude. As a communicative process involving "reciprocal imitation," their circulation does not require any explicit verbal cues.[23] Contagion is a bodily affair consisting mostly of gestures, quivers, signs, sounds, tip-offs, and waves. This imitative contagion moves rapidly and grows in intensity as the crowd expands, imparting a feeling of invincible power. The following passage by Tarde describes how reciprocal and repetitive imitation, the constitutive trait of all social interaction, suddenly transforms a heterogeneous assembly into a single unified entity and force:

> It is a gathering of heterogeneous elements, unknown to one another, but as soon as a spark of passion, having flashed out of one of these elements, electrifies this confused mass, there takes place a sort of sudden organization, a spontaneous generation. This incoherence becomes cohesion, this noise becomes a voice, and these thousand men crowded together soon form but a single animal, a wild beast without a name, which marches to its goal with an irresistible finality.[24]

Thus, the two paradigms of atavistic regression and hypnotic suggestion come together in Tarde's description of contagious crowd behavior. They disclose the fragility of human reason and goodness, a rather dismal picture of human nature.

Taken together, these three tenets give rise to a set of anti-egalitarian and antidemocratic propositions marked by overt displays of racism and misogyny. First, to the extent that being in a crowd initiates the process of deindividualization, crowds jeopardize the liberal notion of a free and autonomous individual, the bedrock of social ontology, moral responsibility, and economic calculation. Second, every crowd is a potential mob, and every mob is susceptible to disorderly and riotous

● 22. Gabriel Tarde, *The Laws of Imitation*, trans. Elsie Clews Parsons (New York: Henry Holt, 1903), 87. Cited in Barrows, *Distorting Mirrors*, 139.
● 23. According to Barrows, Fournial and Tarde got this idea from Alfred Espinas's *Les sociétés animals* (Paris: Félix Alca, 1924), 115–119, 132, 142.
● 24. Cited in Barrows, *Distorting Mirrors*, 141.

behavior; hence, the chain of equivalency: crowd-mob-riot. Third, the right to assembly, however central to the republican/democratic project, gravely threatens that project from within by paving the way to demagoguery and authoritarian majoritarianism.[25]

None of this has any basis in reality, historical or social. These are fantastic projections of a group of fearful men in fearful times, weary of the rising tide of egalitarianism and feminism and deaf to the gathering voices of dissent. These psychosocial theories of the crowd had their counterpart in the liberal political tradition, especially within its conservative wing, that justified opposition to universal adult suffrage on the grounds that the working classes, women, and colonial subjects were uniquely susceptible to crowd-like behavior. It would not be difficult to assemble an archive of conservative attacks against a wide range of emancipatory social and political movements based on the rhetorical invocation of one or both of the two paradigms—atavistic regression and hypnotic suggestion. Among them, opposition to universal adult suffrage, to equal civil status, to fair wages, to the eight-hour workday, to women's rights, to freedom from colonial rule, and to many other justified demands for the immediate rectification of glaring wrongs. Further, when it became evident that conservative opposition could no longer repel the march of popular sovereignty—embodied in universal adult suffrage—liberal laws and institutions designed to neutralize the people's capacity to act collectively appeared. This adaptive reaction is evident in James Madison's defense of American bicameralism and "a well-constructed senate," both of which he believed necessary to fend off the crowd-like behavior of the people or their representatives, assembled in a single house. The people, Madison feared, would be too easily "stimulated by some irregular passion, or some illicit advantage, or misled by artful representation of interested men." According to Madison, the genius of the American system of representation, unlike those of the ancients, "lies *in the total exclusion of the people in their collective capacity.*"[26]

Distressingly, the fears and prejudices of men of the past are still with us and can be heard in the panicked dismissals of populism and populist movements that have come to dominate liberal democratic theory in Europe and the United States.[27] Starting with Plato's image of the demos as "a great beast,"[28] running through Madison's insistence on a "well-constructed senate," immune to the lures of collective sentiments, and into our own time, a deep and abiding anticrowd strain animates Western political thought.[29] With rare exceptions—Machiavelli,

25. Both liberals and conservatives have this anxiety about the republican form of government, even though they have no desire to restore the monarchic form of government.
26. James Madison, *The Federalist: From the Original Texts of Alexander Hamilton, John Jay, and James Madison* (New York: Modern Library, Random House, 1937), 413.
27. See Dilip Parameshwar Gaonkar, "They, the People: Overlooking the Populist Complaint," *Berlin Journal* (Fall 2017): 61–65.
28. Plato, *Republic,* Book 6, 492–493d.
29. The impressive extent to which America's founding fathers were preoccupied with a fear of the mob while drafting and subsequently ratifying the Constitution is copiously documented in *The Federalist Papers.* For a

Spinoza, and few others—there is hardly a political thinker who does not consider the bridling of the multitude an essential objective of constitution making and institution building. As Taine's terrifying historical account shows, the fear of crowds, mobs, and mass gatherings intensifies after the French Revolution. Recognizing the ubiquity of modern crowds, especially in industrial cities, Taine's disciples in the social sciences—Sighele, Tarde, Le Bon, and many others—blur the distinction between specific aristocratic fears of the demos and generalized psychosocial anxieties about the crowd. This blurring enables the old aristocratic suspicions of the demos and democracy to endure underneath a more palatable scholarly garb, as a meritocratic critique of the masses.[30]

Second Explanation: Rioting and Socioeconomic Conflict
Despite the pervasive rhetoric of "one people, one nation," there is no such thing as a conflict-free society or polity. The socioeconomic explanation links the phenomenon of rioting to the inescapable social conflicts constitutive of any society divided along axes of difference: economic, ethnoracial, religious, linguistic, or geographic. Social conflicts arise out of many kinds of difference and manifest in many forms, but there are nonetheless two dominant sources: economic inequality and ethnocultural divisions. In virtually every known political community, democratic or otherwise, a small group of elites controls a massively disproportionate share of income and wealth, rank and status, and opportunity and affordance, at the expense of the vastly more numerous non-elites. The ensuing structural inequality and exploitation of the many by the few is a permanent source of social conflict and class antagonism. Moreover, while non-elites greatly outnumber elites, the latter invariably steer the economy, polity, and culture. This imbalance makes conflict between these two broadly constituted but internally heterogeneous groups indelible. Thus, the issue is not whether such a grossly unfair system of stratification gives rise to social conflict but rather how that conflict manifests and how it is managed, especially in a democratic polity.[31]

detailed account of the anticrowd strain in Western political thought, see J. S. McClelland, *The Crowd and the Mob: From Plato to Canetti* (London: Unwin Hyman, 1989).

- 30. See Ernesto Laclau's discussion of the "denigration of the masses" in part 1 of his *On Populist Reason* (London: Verso, 2005).
- 31. There are multiple explanations as to how social inequalities arise (anthropological, structural, and causal) and justifications (economic, normative, and theological) as to why they are unavoidable and even necessary. In all the speculation and analysis, rival theorists from Plato to Rousseau and from Marx to Rawls come to an overwhelming consensus around one point: whatever its causes, explanations, and justifications, social inequality becomes dysfunctional, dangerous, and destructive once it crosses a certain threshold. Where that threshold lies is not easy to specify. Culturally and historically, it is elastic and variable, but within the social imaginary of any given people, it is perfectly legible and palpable. At that inflection point, when social inequality becomes intolerable, class antagonisms slip out of the mediational frames of legislative assemblies and judicial chambers and surface in the streets and squares. We are at such an inflection point today.

The social conflict that structures the relationship between elites and non-elites is also intensified and dest bilized by social change. In advanced capitalist societies, the technological, economic, and organizational innovations promoted by elites in the name of progress and prosperity are constantly transforming the existing modes of social reproduction and their corresponding ways of life. These transformations, especially when they are sweeping and radical, can perilously destabilize the status quo, further straining the already unequal relation between elites and non-elites. Even when these changes succeed in increasing the wealth of a given nation, they often exacerbate the relative inequality between the two groups. It might very well be the case that, in the long run, some of these changes—scientific and technological as well as socioeconomic —benefit the non-elites. There is hardly any question that the life expectancy of non-elites, along with that of elites, has steadily increased over the last three hundred years. The same can be said about the rise in literacy and, to some extent, the alleviation of stark hunger.

However, such an enlarged temporal horizon has little resonance for those recurrently caught in the so-called "Engels' pause," the hiatus between the two great transformative movements that Karl Polanyi described.[32] According to Polanyi, the first movement is the societal transformation triggered by industrial capitalism. After a delay, the second movement is the political response to the derangements and negative externalities caused by the first. As a rule, the disruptions and instabilities that accompany radical changes in existing modes of social reproduction pose significantly greater socioeconomic risks, hardships, and suffering for non-elites than they do for elites. Given the dynamism of capitalism today, we seem caught in a suspended "Engels' pause," wherein the livelihoods of the non-elites are in perpetual jeopardy and, if any relief comes, it is only ever fleeting. Evident in the short span of time between the financial crisis of 2007–2008 and the COVID-19 crisis of 2020, the lower strata are unable to recuperate from the effects of one disabling blow before the next one lands. Due to their limited resources, non-elites cannot wait indefinitely for Polanyi's second movement to mitigate the negative externalities of opaque and distant structural changes wrought by, among other things, new technologies, the global integration of markets, and the miasmal logic of financialization. With or without a clear agenda or a full understanding of what is to be done, non-elites must act on their own. Throughout modernity and into the present day, this kind of conflict is the preeminent motive and force behind a multitude of social movements, direct actions, and eruptive riots.

The other dominant source of social conflict arises from ethnic, racial, religious, and cultural differences. In terms of race and ethnicity,

---

● 32. Robert C. Allen, "Engels' Pause: Technical Change, Capital Accumulation, and Inequality in the British Industrial Revolution," *Explorations in Economic History* 46 (2009): 418–435. I am indebted to Craig Calhoun for drawing my attention to this concept. Karl Polanyi, *The Great Transformation: The Political and Economic Origins of Our Time* (1944; repr., Boston: Beacon Press), 157.

religious beliefs, cultural values, language, geographical attachments, and lifestyle preferences, no polity is homogeneous. The idea and the ideology of "we, the people" or "one people, one nation" is neither self-evident nor permanently fixed. It is not a fiction, an empty signifier, as Claude Lefort and Ernesto Laclau opine, but a historically sediment-ed construct suffused with tradition and prejudice (à la Edmund Burke) that is always open to ideological contestation and reinterpretation.[33] In a telic sense, "we, the people," the imagined collective agent so closely aligned to the democratic project, are always in the making, dedicat-ed to forging and nurturing a solidarity amid differences. Constantly making and remaking the people is a daunting challenge as it calls forth competing narratives of who the people are, of where they came from, and of where they are going. It is an ostensibly historical exercise but one that is shrouded in myth and fraught with fiction. Despite the reas-surances of cosmopolitan humanism and liberal constitutionalism, the self-hermeneutics of "we, the people" are contingent, fragile, and vul-nerable. The threat of ethnocultural identity (however fictitious) and its disturbing claims to priority can never be fully expunged. The viability of a stable polity depends on maintaining a delicate balance between the dominant majority and significant minorities. This task becomes complicated in any democracy doctrinally committed to popular sov-ereignty, universal adult suffrage, and the material enactment of each through free and fair elections. The perennial temptation for an ethnic or a religious majority to attack one or more minority groups and rele-gate them to the status of second-class citizens is the looming threat of ethnonational majoritarianism, the Achilles' heel of democracy.

Two factors exacerbate ethnocultural conflicts: the presumed intima-cy between the democratic project and the nation-state form, and the relentless social acceleration caused by capitalism. In modern times, nationalism has been and continues to be the most potent solidari-ty-building engine. However, while nationalism unifies people around a constitution and some shared ideals, it can also divide and fracture them along other lines. Being so closely aligned with the nation-state, democracy can easily become embroiled in exclusionary politics. Democratic institutions, forms, and practices associated with elections and party systems are especially prone to polarization and exclusion. In the heat of electoral campaigns, minorities make for ready scape-goats, their exclusion a small price to pay for the ethnonational rhetoric that can excite and unify a majority. The social acceleration that goes hand in hand with rapidly changing modes of capitalist production and market integration can further exacerbate the conflict between major-ities and minorities. When members of the majority become casualties of massive economic transformations, they can blame their econom-ic woes on an already-marked minority. This kind of conflict between majority and minority can mask the more enduring conflict between elite and non-elite. Today, we see this displacement when majoritarian

---

●   33. Claude LeFort, "The Question of Democracy," in *Democracy and Political Theory,* trans. David Macey (Minneapolis: University of Minnesota Press, 1988), 9–20; and Ernesto Laclau, "The 'People' and the Discursive Production of Emptiness," in *On Populist Reason,* 67–128.

ideologues blame the loss of blue-collar jobs on the arrival of immigrants and refugees rather than on the global integration of markets and new, more efficient, technologies. By the same token, majoritarian ideologues cast any reduction in entitlements and benefits for the majority as a consequence of the diversion of national funds to undeserving minorities rather than as the result of neoliberal policies that serve the interests of global elites.

Thus, these two dominant types of social conflict—economic inequality and ethnocultural divisions—intersect and combine in unexpected ways to produce a bewildering, sometimes lethal, array of political conjunctures. Whatever the specific nature of that combination, socioeconomic inequality, which is growing at an exponential rate all over the world, remains the primary source.

II. Rethinking Direct Action

The expression "direct action" has a long and complex genealogy in radical politics. It may be broadly defined as a type of collective political action initiated and carried out by a given group of people seeking redress for their grievances. To draw on the contemporary theoretical vocabulary, direct action begins with what Laclau calls a "demand" for the correction or removal of what Rancière calls a "wrong."[34] In modern capitalist societies governed by democratic or quasi-democratic regimes and with varying degrees of commitment to liberal traditions and values, direct action comes in a multitude of forms: labor strikes (general as well as wildcat), hunger strikes, protest marches and public assemblies, demonstrations and rallies, vigils, picket lines, sit-ins, boycotts, and human blockades. While a similar ensemble of practices can be deployed under authoritarian regimes, the physiognomy (modes of manifestation) and temporality (modes of unfolding) critical to direct action's sustainability are severely compromised by the constriction of public spaces, the swiftness of crackdowns, and the general ethos of intimidation. These limitations cause direct action mobilizations to fizzle quickly or, rarely, to transform into broader revolts.

As indicated earlier, direct action is not the only way in which a given people can seek redress for their grievances. There are two other conventional routes, both nonagitational: the electoral/legislative and the judicial. Direct action is the third option, exercised by those who believe, on the basis of their past experiences, that the legislature and the court will not serve their interests in an effective and timely fashion. In fact, those very institutions are often its targets. Direct action targeting the legislature usually involves a demand to pass an appropriate law to rectify a wrong, as

34. Laclau, *On Populist Reason*: "We will call a demand which, satisfied or not, remains isolated a *democratic demand*. A plurality of demands which through their equivalential articulation constitute a broader social subjectivity we will call *popular demands*—they start, at a very incipient level, to constitute the 'people' as potential historical actor" (74). Jacques Rancière, *Disagreement: Politics and Philosophy* (1995; repr., Minneapolis: University of Minnesota Press, 1999): "Politics is always at work on the gap that makes equality consist solely in the figure of wrong" (62).

was the case with the US Voting Rights Act of 1965. Direct action target- ing the court usually involves a public denunciation of its rulings as unjust; such are the public outcries in response to the acquittals of numerous police officers charged with killing innocent and unarmed people of color in the United States. In these cases, direct action functions as a source of external pressure to extract a specific result rather than as an organized and steady march through institutions to transform them from within. Direct action is not usually geared toward changing the composition of the legislature by campaigning to elect sympathetic representatives, al- though some of the people involved in any given direct action might also be concurrently engaged in electoral/legislative campaigns or judicial appeals and litigation to promote the same agenda. However, overlapping membership neither defines nor compromises direct action; it reiterates the fact that direct action is part of a larger ecology of political mobilization and transformation.

To be sure, there are alternative theories that place direct action in a differ- ent relationship to this larger ecology of transformative politics, especially vis-à-vis the apparatus and institutions of the state. David Graeber, for instance, while tracing direct action's genealogy back to a certain pacifist version of anarcho-syndicalism, claims that this strand of direct action refuses to recognize the state and its claim to adjudicate: "In its essence direct action is the insistence, when faced with structures of unjust au- thority, on acting as if one is already free. One does not solicit the state. One does not even necessarily make a grand gesture of defiance."[35] By contrast, Partha Chatterjee offers a Foucauldian view of *the politics of the governed* that takes the state and its apparatus of governmentality as the primary addressees. While Chatterjee does not invoke the concept of direct action, his account shows how slum dwellers in Gobindapur Rail Colony Gate Number 1 (Calcutta) secure basic services (water, electricity, and public health clinics) from the city and state through collective political action. Skeptical of their political weight within the institutional orbits of the legislature and the court, the slum dwellers rhetorically engage and exploit the very logic of governmentality by other means. Instead of rejecting the label, the slum dwellers embrace their classification as "illegal" squatters, leverage the legitimacy that comes with constituting an identifiable "pop- ulation group," and seek to imbue the empirical category with *"the moral attributes of a community."*[36] Precisely because of their ambiguous legal status, they must agitate to secure basic services as a community. Once their status becomes more stable and their basic needs are met, collective political action gives way to individual consumption. Thus, a direct action politics of the governed operates by simultaneously making a demand and constituting a community that, in the eyes of the state and within the realm of political society, is entitled to make such a demand.[37]

● 35. David Graeber, *Direct Action: An Ethnography* (Oakland, CA: AK Press, 2009), 203.

● 36. Partha Chatterjee, *The Politics of the Governed* (New York: Columbia University Press, 2004), 57.

● 37. This is central to Chatterjee's distinction between the "political society" and the "civil society." The former signals a realm that is distinct from the latter grounded in legal and legislative norms.

I am not interested here in evaluating the comparative merits or in reconciling the divergent claims of these theories of direct action. Today, direct action, like politics in general, takes place in the shadows of modernity's two leviathans, the market and the state. Even though direct action's goals, strategies, and practices—as well as the class composition of its proponents and their addressees—vary massively across and within nations, regions, and cultures, they necessarily unfold in public spaces saturated with economic logics and structured by governmentality. Irrespective of whether direct action protests are triggered by police brutality, a culture of sexualized violence, government corruption, nuclear power plants, or imposed austerity measures, the market and the state cannot be ignored. In almost all cases, oppositional direct action cannot succeed without simultaneously challenging and pressuring both.

In this context, direct action has four salient features. First, *direct action is a collective endeavor.* While it is conceivable that a solitary individual could engage in direct action—as in the case of a "hunger strike" or something analogous to Henry David Thoreau's ingenious acts of civil disobedience—it is mostly a collective enterprise. A hunger strike or an act of self-immolation can be regarded as an individual act only in a technical sense. Such acts occur, or to be more precise, are staged, in public places. Mahatma Gandhi, the real hunger artist in contrast to Kafka's fictional one, went on hunger strikes more than a dozen times during his long career as the leader of the Indian independence movement. He had an uncanny capacity to stage them at the optimal time and place, always before the eyes of the people and the press, exerting the maximum amount of pressure on the British imperial government. Unlike Gandhi's carefully orchestrated hunger strikes, Mohamed Bouazizi, the Tunisian street vendor who set himself on fire after a municipal inspector confiscated his produce cart, appears to have acted entirely on his own.[38] He complained to higher officials, but he was ignored. Upon being deprived of any official channels for a redress of his grievance, Bouazizi, standing right in front of the governor's office, surrounded by traffic, set himself on fire. To be sure, in sheer anger and frustration he acted alone, but he acted publicly. It is precisely the publicness of his act that triggered the series of collective protests that would culminate in the Tunisian democratic revolution and incite the Arab Spring. These seemingly individual acts of protest are not ritual acts of moral cleansing, nor are they a withdrawal from worldly entanglements. They are exemplary acts of public pedagogy addressed to one's community and to the world at large.

Second, *direct action is an invitation to assemble and to act in concert.* It involves exercising the right to free speech as well as the right to assemble. The alignment of these two rights, not always harmonious, reiterates the collective character of direct action. In direct action,

---

38. Those who followed the story will recall that the intensity of Bouazizi's response was due in part to the fact that the inspector who confiscated his cart was a woman. Another instance of the messy interplay between economic and social divisions.

assembly both precedes and exceeds the untrammeled exercise of free speech and expression. The modern right to freedom of speech uneasily incorporates two classical notions of free speech: *isegoria* (the equal right of citizens to speak and participate in deliberation and decision-making in democratic assemblies) and *parrhesia* (fearless speech, to say whatever one pleases without regard to occasion, audience, and perlocutionary effects).[39] The latter, unlike the former, is not central to the democratic project or to popular sovereignty. As in the case of Platonic Socrates, *parrhesia* can be deployed to denounce democracy, to tell the truth about *isegoria* and why it is untenable.[40] Truth-telling, moreover, does not require a collective agent, plural or unified. To assemble is to anticipate the emergence of a collective agent, not a truth-teller but a political claimant. An act of assembling in the name of the people is always an enactment of popular sovereignty and thus part of the democratic project.[41] This is the distinction Judith Butler rightly draws between the voiced "we" and the enacted "we" implicit in the phrase "We the People": "*the assembly is already speaking before it utters any words*, that is by coming together it is *already* an enactment of popular will; that enactment signifies quite differently from the way a single and unified subject declares its will through a vocalized proposition."[42] As opposed to the abstract unity of a vocalized "we"—an empty signifier sutured out of a heterogeneous social field (à la Laclau)—an assembled people, a crowd, is always a concrete multiplicity.[43] To assemble, as Butler notes, is to engage in "plural action, presupposing a plurality of bodies who enact their convergent and divergent purposes in ways that fail to conform to a single kind of acting, or reduce to a single kind of claim."[44] While the enunciated unity of "We the People" can echo through history in its numerous iterations in a citational chain, the enacted "we" is fugitive and contingent, always destined to dissipate and disappear.[45]

To assemble in the name of the people is to proceed "as if" popular sovereignty, in its multiple and irregular manifestations, supersedes the constitutionally or electorally delegated sovereignty of the state. Even when a state promises to uphold the right of assembly, the people engaged in direct action do not see assembly as a right that the state can legitimately extend and withdraw. Even as they address and petition the

●   39. Teresa M. Bejan, "The Two Clashing Meanings of 'Free Speech,'" *The Atlantic*, December 2, 2017, https://www.theatlantic.com/politics/archive/2017/12/two-concepts-of-freedom-of-speech/546791.
●   40. This is clearly stated in Plato's two dialogues, *Gorgias* and *Protagoras*.
●   41. See Dipesh Chakrabarty, "'In the Name of Politics': Democracy and the Power of Multitude in India," *Public Culture* 19, no. 1 (2007): 35–58.
    42. Judith Butler, *Notes Toward a Performative Theory of Assembly* (Cambridge, MA: Harvard University Press, 2015), 156.
    43. See Gaonkar, "After the Fictions": "The category of people is a collective remainder, ever present and operative, something that exceeds all (real, imagined, and hailed) identities. People precede them both as a source and survive them as the reminder as they pass through these identity forms."
●   44. Butler, *Notes*, 157.
    45. While an enacted "we" cannot be idealized and fixed, it does leave a trace, as Benjamin Arditi astutely observes, in the manner of a "vanishing signifier." See Benjamin Arditi, "Insurgents Don't Have a Plan, They *Are* the Plan: Political Performatives and Vanishing Mediators," in *The Promise and Perils of Populism*, ed. Carlos de la Torre (Lexington: University of Kentucky Press, 2015), 113–139.

state, an assembled people act under their own authority and claim their right to be heard, once and forever. It is precisely in this spirit that Butler says that "freedom of assembly may well be a precondition of politics itself, one that presumes that bodies can move and gather in an unregulated way, enacting their political demands in a space that, as a result, becomes public, or redefines an existing understanding of the public."[46]

Third, *direct action insists on publicity.* Visibility is its calling card, and public making and remaking are its vocations. Even when direct action takes place under the cover of darkness, its resonances are not contained within the quiet of night. Its ends are neither secret nor conspiratorial. Direct action is part of a longer and larger tradition of democratic display predicated on the various ways the people reincarnate themselves as a collective sovereign agent. The roots of this tradition—its myriad forms, rituals, and practices—stretch back to a period well before the French Revolution.[47] Shakespeare, among others, provides us with an extensive repertoire of how people make their political presence seen, heard, and felt. *Coriolanus, Henry VI*, and *Julius Caesar* all include scenes of popular agitation and uprising that show the people on display.

The publicity sought and engendered by direct action is of a different order from even the wilder polemical strands of public attention garnered through deliberative discourse—characteristic of the public sphere as theorized by Jürgen Habermas and Michael Warner. In Habermas's much cited account, the bourgeois public sphere is the privileged site of democratic will formation by means of discourse-centered publicity.[48] The initial set of criticisms leveled against Habermas's normatively motivated account of the public sphere focused on a series of historical exclusions.[49] On public matters, workers, women, and colonial subjects were not permitted a voice. If they did somehow manage to speak, they were not heard. This critique of exclusions, however valid, often imagined public voices as disembodied and unmarked. Upon

---

- 46. Butler, *Notes*, 160.
- 47. However, with the coming of the French Revolution, this performative dimension of the people's power crystallized into what Pierre Rosanvallon calls "people as event." Rosanvallon's characterization has a negative connotation insofar as it marks an institutional failure: the inability of the French, unlike their American revolutionary counterparts, to translate the doctrine of popular sovereignty from a common longing into a practical instrument of governance—namely, the representative system. This failure to channel revolutionary energy into an institutional form would, in turn, lead to a reign of terror. See Pierre Rosanvallon, Democracy: Past and Future, ed. Samuel Moyn (New York: Columbia University Press, 2006), 91–94. Recently, Jason Frank has questioned the frequently cited thesis that Americans were able to use constitution making and institution building to neutralize the tradition of performative displays of popular sovereignty. He notes that the constituent power of the people and its periodic invocation by the postrevolutionary crowd did not disappear with the founding of the republic but remained a vital option for foregrounding and problematizing the contentious and unbridgeable "gap between the established institutions of representative government and the public they claimed to represent." See Jason Frank, *Constituent Moments: Enacting the People in Postrevolutionary America* (Durham, NC: Duke University Press, 2010), 09.
- 48. Jürgen Habermas, *The Structural Transformation of the Public Sphere: An Inquiry into a Category of Bourgeois Society*, trans. Thomas Burger with the assistance of Frederick Lawrence (1962; repr., Cambridge, MA: MIT Press, 1989).
- 49. See Craig Calhoun, ed., *Habermas and the Public Sphere* (Cambridge, MA: MIT Press, 1992).

entering the public sphere, the once excluded would formally become an equal citizen, free to avow specific opinions and express particular interests, but ultimately subject to the immanent normative protocols of public speech and reason. By contrast, another group of Habermas's critics, germane to our present discussion, drew attention to the fact that the public sphere is also sustained by a tangible platform made up of coffeehouses, bazaars, parks, streets, and squares—all gathering places for crowds, mobs, and the multitude. Here, the people appear and sometimes erupt in all their ill-defined publicness. They challenge the very premise of general persuasion, the tattered legacy of unreconstructed ancient rhetoric, and question its capacity to discursively reconcile differences and attenuate conflicts across race/ethnicity, religion, class, and gender. While a Habermasian public sphere can try to retreat into an abstract and imagined discursive space, wherein the free and attentive minds of strangers commingle and engage, it can never fully extract itself from the material machinery of print and media, nor can it obviate the gatherings of bodies in common spaces, where the people speak, listen, read, deliberate, agitate, and, sometimes, riot. These gathered bodies generate more than speech and discourse. They generate excesses of all sorts—of solidarities, of equalities, of desires and affects, of hopes and promises, however fleeting their duration.

The double logic of the public sphere—the simultaneous abstracting from and displaying of the people—is also evident in the writings of Benedict Anderson and Michael Warner. For Anderson, a modern nation, an "imagined community" of strangers, emerges out of the shared protocols of dispersed daily newspaper readers, the putative citizens, spread across a large territory beyond the reach of direct contact. For Anderson, the print-mediated public sphere is critical to fostering a "deep horizontal comradeship" among stranger-citizens.[50] Warner goes even further and argues that a public can be said to exist simply by strangers paying "attention" to a common "text" as it circulates through shared social contexts and across common interests.[51] However, this powerful drive toward abstraction and large-scale integration is continually interrupted by assembled bodies in public spaces. The once discourse-centered and now screen-mediated public sphere and embodied public assemblies and crowds continually feed off each other. In fact, the publicity sought by public assemblies emerges through the network and infrastructure of public media. Still, the discursive or screen-based representation of assemblies and crowds in motion can never fully capture their affect and viscerality.

Fourth, *direct action is ambivalent toward unqualified disavowals of violence.* Direct action's liberal critics often denounce and reject it on account of its alleged affinity to violence. Since direct action necessarily involves embodied collective action, assembling and marching

50. Benedict Anderson, *Imagined Communities: Reflections on the Origin and Spread of Nationalism* (London: Verso, 1983).
51. Michael Warner, *Publics and Counter Publics* (New York: Zone Books, 2002), 65–124.

in a crowd formation is one of its distinctive and enduring features. If one were to view crowd formations and action, as liberals tend to do, from the lens of the late nineteenth-century crowd psychologists—who energetically promoted the dubious crowd-mob-riot equation—then it is easy to surmise that direct action leads to wanton destruction of property and loss of life. However, this equation is not grounded in historical reality except in the case of genocidal riots, which are frequently orchestrated from above by political elites competing to seize the state apparatus.[52] A wide majority of political protests, ranging from those aligned with disciplined and agenda-driven social movements to spontaneous eruptions triggered by quotidian transgressions that have overtaxed the patience of the aggrieved, do not result in willful property destruction or bodily harm. Historical studies of riots show that, when it does occur, the destruction of property is more often targeted than random. Furthermore, any loss of life is far more often the result of the excessive force of a militia (or police force) deployed to quell the riots than it is a consequence of a riot's internal violence.[53]

Even though the charge of violence continues to haunt the politics of direct action, many of its proponents—including two of its most renowned twentieth-century practitioners, Mahatma Gandhi and Martin Luther King Jr.—explicitly disavow the use of violence in the struggle against political oppression and social discrimination. Today, the parameters of what counts as direct action are largely set by the theory and practice of Gandhi and King. In both cases, the rejection of violence was principled and strategic. Both, but especially King, understood direct action within the context of a modern political imaginary in which a democratic form of government committed to liberal values has already taken hold. In order to situate direct action in this way, they first had to respond to liberal democratic critics skeptical of the necessity and desirability of direct action.

Those critics believe that, while economically advanced modern liberal democracies have not fully eliminated social conflicts stemming from economic inequalities and social discrimination, they continue to address and mitigate those conflicts in two ways. First, they claim that these liberal democracies have formulated a meritocratic ideology that justifies the unequal distribution of income and wealth through the equal distribution of opportunities. Second, they claim that these liberal democracies provide two accessible and peaceful avenues for redressing social grievances: the legislature and the courts. Thus, they assume

52. Genocidal riots can be explained but not justified. They pose a real problem for the direct action theory. This is one of the reasons why many proponents of direct action embrace and promote "nonviolence" as both philosophy and strategy. On how democratic majoritarianism is susceptible to genocidal temptations, see Michael Mann, *The Dark Side of Democracy: Explaining Ethnic Cleansing* (Cambridge, UK: Cambridge University Press, 2005); Mahmood Mamdani, *When Victims Become Killers: Colonialism, Nativism, and the Genocide in Rwanda* (Princeton, NJ: Princeton University Press, 2001); and Arjun Appadurai, *Fear of Small Numbers: An Essay on the Geography of Anger* (Durham, NC: Duke University Press, 2006).

53. See Mark Harrison's account of the Bristol Bridge Riot of 1793 in his *Crowds and History: Mass Phenomena in English Towns, 1790–1835* (Cambridge, UK: Cambridge University Press, 1988), 271–288.

that in advanced Western democracies—given the institutionalization and protection of liberal rights, the sanctity of the rule of law, an inclusionary history and character, and a robust public sphere—there is no need for any aggrieved group, socioeconomically or ethnoculturally marked, to exercise this unstable and potentially violent "third option." Without endorsing their tactics, liberal and deliberative democrats might understand why an aggrieved group would resort to direct action in a fledgling or corrupt democracy, or in a democracy that has turned "authoritarian and majoritarian." However, they are unable to imagine a compelling rationale for direct action in a mature and well-functioning democracy.

There is a deep historical amnesia involved in this way of thinking. What is forgotten here is the story of how each of the defining features of mature democracies, including the coveted liberal package, were fought for and secured through some type of direct action. Historically, to enhance democracy and to arrest its degeneration, people have turned to direct action. Because that tradition is alive today, liberal and deliberative democrats, despite their deep and abiding anxieties about direct action, are forced to recognize that the politics of protest are an integral part of democratic struggle. They cannot summarily dismiss direct action as antidemocratic.

But neither can they fully embrace direct action's broad and heterogeneous repertoire of forms, genres, and practices. They remain cautious, accepting some aspects and instances of direct action while condemning others. The distinction between the acceptable and the unacceptable usually turns on two criteria. Any direct action associated with organized social movements, with a substantive agenda and accountable leadership, is deemed acceptable and sometimes even recognized as unavoidable. By contrast, unorganized, leaderless, and relatively unplanned (if not wholly spontaneous) eruptions of discontent—the kinds of assembly that are more likely to turn into riots—are rejected as counterproductive and senseless. Within the liberal democratic imaginary, riots have no redeeming social value. They harm the cause that is being espoused, provided a cause is even legible amid the mayhem; they disfigure the grievance that is being articulated. More than anything else, riots are denied their claims to liberal legitimacy because they are destructive and violent. This is the second criterion for distinguishing between acceptable and unacceptable modes of direct action: the possibility and intimation of collective violence.

It is precisely on this point that there is a felicitous convergence between liberal anxieties about certain undesirable types of direct action and Gandhi and King's strong espousal of nonviolence. Whatever their philosophical commitment to nonviolence, Gandhi and King were hyperconscious of liberal anxieties and reservations. They also appear to have internalized the conservative equivalency of crowd-mob-riot. Gandhi knew that there was no way to secure India's independence without mass mobilization. Spearheading the independence movement, the liberal wing of the Congress party, relying on a negotiated constitutional route, had barely made any headway toward domin-ion status, let alone full independence, before Gandhi's arrival from South Africa. Gandhi, arguably the first major mass politician of the twentieth century, knew from the beginning that mass mobilization re-quired drawing and assembling huge crowds of people, leading them on marches, long and short, and thus incarnating the popular will to seize independence. His task was to sanitize the crowd, to make them peaceful, disciplined, and orderly, and hence to cast the movement as acceptable and respectable in the eyes of liberal nationalist elites as well as liberal sympathizers within colonial circles. In a different time and place, King, Gandhi's spiritual disciple, would emulate the same strategy with an added complication: he was making his case on behalf of an aggrieved racialized minority rather than on behalf of an over-whelming colonized majority. During the US civil rights movement in the 1950s and 1960s, King would further sanitize direct action and make it palatable to a different set of reluctant liberal sympathizers.

Gandhi and King labored to exclude, not always successfully, riots and riot-like episodes from the direct action that they initiated. They broadcast the claim that they were driven to direct action because they had been excluded from the more conventional avenues for articulat-ing their demands and seeking redress for their grievances. More than anything else, they wanted to avoid the usual "law and order" charge that they were brazenly stirring up crowds and inciting riots. Toward that end, both Gandhi and King emphasized the long and strenuous training required of a practitioner of direct action. They wrote exten-sively on the philosophy and the practice of nonviolent direct action. Among other things, they explained how a satyagrahi, an exponent of nonviolent resistance, must respect the law even while disobeying it, voluntarily submit to arrest, and allow the force of truth to guide their words and actions; a satyagrahi, moreover, must not harbor anger and resentments, even in the face of unjust provocations, and should never retaliate.[54] King shares and elaborates similar principles in his famous "Letter from Birmingham Jail" (1963). Paramount among them, the need for cleansing and self-purification before one engages the opponent with patience and compassion: "Are you able to accept blows without retaliating?" "Are you able to endure the ordeals of jail?"[55] The angry beast in the soul of the oppressed had to be tamed and expelled before one's oppressors could be vanquished by the forces of truth, justice, and love. This example shows the extent to which Gandhi and King had subconsciously internalized Taine and Le Bon's shared thesis about the loss of individual reason and the volatility of affective contagion in crowds. Without proper self-control, even those individual activists deeply committed to nonviolence could be swept up by a crowd's affect-ive charge and quickly lose their composure and compassion. Afraid of contagion, Gandhi would often call off his direct action campaigns when they turned unruly and violent.

● 54. Mahatma Gandhi, *Non-Violent Resistance (Satyagraha)* (1951; repr., New York: Dover Books, 2001). See section 2, "Discipline for Satyagraha," 37–101.
● 55. Martin Luther King Jr., "Letter from Birmingham Jail (April 16, 1963)," in *Why We Can't Wait* (New York: Penguin, 1964), 64–84.

The transition from Gandhi to King is critical. With King, operating under an avowedly liberal democratic regime rather than under a quasi-liberal imperial formation, direct action as the paradigmatic mode of movement-based peaceful mobilization became a respectable platform from which the oppressed and the excluded could speak and be heard.

III. Alternative Genealogy

However, an alternative (not necessarily violent) genealogy of "direct action"—of crowds, riots, and popular uprisings—continues to haunt the Gandhi-King paradigm. This different genealogy looks to the molecular rather than the molar and the local rather than the national to explore direct action's horizons, temporalities, and addressees. The recuperation and articulation of this alternative genealogy began in England in the 1960s with the work of social historians loosely affiliated with the intellectual projects of "people's history" and "history from below," including E. P. Thompson, Eric Hobsbawm, and George Rudé. In his famous essay "The Moral Economy of the English Crowd in the Eighteenth Century," Thompson offers an account of crowds and riots that radically differs from the one popularized by the late nineteenth-century crowd psychologists.[56] Without mentioning Taine, Le Bon, Sighele, and their contemporaries by name, Thompson effectively demolishes their vacuous crowd-mob-riot equation. According to Thompson, previous accounts of popular action, riots, and uprisings had not regarded common people as rational and purposive historical agents. Instead, these accounts dismissed any collective political action undertaken by common people as either irrational or a spasmodic response to external stimuli. They turned to hunger (the "rebellion of the belly"), for example, to explain the food riots that were frequent and pervasive in Europe in the decades preceding the French Revolution.

Thompson corrects this view. He shows that even during the eighteenth century, hunger alone never provided sufficient grounds for rioting. Early modern European food riots, while provoked in each case by very specific local causes and circumstances, were shaped by the larger forces transforming a quasi-traditional society based on a predominantly agrarian and partly mercantile political economy into a modern industrial society driven by the logic of capitalist accumulation. Stemming from broken promises and unmet expectations that were once taken for granted, a palpable feeling of disappointment and perplexity hovered in the background of each riot. Thompson shows how people's uprisings were the result of perceived transgressions against the existing moral economy in a given community.[57] When a moral economy is disrupted and violated, the aggrieved common people gather in crowds to protest. Occasionally, protesting crowds would turn into a riot. Far from irrational, the men and women in the crowd were acting on the

56. E. P. Thompson, "The Moral Economy of the English Crowd in the Eighteenth Century," *Past & Present* 50 (February 1971): 76–136.
57. Thompson understood the basis of any such moral economy to be "a consistent traditional view of social norms and obligations, of proper economic functions of several parties within the economy" (79).

assumption that they were "defending traditional rights and customs; and, in general, that they were supported by the wider consensus of the community."[58] They actively sought to enlist support from local clergy and other authorities for their cause. Any loss of life or bodily violence was rare. These riots did occasionally lead to the destruction of property, but it was planned and targeted, not random. For instance, instead of wantonly looting a bakery, rioters would set a fair price, popularly known as the "riot price," and confiscate loaves of bread while compensating the baker accordingly. Here, the riot or the threat of the riot functions as a mechanism for influencing and controlling the market, as a mode of collective bargaining, by the common people.

Rioting, especially politically motivated rioting, is not a new phenomenon. It has existed since people began to live in settled and stratified political communities. It is easy to dismiss riots as futile, destructive, and self-defeating but difficult to explain their ubiquity and frequency. With the onset of modernity (now the onset of global modernity) and its promise of "democracy to come," riots appear to be multiplying instead of declining and disappearing. The "inclusive" liberal democratic strategy by itself does not obviate riots. They are a crucial and unavoidable feature of the contemporary ecology of protest.

Aside from the so-called "wallet issues" that vex non-elites the world over—the prices of food, fuel, medicine, rent, public transportation, school supplies, and other basic, though variable, necessities—individuals also share a simmering discontent over their sheer powerlessness. Their voices are unheard, their demands are ignored, their actions are scorned, and any vestige of citizen efficacy has evaporated. This feeling of marginalization and abandonment might result in a temporary withdrawal from democratic participation, or it might stir up exclusionary xenophobic politics and the promise of an easy fix. The only way to fight these negative tendencies is to stop reiterating liberal pieties and renew the demos. Any such renewal demands embracing direct action and harnessing its many forms, genres, resources, and energies rather than anxiously tolerating its fitfulness and struggling in vain to extinguish its eruptions.

Acknowledgments
In writing this essay, I am indebted to Charles Taylor, Craig Calhoun, and Liam Mayes for numerous conversations on the fate of democracy today. I am especially indebted to Liam, who read and edited numerous drafts of this essay. He also served with me as the co-producer of the open archive video installation Riot After Riot: Real and Imagined, screened at the exhibition titled Riots: Slow Cancellation of the Future, ifa Gallery Berlin, January 26–April 1, 2018, and at ifa Gallery Stuttgart, April 27–June, 24, 2018. I would also like to thank Natasha Ginwala, Gal Kirn, and Niloufar Tajeri for inviting me to participate in their innovative multimedia project on riots.

● 58. Thompson, "Moral Economy," 78.

Revolts, Resentment, Resignation: Five Theses on the Negative Dialectics of Post-Marxist Socialism

Thomas Seibert

I

The following essay discusses the Hamburg riot of July 7, 2017, and tries to understand it as an articulation of the mode of existence called "revolt." It takes the riot as a borderline case of the political that is itself neither political nor nonpolitical: like many others, the Hamburg riot was the communication of a resistance to communication itself—that is, to society as such. The specific mission of the riot was precisely *not* to enter into negotiations, not even with the political Left. My five theses are preceded by a description of the Hamburg events.

0.

The context of the July riot was the summit of the G20 states, which took place on July 7–8, 2017, in the Hamburg Trade Fair and Congress Center. The summit was significant in three ways. First, it gathered representatives of the two opposing political tendencies in imperial politics. One tendency (represented by Trump, Putin, Erdoğan, and, mediating to the second tendency, Xi Jinping) seeks to solve the crisis of the neoliberal empire by returning to classic imperialist (that is, nation-state-centered) policies that internally stage themselves as policies of charismatic leadership. The other tendency (represented by Merkel and Macron) continues to hold onto an imperial course, but in this case, it is the imperial course of a multilaterally organized world order, "Empire."[1] Second, the summit was significant in its failure: it could not solve the struggle of the two tendencies and thus became a symptom of the continuation of the crisis of Empire and the stagnation of all attempts at a solution. Third, the meeting in Hamburg was significant because it was the first summit since Genoa in 2001 to take place in a big city and, especially, in a city with a strong Left and radical Left tradition. For example, the fairground where the rulers of Empire met borders the Schanzenviertel, where the famous autonomous center Rote Flora is located.

0.1

In a survey of Hamburg residents in July 2017, 74 percent disapproved of hosting the summit in the city, 87 percent found costs far too high, and 73 percent did not expect relevant results; they were right.[2] The politico-police leadership of the city was prepared for one of the largest police operations in the history of the Federal Republic of Germany. It occupied the city with 31,000 police officers and established a restricted area of 38 square kilometers in which any political assembly was prohibited on the summit days. The area included reserved "red" and "yellow" zones; the first was reserved for summit participants and people entitled to access, the second for residents and post and care

1. I refer to the concept of Empire as developed by Michael Hardt and Toni Negri. The concept and the thing in itself are basically defined by the sentence "The problematic of Empire is determined in the first place by one simple fact: that there is world order." Michael Hardt and Antonio Negri, *Empire* (Cambridge, MA: Harvard University Press, 2000), 3. I would like to stress the point, already made by Hardt and Negri, that the imperial project is motivated not only by the necessity of governing the globalization of capitalist production but also by the politico-ideological need to govern a historical epoch pretending to realize the "end of history."

2. *Hamburger Morgenpost*, July 6, 2017. For more information, see Karl-Heinz Dellwo, Achim Szepanski, and J. Paul Weiler, eds., *Riot: Was war da los in Hamburg? Theorie und Praxis der kollektiven Aktion* (Hamburg: Laika, 2018).

services. A third zone included the area around the Elbphilharmonie, where summit participants were to celebrate with a performance of Beethoven's "Ode to Joy." A special prison for 400 prisoners with its own courtrooms was built to detain riotous persons. Already, in the run-up, massive warnings were issued about the arrival of protesters from Germany and abroad who were "willing to use violence."

0.2

The protests began on Sunday, July 2, with a demonstration of 10,000 participants organized by moderate NGOs. On the same day, however, the police—in an open breach of law—stopped the construction of an overnight camp. With the first police attacks came the first activist injuries. The day after, the politico-police leadership of the city was legitimized ex post facto by the Hamburg Administrative Court: the first submissive act by the judiciary. On Wednesday, July 5, artist protests followed; that evening and the following day, a "countersummit" with around 1,500 participants took place.

On the evening of the second day of the countersummit, the Rote Flora called for the demonstration G20: Welcome to Hell. At 7:00 p.m., 12,000 demonstrators gathered, including some 600 in masks. When they refused to remove their disguises, several hundred policemen with water cannons invaded the crowd shortly after the march started. It was obviously their aim not to arrest but to corporally punish riotous behavior. Nevertheless, the police were defeated. The brutally battered demonstrators reorganized a little later: relatively unhindered, 8,000 people moved to the Reeperbahn, and scattered groups burned cars and barricades, destroyed shop windows, and attacked police officers.

The police suffered its second defeat on the following day, Friday, July 7—the day of the blockades. Thousands of people were always three steps ahead of the police and their water cannons and scavengers, obstructing the trips of state guests, forcing them to take detours, and delaying the course of the summit. Violent clashes broke out in various places across the city, police vehicles burned, shop windows were broken. The police cleared streets with water cannons.

At 7:00 p.m., around 500 demonstrators in the Schanzenviertel district set up barricades, set fire to them, threw firecrackers, and armed themselves with iron bars. The police responded two hours later with action forces and water cannons on Schulterblatt, the core of the district. They used gas grenades and fired a warning shot but were then driven back by protesters throwing stones and bottles. Then special forces squads (SEKs) equipped with machine pistols entered the game—according to their commanders, they were given special permission to use the firearms for self-defense. At this point, what today is called the Hamburg riot began: shops were looted, cars were set on fire, and police officers were attacked and pelted with stones thrown from occupied houses. All this was done by a crowd numbering in the hundreds, composed mainly of migrant youth and activists from the autonomous, anarchist, and insurrectionist Left. Step by step, the SEKs cleared nine of the occupied houses, shooting rubber bullets at activists on the rooftops. All the while, police helicopters circled streets lit by their headlights, the noise of their rotor blades dominating the soundscape.

The performance *1000 GESTALTEN* was a form of creative protest in the context of G20 at Burchardtplatz, Hamburg, on July 5, 2017. Photograph by Miguel Ferraz.

The following day, Saturday, July 8, more than 70,000 people marched to Millerntor without major incidents. Another clash took place in the Schanzenviertel in the evening; the police quickly brought it under control.

1.

I see the riot as an articulation of the mode of existence that I call "revolt." The revolt encompasses much more than the riot, which marks its *collective inner turning point*. The revolt begins not with the riot but instead with the murderous game of *terror*, which is the most extreme articulation of revolt. In this ambiguity, the revolt today expresses what Hegel called "the life of the spirit," which "shrinks from death and keeps itself untouched by devastation" but "endures it and maintains itself in it. It wins its truth only when, in utter dismemberment, it finds itself."[3]

1.1

I start my little phenomenology of revolt with terrorism because the current world is best understood in light of the challenges terrorism creates. Abstracted from its empirical bonds to politico-ideological projects and economic interests, a terrorist attack is played out by (more or less) arbitrary individuals articulating their desire for the tran-scendence of the given world by threatening (more or less) arbitrary people with death at (more or less) arbitrary places. Self-empowering, they rely on nothing but a willingness to die and a desire to take as many others along as possible. Therefore, in its pure form, a terrorist attack resembles what the French writer André Gide called an *acte gratuit*, an act posed not against a specific social, economic, or political deter-mination but against determinism as such.[4] For us, then, to overcome terrorism means to search for radical, different ways to express that attitude.

1.2

However, the challenge of suicide bombing is deeply interwoven with its counterpart, the cybernetic upgraded anti-terrorism of the state, which tends to free itself from all legal restrictions. Anti-terror functions as the last point of convergence for neoliberal Empire pretending to rule the end of history. Proclaimed in the 1990s, the end of history and of its Empire has meanwhile lost (almost) all of its shine. Imperial power today is therefore limited to granting privileged subordinates exclusive protection against the horrors of post-history, especially the horrors of terror. Far more people are paying for anti-terror with their lives, with their injuries, and with the destruction of their goods than in all terrorist attacks put together.

1.3

Empire tries to govern an interconnected set of globally relevant pro-cesses of socialization. The first of these processes is the becoming worldwide of the world itself, for which the concept of globalization

●   3.   Georg Wilhelm Friedrich Hegel, *Phenomenology of the Spirit*, trans. A. V. Miller (Oxford: Oxford University Press, 1977), 19.
    ●   4.   André Gide, *The Vatican Cellars* (London: Penguin, 1976).

stands. The priority of globalization is shown in the fact that all of the other processes of socialization are also processes of globalization. Continuing: the second process is the capitalization of the world, which in itself is (third) the process of our proletarianization. Both find their own place in (fourth) the urbanization of the world, through which the difference between city and countryside disappears. The driving force in all these processes is (fifth) the cyberneticization with which the world becomes a circuit of circuits. The common result is (sixth) the precarization of life in all its material and symbolic conditions. Globalization is then subjectively experienced through (seventh) the process of individualization. However, it does not make us unique, self-centered individuals; rather, it places us in a competitive position where we are forced to compare our behavior to that of others or, more precisely, to the average of their behavior. This is (eighth) the mediocritization that is sociologically realized in the hegemony of the global middle class. The pull of the middle class also governs those who have no chance of belonging to it: the marginalized in all countries. They bear the expenses of the imperial way of life.

2.

These processes of globalization require imperial governance and governmentality because they are invariably processes of crisis: processes of the capitalist crisis, the crisis of work, the crisis of migration, and the ecological crisis. The crisis of capitalism lies in its inner vicious cycle, in which capital can only reproduce itself by reproducing its immanent negativity: class struggle. The question then is not to overcome class struggle but to turn it into capitalist reproduction: a turn that is never sufficient and therefore fuels capitalist crises. The crisis of work lies in the fact that on the one hand, work under capitalist conditions promises a secure income and a coexistential recognition (and therefore integrates class struggle into capitalist reproduction); but on the other hand, it is available for fewer and fewer people. The ecological crisis forms the horizon of all other crises because it could render the earth as uninhabitable as the moon. The already tight deadline is shortening daily. These crises are currently performed in the crisis of migration, which, as the largest movement of people of all time and the front line of class struggle, systematically deterritorializes people individualized by their own nothingness: the dispossessed of Empire.

2.1

The fact that the crisis processes of Empire are in themselves crises of individualization is manifest in the crisis of social relations, including the crisis of elementary relationships like friendship and love. This leads us directly into the crisis of the ethical and consequently into the crisis of the political, which is not accidentally articulated in the double crisis of religion and secularity.

2.2

The double crisis of religion and secularity leads back to the crisis of terror and anti-terror, and thus to the coming out of each other and

A policewoman at Rote Flora after the police attacked the G:0: Welcome to Hell demonstration July 6–7, 2017. Photograph by Miguel Ferazz.

going into each other of all crises: the crisis of history.[5] It lies in the fact that history has ended without being completed—that is, without having fulfilled the promises that enable us to speak of a singular history and of a possible end of history. The clearest symptom of the crisis of history lies in the flippancy with which it is shrugged off.

2.3
In fact, Empire is called Empire because it knows no boundary, no outside, and no other: "There Is no alternative!" Seen from the Western

5. For a systematic philosophical investigation into the crisis of history, see Thomas Seibert, *Zur* Ökologie *der Existenz: Freiheit, Gleichheit, Umwelt* (Hamburg: Laika, 2017).

theological-metaphysical tradition, Empire therefore is immanence in itself, an interior without an exterior that tries to erase every trace of transcendence. For that very reason, and this is the all-important point, Empire (at least at this point of its own history) has found its main challenge in terrorism. Based on this idea, terror is the only transcendence left over: the transition from a self-contained inner to an outer, which is a mere vain nothingness. Terror is revolt in the form of active nihilism. This is the reason that the crisis is not terrorism for the sake of fundamentalism but the other way around: fundamentalism is simply for the sake of terrorism.

3.

Terror, as the transcendence of last resort, also retains a last vestige of the transcendental event, in which for Hegel (though not only for Hegel) the purposeless becoming becomes "world history" in its true meaning: the life-and-death struggle for recognition. Hegel calls it a "struggle for recognition" because its fighters try to communicate their own freedom to each other and thereby try to achieve their recognition as free beings.[6] Only with the risk of death do the fighters prove that they can detach themselves from the natural compulsion for self-preservation and, thus, from mere life in order to affirm themselves as free. It is this existential detachment from the compulsion to self-preservation, in its pure meta-ethical sense, that is perverted by today's terrorists.

The dilemma at the bottom of Hegel's reconstruction of history's first struggle lies in the fact that one of the two combatants evades this existential probation and, for the sake of survival, becomes a servant of the other. From this constellation, world history receives its tendency, its inner drive—of course, not in the sense of an empirical cause but in the sense of the logical starting point for the philosophical reconstruction of history's bloody ups and downs. Exactly in this sense, the constellation itself is to be found in all kinds of social struggles, not only in class struggle but also in all kinds of power relations, those based on class as well as those based on gender, ethnicity, or race. In all of these cases, we have to understand that freedom always provides the possibility of self-neglect, which itself is an act of freedom. All history, and therefore all society, is always a history and society of voluntary bondage or voluntary servitude. This is the scandal in which the revolt reignites, in which the revolt and thus the riot find their own morality.

3.1

In fact, the relationship between domination and bondage is unsatisfactory for all participants. The survival of servants depends only on the arbitrariness of their masters. The masters themselves have gained recognition by their servants, but it is a worthless recognition—simply because it is given only by a servant. While the masters have only their readiness for death, the servants are aware of their opportunity for freedom through self-mastery and world domination achieved by their work. Thus their struggles, however confused, become "political" struggles in the eminent sense of the term: struggles of world history.

●   6. Hegel, *Phenomenology of the Spirit*, 104–111.

THOMAS SEIBERT

For Hegel, the French Revolution marks the sublation of this drama: the killing of the king is the overcoming of the master and therein the end of the story—that is, the end of the dialectic of domination and bondage. This is where Marx and Nietzsche, Hegel's most important critics, come in.

3.2

Marx criticizes bourgeois society from the perspective of collective practice and recognizes in its capitalist form a specific alienation, one that the servant is able to remove dialectically. Nietzsche goes a step further. For him, the societies of the free and equal, politically and philosophically legitimized by Hegel and Marx, are in truth only societies of servants without masters. He works out his criticism from the perspective of singular existence and recognizes in its proletarian-bourgeois form not only a specific but also a generic alienation. By this he means an alienation that cannot be sublated dialectically and therefore remains the medium of existential revolt—in other words, a revolt that even in its plurality remains the singular revolt of an individual.

Marx and Nietzsche became the main proponents of widely endorsed lines of criticism. Marx's line is called "social criticism" and politicizes (in addition to class alienation) many other alienations, especially those of gender and generation; of ethnic, racial, and linguistic origin; and of sexual and spiritual orientation. Nietzsche's line is called "artists' criticism" because it takes the purposeless expenditure of art as pars pro toto for the freedom of existence.[7] Early on, these two lines of criticism disputed over the demarcations between specific and generic alienation. In this sense, it is no coincidence that now three voices of the Surrealist movement have their say: to this day, this disagreement is one of the decisive forces in the mediation between social and artistic criticism.

3.3

Nietzsche has also taught us to recognize the historically most powerful force of revolt and its great danger, which he has called the "spirit of revenge": those who revolt most often take revenge on those whom they rightly and wrongfully hold responsible for their misery. This revenge is not only directed toward the masters or to competing servants but also applies to the whole of life and the earth. This connects the revolt to work as the mode of existence that today devastates all of our lives and our entire world. Artists' criticism following Nietzsche then showed that revenge feeds on at least three basic existential *"Befindlichkeiten"*:

7. The concepts of "social criticism" and "artists' criticism" and the difference between "specific" and "generic alienation" have been developed by Luc Boltanski and Ève Chiapello in their fundamental study *The New Spirit of Capitalism* (London: Verso, 2018). Their main thesis is that the world historical meaning of the May 1968 revolution lies in the way this revolution mediated between these two forms of criticism, and that the neoliberal counterrevolution therefore has to be understood as a reintegration of the specific achievements of this constellation into capitalist reproduction.

I

fear, disgust, and boredom.[8] These basic conditions reflect our specific as well as our generic alienation, above all the alienation that results from our condemnation to death, to desire, and to violence. Today, fear, disgust, and boredom are the basic conditions of the servants without masters and their imperial way of life; they are therefore more powerful than ever before in history. As such, they include, of course, more concrete societal *Befindlichkeiten*, such as the feelings of injustice or exclusion.

From these feelings, it is also understandable why terror and revolt are not specific to a particular religion but symbolically legitimize themselves through nationalism, racism, sexism, and from certain socialisms, as well as from struggles for survival that have escalated into open violence. However, fear, disgust, and boredom also explain why the revolt can exist without any legitimacy, as is the case of a rampage or a suicide: they too are more common today than ever before. Still, they explain how and why revenge is associated with its adversary, imperiousness.

4.

Like terror, rampage, and suicide, the riot also belongs to the revolt. It finds its classic formulation in the famous "pistol phrase" of André Breton:

> The simplest Surrealist act consists of dashing down into the street, pistol in hand, and firing blindly, as fast as you can, pull the trigger into the crowd. Anyone who, at least once in his life, has not dreamed of thus putting an end to the petty system of debasement and cretinization in effect has a well-defined place in that crowd, with his belly at barrel level.[9]

The riot becomes the collective *inner turning point of revolt* because and when social and artistic criticism come together and mutually criticize each other. During the looting in the Hamburg riot, this is clear in the case of the stolen flat-screen TVs. While some rioters—with a kind of sociocritical perspective—recognized the TVs as a good to acquire, others threw them directly into the fire as—from the perspective of artistic criticism—an obstacle to their transcendence beyond the actual existing world. This shows what possibilities the politics of the riot opens up as a borderline case of the political. Most recently, this potential is visible in the Arab Spring, in certain moments of revolts in southern Europe, and currently in a growing number of countries like Algeria, Lebanon, Iran, Iraq, Sudan, Chile, or Haiti.

8. The meaning of the German term *Befindlichkeit*, philosophically enumerated by Martin Heidegger in *Sein und Zeit*, unfortunately is not preserved in its English translation "mental state," because it also contains the meaning of *sich befinden in* (to be located in) through which "*Befindlichkeit*" becomes a basic element of existence—that is, as "being-in-the-world." Unfortunately, the term "state of mind" is used in the English translation of Heidegger's *Being and Time* (1964; repr., Oxford: Oxford University Press, 2001).
9. André Breton, *Manifestoes of Surrealism* (Ann Arbor: University of Michigan Press, 1969), 125.

4.1

Of course, the riot is also led by resentment and, of course, it is also primed by fear, disgust, and boredom. That is why we cannot stop at the riot. This was clearly demonstrated by the Chemnitz riot that began on August 26, 2018, the political counterpoint to the Hamburg riot. On this and the following days, young and socially marginalized Germans repeatedly attacked migrant residents in the city. As in Hamburg, the police were initially unable to stop the violence. Of course, the Chemnitz riot was as clearly on the political right in its social composition and orientation as the Hamburg riot was clearly on the left: this difference is crucial. There are further meaningful differences as well—for example, the different attitudes toward the use of violence: the violence was against marginalized subjects in the case of Chemnitz and against the armed forces of state power in the case of Hamburg. Phenomenologically, however, the Chemnitz riot cannot be reduced to its political coding, because it too not only attacks particular social relationships but also acts against being-related-in-society as such. We can fix this phenomenological ambiguity in three theses:

1. Like rampages and suicide, riot and terror in their pure forms are articulations of an existential revolt against specific and, more importantly, generic alienation.

Sentiments escalate in Hamburg's Pferdemarkt after the police advance with water cannons on Budapester Straße. On July 7, 2017, the Schanze became the center of the riots. Photograph by Miguel Ferraz.

2. Taken politically, specific riots can be associated with the Right (e.g., Chemnitz) and the Left (e.g., Hamburg). The reason for this is that one of the main *Befindlichkeiten* motivating riots is to be found in resentment ("spirit of revenge").

3. Whereas terror in its pure form is neither on the right nor on the left, taken politically, terror is always on the right, even if its protagonists understand themselves as leftists. But armed, or at least violent, struggles identified by state actors as "terrorist acts" need not be acts of "terrorism."

Again, we owe the decisive verdict to Surrealism, this time the group Le Grand Jeu (the Great Game) and its eponymous magazine.[10] It passionately calls for rioting—and at the same time calls for a resignation from revolt. Thereby, Le Grand Jeu understands resignation not as an act of abandonment or pacification but as an existential attitude in

10. Robert Gilbert-Lecomte, Maurice Henry, and René Daumal, *Theory of the Great Game: Writings from Le Grand Jeu Magazine* (London: Atlas, 2015).

which revolt is bracketed and henceforth on the go: as a possibility for existence to be worked out anytime in and as an act of freedom. In order to make this existential attitude come to life, the Surrealists of Le Grand Jeu joined the revolutionary workers' movement of their time and so mediated artistic and social criticism—without letting go of their revolt against the generic alienation, which revolution can change only a little.

4.2

As with the other Surrealists, the alliance of Le Grand Jeu and communism did not last. Nevertheless, we owe another Surrealist, Georges Bataille, for the first reference to another, post-Marxist mediation of social and artistic criticism. For Bataille, socialism was not the end of history and therefore was not the abolition of alienation, but instead was a way to purge the revolt of revenge as well as of imperiousness. His reasoning is as simple as it is striking, empirically problematic yet logically consistent: since fully developed socialism liberates the existential transcendence that he calls "sovereignty" from all forms of hierarchies, the competition for positions of power and property (and the drives for revenge and imperiousness that stem from it) will cease to be politically influential. Of course, the revolt then would not be pacified. But it would now be possible to articulate itself alone in poetry or, perhaps, in beauty. Bataille writes:

> It is less about works in which this beauty could take shape; rather, it is about a force that must possess, who does not want to be separated from this beauty for a moment. And further: provided that the few who are concerned will have the consciousness of this force, chaos and dissonance, of the scale of a world, will not cease to quench the thirst that will plague humanity forever.[11]

4.3

If the riot has its limit in a shooting star, which shines forth only to disappear again in the dark, we must make possible—through reform, reformation, and revolution—a socialism in which riot and revolt can permanently be renewed. It would be a negative-dialectical socialism, in which social criticism and praxis act as an interim that again and again gives way to the primacy of artists' criticism and existence.

5.

The deadline to achieve this socialism is tight. If the clock runs down, the revolt will be as lonely as ever. This does not change anything about its nonnegotiability. On the contrary, the riot would communicate the nonnegotiable. It would offer the power of instantaneous debinding from the present (that is, from voluntary servitude), and it would be the force of anticipation for a real end to history—the anticipation of (not only) Nietzsche's dream of an innocence of becoming in which we could finally abandon history. To be after the end of history is to be before the end of history.

● 11. Georges Bataille, *Die Souveränität* (Munich: Mattse and Seitz, 1978), 86 (my translation).

No One Leaves Delilah —
A (W)rap on Riots

Natasha Ginwala
in conversation with
Vaginal Davis

Natasha Ginwala:
Can you share with us your impressions of the Whittier Boulevard Riots of East Los Angeles of the early 1940s, also known as the Zoot Suit Riots, and their impact on cultural life in LA?

Vaginal Davis:
I saw the original stage production in Hollywood of Luis Valdez's *Zoot Suit* at the Aquarius Theater when I was in high school. Being in the MGM—Mentally Gifted Minor—program of the Los Angeles Unified School District, I was able to see a lot of theatrical and cultural events for free. Back in the 1970s, there was still a social conscience in the United States. That is all gone now.

Later, *Zoot Suit* had a short-lived run on Broadway, and I believe they made a film of it that was just documentation of the stage run.

The Sleepy Lagoon Chicano race riots of Los Angeles in 1943 are fascinating on so many levels. They took place not only in California but also in Texas and other states where there was a large Chicano presence in the 1940s. The zoot suiters and pachucas had a very distinctive style. With my punk pop group ¡Cholita!, The Female Menudo, I co-opted looks first made popular by the pachucas back in the 1940s. The pachucas were the first to wear skirts above the knee and overdraw their lip line. And the racism of that time was reflected in people being so evil toward those wearing this look. With ¡Cholita!, we were sort of combining the earlier pachuca style with a mid-1970s girl gang "I'm gonna jump you" look.

Are you familiar with the St. Louis race riot of 1917 that affected the activism of the legendary Josephine Baker? Those riots scarred Baker for life. Baker was also a performer I got to see live in the 1970s, thanks to MGM, along with Marlene Dietrich, Eartha Kitt in *Timbuktu!*, and *The Magic Flute* at the world-famous Shrine Auditorium, which was my first experience with grand opera and a major influence on my performance work.

Josephine Baker, c. 1936. Courtesy of PictureLux/The Hollywood Archive/Alamy Stock Photo.

NG: Josephine Baker went on to work as a civil rights activist and especially focused on the prolonged impact of racial violence—like you, through her performance style and through renegotiating representations of the "exotic" entertainer. She was troubled by the early experience of the St. Louis race riots and ran away from home soon after. Would you elaborate on her influence on your performance work?

VD: When the East St. Louis race riots happened, I think Josephine was just about ten or eleven years old. It was horrific. Those riots also affected Miles Davis, who was from St. Louis as well. The ability of those people to attack and scream at the Blacks—men, women, and children—in St. Louis affected her very much. I think that's one of the things that led to Josephine Baker wanting to leave America altogether.

NG: How would you characterize the impact of the Watts Riots and the role of artists, writers, and jazz musicians who responded during that time? Would you say that the punk scene and zines you produced later responded to the systemic violence unleashed at the time?

VD: One of my professors at UCLA, Oscar Saul, who adapted *A Streetcar Named Desire* to the screen, taught regular poetry and writing workshops at the Watts Towers in the 1960s and 1970s. Liberals at that time put their penis where their mouth is and didn't pay lip service to social issues but got their hands and feet dirty by going into direct, selfless action. Oscar Saul was one of the first people to encourage my writing, telling me that I didn't realize how good it was.

Having lived through the first riots in 1965 certainly influenced my zine writing and contributed to my writing having a militant, whimsical edge.

NG: The Stonewall Riots or uprising (1969) had a global resonance for the queer and trans community and for the human rights movement more broadly. Who were some of the heroines you recollect from then?

VD: Marsha P. Johnson and Silvia Rivera are certainly two figures from that period who have always stood out and who I've always seen as role models. Also Jim Fouratt, who was not only at Stonewall but who also crisscrossed with the New York City punk and early queer scenes, as he was the manager of Danceteria and was a big supporter of those of us who were part of the zine movement. In any scene of interest, you will find Jim Fouratt. He is still an elegant fixture of anything interesting happening in New York City and a tireless warrior priest. Also Peter Hujar's muse John Edward Heys, who lives in Berlin and who created the early gay rights magazine *Gay Power*, which featured photography by a then unknown Robert Mapplethorpe.

Vaginal Davis, *That Fertile Feeling*, 1982. Directed by John "Quasi" O'Shea and Gomorrah Wednesday (AKA Keith Holland), edited by John "Quasi" O'Shea. Courtesy of the artist.

NG: Linking with the 1980s and the 1992 LA Riots, can you tell us about your neighborhood, Koreatown, and the parties and HAG Gallery's DIY shows that you ran, which brought in music, entertainment, socializing, sex, and creativity as a way to deal with class ruptures and racism?

VD: I lived in the old ethnic neighborhood that is now called Koreatown. Before, the neighborhood that I lived in was the old

FERTILE LA T

JACKSO

MAGAZINE

inside rob lowe's body parts
- p. 15

alan carr plays
with charlie sexton -p. 17

party down with jul
and paul fortu

omar's men, erotica & more

harvest issue

$1.00 - US   £ c.50

YAH
N

Vaginal Davis. *Fertile La Toyah Jackson Magazine*, 1982–1991. © Vaginal Davis.
Courtesy of Dan Gunn.

e
6.

Irish section of Los Angeles. And it had this wonderful bar called the Daughter of Rosie O'Grady. It was like an SSI [Social Security Insurance] bar where the drinks were very inexpensive. What people don't really know in terms of class consciousness is that a lot of whites that lived in the inner city were too poor for white flight into the suburbs or exurbia, so the owner of the Daughter of Rosie O'Grady stayed in the neighborhood as it went from being an Irish neighborhood to a Korean neighborhood that also included Latinos—and not just Latinos from Mexico but Latinos from Central America. When the owner of the Daughter of Rosie O'Grady died, some Vietnamese ladies took over the bar, and it was called the Monte Carlo II, even though there wasn't really a Monte Carlo I. I hosted a party for my film *The White to Be Angry* and Bruce LaBruce's film *Skin Flick*, which they screened at the Directors Guild Theater as part of the Outfest Film Festival [Outfest 99], and that's when I first met Susanne Sachsse, the fearless leader of the CHEAP Kollektiv. She was in Los Angeles with Volker Spengler, the [Rainer Werner] Fassbinder star on tour with the Berliner Ensemble production of Brecht's *The Resistible Rise of Arturo Ui*. The cast all came to my party at the dive bar Monte Carlo II, including Susanne, Volker, Martin Wuttke, Konstantin Achmed Buerger, and Margarita Broich, who thought she was sharing some hashish with a local woman but was actually smoking a cigarette dipped in crack cocaine. Margarita had a bad reaction and had to be rushed to the emergency room. The parties I would host during this period were unique in that my crowd would mix debutants with people just released from prison.

The person that owned the beautiful, gigantic apartment building I lived in during this period in Koreatown was a woman named Mrs. Ritchie. Mrs. Ritchie was a Eurasian woman who only rented to artists. She didn't care how much money you made, you had to have the right energy to live in her apartment building. Mrs. Ritchie couldn't care less if an apartment stayed empty for three years. After the 1992 riots and the [Big Bear] earthquake, I needed an apartment because the one I had been living in had been damaged during the earthquake. Luckily, Mrs. Ritchie liked me, and I got my dream apartment. It was huge, three bedrooms, two baths. I had a balcony that faced the Hollywood sign and the Griffith Park Observatory and a terrace where on a clear day, you could see all the way to Catalina Island.

NG: You made these sort of no-budget or small-budget blaxploitation films, queer zines, and a home gallery. Can we talk about that?

VD: Well, when I was living in my beautiful, gigantic apartment in Koreatown, that was the main office of my movie studio Mateo, Gobulin, Mathu. I wanted it to have the initials of Metro Goldwyn Mayer. I made all my no-budget, low-budget films there, and even some of the films that I starred in, like Bruce LaBruce's *Hustler White*. My scenes from *Hustler White* were filmed in that apartment. But before I lived in Koreatown, I lived on the Sunset Strip, in a building called La Via Rosa. That apartment was where I had my home gallery, the HAG— small, contemporary, haggard. It was a tiny apartment, but I decided to have openings every six weeks at this space because the walls were so big and they were just perfect for artwork. The main reason I opened the gallery was not that I wanted to become an art gallerist. I only opened it because I thought maybe I could get a boyfriend if I had openings and little regular parties and happenings there. But as with everything that I tried to do, it backfired, and I didn't meet anyone for a relationship. Also at this time, when I had the HAG Gallery in the 1980s, I was doing my zine, *Fertile La Toyah Jackson*. Back in those days, I had a day job. I actually worked at UCLA's Placement and Career Planning Center. My boss was William Locklear, the father of actress Heather Locklear. Heather and I were in the same graduating class at UCLA.

NG: You also wrote for *LA Weekly*, right?

VD: Yes, I'd been writing for *LA Weekly* since I was sixteen years old, because it was the only place where people who were strange, weird, and freaks could get a job. Of course, later the *Weekly* became corporate, so they would just get interns from Harvard, but back in the 1980s, it was where all the people who couldn't really get a job anywhere else worked. I was a regular contributor there, even when I worked at UCLA's Placement and Career Planning Center in a building that was designed by Frank Gehry. I had access to a free Xerox machine, and that was like having a grant. Because with that free Xerox machine, I could make my magazine. I just made as many copies as I would get orders for. Looking back now, it seems bizarre that a magazine that was just xeroxed and stapled together would get orders from all over the world.

. . . tell me sumpthin' good!

Floated into the opening of a
trendy new ex underground
celebrity hangout which shall
remain nameless because I've
been sworn to secrecy that
I won't divulge their all
too-secret location and name
since it could prompt the
police to closedown this
racy speakeasy. But I will
give out a few clues to its
whereabouts because I could
never keep a secret. The
club is on the West Hollywood/
Bev Hills, LA border and this
place useta be an infamous
Bathhouse. Enough already I
can't go on any further.
Well one thing I can say
is that all the boys were
delicious, tanned to perfection

all pumped Nautilis pumped
ing very very little.

vicious

lies

hear-say

speculation

pussi washington at t
of morgan mason's new

pic by beulah luv

Anyway that slutty
Bridgette Nielsen was there
seriously making out with a
few of those sexy Nina Blanchard
boy models and left with young
male starlet James Mathers
(Who has a sexy nude scene in
that movie Aria with Brigette
Fonda, Peter's little girl and
Jane's niece.) Joining the
couple was a non-descript model
type with a very beefy
body, so I'm sure that turned into a
delicious 3-way. My guess
is that the boys got more into
each other and left Bridgette
with a wet muff. The

dor

e

y

ru

Other action that night was fat
and gross troll of trolls Alan Carr
making an oink oink of himself trying to
talk Charlie Sexton into going home
with him and his entourage of sexy
male escorts. What nerve.
Isn't he just being a little greedy
He already had 4 beautiful blond surfe

wanted to add dark hai
to the harum. Well Ch
lite but graciously de
offer.

is this famous man?

sing all I have to say is if you're sitting back reading this column wis
e glamorous social life that I do, thank the heavens above that you
e unknown unknown nobody because in all actuality you're not missing anvt
best evenings are spent at home reading a good book

RETAIL SLUT

7517 Melrose Avenue

Hollywood

(213) 655-6576

true debs

models: kayle hilliard, albe

~~styling~~ ~~rick~~ ~~castr~~

styling rick castro

NG: I want to talk about your musical side and all these amazing bands, like the punk pop band ¡Cholita! The Female Menudo and Afro Sisters. Were these in any way responding to the subtext of the riots and of systemic racism? How would you define the relationship there?

VD: I would say that there is a relationship, because I'm a child of the first uprising in 1965, the uprising in Watts. My family moved to Los Angeles in the 1940s, I guess as part of that second wave of what was called the Great Migration, where a lot of Blacks from the American South moved to the North for jobs and to escape Jim Crow. The ones that moved to LA from the South, the first group of Blacks in the teens and in the 1920s, were the Black French Creoles. The only places where Blacks and other minorities could live in Los Angeles— because they had these covenant laws that were very strict and horrible—were basically Watts or East Los Angeles. My mother was a Black Creole from Louisiana, and we were vis-

Vaginal Davis, *The White to be Angry*, 1999. Directed by Vaginal Davis, cinematography and editing by Lawrence Elbert. Courtesy of the artist.

iting my mother's godmother in Watts when the uprising happened. Because of the curfew, we were stuck in Watts during the uprising. I think it lasted about six days or so. And even though I was quite young, my main memory from the 1965 riots was my mother taking me out on the street to look at the soldiers and the big tanks coming through the neighborhood. For a small child, it was extremely frightening to see soldiers and tanks and smoke everywhere. And after the curfew had been lifted, we went back a little bit farther north from Watts to Mid-City Los Angeles, where my oldest sister lived, around Pico Boulevard. Even in this neighborhood that didn't have the largest Black population—it did have a sizable Black population, it wasn't exactly Watts, but it was still close to South Central LA—there were soldiers, there was the National Guard. This had an effect on me, and it just stayed with me. When I became part of the punk scene, I started doing all my little natty art bands. I used the Afro Sisters as a vehicle to let out a lot of my anger from growing up very poor in the inner city.

Afro Sisters started in the late 1970s, and then in the mid-1980s, I started ¡Cholita! The Female Menudo because I had never really explored my Latin roots. I'm biracial on my father's side—he was born in Mexico. That's when I started to only listen to K-LOVE Radio Amor, this Latin music radio station

The response of the first issue of Fertile LaToyah Jackson, The Magazine was staggering. Our phone keeps ringing off the hook. Thanks for all the cards and letters and the words of encouragement. Fertile loves her fans and is warmed at the reception of her magazine. Fertile is a woman with a lot on her mind. We hope you enjoy reading about Fertile and the exploits of the Afro Sisters. Remember! Fertile La Toyah Jackson is the woman and the magazine everyone is talking about.

Fertile La Toyah Jackson, the living, breathing TV movie, rock video, xxxxwoman and magazine is published whenever Fertile becomes so indignant, so frustrated with the goings on of our critical times of which we live that she feels its time for her to make comment. Fertile La Toyah Jackson magazine-7850 Sunset Blvd #110 Wxx West Hollywood, CA., 90046. Make all inquiries to that address.

STAFF
Editor-In-Chief-Miss Vaginal Creme Davis
Photo Editor-Beulah Luv
Contributing Editors Urethra Franklin, Clitoris Turner, Cherry Jefferson, Pussi Washington, Vulva Jones
New York Editor-Saliva Johnson
Paris Editor- Sucretion Williams
London Editor- Ovaries Smith

Cover photo of Fertile La Toyah Jackson
By Beulah Luv

pic by Jackie Diverse

ADVERTISE! ADVERTISE! THE KING AND HIS KINGDOM! Yes. Advertise in Fertile La Toyah Jackson, The Magazine. Rates are cheap and with a circulation of 40,000 readers in the United States alone an ad in Fertile is worth its price in gold. So call Vaginal Davis at (213) 851-7743 we have our own art department who can create that special ad for you or just give us one that is camera ready. Y'know Fertile La Toyah Jackson is a camera ready kind of black woman.

AD RATES	
whole page	$25.00
half page	15.00
business card size	5.00

What have you got to lose? Nothing but your composure.

2

1

that would play artists like the immortal Vikki Carr. I started to write songs in Spanish even though my Spanish is very limited. But that didn't stop me from writing songs in Spanish and collaborating with Alice Bag—Alicia "Alice" Armendariz—who was in one of the earliest of the LA punk rock bands, the Bags. I started to do ¡Cholita! The Female Menudo around the mid-1980s, and it continued to the end of the last century. The Afro Sisters went on from 1978, and our last show was 1990. Then I formed the positive punk band called Pedro, Muriel & Esther (PME). I think ¡Cholita! and Pedro, Muriel & Esther are the two bands I'm more identified with in terms of the queercore music scene.

NG: Did you directly experience the Whittier Boulevard Riots of East Los Angeles, which were in 1970, I think?

VD: No, not directly. During those riots in the 1970s, my family had already left East LA, and we were living in Mid-City LA. But this is from Chicana activist and artist Harry Gamboa Jr., from his "Misses and Other Unknowns," his mailing list where he sends all these really wonderful snippets. Harry Gamboa Jr., besides being a Chicano activist, performance artist, and photographer, is also one of the cofounders of the Chicano artist collective ASCO. So Harry shares:
"In 1971, I was marching with many young people in East Los Angeles during a peaceful protest against the politically motivated assassination of journalist Ruben Salazar, a prominent voice on behalf of the Chicano community who had been shot to death by a police agent. The calm and silence of the protest demonstration was shattered when more than a dozen police officers opened fire with riot shotguns using live ammunition, resulting in many fallen and dead. The subsequent reactionary mainstream news reports that fan the false flames of negative stereotypes against Chicanos and mass arrests that followed, along with the martial law-like tactics that were enacted, created a toxic environment of oppression. The shock that such extreme measures of power would be utilized on American citizens of Mexican descent to counter the increasing social and political awareness of my peers caused me to reflect on my lack of documentary imagery to illustrate what I had witnessed to be an absolute atrocity against the nonviolent group of youth."

NG: Another good friend of yours, José Esteban Muñoz, has written on your "terrorist drag" and the film and concept album *The White to Be Angry*. *The White to Be Angry* is such an important work, and I wonder also about its relationship to "terrorist drag." How do you think of that work in relation to this topic and the experience of racialization as well?

VD: I met the late Dr. Muñoz in the early 1990s during my retrospectacle at the Anthology Film Archives in New York. He started to come to my events, taking notes and writing about the kind of work that I did. That led to him writing his book *Disidentifications* [subtitled *Queers of Color and the Performance of Politics*] and doing a chapter on my work called "The White to Be Angry." *The White to Be Angry* is not only the title of my little "omnibus film," but it's also the title of my art, punk, rock band record album with Pedro, Muriel & Esther. José came up with that tag "terrorist drag." I'm worried every time I go to the States that someone is going to look on the computer when you have to go through a check and see: "This person before me, trying to get into our country, is a terrorist!" That was José writing his opinion, and he labeled it a "terrorist drag."

NG: Throughout this project, I've been thinking a lot about a line by Audre Lorde, where she says "the process of learning is something you incite, literally incite like a riot."[1] I found that extremely useful, and it guided this project, the exhibition and the program. I was recently watching the documentary *Audre Lorde: The Berlin Years 1984 to 1992*, and it shows Audre Lorde and her partner creating this amazing unity within the Afro-German community in the city.

VD: I wish I was living in Berlin during the Audre Lorde era. Saint Audre Lorde, I might add—she is my insurgent muse. When I was doing a club in Los Angeles and I had a 1920s speakeasy called Bricktops!, I took on the guise of Ada Smith, a.k.a. "Bricktop," the proprietor of Bricktop in Paris, Mexico City, different cities throughout the world from the 1920s until she died in the 1980s. My co-conspirator in this club was a young British boy named Andrew Gould. And I renamed him, when he would DJ with me, Audre Beardsley, in honor of Audre Lord.

I survived the 1965 riots and the 1992 riots. Oh my God! That one was *whoo...* And that's why I left Los Angeles before the next one comes. They always come in a cycle of twenty to twenty-five years. But what is gonna happen next, it's gonna be beyond anything. Los Angeles is always the epicenter of explosive things.

1. Audre Lorde, *Sister Outsider: Essays and Speeches* (New York: Ten Speed Press, 2007), 98.

Ideologies of Riot and Strike

Joshua Clover

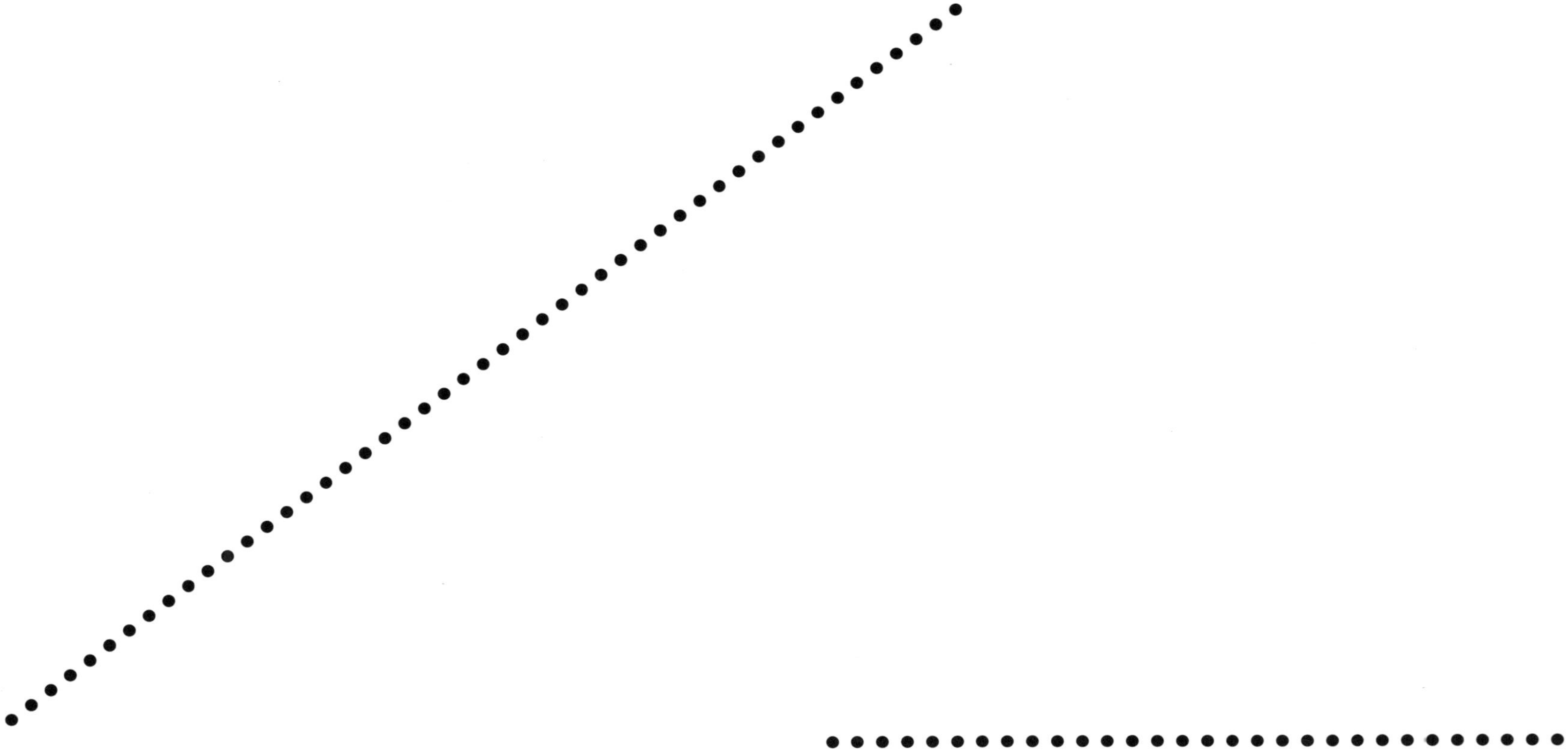

JOSHUA CLOVER

I

Part 1: History and Change

"Riot" and "strike" are persistently treated as both the orienting forms of social contest and as a binary opposition. I do not mean to suggest some sort of originary ideological formation within that pair. I simply want to point to how it gets seized upon—notably in the early industrializing nations—to develop an enchained array of ideological oppositions, each reinforcing the others. These oppositions structure a fairly broad swath of political thought, particularly regarding how social struggle unfolds and how it is understood. While this essay largely attends to the United States, it is neither because the ideologies it considers are unique to that nation nor because they necessarily originate there. At a minimum, we might say that they have been consolidated, repackaged, and recirculated within the context of the United States in such a way that a hegemon functions as a global entrepôt for ideology.

There is at least one sense in which the ideological developments in the United States could be expected to be both exemplary and in advance of developments elsewhere. Because the contemporary ideology of riot has developed in a largely complementary correspondence with that of strike[1]—in a purported antinomy we can formalize as

$$riot{:}strike$$

—the strength and direction of (generally national) labor movements has played a major role in shaping their dual trajectories. By the same token, the historical forces that have provided the conditions of possibility for labor movements have also produced the intensive market dependency and extensive exclusion from the formal wage that pushes populations toward riot. It is predictable that a national economy at the most advanced—which is not to say the highest so much as the most sclerotic—stage of capitalism would have pushed the accompanying ideological *preliefs*, the beliefs that precede belief, into a similar overdevelopment.

Most striking in this situation is the serial transcoding of the riot:strike pair into further purported antinomies, an activity that, in a double action, both exports the ideologies of riot and strike to other pairings and returns the ideologies of the new pair x:y to reinflect riot:strike. The transcodings proliferate; it

1. The examples of this development are durable and many. For one important consideration, see Charles Tilly, "Speaking Your Mind Without Elections, Surveys, or Social Movements," *Public Opinion Quarterly* 47, no. 4 (Winter 1983): 461–478.

is almost enough to make one believe in the endless chain of signifiers along which signification slides, meaning perpetually deferred.

The long-standing pair of riot:strike pair has been propositionally opposed since the mid-nineteenth century. I have been writing about related matters for some time and hope I will be forgiven the exigency of referring to that earlier research in passing as this essay moves toward its own ends. One main motion of the New Riot Studies has been to pass through the ideological layer to arrive at and to redescribe what riot and strike *are*—as tactics that develop out of changing political-economic dispensations and that seek to intervene within and against them.[2]

No pursuit of the objective character of these activities can detach them from their ideological layers; to imagine such a thing would be to imagine that ideology is merely a correctable error in the mind of the individual rather than an expression of real conditions, however inverted or distorted or reified. That said, we can follow the chain of ideological development and note the distance between its form and the activities it arises from and recasts. Before doing so, it is worth stating plainly that riot and strike do not form an antinomy in actuality; respectively understood as struggles of circulation and production, the latter emerges dialectically from the former in the late eighteenth century. As strike wanes in the West and riot reasserts itself, they do so profoundly changed.

However, even if the concrete activities of participants in riot or strike had not changed in the last two centuries (which they have), their significance—their political contents—would still be subject to history and thus to the possibility that their meanings could change (which they also have). I offer, by way of analogy, the mass strike, understood by communist thinkers in 1873 as an irredeemably weak tactic of anarchists and a mere three decades later put forward as among the most powerful weapons in the revolutionary communist arsenal. Rosa Luxemburg offers a characteristically clear-eyed account of this, which concludes, "it is not by *subjective criticism* of the mass strike from the standpoint of what is desirable, but only by *objective investigation* of the sources of the mass strike from the standpoint of what is historically inevitable, that the problem can be grasped or even discussed."[3]

2. Here I refer to the renascent studies of riots in the twenty-first century, especially in the aftermath of the global economic collapse of 2007–2008. This field includes (but is scarcely limited to) contributors to this volume and to the 2019 "Riot as a Global Political Concept" conference at Instituto de Altos Estudios Sociales (IDAES), Universidad Nacional de San Martín in Buenos Aires.

3. Helen Scott, ed., *The Essential Rosa Luxemburg* (Chicago: Haymarket Books, 2008), 118 (emphasis in original).

That recognition, so fundamental to materialist method, has nonetheless proved elusive to many who identify themselves as being able to reassess political dynamics according to real conditions. They see themselves as alert to historical change—the irreducible kernel of materialist method—and yet obtain unchanging results regarding tactics no matter the year, the location, or the balance of forces. It is this phenomenon, wherein the conclusions are functionally transcendental, inalterable in the face of great historical alterations, that led C. Wright Mills to identify for the Western labor Left the "labor metaphysic." Against that metaphysic, it is obvious that the meanings of any form of struggle, riot, or strike, as well as their relations to each other and their relations to the transcoded pairs regularly accompanying them, are neither self-evident nor static *except within the realm of ideology*. It is ideology that renders all that is exposed to transformation by the forces of material history to instead be fixed and sequestered in the amber of idealism. Riot means *this*, strike means *that*, such will ever be the case!—this sentiment is the veritable seal upon the brow of the ideologue. Of course these *idées fixes* are themselves historical. Appearing where they did not previously exist, shaped by real conditions, they swiftly take on the force of self-apparent truths, *socialist common sense*, for the ideologues whose self-recognitions and political roles depend on them. More distressingly, they are then put on offer to those new to political movements and in search of an orientation, a path forward. As is the habit of ideological suppositions, they are treated as a series of royal roads to revolutionary wisdom rather than the dead ends that they are.

Part 2: The 1960s and All That

The uneven but ongoing pacification of the labor strike, conducted over the last century, has altered the meaning of the riot:strike pairing. In the United States, crucial moments include the Treaty of Detroit at exactly mid-century and, later, the sometimes grudging but increasingly prevalent collaboration with capital that has characterized organized labor since the 1970s. The decrease in the militancy of strikes, and the corresponding diminution in violent repression of labor actions, has allowed for a widespread amnesia regarding the violent history of strikes, which historically often tended toward the status of military engagements (one need only recall the example and the name of the Colorado Coal Wars). More recently, strikes have become associated with a steadfastly nonviolent approach, with the peak moment of confrontation perhaps appearing as a scuffle over someone crossing a picket line (that this has come with an increasing sensitivity to rhetorical "violence," as when calling somebody a "scab," etc., is an underremarked fact).

For this reason, among others, the axis of riot and strike has shifted such that the two poles may now align with violence and nonviolence. This is nowhere more evident than in legal codes, which have long entrenched the presence of violence in their definitions of the (always illegitimate) riot while defining strikes as "legitimate" because of their absence of violence. The ideology that understands riots and strikes, respectively, as violent and nonviolent, illegitimate and legitimate, has been in part produced by legal regimes that are themselves products of concrete historical events, including successful riots and militant strikes. This ideology is thus in service to those legal regimes and, more broadly, is in service to the state monopoly on violence. This in turn inflects purportedly ethical or strategic claims on behalf of nonviolent approaches and, implicitly or explicitly, on behalf of legitimate or legalistic forms of struggle: *we cannot usher in an epoch of emancipation by setting loose brutality, we cannot win by inviting state violence, we will not appeal to the masses if we are perceived as willfully dangerous*, and so forth. These positions, ingenuously or not, are a submission to state and capital. The pacification of the strike and the exclusion of the riot from the sphere of the properly political together are, among other things, a patent desire of the state and of the bourgeoisie. Any adherence to or repetition of these ideas, no matter how framed or intended, partakes of such desires.

This modern alignment of riot and strike with violence and nonviolence provides to some degree an explanation for the willingness to identify more ambiguous actions with the latter, as in the case of "Human Strike," "Strike Debt," et cetera. Bracketing the always contentious issue of "productive labor" and what it includes, many self-named strikes do not seem to involve the withdrawal of labor. One should not make too much of this, but we might note nonetheless that the logic of designating these actions as strikes comes not just from the charisma that strikes accrued during their period of greatest success but also from the ways that these actions are *not riots*—the ways that they feature generally nonviolent withdrawal and refusal, and treat these features as part of a strike's constitution. Whether this naming practice further consolidates the ideology of riot and strike is uncertain; however, it is inarguable that such a naming practice depends in part on such an ideology being already in place, already naturalized.

This alignment that might be formalized as

riot:strike::violence:nonviolence

has proved relatively durable. Similarly durable has been another transcoding according to the axis of race or racialization. Here I draw on Colleen Lye's remarks introducing Max Elbaum and his history of the New Communist Movement.[4] *Revolution in the Air* tells the history of Students for a Democratic Society (SDS), of which Elbaum was a member, and its historic split in 1969—a moment that substantially recast the social contest in the United States in the 1960s and set the terms for a similarly large upheaval in the 1970s.[5]

As Lye notes, the canonical Left's account of the 1960s in the United States was for a long time set forth by representative texts such as Todd Gitlin's *The Sixties: Years of Hope, Days of Rage*. In that telling, the later rage despoiled the earlier hope, dividing the decade temporally into first a good 1960s and then a bad 1960s. Excessive militancy—violence rather than organization—is here understood to have undone the gains of the political struggle, forming a nimbus around the antiwar movement.

This account rests uncomfortably alongside the verdict offered on the decade from within ethnic studies, a set of disciplines famously founded (at San Francisco State University, at the University of California, Berkeley, and elsewhere) by third-world and black student "strikes" that foregrounded the threat of violence and the actuality of confrontational direct action. In this account, the late 1960s were, if not preferable, at least necessary in overcoming the limits that developed within and against the civil rights movement. "In the origin story of ethnic studies," notes Lye, "the line dividing the early sixties from the late sixties was racial—that is, a problem of the constitutive exclusion of liberal progressivism or liberal reformism. At a tactical level, nonviolent vs. militant forms of protest; at a theoretical level, the problem of how to conceive of the relation between racism at home and imperialism abroad."[6]

So then: there are two accounts of the political vector that characterized the decade, everywhere different and often directly opposed. The events of 1968–1969 bear this level of detail because it is within that crucible that this extended transcoding was set in place. The split in SDS reflects this division clearly enough. Per the unsigned report, "SDS Convention Split: Three Factions Emerge," the faction comprising the Progressive Labor Party (PL) and the Worker-Student Alliance Caucus, potentially a majority, was nonetheless excluded by the newly formed Revolutionary Youth Movement, in part for failing to address the demands of and for ethnic studies

4. Colleen Lye, "Introduction to Max Elbaum" (public talk, April 26, 2019, University of California, Berkeley).
5. Max Elbaum, *Revolution in the Air* (New York: Verso, 2002).
6. Lye, "Introduction to Max Elbaum."

(particularly for open admissions). Members of the Black Panthers, including Jewel Cook and Bobby Rush, denounced PL for inadequate support of black liberation struggles. In Lye's summary, "The coexistence of Gitlin's liberal account and ethnic studies' racial account... meant first that there was a false parallel between the two binaries each established (around violence and race) and that therefore there was an invidious racialization of militant protest." This then allows for the next extension of our formalization, which now can be configured as

riot:strike::violence:nonviolence::black:white.

However, the black:white dyad is an ideological convenience, albeit one again affirmed, by intention or not, in the reception of the contemporary Afropessimist discourse, specifically in the works that insist on an essential incommensurability between antiblack racism and all other racisms. The dyad forms an antinomy only in the racial imagination; its limits are particularly clear regarding the late 1960s. We might take as exemplary the united struggle of the Third World Liberation Front and the Black Student Union, first at San Francisco State University and then across the nation, to found an ethnic studies department within the university—a movement insep- arable from the antiwar movement and all the struggles in its nimbus. This specific example is indicative of the way that the black:white dyad, in exactly the moment it is presumed to reinforce arguments about political violence, functions more broadly to disguise the participation of those racialized as neither black nor white and identified with the "third world," particularly in this case with Southeast Asia, with Asia more broadly, and with the Bandung nations.[7] More usefully, the dyad should comprise something like, on the one side, those recognized as subordinated according to racial logics and, on the other, those who are not subordinated in such a way, or those treated as racially unmarked according to the self-nat- uralization of white supremacy. This allows the last relevant transcoding, which reveals that the chain of pairings is in truth closer to a loop—configured as

7.   Moreover, it is scarcely the case that some sort of racial unanimity prevailed. The victorious slate within the Revolutionary Youth Movement had already begun to form the Weathermen, later the Weather Underground. Made up almost entirely of white people, the Weathermen would shortly foment the aforementioned Days of Rage, an event famously denounced by Fred Hampton (leader of the Chicago chapter of the Black Panthers) for being "anarchistic, opportunistic, adventuristic, and Custeristic." It would thus be inaccurate to suggest that the opposed accounts of the 1960s were unfailingly raced.

riot:strike::violence:nonviolence::black:white::race:class.

Part 3: New Riot Studies

Some aspects of this derivation and consolidation of the ideologies of riot and strike are relatively apparent and well-recognized, in ways that perhaps do not deserve the name "ideology" aside from their naturalization as self-evident truths. We "know," for example, that riots are racialized—at least in the United States, the United Kingdom, and Western and Central Europe, if not farther afield as well. Less apparent is the knowledge that labor strikes are racialized in a less recognized way within the sphere of ideology, where abstractions like "the white working class" hold sway. Here I do not mean to suggest that divisions within the proletariat are purely ideological and are purpose-built to threaten class solidarity; instead, the divisions are the ideological sedimentation of the definite relations necessary to reproduce class society. As part of this process, these divisions operate in that familiar manner of thought-before-thought, preceding and eluding conscious knowledge or opinion; one example of this is how racialization is entangled with the relative legitimacy of struggles and with how people assess the risk of participation. We might recognize, in turn, that these insistently produced and maintained chains of association have forged indirect agreements between the "organized" Left and the state about preferred forms of struggle. Both Right and Left recommend peaceful actions with closely delineated demands conducted within a legalistic framework—an approach to social contest that aspires to universalism while being always, through the concrete histories to which ideologies correspond, premised on implicit racialization.

These recognitions are fundamental to the nascent field I previously called New Riot Studies—its roots in 1992 Los Angeles, grown in the ashes left by the fires in Tottenham and Ferguson and Hamburg, commingled with the embers of the Occupy movement, the Arab Spring, the Gilets Jaunes, a series of waves sweeping across Latin America, the planetary foment of 2019, and so on. However, while we may begin with riot, this does not mean we must end there. The New Riot Studies is equally founded on the capacities for an expanded sense of riot to provide a heuristic for revisiting related issues, and it is in this gesture that the chain of transcodings becomes particularly useful, as one may enter or pause at any moment.

Indeed, as a matter of inquiry—or perhaps of necessary polemic—this chain of transcodings can shed light on the renewed debate that sets class and race in opposition. In the United States, the charged arena for this debate is that marked by the Left variant of the culture wars, in which—to use the pointedly inadequate terms of art—*class reductionism* and *identity politics* are set at each other's throats (the latter term designating, plainly enough, a number of so-called identities in addition to race, though it is striking how consistently race is asked to stand in for that multitudinous array, an enforced exemplarity mobilized in the present by global struggles around immigration). Thus we might say that a pivotal claim of New Riot Studies, that riots are a form of class struggle—conditioned by class composition and recomposition, and by structural relations to the mode of production (which includes what I have elsewhere called *the production of nonproduction*, the intransigent negation within progress's death march)—serves not simply to illuminate the matter of what riots are but also to point to the false antinomy of race and class.[8]

This is a necessary outcome of formalizing the chain of transcodings: once a single purported antinomy loses its character of static opposition, the other pairings are equally subject to such a fate. We can see this lurking volatility and its effects in Lye's clarifying assessment of the 1960s debates, wherein Gitlin's liberal account and ethnic studies' racial account formed a complementary antinomy that ignored the extent to which the sixties needed to be understood as another chapter in an ongoing unresolved dialectic of a slaveholding, settler-colonial republic wherein racial ascription and oppression have persisted long beyond the formal abolition of slavery and the passage of formal civil rights legislation.[9]

I might amend this assessment by proposing that, if we understand riots as the concrete social experience wherein the invidious alignment of race and violence is imagined to find its highest expression, the contrary recognition of riots as a form of class struggle interrupts and, in truth, annihilates the series of transcodings—allowing us not, for example, to refute their racialized character but to see the unity of race and class.[10]

One need not enforce a priority between the two categories to affirm that class can only reproduce itself via the production of differential valuation of lives, a differential across which value flows according to the possibilities of unequal wages and ensuing wage arbitrage. Karl Marx notes this

8. Regarding the production of nonproduction, see Joshua Clover, *Riot. Strike. Riot: The New Era of Uprisings* (New York: Verso, 2016), 28.
9. Lye, "Introduction to Max Elbaum."
10. Gender is conspicuously absent here. For a preliminary approach to some possible reasons for this, see Clover, chap. 9, "Riot Now: Square, Street, Commune," in *Riot. Strike. Riot.*

clearly in his 1869 "Resolution on Relations Between the Irish and the English Working Classes" as well as his letter to Ludwig Kugelmann written the following year. Drawing on this account in "White Blindspot" (the essay that bequeaths us the term "white privilege," originally "white-skin privilege"), Noel Ignatin and Theodore Allen conclude, "Now, if Marx could correctly observe that the Irish workers formed a 'very important section of the working class in England' in 1869, what are we to say of the position of the Negro workers in the American working class in 1967?"[11]

The argument is in some sense quite simple. Class relations as we know them—which is to say, capitalist relations of production—being an unnatural aspect of social existence, must be reproduced in order to exist. The expropriation of surplus value from one class by another is both a consequence of these relations and the way in which they are reproduced. Since the rate of surplus value is determined in part by the level of wages, and since the increase of this rate offsets the negative effect on profits of a rising ratio of machines to human labor power, the ongoing reproduction of capitalist relations does not simply thrive on but *requires* the capacity to drive down wages, a capacity, in turn, dependent on the differential valuation of certain subjects. While race has provided a dramatic example of this unequal valuation, the production of this differential is conducted as well with reference to gender and the abjection of feminized labor; to the displacement and the genocide of indigenous peoples; and further with reference to sexuality, religion, documentation status, and more. These differential valuations of given subjects, also being in no way natural, must be produced by ongoing state and social violence, which includes, for example, the specific activities of the police but also the ongoing structural subordinations that we name as racism, patriarchy, and so on. Again, this is not to claim that wage arbitrage is the only basis or explanation for these modes of subordination, that racism and patriarchy are purely economic phenomena, et cetera—but only to make the far humbler claim that capital's self-reproduction depends on them and that their function is now irrevocably entangled with capitalist logics.

It is clear that the differential valuation of, for example, black labor depends on the differential valuation of, for example, black lives—it is the imposition of diminished life chances that compels a willingness to accept diminished wages (a truth captured in the name of the movement Black Lives Matter, with its origins in the dire knowledge that police are charged with making black lives matter *less*). Consequently, the driving

●   11. Noel Ignatin and Theodore Allen, "White Blindspot," https://www.marxists. org/history/erol/ncm-1/whiteblindspot.pdf.

down of black wages is inseparable from the exclusion of black subjects from the wage; cheaper racialized employment is only assured by higher racialized unemployment. This fact, while it may be self-evident, has analytical consequences that have not yet been fully explored by many who weigh in on the race/class debate. It makes visible, for example, the manner in which exploited populations and surplus populations—the "working class" and those who are "structurally unemployed" or unemployable—are, in truth, two sides of one phenomenon within capital, even if one side never appears to take part in capitalist production. This circumstance can also be described by noting that the orienting populations of strike and riot—the exploited and the excluded, those who labor directly for capital and those sequestered in the realm of market dependency without access to the formal wage—together constitute a whole, each requiring the existence of the other, even as the development of the forces of production ineluctably alters the ratio between them in a racialized expression of what Marx calls "the moving contradiction" of capital.

Race, to summarize this point, is among other things a mediator of *the unity of the employed and the unemployed equally as class subjects.* That is to say, it constitutes them as a complete structural position necessary for surplus value extraction. Supposedly color-blind class can only be reproduced through the violence of racial subordination (as well as the array of other modes of subordination mentioned). Therefore, the suggestion that class can be treated autonomously from race, that capital's exploitation can be treated as distinct from racial animus and subordination (an argument that circulates within parts of the contemporary socialist Left, presented regularly by, for example, Walter Benn Michaels and Adolph Reed), can only be a solecism. Its analytical error is complementary to a "common move in an important strand of contemporary black critical theorizing known as Afro-pessimism," as Nikhil Pal Singh puts it (referring to the contemporary theorists who have most directly taken up Orlando Patterson's idea of "social death"). This move offers "a kind of inversion in which slavery and the antiblackness that proceeds from it are the excluded ground for politics as such," a mode of white supremacy treatable as anterior to class and capital, to the demands for surplus value production.[12]

The line of reasoning herein has endeavored to understand race and class as a dialectical unity. This unity goes by the name of *the proletariat*, which is also riven and unified by the other modes of differential valuation, of inclusion and exclusion from the circuits of capital's expanded reproduction. The

12. Nikhil Pal Singh, *Race and America's Long War* (Berkeley: University of California Press, 2017), 77.

riot, a contestation of precisely this social arrangement, is thus—even when it appears oriented by race—necessarily at the same time a form of class struggle. This is not to adduce a single determination to riot as a historical phenomenon, nor is it to impute a lone Impulsion or rationale to participants, any more than white supremacy exists as a singular and conscious idea. Indeed and instead, much as we refer to the idea of structural racism, we might usefully refer to the riot as *structural class struggle*.

Readers will note, I hope, that this final effort to understand race and class as a dialectical unity features the other elements of our chain of transcodings as well: violence and nonviolence, black and white, riot and strike, disclosing each in turn as a unity. This is the minimum program of the New Riot Studies: it is dialectical or it is nothing.

"They Been Jealous, Must Be"— Toxic Sovereignty, Dispossession, and the Extimacy of Riots

Elizabeth A. Povinelli

1.

The genealogy of riots and modernity has been written as a series of interconnected social histories and political possibilities ad nauseam: the rise of the city, the rise of modernity; the emergence of stranger sociability, anonymity, and abstract nationalism; the flash of the crowd; the riot versus the uprising, the rampage versus the revolution, the populace versus the demos. Riots, strangers, uprisings, modernity, the city, the mega-city, the mega-riot of populism—theorists have tangled and untangled cause and consequence, moral imports, political expediencies, and social outcomes.

In 2007, a two-day riot broke out in Belyuen, Australia—a small, rural, Indigenous community near Darwin—after which some fifty people, out of the extended family of about two hundred who lived there, fled for their lives as their houses were overrun in the riot or burned. Initially aided by the Northern Territory government, they moved some 200 kilometers south to what settlers considered their traditional lands. For four years, people moved between tents in these remote lands and overcrowded government houses in Darwin. In the aftershocks of these two riotous days and the social dislocation they created, "Karrabing" emerged as a concept and a social fact. In the Emmiyengal language, *karrabing* refers to the moment when the vast saltwater tides that characterize members' coastal lands reach their lowest point and are about to return. The conditions submerged in the seas reveal themselves—reefs, mudflats, mangrove roots—and the nurturing possibilities they hold. Around 2008, the families who fled Belyuen chose this term for a media project that they hoped would provide social and economic stability for themselves and a political vision for how Indigenous people should relate to each other and their ancestral lands. The resultant Karrabing Film Collective uses filmmaking and installation as a form of self-organized reflection on the socioeconomic and political conditions of contemporary Indigenous life. The collective includes approximately thirty Indigenous members—most of whom live in the Belyuen community—and myself.

Years later, the Karrabing Film Collective produced a documentary video, *The Riot*, to accompany a map and barbed-wire installation in which two more of our films were embedded, *Night Time Go* and *The Jealous One*. The installation was for Natasha Ginwala's paradoxically titled exhibition *Riots: Slow Cancellation of the Future* at the ifa Gallery Berlin. Was the riot that created Karrabing just another eruption in the "slow cancellation of the future"? Or was it exemplary of a certain Western critical theoretical hope for a mode of violence linked to the persistent renewal of the voice of the demos and the rectification of systemic injustice? More, how might this specific social event tell us something not merely about the sociology of riots but about an Indigenous understanding of the grounds on which violence occurs—grounds formed at the tectonic intersections of decades of settler governance and its tactics of recognizing the other but disavowing itself? How does a riot reappear outside a city, stranger sociality, nationalism, and populism and inside a space of Indigenous refusal? And how might one reconsider the political nature of the riot—or whatever we call this particular rampage—from the point of view of the target of the riot? In

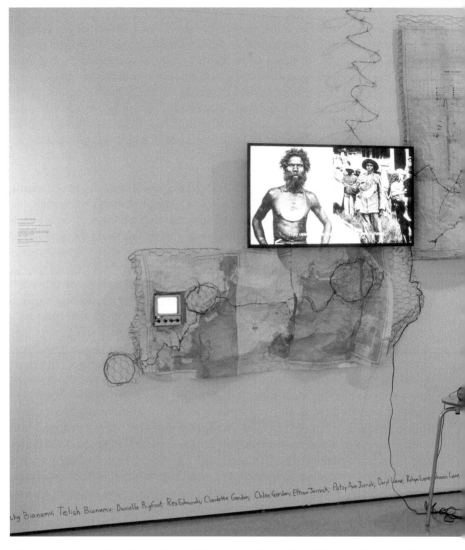

cky Bianamu; Telish Bianamu; Danielle Bigfoot; Rex Edmunds; Claudette Gordon; Chloe Gordon; Ethan Jorrock; Patsy Ann Jorrock; Daryl Lane; Robyn Lane; Sharon Lane

other words, while Elias Canetti looks at the role of the state in inciting crowd violence and Dilip Gaonkar looks at the ambivalence of the populace and the multitude, the crowd and the riot, in liberal political theory, we rarely see a discussion of the potentiality of violence where violence strikes.[1] And finally, what is the relationship between the riot and the political event once, as Ginwala's artful title suggests, the temporality of political and social eventfulness is pressured?

2.

The scene of the riot, the Belyuen Community, is dispersed across a series of historical acts. Act 1 is the Delissaville Settlement, established as an Indigenous internment camp in the late 1930s. Located in the middle of the Cox Peninsula, on the western side of the Darwin

●   1.   Elias Canetti, *Crowds and Power*, trans. Carol Stewart (New York: Viking, 1962);Dilip Parameshwar Gaonkar, "After the Fictions: Notes towards a Phenomenology of the Multitude," *e-flux journal* 58 (October 2014), https://www.e-flux.com/journal/58/61187/after-the-fictions-notes-towards-a-phenomenology-of-the-multitude.

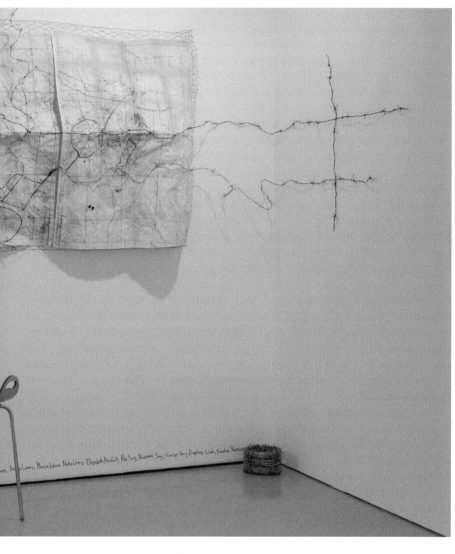

Karrabing Film Collective, "They Been Jealous," 2018, installation view of *Riots: Slow Cancellation of the Future*, 2018, at ifa Gallery Berlin. Photograph by Wataru Murakami. Courtesy of the artists/ifa Gallery Berlin.

harbor, Delissaville was formed to contain Indigenous groups whose lands stretched some 250 kilometers along the coastal region from Cox Peninsula to the south side of Anson Bay. Delissaville/Belyuen was never large; its population has fluctuated between some 150 and 250 people since its creation. Most residents have been from four language groups—Menthayengal, Emmiyengal, Wadjigiyn, and Kiyuk—each with specific land-based patrilineal ancestral sites, the main ones being Kugan (Honey), Mudi (Barramundi), Mortumortu (Long Yam), Durlg (Sea Monster), and Ingarrainy (Greenback Saltwater Turtle). These language groups were collectively referred to as the Wagait, or saltwater people. All had long-standing ceremonial, kinship, and hunting paths that extended from their southern coastal regions to the Cox Peninsula. Of critical importance during the internment years were a series of underground water tunnels linking Anson Bay to Cox Peninsula and to one of its aboveground water holes located at the center of Belyuen.

By the mid-1970s, elder Indigenous men and women had utilized existing ancestral ceremonial logics and connections to the land they were locked up on to cultivate forms of Indigenous belonging in settler dislocation.[2] Their creativity is part of what Barbara Glowczewski sees as a general Indigenous power to construct *ancestral newness*—a temporality that offers an ancestral continuity to historical discontinuities, a power that is conversant with Felix Guattari's ecosophy as well as his and Gilles Deleuze's understanding of univocal original multiplicity.[3] Aileen Moreton-Robertson has located the source of this power in a form of Indigenous ontological belonging ("I Still Call Australia Home").[4] Delissaville elders' ability to harness the differential between ancestral continuity and always unfolding actualities formed the reasoning for why, when asked in 1974 which Indigenous people should hold Cox Peninsula lands, the elder men and women (including Tom Imabulk Lyons, who anthropologists would later identify as the true, real, or proper "traditional owner") answered "all of us," given the rich connectivities that joined the different groups interned at Delissaville.

Karrabing members describe this dynamic as the continual play between the ancestral beings who manifest themselves at well-known sites (say, the Mudi, Durlg, and Kugan sites) and those that are underground, as well as the play between the distinct and separate nature of an ancestral site and the original interconnections to other sites based on the ancestral histories that put them in place—the Mudi is where it is because of its sister Mudi that is somewhere else. The original and irreducible play between what Linda Yarrowin calls "separate-separate and connected" is manifested in ceremonial and linguistic practices. For example, a year after a person's death, the family should hold a *kapug* in which the deceased's clothes—and other items holding the person's sweat/spirit—are torn, burned in a small hole, covered, and danced on. But the immediate family can neither touch the clothes during the ceremony nor burn them, lest the deceased slip into them through the smoke. Instead, an uncle or cousins from adjacent lands must carry out the ceremony for the family. In a panel accompanying the installation at ifa, Linda Yarrowin and Cecilia Lewis, Emmi women from Mortumortu and Nunggudi, describe a similar mode or obligated reciprocity in language in terms of respect.[5]

2. For more, see Elizabeth A. Povinelli, "The Poetics of Ghosts: Social Reproduction in the Archive of the Nation," in *The Cunning of Recognition: Indigenous Alterity and the Making of Australian Multiculturalism* (Durham, NC: Duke University Press, 2002), 187–234.

3. Barbara Glowczewski, *Indigenising Anthropology with Deleuze and Guattari* (Edinburgh: Edinburgh University Press, 2019).

4. Aileen Moreton-Robinson, *The White Possessive: Property, Power and Indigenous Sovereignty* (Minneapolis: University of Minnesota Press, 2015).

5. This conversation reiterates ideas originally published in *Specimen: The Babel Review of Translations*, http://www.specimen.press/writers/karrabing.

Elizabeth A. Povinelli: So, in the beginning, there were many languages. Did all of these languages present a problem to them?

Cecilia Lewis: No, it didn't, because they knew all these languages. Like my mom's mom knew the whole lot of the languages we've been discussing. [...]

EP: Do you think that she just understood all these languages, or something more... like I was thinking about how those old women taught us to say to Burn-the-Rubber, "nira" (Maranunggu/cousin), but to say to Daboi's brothers, "pannin" (Emmi/cousin), and to Mortimah, "arritu" (Batjemalh/cousin). Why? [...]

CL: Yeah, but here we think that when you speak to that person in this way, you connect or articulate, you and him—when you speak their language to them, the other person comes inside you and you go inside of them. You are thinking of/with/through that other person.

EP: Like that old woman now. When me, I say "malabat" instead of "mebela," I can't help but think about that day we went hunting. [...]

Angelina Lewis: And don't forget about ceremony... And about people sitting around a fire and swapping stories...

CL: One group tells their side of a story, like the various ways the Sea Serpent story is told depending on where you live. And all the stories are similar but different, and so you need to tell what the Dreaming did from your country's perspective, and you begin to see how it connects to what happens in another country—or how it's different—such as whom he fought or didn't fight. So, Marriamu, Emmi, and Mentha, and Wadjigiyn with the Dog Dreaming, are connected by the story that crosses their countries.

Linda Yarrowin: As with marriage, ceremony, sweating in a place—by doing this, you join the places that these activities cross over, but you also keep your own people and places strong. That is why people were strong before white people came. They respected the other person because they were connected inside and outside.

These modes of obligated interdependencies among distinct and separate ancestral beings, languages, and places were what allowed Linda, Cecilia, and Angelina's grandparents and great-grandparents to transform the internment landscape of Delissaville into an ontological space of belonging via the underwater reaches of Belyuen.

As part of our ifa installation, the film *Night Time Go* played on a black-and-white monitor, embedded in a montage of chicken wire, barbed wire, and land maps. *Night Time Go* is an exploration of the settler state's attempt to remove Indigenous people from their lands during World War II by truck, train, and rifle, and shows the refusal of Linda, Cecilia, and Angelina's grandparents and great-grandparents to be detained. At the core of the film is the escape of Karrabing ancestors from a war internment camp on September 19, 1943, and their journey of more than 300 kilometers back to their coastal homelands. The film begins by hewing closely to the actual historical details of this journey but slowly turns to an alternative history, in which the group inspires a general Indigenous insurrection that expels settlers from the Top End of Australia. This potentiality never actualized. Instead, some three to four years after the war, these men and women and their children returned to Delissaville, where their rights to move, marry, seek employment, drink, and keep or lose their children were controlled by the settlement's superintendents.

Indigenous people in the Northern Territory, like the ancestors of the Karrabing, were declared wards of the state in 1957, although they had long been treated as such. Their status did not officially change until 1964, though even then the change was in language only. It was not until a 1967 referendum that Indigenous people in Australia were given the "right" to be counted as part of the "people" and to vote. In Jacques Rancière's terms, 1967 marked a moment of politics: when those who were a part but had no part came to enter and thus change the composition of the demos.[6] But only in part—since it was, in Rancière's terms, the police (state) that recognized them (only to a degree) in the first place, as it excluded the range of other rights for which they had to (and did) fight. The day-to-day lives of Indigenous men and women remained under the practical control of settler superintendents until what we might call Act 2.

It was not until 1976—in the wake of decades of social, economic, and land rights protests and rioting, whose language and tactics mixed elements from local and international anticolonial movements—that the federal government passed what was considered the first piece of legislation giving Indigenous people in the north "self-determination." The Land Rights Act (LRA) never, however, left self-determination to the Indigenous subject. Instead, the LRA stipulated the form that self-determination could take—namely, it offered a set of definitions devised with British social anthropologists. Anthropology claimed to translate the social nature of Indigenous land rights, but in reality it often adjudicated between what these anthropologists considered to be "authentic" tribal forms and what they thought of as "corrupted" ones.

In a series of judgments stretching across two hearings on a land claim between 1976 and 1995, the Belyuen community (like many others) was divided according to the severing logics of definitional power: those who were recognized by settler law as traditional owners and those who were not. Under the cover of self-determination, the settler state legislatively codified anthropological theory of precolonial politics: namely,

---

●   6.   Jacques Rancière, *Disagreement: Politics and Philosophy* (Minneapolis: University of Minnesota Press), 1999.

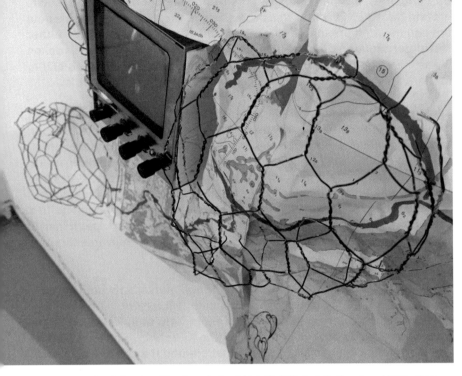

Karrabing Film Collective, "They Been Jealous" (detail), 2018, installation view of *Riots: Slow Cancellation of the Future*, 2018, at ifa Gallery Berlin. Photograph by Elizabeth A. Povinelli. Courtesy of the artists/ifa Gallery Berlin.

the absolute and irreducible primacy of "the local descent group"—the clan and its totem—as the sovereign ground of the Indigenous demos. Although the original bias toward strictly patrilineal clans gave way to other forms of descent (matrilineal, cognate, and indeed a whole host of anthropological social algebras), settler law was immovable when it came to the linkage between recognition and sovereignty. To be "recognized" as a traditional Aboriginal owner, claimants had to form themselves as separate, internally independent social units with hard land boundaries; that is, in the form of the nation-state. The original and irreducible connectivity among peoples, places, and ancestral sites was legislatively ignored and often anthropologically ridiculed as "historical" or "postmodern."[7] Swept into this anthropological disregard were the ontological modes of belonging through original and multiple connectivities that Karrabing ancestors utilized to ontologically survive vicious settler assaults.

As Rex Edmunds, senior Emmi man from the Mudi clan, says in *The Riot*, the Land Rights Act "forced people to say, this land is just for that people and certain people got... and you have traditional owners for that little area and traditional owners for all kind of little areas" without any recognition of the multiple, original interconnectivities of lands and peoples. The slow erosion of such respect and regard under the regimes

7. See Peter Sutton, *Native Title in Australia: An Ethnographic Perspective* (New York: Cambridge University Press, 2003).

of genocide, assimilation, and self-determination create a social ground for riot. Not that it was better before the LRA. Edmunds rejects the choice often presented to him and other Indigenous people—either self-determination of the LRA kind or assimilation. He notes, "I reckon it was worse before Land Rights." And it was: up until at least the 1920s, settlers still went on safaris whose game was Indigenous people.

Karrabing as a concept and a form of sociality emerged from this history; it follows from parents' and grandparents' arguments for the original, multiple modes of connectivity and separation. Composed of three language groups and eight major dreaming clans, and encompassing coastal regions stretching across hundreds of kilometers, Karrabing counters with an irreducible play between separation and connectivity— of a separation possible only through an original interdependency. To a settler sovereignty of sealed subjects, ancestral or otherwise, it insists on an irreducible interdependency, a both/and rather than an either/or.

3.

Like many political theorists, the Karrabing are interested in both the contemporary conditions of riots and the political future of riots—whether riots cancel the future or create a more just form of it. *The Riot* begins with reflections by various members of the Karrabing Film Collective on how they define the social disruption that created the collective as such.

Rex Edmunds: **We had a riot at Belyuen.**

Elizabeth A. Povinelli: **What do you call it, riot, violence? What do you call it?**

Daphne Yarrowin: **I say violent, terrible.**

Angelina Lewis: **Riot... riot?**

EP: **What do you call it?**

AL: **I don't know what you call it.**

Linda Yarrowin: **That terror.**

EP: **Terror?**

LY: **Not terror, what do you call it?**

EP: **Terror is a good word, aye?**

The video then lays out what happened, when it happened, and the condition of homelessness and precarity in which the fifty or so targets of the riot/violence/terror found themselves. Emminu? Why? What for? What caused half of the Belyuen community to attack the other half, when virtually everyone living there is connected through marriage, ceremony, descent, and common enough living conditions? Across a set of interwoven conversations, Karrabing members lay out a harrowing scene: people hiding in attic crawl spaces, running through the bush, fighting for their lives, then piled up in government housing in Darwin or living in tents along the coastline some 200 kilometers away. From the other side of this riot, no redemptive cleansing—no purified voice of the people—can be heard. Terror seems the right word.

Three reasons are given in *The Riot*: jealousy, boredom, and the never-ending settler upending of social life. The conversation quickly turns away from the question of what to call the "event" to a discussion of the causes of the event.

In the way that it is used among the Karrabing and their extended network, "jealousy" certainly covers the English understanding of covetousness. Angelina Lewis notes this in the video when she says that jealousy is when someone "wants what that other person has but they think they can't get it." They are jealous of that—an object, affection, attention, or mode of life. Sheree Bianamu and Rex Edmunds note that one cause of the riot was jealousy over the shooting and butchering of five head of wild cattle. The jealousy wasn't over the meat per se but over a way of life revolving around the skills of hunting (which includes all forms of food gathering). And these skills are not merely being a good marksman, a clever mudcrab collector or yam digger, et cetera, but a set of social interconnectivities that animate the activity: having an elder to teach you, knowing who to share the foods with, knowing where to go in the first place and when. As Rex Edmunds says, "That's how we learn people, too, in another way."

It would be wrong, however, to think that the world could be cleansed of jealousy through the proper education of people. Jealousy is not something that emerges only when the world falls apart. Jealousy set the world in place—it put various ancestral beings where they can now be found; it created an insatiable affective current through the most socially healthy of spaces. Why are Parunga (Wallaby) and Mele (Porpoise) located next to each other? Because the latter was jealous of the beauty of the former's baby and they fought, shaping the land and how each of the animals now look. Why are Mukmuk (Owl) and Kerraguk (Pigeon) adjacent to each other? Because they were jealous of each other's song and time for singing. Why is Durlg (Sea Monster) where he is? Because he was jealous of others having fun in a corroboree. In *The Jealous One*, an Indigenous man weaves through bureaucratic red tape to get to a mortuary service in his traditional country while a fight breaks out when another man is consumed with jealousy over his wife. The two stories meet in a dramatic and explosive final encounter. *The Jealous One* is based on a traditional story that connects the traditional lands of the Karrabing, but it also asks who is the jealous one now: the land, the men, or the settler state?

The Riot is cut throughout with scenes of different sorts of rioting—rioting in southern city suburbs like the Indigenous suburb of Redfern in Sydney, rioting in small and large remote Indigenous communities, mass political protests with rioting along their edges. Sheree and Gavin Bianamu, two young Karrabing adults, note a second reason for riots in small communities like their own: boredom. People get bored in rural Indigenous communities; boredom is part of a more general malaise characterizing the affective interpretation of the difference between rural and urban life. E. P. Thompson, in *The Making of the English Working Class*, discusses the enclosures and restrictions during the Industrial Revolution in conjunction with the pull of new manufacturing techniques. Certainly the rise of the European city was due to complex balances of push and pull from rural areas. The contemporary enclosures of agricapitalism took over farming, the collapse of manufacturing ruralized the suburb (as witnessed in the United States). Those still in suburbs and rural areas are left without jobs but also in the outer glow of the city, its promise of excitement even if one's race means poverty there. One of the supposed pull factors is that megacities are where mega-rioting emerges. Gavin Bianamu says, "Sometimes we tease each other to make each other wild for no reason. And we say ah, just jokes, you know jokes," even though everyone knows that jokes, as Gavin's sister Sheree says, can lead to people looking for a punch. Boredom demands an event. And for those who might ask why youth don't get a job or go out hunting, Rex Edmunds has often reflected on the intensifying intersection of economic and policing factors.

Act 3 can be said to have started in 2007, when the federal government declared a national emergency over Indigenous communities in the Northern Territory. The Northern Territory Emergency Act, widely referred to as "the Intervention," rode on the back of a report, *Ampe Akelyernemane Meke Mekarle (Little Children Are Sacred)*, commissioned by a Northern Territory Labor government. The hysteria around the abuse of children in rural and remote Indigenous communities was national and intense, no matter the fact that no comparative statistics were cited about sexual dysfunction or family structure in settler communities. The stated intention of the Intervention was to normalize Indigenous affairs by normalizing supposedly dysfunctional family and sexual practices relative to non-Indigenous public norms and by normalizing labor and property practices relative to neoliberal market norms.

The Intervention itself consisted of almost nothing pertaining to child welfare but instead imposed a set of legislative changes to federal laws governing Indigenous land tenure, welfare provision, and legal prosecution, in addition to a broadly public reevaluation of the purpose and value of Indigenous self-determination. The AU$587 million package came into effect with the passage of the Northern Territory National Emergency Response Act 2007 by the Australian Parliament in August 2007. The nine measures contained therein were as follows: the deployment of additional police to affected communities; new restrictions on alcohol and kava; pornography filters on publicly funded computers; compulsory acquisition of townships currently held under provisions of the Native Title Act 1993, through five-year leases with compensation on a basis other than just terms (the number of settlements involved remains unclear); commonwealth funding for provision of community services; removal of customary law and cultural practice considerations from bail applications and sentencing in criminal proceedings; suspension of the permit system controlling access to aboriginal communities; quarantine of a proportion of welfare benefits to all recipients in the designated communities and of all benefits to those who are judged to have neglected their children; and the abolition of the Community Development Employment Projects.

Rather than rationalizing Indigenous welfare, Tess Lea has argued that the Intervention was just another instance of "wild policy," the "feral unfurlings of bureaucratic ganglia" into Indigenous worlds. Fifteen months after this flood of money was announced, one of the major initiatives, the Strategic Indigenous Housing and Infrastructure Program, was "imploding from one cost blow out revelation after another, with claims of funds being siphoned into consultancy fees, of bloated bureaucrat fiefdoms, and confected pre-build construction figures."[8] Meanwhile, following a strategy begun in the 1990s, the Northern Territory government diverted large parts of federal funds meant for rural and remote Indigenous communities into the general revenue, especially for the upgrading and expansion of the police force. This expansion then allowed searches of Indigenous homes in rural areas, usually conducted without warrant or specific provocation, under the "special measures" of the legislation.

Belyuen and other rural and remote communities became caught in a cycle of police surveillance and harassment, proliferating lifestyle fines (driving unregistered vehicles in remote bush lands, drinking in one's own home), and debt incarceration, all similar to that characterizing many brown and black communities in the United States.[9] The mechanical and hunting skills of elder men and women have now became an economic hazard—the pride of knowing how to make a vehicle work long after its use-by date in order to bring families to remote outstations has become a cash crop for police and state. New forms of hunting emerge: the police hunt for hidden grog and dodging vehicles, Indigenous residents use phones and hand signals to find hidden patrol vehicles.

The genocides and internments, the legislation of a conditioned self-determination, the declaration of a national emergency: these events characterized the lifeworlds of the men and women at Belyuen I have known since 1984, a span of only thirty-five-odd years. And thus it is no surprise that the final, or perhaps original, cause given for the riot/terror/terrible violence is "the never-ending, upending," or what Glen Coulthard describes as "ongoing dispossession"—recognition as dispossession.[10] If boredom takes its punch, how much more does the

8. Tess Lea, "From Little Things, Big Things Grow," *e-flux journal* 58 (October 2014), https://www.e-flux.com/journal/58/61174/from-little-things-big-things-grow-the-unfurling-of-wild-policy.

9. See Melinda Hinkson and Thalia Anthony's recent piece in *Arena* detailing the relationship between the "expanding law-and-order complex that has increasingly penetrated NT Aboriginal communities over the past decade" and the murder and massacre of Indigenous people during the early nineteenth century. Melinda Hinkson and Thalia Anthony, "Three Shots," *Arena* 163 (December 2019): 16.

10. Glen Coulthard, *Red Skin, White Masks: Rejecting the Colonial Politics of Recognition* (Minneapolis: University of Minnesota Press, 2014); Elizabeth A. Povinelli, *The Cunning of Recognition: Indigenous Alterities and the Making of Australian Multiculturalism* (Durham, NC: Duke University Press, 2002).

Karrabing Film Collective, "The Jealous One" (film still), 2017.
Courtesy of the artists.

state-sponsored experimentation in and on the lifeworlds of Indigenous people take? As Tess Lea discusses, this "wild policy" is a form of trickery in which the state depends on supposed Indigenous dysfunction to justify regrettable necessary acts *for their own good*.[11] Small to major disturbances are normalized but—like a gutted, rutted road—nevertheless felt, nevertheless disruptive of the constant countermeasures to set or keep in place the good life.

Beyond the event, the upending of state policy, the riots, the punch is what Linda Yarrowin calls "the terror," a term encompassing not only the event but an ongoing intensification-but-not-event as such. Intense fear and dread as noun and intransitive verb. Such a state can characterize

11. Tess Lea and Paul Pholeros, "This Is Not a Pipe: The Treacheries of Indigenous Housing," *Public Culture* 22, no. 1 (January 2010): 187–209.

encounters with nonsettler beings—such as *munggul*, a *derrabrek* gone wrong, bad clevermen—who act for a reason, a purpose, even if one can only glimpse those reasons or purposes at the edge of one's social world. But they offer protocols for knowing-acting. Against such an affect, Cecilia Lewis proposes another: stubbornness, as a form of remaining that belies liberal resilience.[12] "They think they can force us to change. But no matter what they take away, we still will find a way of staying the same."[13]

4.

A certain form of violence has long captured the imaginary of modern political theorists. From Benjamin's divine violence to Fanon's absolute violence, hope has been placed in the flash of refusal that burns a landscape of domination and seeds a new, more just demos. Of course, in

- 12. Elizabeth A. Povinelli, "Stubborn," with illustrations by Clara Bessijelle Johansson, *e-flux journal* 96 (November 2018), https://www.e-flux.com/journal/95/228045/stubborn.
- 13. Cecilia Lewis to Elizabeth A. Povinelli, 2008.

actuality the demos (we the people) is always a part of the demos (we as opposed to you). The fury of the riot is sparked by *an opposition to* Muslims, Blacks, whites, settlers, Hindus, the wealthy, political classes, et cetera. Rancière figures this eruption of the part as the irreducible renewability of democracy, a result of the play between the police and politics. As for Laclau, for Rancière the riot does not so much consolidate as constitute the people—a phoenix that rises from the violence as if the violence had been stoked on its behalf, rather than as if it had been the cauldron of its formation. The queer public did not precede Stonewall but was made from it. The Brown Commons emerges and renews itself in the constant refusals of white supremacy.[14]

It might then be useful to rethink a tendency within Western critical theory to characterize riots that become revolutions as righteous violence and those that do not as wrongful acts of terror. This characterization lodges a hopefulness in the riot. For instance, the historic emergence of the Karrabing from the terror of a riot seems to reinforce the hope of violence. Even the target of a wrongful rampage can be the cauldron of a new form of political imaginary!

But before one celebrates too loudly, two cautions. The first remembers that for all the Karrabings that arise from the ashes, countless others simply burn. The second takes seriously what my colleagues insist are the affective conditions shaping all geosocial realities—namely, the movement of jealousy across separate-separate and connected realities. But this original affect does not necessarily manifest as riot or manifest in the content-form of the riot. The Belyuen riot was intensified by the fact that the settler state only "recognized" those parts of Belyuen social reason that suited it. Thus the state structured the content of the riot in the sense that it provided an architecture for jealousy—who was attacking whom. Rather than confirming or negating the potential link between a form of violence and the hope of political democracy, Karrabing's understandings of the riot point to new forms of affect, epistemology, and obligation relative to one's internal outside.

> Linda Yarrowin: As with marriage, ceremony, sweating in a place— by doing this you join the places that these activities cross over, but you also keep your own people and places strong. That is why people were strong before white people came. They respected the other person because they were connected inside and outside.

Karrabing is not somehow exempt from the difficulties of balancing the play between separate-separate and connected—from the difficulties of keeping individual places strong by keeping the places they are connected to strong despite oppressive policing and economic bullying. But succeeding or failing at various points of the day is far different from the terror of a settler state that disavows "both/and" for the terror of the "either/or."

14. See the work of José Muñoz and Fred Moten.

Riot Act, April 29, 1992

Ai Ogawa

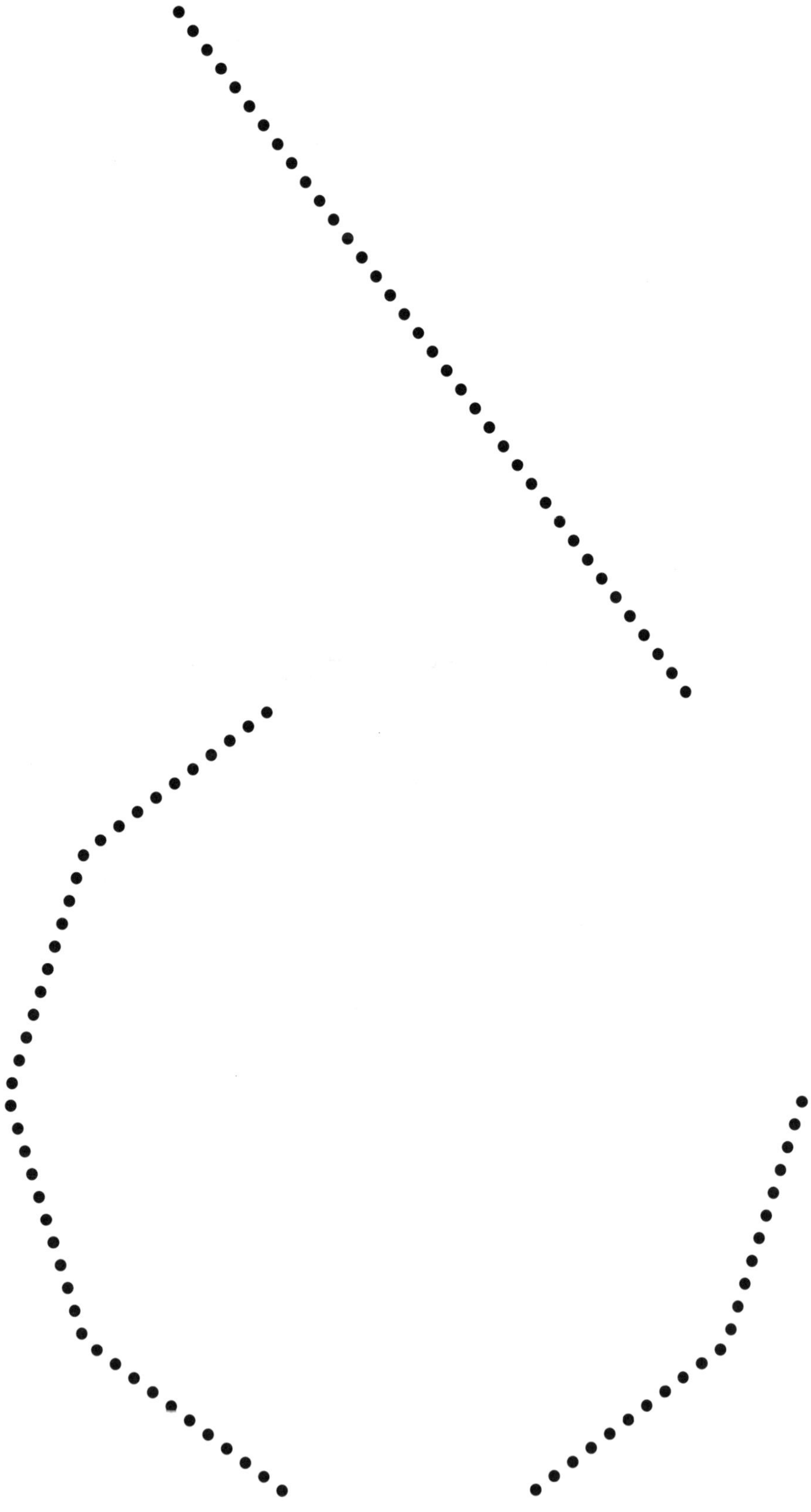

I'm going out and get something.
I don't know what.
I don't care.
Whatever's out there, I'm going to get it.
Look in those shop windows at boxes
and boxes of Reeboks and Nikes
to make me fly through the air
like Michael Jordan
like Magic.
While I'm up there, I see Spike Lee.
Looks like he's flying too
straight through the glass
that separates me
from the virtual reality
I watch everyday on TV.
I know the difference between
what it is and what it isn't.
Just because I can't touch it
doesn't mean it isn't real.
All I have to do is smash the screen,
reach in and take what I want.
Break out of prison.
South Central homey's newly risen
from the night of living dead,
but this time he lives,
he gets to give the zombies
a taste of their own medicine.
Open wide and let me in,
or else I'll set your world on fire,
but you pretend that you don't hear.
You haven't heard the word is coming down
like the hammer of the gun
of this black son, locked out of this big house,
while massa looks out the window and sees only smoke.
Massa doesn't see anything else,
not because he can't,
but because he won't.
He'd rather hear me talking about mo' money,
mo' honeys and gold chains
and see me carrying my favorite things
from looted stores
than admit that underneath my Raider's cap,
the aftermath is staring back
unblinking through the camera's lens,
courtesy of CNN,
my arms loaded with boxes of shoes
that I will sell at the swap meet
to make a few cents on the declining dollar.
And if I destroy myself
and my neighborhood
"ain't nobody's business, if I do"
but the police are knocking hard

at my door
and before I can open it,
they break it down
and drag me in the yard.
They take me in to be processed and charged,
to await trial,
while Americans forget
the day the wealth finally trickled down
to the rest of us.

Pat–Riot–Against the Slow Cancellation of the Future
Ala Younis

Ala Younis, *Pat-riot-against the slow cancellation of the future*, 2018, detail

Behind the food trucks in Sharjah, Lara kneels as she explains the project she's curating for Sharjah Biennial 13's intervention in Palestine. The commissioned artists are "unearthing" problems the occupation has hidden in the land. One artist is tracing the radioactive waste buried in the West Bank villages. Another is investigating the Palestinian businesses that provide cement products to build Israeli settlements. The details they bring to light will surely make people angry.

"Beware of building anger destined for self-suppression—self-suppression that could then be normalized," one of us said. "Beware of curating anger, especially without the necessary tools to guide the angry to use this anger and fight back."

"Beware of anger if it can only vent as desperation."

•

"They came to the martyr's condolences tent and beat his father," someone else said. "People became angry, and so the Palestinian police came to restore order, treated people as rioters." Another picked up on the conversation: "The martyr was killed because he had thought of alternative ways to use anger. He was brewing his and other Palestinians' resentment of Israeli occupation into a knowledge of practicalities against the occupier; he thought to take people on bus tours around places in Palestine where interesting forms of resistance had erupted in the past, and through the bus microphone he gave concise information on what was successful in the strategies the resistance groups came up with. He wanted to learn, to teach people how land can be an agent, how our knowledge of the land can be a tactic to demonstrate our resistance against the occupier."

He was known as "the educated martyr"; he was also called "the intellectual caught in the clash."

The martyr had published a few articles online in which he strategized the accumulation of small efforts. He saw ways to instrumentalize the hardship of living under occupation to interrupt the occupier's schemes of dominance over the land. He believed in the method of giving up on the land temporarily for the sake of gaining time. He retreated when attacked, attacked when his enemy retreated. He liked to plan escapes with stops or places for rest, he thought of dispersed micro-operations that spread horizontally, of small triumphs achieved through collective work. "This is an effort that is possible, and that will weaken the occupation's forces," he wrote. He was thirty-three years old when he was assassinated in March 2017 near Ramallah. For a few weeks after, his online articles spread widely.

His name, his fist, and the title of his article "Live as a porcupine, and fight like a flea" (2013) were sprayed across walls in Amman after his assassination. Next to his name, someone sprayed a hashtag, #almushtabik (the-caught-in-clash), his other nickname.

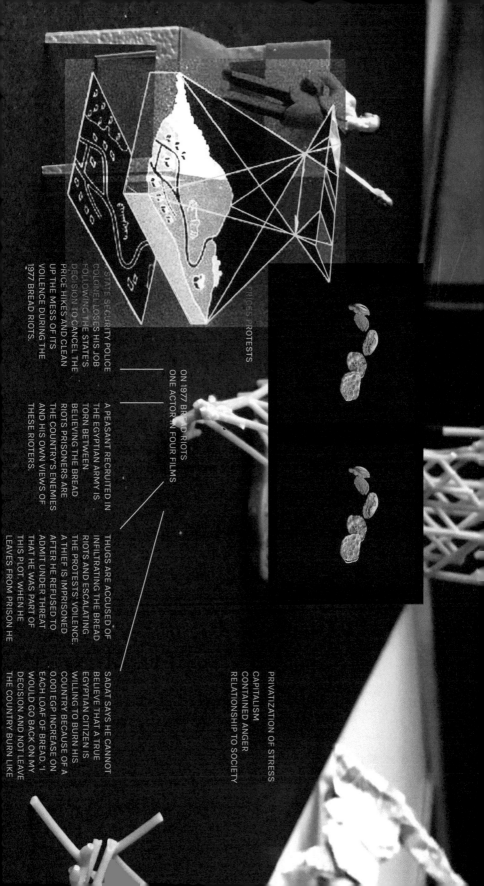

STATE SECURITY POLICE COLONEL LOSES HIS JOB FOLLOWING THE STATE'S DECISION TO CANCEL THE PRICE HIKES AND CLEAN UP THE MESS OF ITS VIOLENCE DURING THE 1977 BREAD RIOTS.

PRICES PROTESTS

ON 1977 BREAD RIOTS ONE ACTOR IN FOUR FILMS

A PEASANT RECRUITED IN THE EGYPTIAN ARMY IS TORN BETWEEN BELIEVING THE BREAD RIOTS PRISONERS ARE THE COUNTRY'S ENEMIES AND HIS OWN VIEWS OF THESE RIOTERS.

THUGS ARE ACCUSED OF INFILTRATING THE BREAD RIOTS AND ESCALATING THE PROTESTS' VIOLENCE. A THIEF IS IMPRISONED AFTER HE REFUSED TO ADMIT UNDER THREAT THAT HE WAS PART OF THIS PLOT. WHEN HE LEAVES FROM PRISON HE

SADAT SAYS HE CANNOT BELIEVE THAT A TRUE EGYPTIAN CITIZEN IS WILLING TO BURN HIS COUNTRY BECAUSE OF A 0.001 EGP INCREASE ON EACH LOAF OF BREAD. 'I WOULD GO BACK ON MY DECISION AND NOT LEAVE THE COUNTRY BURN LIKE

PRIVATIZATION OF STRESS
CAPITALISM
CONTAINED ANGER
RELATIONSHIP TO SOCIETY

I took a photo of the graffiti before the sun went down. She said, "Many people posted things on this martyr on Facebook, pretending they knew him. They faked a relationship with him, just to join the trend."

The spray paint was later covered with yellow paint—a confrontation hidden in this form of writing and unwriting on public walls in the side streets of Amman.

•

Looking into the camera of a mobile phone extended on a selfie stick, a group of young men sang like a pop-up choir in the streets of Cairo. They performed short satirical pieces that criticized the state's tight grip on social and political conditions. They posted videos of their performances on YouTube. Then they were arrested.

In solidarity, people hiding their eyes behind their mobile phones took a riot of selfies that swept the walls of social media, along with the hashtags #shaken_by_the_mobile_camera and #street_kids. The rioters wanted to deluge social media space with multiple variations of a single image, but with the face of the person who protests remaining unidentifiable.

A Google doc from the spring of 2011 carried the names of the Friday demonstrations that took place in Arab cities. The list of cities grew as they appeared in the news. The names of their protests were cloned from one city's Friday to another. The document also included the counterdemonstrations of pro-regime crowds meant to illustrate their presence on the ground too. Most of the names and dates of demonstrations were found in the titles of their YouTube videos.

The demonstrations had names like "Your silence kills us," "The last chance," "The path correction," "The one demand," "The martyrs of the Arab truce extension."

The demonstrations and the anger were always televised. They were often described from both sides, for and against. They were highly performative—often shockingly spectacular. Their unexpectedness was growing, somehow, banal. Confrontations with the opposed governments (or governing systems) were happening on the way to, during (on social media), or after the return from the protests.

Mark Fisher has written, "The slow cancellation of the future has been accompanied by a deflation of expectations."[1] The Google doc has not been updated since February 2012.

•

Riots in front of the Intercontinental Semiramis Hotel in Cairo continued for a while in the first half of 2013. When the rioters attempted to enter the hotel, they were sent away by the hotel chefs in their white coats, who fought back. The clashes were caught on mobile cameras; they looked like absurd scenes from fiction films.

We were looking to book a hotel in Cairo. We had to avoid the Intercontinental and the hotel opposite so that our short stay would not be swept up in the chaos of the riots.

People analyzed these riots on social media. Some wrote that the riots began so that real estate prices would drop, that someone in power

•   1.   Mark Fisher, "The Slow Cancellation Of The Future," MaMa, Zagreb, May 21, 2014, https://youtu.be/aCgkLICTskQ.

PRICE HIKES AND CLEAN UP THE MESS OF ITS VOILENCE DURING THE 1977 BREAD RIOTS.

RIOTS PRISONERS ARE A THIEF IS IMPRISONED AFTER HE REFUSED TO ADMIT UNDER THREAT THAT HE WAS PART OF THIS PLOT. WHEN HE LEAVES FROM PRISON HE BECOMES A DRUGS LORD.

COUNTRY BECAUSE OF A 0.001 EGP INCREASE ON EACH LOAF OF BREAD. 'I WOULD GO BACK ON MY DECISION AND NOT LEAVE THE COUNTRY BURN LIKE THIS. ALL GOVERNMENTS MAKE MISTAKES.'

SHAKEN BY A MOBILE CAMERA

UPRISING OF THIEVES

THE REBELS (1968) - PATIENTS' REBEL. RIOTS IN THE TEWFIK SALEH QUARANTINE. THE FILM IS CENSORED AS IT WAS FEARED TO BE READ IN RELATION TO POLITICAL CONTEXT.

THE LONG DAYS (1980) - THE REBELS DEMONSTRATE, THROUGH TEWFIK SALEH THE EYES OF THE NEW REGIME, THEY ARE PORTRAYED AS REVOLUTIONARIES.

ALEXANDRIA, AGAIN AND FOREVER (1990) - TEWFIK SALEH AS PART OF THE SIT-IN YOUSSEF CHAHINE PROTESTS AT THE SYNDICATE FOR EGYPTIAN ARTISTS. SOME ARE JOINING A HUNGER STRIKE DEMANDS THAT THE SYNDICATE REMAINS INDEPENDENT OF THE STATE INTERVENTION IN CHOOSING ITS ADMINISTRATION.

OCCIDENTAL (2017) - NEIL BELOUFA CONSTRUCTS RIOTS. HE NEIL BELOUFA USES A RIOT AS A BACKDROP TO A SUSPENCE THRILLER AT A HOTEL. IT AGITATES THE VIEWERS' SELF DELIVERANCE TO RACISM AND EXTREMISM, PARTICULARLY AS THE RIOT LEADS TO THE DESTRUCTION OF A PROPERTY.

AL ASWAR (1979) - DEMONSTRATION, RIOT, UPRISING. MOHAMMAD SHUKRI JAMIL. WOMEN IN FRONT. SHORTER IN DURATION IN THE FILM THAN IN THE FILM STILL IMAGE.

paid rioters to target this hotel overlooking the Nile, at the corner of Tahrir Square. The hotel's resistance thwarted the riots' success.

In January 2018 someone told me that people are still split over what happened there. But in the videos posted on YouTube at the time, the rioters were deliberately described as "demonstrators," a name that was given to the revolutionaries that peacefully sat in Tahrir Square in January 2011.

Neither these demonstrations nor Tahrir's were bread riots, like those of 1977 that President Sadat called the "Uprising of the Thieves," when hundreds of thousands of people rose against the increase in bread prices due to Sadat's acceptance of the International Monetary Fund (IMF) and World Bank mandate stopping the subsidization of basic foodstuffs. We came to hear more on the 1977 bread riots when the events in Tahrir in 2011 took on an unexpected dimension, particularly when the people demanded bread, liberty, and social justice. Or when the people demanded the fall of the regime.

We linked the 2011 events in Tahrir Square to what we had seen of archival footage of the bread riots—included in fiction films but left unexplained—unsettling the process of piecing together a memory of the riots for those who were not involved in them. In fact, there were four films starring the same Egyptian actor, Ahmed Zaki (1949–2005), made in the decade that followed the bread riots that depicted them, each offering a vastly different point of view.

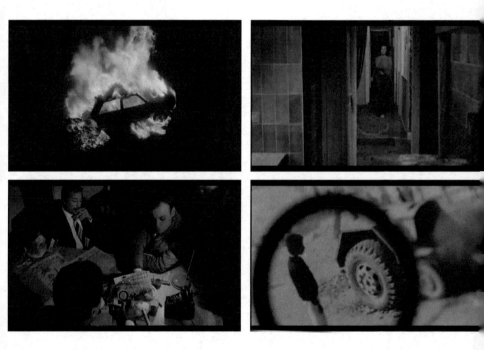

In *Wife of an Important Man* (1987), directed by Mohammad Khan, Zaki plays a police colonel who violently interrogates the students suspected of calling for the riots. When the state wants to clear itself of the violence that was practiced in these interrogations, he is dismissed from his job. "We are the ones who protected the country," the colonel cries when he loses power. In the film, we see the struggle over how to see these riots from domestic space; his wife feels alienated from what is happening on the street as much as from her husband's violent anger. She is also a witness, or a victim, of his resentment of the retreat from a politics that had once empowered him to suppress rioters. He is hurt by a punishment that deprives him of the power to punish.

In *The Innocent* (1986), directed by Atef Al Tayeb, Zaki plays the role of a peasant recruited into the Egyptian Army who is torn between being faithful to his personal beliefs and carrying out the orders he receives from his superiors. He is first faced with such a dilemma when a group of bread rioters is brought to the prison where he works as a guard. In the group is his neighbor, a student who "cannot be any enemy to the country," he thinks; "he is the one who had convinced me that serving in the army is serving the country." Siding with his friend, the soldier becomes one of the rioters, who are shown no mercy when they are punished.

From the opening scenes in *The Emperor* (1990), directed by Tarek Al Eryan, thugs are said to have joined the riots after the students have withdrawn. Zaki plays a thief who confesses he had used the disorder of the riots for robberies. Though his crimes sent him to prison fourteen times, he says he prefers to *now* be a political prisoner rather than a prisoner for a crime he did not commit. Afterward, he awaits impatiently in prison for his acquittal. He tells his collaborator, "This is the time to be out, there is so much to be done out there now," referring to how Sadat's opening to neoliberalism offers great opportunities for all sorts

of investments—he regrets being in prison at a time when these opportunities await cunning people like him. When he is out, he quickly

gets in with new business lords and soon becomes a drug lord himself.

Zaki's role in another film directed by Mohammad Khan, *Days of Sadat* (1991), illustrates the views of President Sadat himself, whom he plays. On the rioters of 1977, he says, "It cannot be a true Egyptian citizen who is willing to burn his country for a 0.01 EGP increase in sugar prices! I would prefer to go back on my decision [of raising prices] and not leave the country to burn like this." As someone with neoliberal inclinations, he claims the riots were motivated by communists and infiltrated by thieves. The riots stop only when he acknowledges that "we made a mistake. All governments make mistakes." After two days of riots, the price hike is cancelled.

•

A recording of a radio report on angry incidents in the south of Jordan is posted online. The recording must be from sometime after 1990 because it speaks about taking in refugees from Iraq. It speaks of how the country is burdened by this economic challenge.

"We are in a difficult situation," says the Jordanian official in the report. Had Iraq not entered two wars by now, our economy would not have drowned. "But you, the bearers of the Arab revolutionary flag, cannot be the ones who bring disorder to this country."

Riots mostly erupted in response to "reforms" requested by the World Bank and/or the IMF in return for new loans to Jordan and other countries. Prices of goods and services were getting higher while the IMF requests encouraged private investments, privatization, and the weakening of currencies.

The radio recording links to another page that features a story on a folder "accidentally" left on a table to inform a Jordanian state official of potential riots that would soon take place in the country. The government received this foreign intelligence report on the imminent riot and took measures to contain the brewing anger. It fought against the riot-to-be through a counterpatriotic rhetoric: if you riot, then you cannot be a patriot; if you are a patriot, then why do you riot?

It was terrifying to learn that the authorities had received a report predicting future riots. Just like the algorithmic machines that automatically detect, report, and flag random people's words, expressions, or statements.

The riots could cancel the hike in prices, but the prices would nevertheless slowly rise afterward, with no riots in sight.

•

In a "highly stylized" video by Neil Beloufa, the streets of Paris are taken over by barricades and furious protesters. An eccentric and improbable couple take refuge in the Hotel Occidental. As the hotel staff grow increasingly suspicious of the couple, a series of absurd events unfold, provoking homophobia, racism, misogyny, terrorist threats, and political manipulation. Beloufa's production used professional actors and was shot in the artist's own studio. He made the film's retro scenery recall 1970s cult cinema, while cell phones and surveillance cameras situate it squarely in the present. With its eclectic range of influences, this genre-bending film reflects satirically on the uneasy context of our time. The protagonists' suspenseful stay at the hotel is shaped by signs and signals from the actors and in the film's score that arouse the viewer's suspicion. Strikingly fake visual and sonic features play "mischievous games" with audience expectations. When the hotel is blown up, we are inclined to blame the odd couple. The rioters on the street also speak of this possibility, based on the description of the two protagonists. In other words, we the audience (just like the rioters) accuse two men of blowing up a hotel only because we did not understand them and could not see the full picture.

While my short synopsis relates the video to cinema, I see this manipulative plot as more similar to scripts of Arab drama series produced between the 1960s and the early 1990s, when television stagecraft was the vernacular of Arab opinions, and when directors were making us suspicious—in one series, about a crime set in a hotel, every character (at some point or another) seems to be the person who committed the crime. The viewer's expectation of future events in the series was shaped by how it was written to "direct" our expectations.

•

I was eleven and in a hotel elevator when another kid pressed all the buttons just as he left for his floor. His intervention delayed the remaining riders as the elevator proceeded to stop at every floor. I can't

remember if I ever tried this same trick or stepped into one of these "directed" trips, but instead of going up to my floor, the elevator took me down to the basement. The elevator doors opened onto the hotel's kitchen, where a chef stood wearing his white uniform. He stuck his head into the elevator, saw all the illuminated buttons, and started to scream at me in Greek. I was terrified—not just of the unfamiliar world outside the open elevator door, or of the violence of fighting in a language that I did not speak, but also of the idea that someone would unleash their anger on a passerby.

Here was after all the buttons had been pressed in a hotel elevator in Athens, which brought me to the hotel's basement kitchen. The chef was yelling at me in Greek, while my family was taking a picture of my sister with some Egyptian actors who were staying at the hotel.

On this trip, I learned that the Greek currency was devalued to the point that we were paying millions of drachmas for everything, that (Egyptian) actors also appear (as important) outside studio sets, and that we could be caught in the flare-up of someone else's riot.

•

Jordan's acclaimed television series directed by Ghassan Jabri about Bedouins, *Wadha wa Ibn Ajlan* (Wadha and son of Ajlan) (1975), was shot in Athens one decade before my visit. It was the country's first drama produced for color broadcast. The series appears to have been filmed in three locations: outdoors, in the desert; indoors, on a set made to look like the desert, with bushes, rocks, and a well; and inside a Bedouin tent. The lead actor was Egyptian and the lead actress Syrian; the Bedouin costumes and production accessories would have traveled with the crew from Jordan.

In his book *Colonial Effects*, Joseph Massad argues that Jordanian soap opera productions such as *Wadha wa Ibn Ajlan*... produced for radio and television, were exported to the rest of the Arab world, launching the Jordanian soap opera genre. Such programs advertising Jordan's Bedouin identity were shown throughout the Arab world from Iraq to Morocco. The fact that Transjordanians of settled and Bedouin origins, Christian or Muslim, were active in promoting Jordan's Bedouin image attests to the inclusive project of Bedouinizing all Jordanians as a form of nationalizing them against the Palestinian national threat that was defeated on the battleground in 1970. As such, the ability of the modern Jordanian and her or his European and Euro-American counterpart to observe the Bedouins and live in their time can take place only if he outlives them, i.e., if he moves through the time he may have shared with them onto a level on which she or he finds modernity.[2]

The series script was adapted in Damascus to premiere as a radio show; its author had not had the chance to hear it until he was on a bus trip from Jordan through Syria to Turkey. He returned to submit the television script to the media department in Jordan, only for the script to be rejected twice. He writes that the censor saw the difficulty of producing accurate sets and perfected accents as a risk that would take away from the authenticity/acclaim of the Bedouin national image. The series was eventually produced (interiors shot in Athens, exteriors in Amman), and when it finally aired on television in several Arab cities simultaneously, the streets were empty of people. The viewership was not obstructed by poor accents or fake interiors; in fact, the series' Bedouin features gained particular popularity in the Gulf. This acceptance also meant that image quality and content of future productions could be shaped further by the money earned by the series' popularity. This meeting halfway was not because people tolerated their own distorted image, but because of an eagerness to see how the media (and actors) could reproduce their image.

•

My uncle starred in a series produced in Dubai, *Hboub El Rih* (The Blowing Wind) (1979). The series was set in Petra, an ancient city in the south of Jordan, around 1948—at the end of the British Mandate for Palestine and the rise of Jewish settlements there. My uncle, originally Palestinian, played the role of a South Jordanian Bedouin from Petra's El Bdoul family, and another actor played the role of a Palestinian revolutionary; the lead actress was Iraqi. These characters challenged the practices of the new settlers as well as the oppressive mandate officers. The title of the series reflects the swiftness of the protagonist, based on a real person who was able to disappear quickly after his raids on the military or militia bases. It is worth mentioning that the first "Arab revolution," against Ottoman rule in the region, had emerged from the south of Jordan in 1916.

The people represented in the events and locations celebrate Jordan's history and remind Jordanians of their own patriotic past. The series was aired again on Jordanian television in 1988, perhaps not only in solidarity with the Palestinian uprising that was widespread in the occupied territories after December 1987, but also in the context of the massive devaluation of Jordanian currency and the burgeoning anger among people of the south, who would rise up again a few years later.

Ala Younis, *Drachmas*, 2018, detail. Scenes from (clockwise): *Laylat Alqabd 'ala Fatma* (The Night of Arresting Fatma), directed by Mohammad Fadhel, 1982, Athens; Cairo; *El 'alm Noor* (Knowledge is Enlightenment), directed by Raphael Bucaily, 1984, Dumu fi 'oyun Wesiha (Tears in Rude Eyes), directed by Yahia El Alami, 1980,

2. Joseph A. Massad, *Colonial Effects: The Making of National Identity in Jordan* (New York: Columbia University Press, 2001).

One Arab currency after another was devalued in the final decades of the twentieth century—with repercussions across the Arab world. The Egyptian pound was worth the equivalent of US$4.00 in 1936, $3.00 in 1950, $2.50 in 1967, $1.40 in 1978, and a mere $0.70 by the 1980s. Elsewhere, a combination of political malaise, a lack of confidence, and speculation surrounding the Lebanese pound all but stripped the currency of its once-envied purchasing power. In the early 1980s, a US dollar was the equivalent of about 3.5 Lebanese pounds; in contrast, a 1987 news article reported a dizzying and exponential depreciation of the currency, which sank from 87 per US dollar down to 505 per US dollar in one year (a drop of 480 percent).[3] Between 1982 and 1987, the Jordanian dinar varied only slightly in value, between US$2.55 and US$3.04. Jordan withdrew its financial support for the West Bank in 1988, however, which led to financial crisis. By 1989 the dinar had dropped 10 percent, to a value of $1.76. In response, Jordanians— especially those of Palestinian origin—tried to exchange dinars for foreign currency or move their savings outside the country. Responding to a similar effect locally, Syria passed a law in 1989—Law No. 24— that imposed severe penalties for such foreign exchanges. During this period, the Gulf would rise as the powerhouse in the region, backed by a stable currency and an influx of investment.

This new prominence of the Gulf coincided with Gulf-based studios' rising interest in dramatic productions. Their investments in film and TV production were reflected in changes to the voices, accents, faces, and topics represented. A Bedouin series on resistance in the Palestine Mandate sustained anger in the region and demonstrated the historical commitment (of tribes) to the Palestinian cause at the same time that President Anwar Sadat signed the Camp David Accords, which led to the Egypt-Israel Peace Treaty in 1979. These treaties incited a wide-spread anger across the Arab world and against Egyptians and their representative offices.

Besides the anger and demonstrations, what is worth noting in this period is the Gulf's gradual takeover and enabling of investments in the region, and the nationalism and patriotism that this power facilitated. As Mark Fisher has warned, the power of these investments is that they destroy the imaginary of income-yielding projects other than those from jobs in or investments from projects capitalizing on the interests of the funder—in this case, the Gulf. However, the drama productions from the Gulf had something else significant in common: the inclusion of modernized interiors and the technologies enabled by their income, and thus their modernization. With the click of a button on a remote control, a hole would open in the floor, or a wall or guards would appear and stop intruders from a distance. These technologies were used in offices and houses, as we see in *Dars Khsousi* (Private Lesson), a Kuwaiti TV series from 1981, where a secretary monitors the engineer she loves through the glass panels that separate their offices. From this monitoring, she learns his preferences in women, food, and other interests and creates a persona for herself using this accumulated surveillance knowledge. Surveillance teaches her how to stage a fake but appealing image for the man she loves. Once she marries him, she no longer needs to pretend.

In another series from 1983, *Khalti Qumasha* (Auntie Qumasha), the same actress plays the victim of surveillance by her mother-in-law. The mother-in-law has installed CCTV systems in her three sons' rooms, particularly to overhear the complaints, plots, and plans carried out behind her back. She hides her equipment behind a sliding fake wall in her room. This means that the mother-in-law is always aware of and prepared to thwart any plans (or riots against her) made by members of her household. This can be nothing but an early depiction of surveillance and (perhaps) algorithmic terror.

Mark Fisher has argued that the growing grip of capitalism flattens ideas and cultural styles by limiting the ability to work, imagine, or experiment with new forms and ideas to projects with profit potential.[4] As investment from the Gulf chews through the Arab film and television industry, we are witnessing a "this slow cancellation of the future" in the form of lost chances to imagine a hideout, a place in which individuals could faintly voice their anger. But what also enables this cancellation is technological control of the spaces that surround us and a profit-oriented mechanism molding history and personal narratives for an overwhelming distribution network. We must pair these cancellations with anger that prompts us to restore, or perhaps make, tools that empower us to stand against this slow cancellation of our imagination of the future.

● 4. Fisher, "The Slow Cancellation Of The Future."

Mnemonic Spatiality of Violence

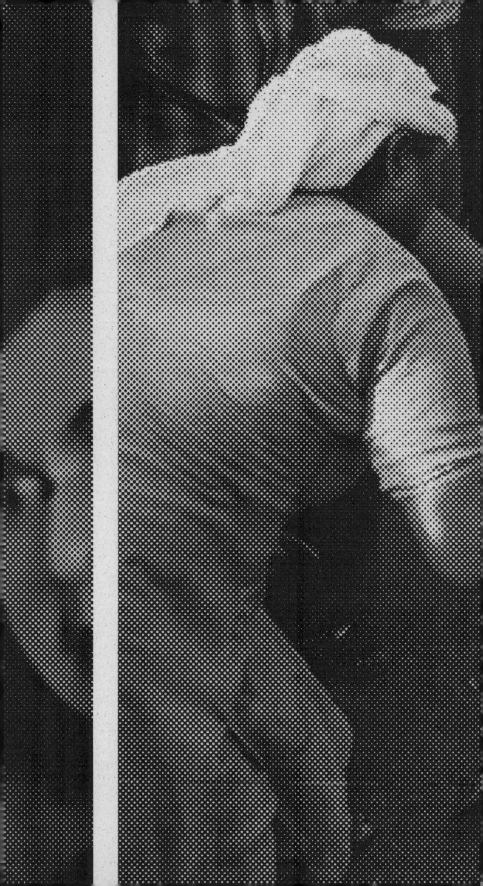

Introduction
Niloufar Tajeri

This section, "Mnemonic Spatiality of Violence," focuses on (post)colonial urbanism as well as neoliberal capitalism and its racial logic of spatial injustices. In his book *Hollow Land* (2017), architect Eyal Weizman looks at the Palestinian landscape not only as a *site* of war but as its very *tool*, enforcing the slow and oftentimes unseen violence carried out by design. "The architecture of Israel's occupation," he tells us, is "a form of slow architectural violence."[1] The concept of the "spatiality of violence" seeks to capture this notion that spatial organization, architecture, and urban design are not merely signifiers or aesthetic representations of power relations, but in fact are their very tool and medium. The "spatiality of violence" looks at space as medium and tool to maintain social inequality and racial violence and at the same time to evoke memories of violence and injustice: space is a *mnemonic* medium, transmitting memories from generation to generation.

Riots communicate rage against multiple forms of violence—visible and invisible, explicit and structural. Violence harming bodies and violence restricting expressions, identities, aspirations, movements, freedoms, safety. It ranges from the most spectacular instances of police brutality to bureaucratic austerity urbanism and data-driven systems of public surveillance. As Nadine El-Enany demonstrates in this section, not all violence is tangible or legible to dominant society or to the legal system.

The exclusion from decent housing, pleasant neighborhoods, good schools, jobs, and social positions primarily experienced by vulnerable and racialized groups (but not confined to them) has slowly developed into grievances that are geographically defined—while at the same time, austerity urbanism shapes ties between social movements and urban uprisings (see Margit Mayer's contribution to this volume). Natascha Sadr Haghighian finds that not only do social movements and uprisings share ties, but both are also targeted, observed, and labeled by police. Here the spatiality of violence is the invisible, racially biased data web in which people are unknowingly trapped, making them more vulnerable to police violence.

When looking not *at* but *from within* the spaces in which riots occur, riots can no longer be understood as "riots" but as uprisings, anticolonial revolts, and resistance movements. Within this context, something else emerges as the actual riot: state acts of violence (policing and displacement of people), private-public vandalism (demolition of housing estates and violent reorganization of space), and corporate looting (privatization of public property) are manifold in the neoliberal

1. Gal Kirn, Niloufar Tajeri, Eyal Weizman, and Anselm Franke, "Forensis Is Forensics Where There Is No Law," *Mute*, December 16, 2014, https://www.metamute.org/editorial/articles/forensis-forensics-where-there-no-law.

project of restructuring cities. As Gal Kirn and I describe, this "riot from above" creates a "spatiality of violence." In the traumatic case of the Grenfell Tower, the spatiality of violence manifests itself as structural neglect and austerity for the homes of racialized people combined with overpolicing of their public spaces. As Nadine El-Enany argues, it is the "slow or structural violence" and the colonial configuration of the state that is a blind spot of the British legal system and that constantly questions the presence of poor and racialized communities (see page 219 in this volume). El-Enany's critical analysis is neatly complemented by the poetic expressions and reflections of Zena Edwards, who mourns for the fallen in riots and the Grenfell fire and shows how "revolving anger" will not cease unless the structural causes of racism and injustice are destroyed (see Zena Edwards's contribution on page 205).

The spatiality of violence also points to the memory of violence and its inscription in everyday urban spaces. The maps and reflections shared by Léopold Lambert show how the memory of the 1961 massacre of Algerians in Paris is carried on in the weaponized spatiality of Paris and in the segregated bodies in the *banlieues*—the spaces that rise up every time violence is most blatantly exercised against racialized communities. Dariouche Tehrani argues that the 2005 revolts in the French *banlieues* were instances of anticolonial resistance and self-defense against a system of structural violence (see Tehrani's essay in this volume). Asef Bayat, on the other hand, presents the possibility for resistance in taking back these same everyday spaces. His contribution investigates the formation of dissent in Cairo in 2011 and in the Arab revolutions more generally, against the backdrop of neoliberal structural adjustments in the Middle East since the 1990s. The "nonmovement" is the wave of the otherwise invisible political subjects that resists structural exclusion by encroaching on the public sphere, making squares and public spaces the "spatial locus" of subaltern struggles in the Arab revolutions.

Gauri Gill's long-term project *1984* assembles a range of voices, including artists, writers, poets, and filmmakers, together with survivors' testimonies of the anti-Sikh genocide. The excerpts re-presented in this section emphasize the dialogue Gill creates between her photographs and resilient modes of response in a notebook and bibliography, countering the void left by necropower. Balbir Singh relates to Gill's work in the terms of "mourning as antagonism" asking, "how does a community deal with state accountability while carrying a common traumatic wound?"[2] This, too, is a question of heritage, communal memory, and monumental loss.

Ruth Wilson Gilmore's statement "Capitalism requires inequality and racism enshrines it" resonates throughout the contributions, asking how riots and revolts inhabit or even lend structure to global metropoles that in turn become the testing grounds for militarized urbanism against

2. Balbir K. Singh, "Unjust Attachments: Mourning as Antagonism in Gauri Gill's 1984," *Critical Ethnic Studies 2*, no. 2 (Fall 2016): 104–128.

vulnerable and racialized groups.[3] There is an essential link between the organization of space to control communities and the riot as both a political response to and a justification for societal and spatial restructuring from above. Urban space is interrupted by the event of the riot, only to be weaponized in its aftermath. However, riots are not only a phenomenon or triggers and reactions; they also communicate a firm disbelief in the myth that the system, the sovereign, and capitalism can be fixed or reformed.

If the system can be neither fixed nor reformed, the riot is a first claim toward self-determination over homes and public spaces, toward having a say or at least security, safety, and rights in one's own living environments. The symbolic acts of destruction of buildings and spaces are acts of expropriation by the oppressors and claims of ownership by the dispossessed, claims that ultimately materialize the demand and the desire to rebuild on one's own terms, based on one's own decisions. To whom does the city belong, and who has the right to the city? Austerity urbanism thrives on the insecurity of the precarious, both inside and outside their own homes. This constant threat of displacement and destruction hovers over people's lives as a consequence of racism, profit-driven urbanism, and urban governance. It is this fundamental experience of the mnemonic spatiality of violence and inequality that triggers urban rage. And it is the fundamental experience and power of urban rage that reverses the status quo—even if just for a brief moment.

3. Ruth Wilson Gilmore, foreword to Bobby M. Wilson, *America's Johannesburg: Industrialization and Racial Transformation in Birmingham*(Athens: University of Georgia Press, 2019), ix.

Riots as Contestations of Neoliberal Urbanism

Margit Mayer

I. The Many Languages of Uprising

The "riot" as an analytical category in social science research deserves some care. As scholarship on collective action has internationalized and as more comparative studies of urban uprisings have been undertaken, it has become obvious that the concept described by the English language media as "rioting" is not so readily translated. In addition to its diverse connotations in different languages and its fuzzy definition, the term has often been associated with particular meanings stemming from its origin as a legal term. For example, in the nineteenth-century German Empire, *Aufruhr* was defined as resistance against the state and thus was punishable as a criminal offense.[1] Similarly, the UK Public Order Act of 1986 defines "riot" as when twelve or more people use or threaten unlawful violence that would cause others present to fear for their safety.[2] Much scholarly work on "riots" has adopted the criminalization associated with the term. Thus, labeling the wave of urban unrest that first broke out in the *banlieues* of Paris (2005), erupted on the streets and plazas of Athens (2008 and 2011), spread from London to eight major cities in England (2011), and ignited in the Stockholm suburb of Husby before spreading to other poor suburbs as well as smaller Swedish cities (2013) as "riots" has usually served to stigmatize these actions as criminal/mob behavior and to deny them political character.

Further, within social science research, definitional boundaries between different forms of protest movements and collective defiance (such as urban uprisings) are unclear. The "riot" label is employed for a host of rather different phenomena, situations, and events. Whether (apolitical) soccer hooliganism; anti-G20 rallies involving broken bank windows, burning cars, and skirmishes with the police; or marginalized youth drawing public attention to their exclusion, deprivation, and discrimination by resorting to "rioting," these actions are scrutinized through the lens of collective physical violence rather than collective action. Or, more precisely, the feature of violence is made relevant for distinguishing (and then penalizing) these forms of action. Referencing the violent aspect of riots in this way serves to depoliticize such actions or, where political motives cannot be denied, to delegitimize them. The role of power and domination rarely matters in such analyses—for example, in research on microsociological variants of violence such as that by Randall Collins or in social-psychological work in the tradition of Gustav Le Bon's work on crowd behavior— as they focus exclusively on what appears to generate the

1. *Das Strafgesetzbuch für das Deutsche Reich* (Erlangen: Verlag von Andreas Deichert, 1876), 34–35, https://reader.digitale-sammlungen.de/de/fs1/object/display/bsb11332537_00044.html and https://reader.digitale-sammlungen.de/de/fs1/object/display/bsb11332537_00045.html.

2. Public Order Act 1986, Chapter 64, Part 1.1, www.legislation.gov.uk/ukpga/1986/64.

violence and not on the motives of participants or on underlying societal structures.[3]

Contemporary social movement studies within the dominant research paradigm assumes that movements are goal-oriented, rational, and strategic. They thus distinguish between spontaneous, disorganized, and temporary phenomena and organized, sustained collective action with clearly defined political goals and evident targets.[4] The shortcomings of such an approach for capturing the plurality of shapes and logics of different forms of collective action were pointed out by Frances Fox Piven and Richard A. Cloward early on.[5] Piven and Cloward argued that disruptive action—that is, actions that interrupt everyday routines and bring normalized or institutionalized processes to a halt—may be not only rational but also strategically sensible and functional toward a (progressive) goal, in particular for social groups that do not benefit from formal politics and have to break through them for their concerns to be noticed.[6]

To urban scholars, it seemed noteworthy that the post-2000 uprisings in Europe have primarily unfolded in urban (central) and suburban (poor peripheral) spaces, where they articulated and resisted spatialized social inequalities and conflicts— thus sharing important context-specific structural dimensions with contemporary urban social movements.[7] This structural context has a lot to add to our understanding of urban uprisings (including those labeled as riots) as it helps identify their political content even where other approaches invisibilize it and helps to deconstruct the racial or ethnic stigmatization of "rioters." In order to gain knowledge about these uprisings that goes beyond the description of regular patterns and that does not lock them into an a priori irrational, deviant, or nonstrategic position, an approach that analyzes them in the context of the hegemonic societal and political regime can be helpful. This would link riots to other forms of urban contestations that also address the deepening spatialized social inequalities that are a defining aspect of contemporary neoliberal urbanism.

3. Randall Collins, *Violence: A Micro-Sociological Theory* (Princeton, NJ: Princeton University Press, 2009); Gustav Le Bon, *The Crowd: A Study of the Popular Mind* (1895; repr., Cardiff: Sparkling Books, 2009).

4. A more recent turn within the dominant social movement research paradigm, the theory of contentious politics, considers "disruptive" collective action (including riots) as an aspect of social movement politics. But the emphasis is still on (1) "interactions in which actors make *claims*," in which (2) "governments appear either as targets, initiators of claims, or third parties." Charles Tilly, *Contentious Performances* (Cambridge: Cambridge University Press, 2008), 5.

5. Frances Fox Piven and Richard A. Cloward, *Poor People's Movements: Why They Succeed, How They Fail* (New York: Pantheon Books, 1977).

6. For a more elaborate discussion and critique of research on riots since the ghetto revolts in US cities, see chapter 1 in Margit Mayer, Håkan Thörn, and Catharina Thörn, eds., *Urban Uprisings: Challenging Neoliberal Urbanism in Europe* (London: Palgrave Macmillan, 2016).

7. Mayer, Thörn, and Thörn, *Urban Uprisings*.

II. Neoliberal Urbanism and Its Contestations

Neoliberal restructuring in the past four decades has wrought enormous changes on urban landscapes, fundamentally altering conditions for those struggling over (the definition of and access to) the city. The Fordist model, characterized by (top-down, bureaucratically governed) public infrastructures and state-underwritten social reproduction, has been gradually dismantled by consecutive waves of neoliberalization, which has also transformed the shape and dynamics of urban contestations. Both the vibrant mobilizations of those discontent with and alienated by the cultural norms and authoritarian ways of the Fordist-Keynesian city and the protests of those excluded from or disadvantaged by the "blessings" of the Fordist model would eventually become appropriated in the consolidation of the neoliberal city.

The global shift toward the neoliberal paradigm began with the austerity politics of the 1980s, which ground away at Keynesian-welfarist and social-collectivist institutions. This initial "roll-back" phase put so-called "old" social issues back onto the agenda.[8] Increasing unemployment and poverty, "new" housing needs, riots in housing estates, and new waves of squatting emerged, while local governments—confronted with intensifying fiscal constraints at the same time that social service expenditures were increasing—became interested in innovative ways to solve their problems. This opened municipalities up to some of the innovative ways that movement organizations (whom they had previously scorned, marginalized, or repressed) tended to issues like youth unemployment and housing decay, among others.

Since the 1990s, "roll-out neoliberalization" has responded to the contradictions and deleterious effects that the previous phase of retrenchment had generated. While the basic neoliberal imperative of mobilizing city space as an arena for growth persisted, municipal policies now foregrounded more supportive mechanisms, such as local economic development policies and community-based programs. These mechanisms addressed social infrastructures, political cultures, and the ecological foundations of the city—but in a way that transformed these conditions into assets useful for the intensifying interurban competition. Also as a result of this competition, new institutions and modes of delivery for social services were fashioned—such as integrated area development and public-private partnerships in urban regeneration as well as social welfare, all with a heavy reliance on and incorporation of civic engagement.

●   8.   On the periodization of the various phases of neoliberalization, cf. Neil
         Brenner and Nik Theodore, "Cities and the Geographies of Actually Existing
         Neoliberalism," *Antipode* 34, no. 3 (2002): 349–379.

These novel urban development policies, accompanied as they were by the de facto erosion of social rights, politicized distributive conflicts around the question of whose city it is supposed to be. The increasingly professionalized, formerly alternative community-based organizations were more thoroughly integrated into neighborhood revitalization programs, while multiplying ranks of "urban outcasts" were sorted into different categories to be "serviced" by such programs.[9]

By the beginning of the new century, urbanization had gone global as financial markets took advantage of deregulation and increased flexibility to debt-finance urban development around the world. But because economic growth rates as well as wages began to stagnate with the dot-com crash of 2001, social divides increased, particularly in the deepening socio-spatial polarization within and between cities. By then, social reforms (such as PRWORA in the United States in 1996 and Hartz IV reforms in Germany) had everywhere replaced welfare with workfare systems, which meant that the new urban, social, and labor market policies had "activated" large parts of the urban underclass into (downgraded) labor markets, thus making *them* responsible for "self-optimizing" and improving the conditions that the new regime had wrought on them.

The bursting of additional financial and real estate bubbles triggered the 2008 financial crisis, which delegitimized the neoliberal project; finance capital in particular was discredited, but it has nevertheless continued to dominate. As the financial crisis was translated (discursively and practically) into public debt, fiscal crises, and intense vilification of state spending, urban neoliberalization was increasingly characterized by a *devolved form of extreme fiscal constraint*. Municipalities were adversely affected everywhere, and many of them imposed advanced forms of austerity politics that dismantled whatever had survived previous rounds of cutbacks and neoliberal restructuring.

Thanks to its dominance, financial capital has been able to delay and weaken attempts to reregulate its operations at the expense of the public purse and future crises. Since then, we've seen neoliberal austerity policies and politics transform, in more and more places, into a *constitutionalized state of austerity* that tends to undermine the institutions and practices of liberal democracy.[10] Instead of seeing the end of neoliberalism (which many have heralded), we are witnessing the continued success of the neoliberal project with its endless marketization and financialization, increasingly taking place

9.   Loïc Wacquant, *Urban Outcasts: A Comparative Sociology of Advanced Marginality* (New York: Polity, 2008).

10. Bob Jessop, "Authoritarian Neoliberalism: Periodization and Critique," *South Atlantic Quarterly* 118, no. 2 (April 2019): 348.

through accumulation by dispossession and illiberal and authoritarian political regimes.

In this current era, the economic and political features that characterize the urban realm shape the contestations and resistance taking place in cities today.

1. Chasing revenues in new ways

The overarching political strategy of city leaders continues to be what it has been since the beginning of the neoliberal turn: the pursuit of *growth first*. That is, urban managers do whatever they can to accelerate investment flows into their city and improve its position in the interurban rivalry.

As manufacturing industries have declined in or left cities of the Global North altogether, the financial sector has expanded in size and influence, and new forms of financial capital, such as hedge funds, private equity, or vulture capital, have gained significance.[11] Growing portions of this financial capital have flown into the real estate sector, which realizes higher interest rates than other forms of capital investment.[12] This transformation of urban economies sets up a new type of competition among cities: those that manage to attract the so-called FIRE industries (finance, insurance, real estate) benefit from the dominance of interest-bearing (financial and real estate) capital. Cities at the bottom of the urban hierarchy, in contrast, find themselves on the receiving end of the deregulated, predatory, and sometimes fraudulent financial institutions preying on their remaining public assets and often conning them deeper into debt. Ordinary cities (in the middle) also seek to raise property values and bring in higher rent payers, ceding more and more influence over the shape of our cities to real estate capital. As real estate values have risen, so has the political power of real estate capital.

City managers everywhere, whether cash-strapped or not, assume they can lure this kind of investment into their city by increasing land values. They incentivize real estate development by rezoning certain areas and by rebranding specific locational assets to attract upwardly mobile and wealthy residents or "creative classes" and artists (if only transitionally). Image construction and city marketing have become indispensable instruments in this game. Ordinary and poor cities find low-cost, symbolic ways to play up their "local flavor"

11. Financial capital in this regime has a target rate of return that is several times greater than the historic norm for profit-producing capital. Worse still, by striving to achieve this target, it leverages fictitious credit and capital on an unprecedented scale. In aggregate, the eventual validation of this massively leveraged capital would demand a total volume of surplus value that far exceeds the productive and exploitative capacity of existing profit-producing capital. See Jessop, "Authoritarian Neoliberalism," 352.

12. Samuel Stein, *Capital City: Gentrification and the Real Estate State* (New York: Verso, 2018).

and attract "creatives" to upgrade their brand. Everywhere the search is on for innovative, more or less low-budget, culture-led efforts to mobilize city space for growth.

In this process, creative and cultural workers have been assigned to enhance the unique brand of a city as their presence is understood to be particularly conducive to creating "indigenous authenticity." Many cities have put in place programs and subsidies for such groups in order to foster their (sub) cultural activities and productions. Often such groups receive support for rehabbing old buildings in former manufacturing areas, in which case the real estate industry can then benefit from their efforts.

Such interim policies have provided opportunities—though in ambiguous ways—to social movement groups that can be fitted into *creative city* projects. But since the outcomes of such programs tend to valorize and upgrade the spaces made attractive by artists or (sub)cultural interim users, their work ultimately creates pressures on other movement groups that lack symbolic resources and leads either to their marginalization and displacement or to their resistance.[13]

2. Privatization—of local state assets, public services, and public spaces

Intensified *privatization* of state assets and public infrastructures, as well as of services (through outsourcing), is another key feature of neoliberal urbanism. Privatization of the local public sector involves both destructive and creative moments—with the elimination of public monopolies for municipal services (such as utilities, sanitation, or mass transit) and the creation of new markets for service delivery and infrastructure maintenance. Privatization first transformed the traditional relationship and boundary between the public and private spheres by rolling back and reorganizing the socially oriented institutions of the public sector. But as collective infrastructures—from public transport and utilities to social housing—became exposed to the market, privatization became financialization. In this raiding of public coffers, often by government-sponsored private companies, urban resources, public infrastructures and services, and social housing estates have become options for expanded capital accumulation by dispossession.[14] Jamie Peck and Heather Whiteside have observed that in US cities, "infrastructure provision, which was integrated and socialized under Keynesian regulation, has since been extensively 'unbundled,'

● 13. Cf. Margit Mayer, "Creative City Policy and Social Resistance," in *Making Cultural Cities in Asia*, ed. Jun Wang, Tim Oakes, and Yang Yang (New York: Routledge, 2016), 234–250.

● 14. Raquel Rolnik, "Late Neoliberalism: The Financialization of Homeownership and Housing Rights," *International Journal of Urban and Regional Research* 37, no. 3 (2003): 1058–1066; Kevin Ward, "Financialization and Urban Politics: Expanding the Optics," *Urban Geography* 38, no. 1 (2017): 1–4.

rated for 'return,' and financialized, in a manner that shifts the locus of power toward bond market networks and away from growth-machine coalitions *per se*."[15]

As mentioned above, land and property play a pivotal role in today's urban economies and politics, so the privatization of this state asset is especially popular, and the extortion of maximal land rent works best when more and more private spaces are dedicated to elite consumption. The impact of privatizing public land and public areas, along with privatizing quasi-public spaces such as train stations or shopping malls, has been to limit access to and make the use of collective infrastructures more expensive. Whole urban centers—from Paris, Manhattan, and London to Singapore and Hong Kong—have become, in the words of the *Financial Times*, "exclusive citadels of the elites." "The middle classes and small companies are falling victim to class-cleansing. Global cities are becoming patrician ghettos."[16]

These enclosures have generated sundry protests and countermovements, from resistance to condo conversions and rent increases to protests against cutbacks of public infrastructures and services. Such cutbacks also underlie the uprisings that have erupted in deprived and often racialized areas, whether the suburbs of French and Swedish cities or inner-city neighborhoods of British cities, though they have often been triggered by police violence. Less spontaneous in appearance are various Situationist-inspired guerrilla actions in and against the (semi-public) privatized spaces of consumption and surveillance or the growing movements to recommunalize water or energy.[17]

Both of the strategies that municipalities pursue in their efforts to thrive under financialization—chasing high-revenue eindustries and privatizing public assets—have the effect of displacing from urban centers the poor as well as wage workers in sectors that generate lower returns than the FIRE sector. In addition, they also enslave small business owners and workers to the revenue expectations of investors and speculators—that is, to rising rents, high mortgages, and growing indebtedness. In more and more cities, these displaced and discredited groups have begun to resist, in more and less political ways, sometimes progressively and at other times in chauvinistic and xenophobic ways.

15. Jamie Peck and Heather Whiteside, "Financializing Detroit," *Economic Geography* 92, no. 3 (2016): 9.

16. Simon Kuper, "International Cities Are Turning into 'Elite Citadels,'" *Financial Times*, June 17, 2013.

17. Andrew Cumbers and Sören Becker, "Making Sense of Remunicipalization: Theoretical Reflections on and Political Possibilities from Germany's *Rekommunalisierung* Process," *Cambridge Journal of Regions, Economy, and Society* 11, no. 3 (2018): 503–517.

3. Entrepreneurial governance

Regarding the way cities govern themselves and their residents, we also have to note novel features of neoliberal urbanism: cities have adopted entrepreneurial forms of governance in ever more policy areas, seeking to make more and more use of presumably more efficient business models and privatized forms of governance. This means that task- and project-driven initiatives (such as developing a particular part of town or upscaling waterfronts or former industrial areas) have become routine, and special agencies have been created to deliver these target-driven initiatives. Especially in places where funding streams from higher levels of government have dried up and local governments are trying to do more with less, municipal governments have increasingly turned to "the markets," sub- and out-contracting, and public-private partnerships. That way, mayors and their partners from the business sector often bypass council chambers, legitimating their rule by making small and constantly changing concessions to particular groups—especially to middle-class and upwardly mobile ones (as opposed to the long-term, tripartistic designs that were characteristic of the previous Keynesian mode of governance).

This trend has transformed municipal planning, embedding within the administrative apparatus informal and cooperative procedures that now involve both (global) developers and participatory citizens, along with the municipality's political and administrative representatives. In this increasingly ad hoc and informalized political process, out-of-town investors, global developers, and corporate flippers have come to play ever stronger roles (as seen above), but the process has also created openings for other "stakeholders," including movement groups that know how to make themselves heard. At the same time, these strategies—and particularly their lack of transparency—have triggered protest, as groups that cannot use these openings object to their exclusion and protest the erosion of representative democracy.

4. Dividing communities by repression and co-optation

To deal with the resulting increase in social polarization, cities have adopted a novel two-pronged policy. During the rollout phase of neoliberalization (the 1980s and into the 1990s), the territorial concentration of what at the time was termed "social exclusion" was addressed with area-based programs—that is, a mix of targeted revitalization programs that were to stop the anticipated downward spiral in "blighted" neighborhoods.[18]

●   18. Margit Mayer, "The Onward Sweep of Social Capital: Causes and
Consequences for Understanding Cities, Communities and Urban Movements,"
International Journal of Urban and Regional Research 27, no. 1 (March 2003):
114.

Since then, these programs have been severely curtailed and superseded by a new strategy consisting, on the one hand, of blunt attrition and displacement policies coupled with repressive and punitive measures and, on the other hand, of more benign programs designed to incorporate *select* impoverished groups and areas into upgrading efforts. The goal is no longer social cohesion, and the effects of these policies polarize cities even further, both in terms of geographies and social groups: policies addressing "upgradable" areas generate uneven sociospatial development, and policies differentially targeting groups and individuals divide residents according to ascribed risk and creditworthiness.

The repressive prong tends to criminalize unwanted behaviors and groups, as well as evict and banish the poor, pushing them to the outskirts or into interstices of blight within the urban perimeter. This repressive side of the neoliberalizing city, with its stricter laws, aggressive policing, and intensifying disenfranchisement hits not just (the growing ranks of) people who are homeless, undocumented, and/or working in the informal sector, but increasingly it also impacts more recent austerity victims who used to inhabit relatively secure middle class positions.[19] With the rise of anti-immigrant populism, some governments have gone so far as to designate majority low-income and heavily Muslim neighborhoods as "ghettos," making them subject to harsh new restrictions and a reduction of benefits (as, for example, in Denmark).[20] A broad spectrum of new movement organizations has emerged to battle these policies, from anti-eviction groups to "solidarity city" initiatives, often joining forces with human rights and anti-racist organizations.

The "benign" prong, on the other hand, is applied in areas that city managers and developers deem to have potential in their search for developable territory, such as (ex-) industrial areas or decaying social housing districts—that is, areas previously stigmatized as "problematic" districts.[21] While they propose that such projects benefit existing residents, these projects only happen in places where a rise in property and investment values is indeed promising. Once these projects "succeed"— frequently by marketing a "wild urbanism" and exploiting the working-class milieu or chic "indigenous authenticity"—in

19. Lynda Cheshire and Gina Zappia, "Destination Dumping Ground: The Convergence of 'Unwanted' Populations in Disadvantaged City Areas," *Urban Studies* 53, no. 10 (2016): 2081–2098; Volker Eick and Kendra Briken, eds., *Urban (In)Security: Policing in the Neoliberal Crisis* (Ottawa: Red Quill Books, 2014).

20. Michala Bendixen, "Denmark's 'Anti-Ghetto' Laws Are a Betrayal of Our Tolerant Values," *Guardian*, July 10, 2018, https://www.theguardian.com/commentisfree/2018/jul/10/denmark-ghetto-laws-niqab-circumcision-islamophobic.

21. These will then be developed/upgraded by entrepreneurial agencies that plan and implement target-driven projects often involving participation from vocal civil actors.

attracting a wealthy clientele, the indigenous poor and vulnerable populations are eventually forced out.[22] Frequently such strategies include participatory measures, presumably to mitigate the conflicts that erupt around them.

In sum, then, neoliberal urbanism denotes a complex configuration of local adaptation to neoliberal regulations such as enforcing low wages and insecure working conditions, restricting tenants' as well as workers' rights, employing debt as a disciplinary technique, and a variety of specifically spatial adaptations of neoliberal tenets. Geographically uneven development is increasingly understood not as an epiphenomenon but as *constitutive* of urban environments that produce and reproduce patterns of inequality. Cities are now seen as spatial systems that distribute their resources across uneven geographies of affluence and deprivation, redistributing wealth upward through land and rent.[23] A variety of activation and mixing policies then focus on the resulting areas of "concentrated poverty" in cities—whereas the "secret gardens" of elite secession and their supervalorized, segregated estates are never asked to "mix" or "integrate." A different set of policies (and rather more funds) are, however, directed at central areas, which are continuously upgraded with expensive, glitzy, and securitized developments, while poorer neighborhoods suffer further cutbacks in social services and suspicious surveillance. At the same time, municipalities are also developing new policies to tap any potential inherent in left-behind, discredited groups and areas while further excluding those without any use. This kind of differential targeting and selective inclusion puts activists and organizers into complicated situations.

III. Resistance to Neoliberal Urbanism: The Case of Stockholm

Viewing "riots" within the context of neoliberal urbanism reveals their linkages with other urban movements and provides a theoretical underpinning that is helpful for exploring the significance of this recurring mode of dissent. Neoliberal urbanism provides the circumstances within and against which a broad spectrum of urban collective actions, from well-organized campaigns and social movements to violent eruptions, have coevolved.

The varied and complex processes of marginalization, exclusion, dispossession, and disenfranchisement that have

22. Alex S. Vitale, "The Safer City Initiative and the Removal of the Homeless: Reducing Crime or Promoting Gentrification?," *Criminology and Public Policy* 9, no. 4 (2010): 867–873.

23. Cf. Fran Tonkiss, "Urban Economies and Social Inequalities," in *The Sage Handbook of the 21st Century City*, ed. Suzanne Hall and Ricky Burdett (London: Sage, 2017), 187–200.

accompanied neoliberal urban development have multiplied the number of grievances around which resistance has arisen, as well as brought new and unconventional actors into the field of contestation, making that field both more heterogeneous and more fragmented. For one, accelerated growth policies have triggered a broad spectrum of struggles against upgrades, displacement, touristification, and/or the violation of housing codes and the like. This heterogenization within the activist field is sharpened by new strategies, such as the creative city policies, that benefit (at least temporarily) some activist groups while impeding others, thus spawning new divisions within the movements.

In spite of their differences, affected groups have recently united against rising rents (e.g., in Germany) and mortgage foreclosures (e.g., in Spain). The exorbitant rise in property values in large cities has triggered veritable tides of tenant and anti-eviction organizing that have aligned with related struggles against gentrification and displacement to resist the speculative transformation of housing markets and to demand cooperative housing associations, remunicipalization, and even the expropriation of big housing corporations.[24] In the context of protests against mortgage foreclosures, incidents of heavy rioting have occasionally occurred, such as in Barcelona in May 2014, when a week of uninterrupted street fighting forced the city government to cancel the eviction of the Can Vies, a social center that had been squatted for seventeen years.[25]

These housing struggles reveal another novel feature of urban protest: the encounter of new adversaries such as unelected technocrats, especially financial technocrats, as well as the global investors and developers behind the financialization of housing markets and big development projects. These adversaries, especially developers and banks headquartered in other countries, are more difficult to hold accountable than the familiar adversary, city government. The invisibility of the people and organizations behind the financialization of housing markets and displacement pressures contributes to the difficulty of building "orderly" social movements with clearly defined demands and addressees.

24. In April 2019 a Europe-wide day of action took place. In Berlin the demonstration of forty thousand also incited the first round of signature collections for the "Expropriate Deutsche Wohnen & Co." referendum. See "Bundesweites Bündnis #Mietenwahnsinn zum Protesttag am 6. April 2019," March 22, 2019, https://mietenwahnsinn.info/demo-april-2019/wp-content/uploads/sites/4/2019/03/pm3-bundesweites-buendnis-mietenwahnsinn.pdf; and Johannes C. Bockenheimer, "Einig im Protest, gespalten bei Enteignungen," *Tagesspiegel*, April 6, 2019, https://www.tagesspiegel.de/berlin/mietenwahnsinn-demo-in-berlin-einig-im-protest-gespalten-bei-enteignungen/24190590.html.

25. Peter Gelderloos, "Precarity in Paradise: The Barcelona Model," *Roar Mag*, June 28, 2015, https://roarmag.org/essays/precarity-in-paradise-the-barcelona-model.

It is more and more rare that municipalities appear as the "adversary," either because they are perceived as increasingly powerless or because cooperation has evolved "between civil society and politics," particularly in cities where movement demands have found advocates in city councils and mayoral offices—as with the "new municipalism" that has emerged in cities such as Barcelona, Zagreb, Warsaw, Bologna, or Berlin.[26] These cities have seen movement groups transfer policy demands, democratic structures, and progressive individuals from the streets into local governments. But these efforts to expand options for citizens to participate in governing cannot distract from the fact that, overall, many civil society organizations suffer from shrinking resources.[27] As austerity has hit not only the traditionally disadvantaged but also, increasingly, youth, students, creatives, and more segments of the middle class, this punitive side of neoliberal urbanism is experienced by more—and different—social groups. Primarily, though, it is vulnerable and "disposable" groups that experience this side of the neoliberalizing city and that may articulate their grievances in sudden uprisings.

The case of the Husby riots highlights how austerity urbanism triggers and shapes (ties between) social movements and "riots." Stockholm's growth pressures led local politicians to plan an expansion of Sweden's Silicon Valley, the so-called Kista Science City, into the multiethnic suburb of Husby. They prepared demolitions of some of the suburb's large housing complexes to make way for this expansion, began renovating other housing (to raise rents) and privatizing public infrastructure, and announced plans to shut down the social center, Husby Träff. Like many other peripheral poor neighborhoods in Sweden, Husby was already the site of a "zero tolerance" strategy as well as police programs against political "radicalization."[28] However, local civil society organizations protested the "renovictions," succeeded in preventing some of these plans from being implemented, and occupied the social center against its threatened closure.

As Sweden has a large number of first-generation citizens who are now part of the "creative classes," as journalists, authors, musicians, and the like, "the suburbs have their own organic intellectuals, who can share their personal experience of structural racism, discrimination, and what it means to

26. Bertie Russell, "Beyond the Local Trap: New Municipalism and the Rise of Fearless Cities," *Antipode* 51, no. 3 (2019): 989–1010.
27. Many have lost state funding as a result of austerity policies or have lost legal status as recognized associations as a result of right-wing pressures; others lose public support as they are criminalized.
28. "Zero tolerance" strategies prescribe the most severe punishment possible for minor offenses—such as small-scale drug use, graffiti, or "antisocial" behavior—under the assumption that this will discourage more serious crimes.

grow up in poor neighborhoods."[29] The movement organization Megafonen (founded in 2008) has been rooted in Husby, giving voice to the grievances of its multiethnic youth, criticizing racial stereotypes in the media, and demanding more representation in the decision-making processes affecting their community. When a sixty-nine-year-old man was shot by police in Husby in May 2013, Megafonen documented what had happened, challenged the police narrative of the event, called a peaceful demonstration, and demanded an independent investigation. Six days after the incident, and after police accused Megafonen of spreading hatred and undermining confidence in the police, a violent uprising started in the area; more than 100 cars were burned during the first night. By the third night, the fires had spread to fifteen further Stockholm suburbs; on the fourth night, they began to spread beyond Stockholm.[30]

Building on five years of practice of combining local social support and political education with national networking, Megafonen was able to act as a clear public voice, as a "megaphone" for those who had turned to "rioting." "This remains the only way of expressing frustration when other democratic avenues are closed... peaceful demonstrations have taken place, but initiatives for dialogue have been left unanswered."[31]

This case illustrates how violent uprisings and social organizations such as Megafonen may be intricately connected. As a "classical" social-movement organization—boasting continuity, collective identity, and an organizational platform—Megafonen saw its public profile significantly enhanced by the uprising; it captured space in the media and public debate it had not previously received, forcing the public and politicians to "look beyond burning cars and to see the reality of unequal citizenship and structural issues."[32] Even where there are no social movement organizations in place at the time of violent uprisings, it is often obvious from the statements of arrested and interviewed participants that their actions had been directed against the deterioration of their living conditions, stigmatization of their neighborhoods, racism, institutional

29. altemark, "On the Fires in the Stockholm Peripheries," May 29, 2013, http://www.libcom.org/news/autonomist-analysis-stockholm-fires-29052013; cf. Jonas Hassen Khemiri, "Sweden's Closet Racists," New York Times, April 20, 2013, http://www.nytimes.com/2013/04/21/opinion/sunday/swedens-closet-racists.html.

30. Carl-Ulrik Schierup, Aleksandra Alund, and Lisa Kings, "Reading the Stockholm Riots: A Moment for Social Justice?," Race and Class 55, no. 3 (2014): 1–21; altemark, "On the Fires"; and Ove Sernhede, Catharina Thörn, and Håkan Thörn, "The Stockholm Uprising in Context: Urban Social Movements in the Rise and Demise of the Swedish Welfare-State City," in Mayer, Thörn, and Thörn, Urban Uprisings, 149–174.

31. Schierup, Alund, and Kings, "Reading the Stockholm Riots," 5, quoting Megafonen homepage.

32. Schierup, Alund, and Kings, "Reading the Stockholm Riots," 15.

discrimination, and systemic harassment by police.[33] The so-called "inarticulate" or "issueless" riots are thus intricately related to the anti-austerity movements across Europe that protest the dismantling of social infrastructures, the lack of political representation and participation, and the absence of meaningful work.

One of the reasons the protests of the Husby residents—and so many similar protests—took on more "riotous" forms lies in the authoritarian and punitive side of neoliberal urbanism. As cities have become ever more securitized and, in some ways, even militarized, as surveillance systems are expanded to track public space and infrastructures, and as the geography of policing has identified certain areas as "unsafe" or "violence prone," the populations of these territories (as well as groups deemed potential threats to cities' competitive functions) have become targets of increasingly repressive state strategies.[34] Ever since the riots in the United States in the 1960s, patterns of urban spatial segregation, in which class, racialization, and the quotidian experience of racist discrimination intersect, have created situations in which some incident of police brutality can spark the blaze of a violent uprising. The neoliberal city has created its own patterns of (racialized) territorial stigmatization, where ethnic minorities and other marginalized, "disposable" groups are concentrated—and are targeted with the punitive instruments of attrition and control, providing countless provocations for pent-up indignation and despair to erupt in violent uprising.

The violence occurring in such contexts has been described as the "language of the unheard" because the social, economic, and political marginalization of these groups makes it all but impossible for them to make their concerns heard in any other way.[35] Only once the violence erupts do the media and politicians focus—though invariably with very different interpretations—on the neglect, discrimination, and injustices characterizing these (sub)urban areas. While in the Swedish case, movement organizations had been articulating the problems of poor suburbs (not just of Stockholm but similarly of Gothenburg and Malmö) long before any riots broke out, in Paris social movement organizations convened *after* the 2005 uprising of youth of color in order to mediate their grievances to the public and to facilitate strategic discussions.[36]

33. Cf. Iris Dzudzek and Michael Müller, "Der Lärm des Politischen: Die Londoner *riots* 2011 und ihre politischen Subjekte," sub\urban 2 (2013): 17–40.
34. Eick and Briken, *Urban (In)Security*.
35. When urban uprisings broke out in a number of US cities in 1964, one of the most well-known proponents of nonviolence in the twentieth century, Martin Luther King, stated that "a riot is a language of the unheard." Quoted in L. M. Killian, *The Impossible Revolution* (New York: Random House, 1968), 109.
36. Stefan Kipfer, "Tackling Urban Apartheid: Report from the Social Forum of Popular Neighborhoods in Paris," *International Journal of Urban and Regional Research* 33, no. 4 (December 2009): 1058–1066.

Unlike the uprisings of the marginalized poor and majority ethnic neighborhoods, leftist or anarchist "riots" use violence as one of many tools within the broader repertoire at their disposal. For example, the tradition of militancy formed in decades of urban struggles to defend old working-class districts (and the alternative infrastructures established within them) from encroaching gentrification has been resuscitated in many European cities. The urban and squatting movements of the 1970s and the 1980s utilized the whole repertoire of actions, from demonstrations and rallies to public education, community organizing, and self-help rehabilitation. They created youth centers or autonomous cultural centers in Zurich, Berlin, Amsterdam, Athens, London, and many more European cities, thereby building strongly politicized neighborhoods with their own institutions as well as interurban and international links between them.[37] But again and again, shifting urban policies toward such neighborhoods, from the 1970s slum clearance via the urban renewal of the 1980s to the gentrification of the 1990s and the yuppification of the 2000s, have also provoked violent battles against these policies and in defense of the movements' centers.

Whether the uprising is spontaneous, violent, and seemingly lacking clear demands or well organized around specific political claims, all these actions are intrinsically related to neoliberal and austere urbanism as they all address the spatialized inequalities and injustices inherent to it. The more the repressive "right hand of the state" meets both disruptive and peaceful demonstrators with excessive force and criminalization, the less the conventional distinction between spontaneous "riots" and organized movements makes sense. Whether expressed in pacifist or militant ways, protests against the neoliberal restructuring of cities across Europe signal that livable and sustainable cities cannot be built by neglecting, marginalizing, or repressing "disposable" areas or their residents.

● 37. Harald Bodenschatz, Volker Heise, and Jochen Korfmacher, *Schluss mit der Zerstörung?: Stadterneuerung und städtische Opposition in Amsterdam, London und West-Berlin* (Wetzlar, West Germany: Anabas Verlag, 1983); Margit Mayer, "Restructuring and Popular Opposition in West German Cities," in *The Capitalist City: Global Restructuring and Community Politics*, ed. Michael Peter Smith and Joe R. Feagin (Oxford: Basil Blackwell, 1987), 343–363; Margit Mayer, "Social Movements in European Cities: Transitions from the 1970s to the 1990s," in *Cities in Contemporary Europe*, ed. Arnaldo Bagnasco and Patrick LeGalès (Cambridge: Cambridge University Press, 1999), 131–152.

Fuel to the Fire

Natascha Sadr Haghighian

NATASCHA SADR HAGHIGHIAN

Natascha Sadr Haghighian, *Fuel to the Fire*, 2017. Courtesy of Ça Ira!

This is an excerpt from the newsprint *Fuel to the Fire*, edited by Natascha Sadr Haghighian, published alongside the artist's installation of the same name at the Tensta Konsthall in Stockholm, 2017. In what follows, sections of Sadr Haghighian's introduction bookend the artist's conversation with Hamid Khan.

Two questions preoccupied me when I first saw the image of Lenine Relvas-Martins's dead body being carried out of his home in Husby on the night of May 13, 2013. Martins had been shot by Piketen (SWAT) police in his own apartment, a fact they first denied. The incident later led to a significant uprising in Sweden.

The first question was why on earth was a SWAT team dispatched to the home of a retired man who waved a knife on his balcony? How, when, and why did the police start to operate this way? Tracing the history of SWAT police leads me to Los Angeles in the 1960s and I find more police violence and more uprisings. The first Special Weapons and Tactics team was formed in the aftermath of the Watts Rebellion in 1965, which was sparked by police harassment in the segregated and impoverished neighborhood of Los Angeles. After their first deployment in an attack on the headquarters of the Black Panther Party for Self-Defense's Los Angeles Chapter in 1969, SWAT immediately captured the hearts of police chiefs all over the United States and eventually the world. It's a success story that ties into what Ruth Wilson Gilmore and Craig Gilmore describe as a

• "political culture of perpetual enemies who must always be fought but can never be vanquished." •

This political culture of perpetual crisis and war is deeply embedded in the racist colonial project and was vividly enhanced by the 9/11 Commission and the War on Terror to create what Toni Negri called the "warfare state."

Looking into the history of policing also means looking at perpetual resistance, upsurge, rebellion and self-defense by the communities that are exposed to the power of police and its violently dispensed warnings to "stay the fuck where you are and obey," or as Tony Platt would put it, to "contain exclusion and abandonment."

And this leads to the second question, which concerns the image itself. Neighbors had held out until 3:00 a.m. to take a picture that would provide visual evidence of not only police killing Lenine, but also lying about it. The neighbors knew that nobody would believe them over the police report and that an image would be more powerful than their verbal accounts.

• How did visual evidence of police violence become the most important tool in creating a legitimacy crisis for law enforcement? •

Indeed, court witness accounts are increasingly only deemed viable when supported by data, or material evidence, a shift

Thomas Keenan describes as a "forensic turn." This turn, as Keenan points out, leads to a whole new genre of reading and interpreting visual evidence.

The growing number of images taken by more and more neighbors have another agency outside of courts and corporate media. They proliferate along social networks in feeds, reposts and shares, multiplying witnesses. They expand the act of witnessing beyond the courtrooms and investigation committees, beyond the limits of segregated neighborhoods, beyond racial frontiers and beyond capitalist visual regimes that seek to monopolize and control what is seen and is to be seen. By looking at these images we all participate in the acts of witnessing and their requests. We can study with and learn from the battleground that these images create, a battleground of interpretations and legitimacies, of different visual regimes, of differently coded ways of seeing and ultimately, a battleground of technologies and access. Mobile phone against the police body camera and drones.

Despite the image and its impact, no one was held accountable for the murder of Lenine Relvas-Martins or for lying about it. An internal police investigation justified the actions of the police and deemed them appropriate. As the activist group Megafonen had stated on its website the day after the killing,

● "This is neither the first nor the last time, this is a system." ●

Megafonen's statement continues, "The police are not there to serve the common people. The police are in our areas to protect the political and economic elites: to scare us, to discipline us..." A statement uncannily similar in its systemic analysis to James Baldwin's writing in his 1966 "Report from Occupied Territory": "The police are simply the hired enemies of this population. They are present to keep the Negro in his place and to protect white business interests, and they have no other function. They are, moreover—even in a country which makes the very grave error of equating ignorance with simplicity—quite stunningly ignorant; and, since they know that they are hated, they are always afraid. One cannot possibly arrive at a more surefire formula for cruelty." How does this impact the legitimacy of organized violence that policing is hinged on, and what does it mean for the legitimacy of police in general?

[...]

SO POLICING IS MORE AND MORE BASED ON PREDICTIVE
METHODS AND SPECULATION?

Hamid Khan is the Campaign Coordinator for the Stop LAPD
Spying Coalition, an alliance with the task of dismantling all
surveillance and profiling practices used by the Los Angeles
Police Department. He also founded the South Asian Network and
is active in several other networks and grassroots initiatives
for immigrant and refugee rights. I meet Hamid in a cafe near
his office in Little Tokyo in Los Angeles to learn more about
the LAPD's practices.

NSH [Natascha Sadr Haghighian]
As part of the Stop LAPD Spying Coalition you have been organizing
against police violence and surveillance in Los Angeles for several
years. My research on the origins of SWAT policing has brought me
to Los Angeles. I'm trying to understand the history of policing as
well as where it is heading. How did the Stop LAPD Spying Coalition
start and what is it up against?

HK [Hamid Khan]
I have been involved in grassroots organizing for over
twenty-five years against the impact of racism, sexism,
homophobia, economic injustices, state violence, and
policing of marginalized communities and communities of
color. I'm an immigrant from Pakistan myself and I have
experienced and seen the impact of human rights violations
and state violence on the community. I was also a founding
member of the Los Angeles Taxi Workers Alliance and
helped organize taxi drivers in Los Angeles for their
labor rights. The Stop LAPD Spying Coalition started
in the summer of 2011 as a result of several community
members and organizations coming together to basically
look at the rapid expansion of the national security
police state and the creation of several surveillance,
spying, and infiltration programs, and the codification
of counterterrorism and counterinsurgency tactics into
everyday policing and its impact on various communities,
social justice movements, and political activists.

These particular tactics are not new in policing and
there has been a use of such infiltration and surveillance
throughout the history of the United States. A lot of
people think that surveillance programs began with
the FBI Counterintelligence programs but actually they
were preceded by several decades with the creation of
Police Red Squads within local law enforcement agencies
starting in the late nineteenth century. The Red Squads
were historically very much anchored in white supremacy
and the old advancement of slavery and segregation. The
Red Squads enforced racist codes of segregation and they
were formed in the aftermath of the Haymarket strikes

The dead body of Lenine Relvas-Martins is being carried out of the building by undertakers and police at 3:00 a.m.

in Chicago in 1886. These were fights for eight-hour workdays and the Haymarket strikes led to the creation of the International May Day observances for workers across the world. Though there was no evidence about the eight individuals who were accused of actually throwing the bomb at the police that killed police officers and civilians in the uprisings in Chicago, there were convictions and four so-called "anarchists," as they were labeled by the state, were sentenced to death. This was a hugely formative event in the future of labor rights across the United States. And due to the impact of the Haymarket strikes, in 1888, the Chicago Police department formed the first covert section within the department, calling it the Red Squads. The goal of these units was to look at policing not only as managing crimes committed on the street but more as ideological warfare. So then the whole methodology of covert policing methods started to expand into other cities, including Philadelphia and New York and also came here to Los Angeles. In LA, we've been able to trace this back to 1923 when there were covert illegal sections created in the LAPD. And one thing that is interesting is that the LAPD red Squads also had a base out of the Chamber of Commerce and there was major funding by the manufacturers' and retailers' associations and various other trade associations. There was a lot of money involved, what we now call the 1 percent and the protection of private property continues as a major trajectory throughout the development of policing in the US.

● Police Red Squads were historically very much anchored within white supremacy and the advancement of slavery. ●

And then of course you see the role of the Federal Bureau of Investigation's (FBI) covert and illegal Counterintelligence Program, also known as COINTELPRO, that started in the mid 1950s. This whole covert operation of the FBI had a mandate to discredit, disrupt, neutralize, and dismantle workers' and labor movements, and various liberation and social justice movements that were seen as a "threat to the American way of life." This program was finally exposed in early 1970s.

In the early 1980s, the LAPD was busted and it became apparent through the ensuing lawsuit that they had infiltrated over 200 nonprofits in the city of Los Angeles. In the investigation around 2 million documents were discovered spying on over 50 thousand people in the social and economic justice organizations and those engaged in local politics. It became clear that they had infiltrated every single local politician, including the mayor of Los Angeles who at the time happened to be a

Black man by the name of Tom Bradley. At that time the United Farm Workers strike was taking place along with the Gallo Winery strike and it was revealed that all the conversations between these strikers and the mayor were being secretly recorded by the LAPD and given to a group in San Francisco called the Western Goals Society, which was an extension of the John Birch Society. John Birchers were based out of Southern California and were known by many as the modern version of the white supremacist group, the Ku Klux Klan. From this you can see the historical connections between policing and white supremacist groups such as the Klan.

Southern California has a long history of organized hate violence and white supremacist groups and the Klan remained active in Southern California. Recently there was a Klan march in Anaheim near Disneyland, which is a big immigrant city. The Klan shamelessly came out and marched in their full regalia, including the hoods and robes. Southern California is known as a hub for one of the largest number of white supremacist hate groups in the country.

NSH

So the formation of the Red Squads has a racist origin, with ties to white supremacist groups and the ruling class. How does the history of the Red Squads connect to the increased militarization of the police today?

HK

In terms of the militarization of the Los Angeles Police Department, these covert tactics that originated in the Red Squads developed to create the concept of the Special Weapons and Tactics teams, or SWAT teams. Although the idea of SWAT itself originated in Philadelphia in the early 1960s, the formal operationalization of the SWAT team began in the LAPD in 1967 by former LAPD chief Daryl Gates, who was a police inspector in the LAPD at the time.

NSH

Yes, in his memoirs Gates proudly recounts how he invented the name SWAT. He first wanted to call it Special Weapons Attack Team but his Boss wanted him to replace the word "attack." So policing is more and more based on predictive methods and speculation?

HK

Yes. He then called it Special Weapons and Tactics. What I would also like to emphasize here is that when we think of militarization of policing, it is necessary to make connections with the US military and the overall militarization of society as well. And the LAPD is a unique model of that. For example, it has been documented that in the late 1980s the LAPD was training the El Salvadoran paramilitary squads. Then more recently, post-2003, there was around seventy marines assigned to the LAPD to learn methods of urban warfare developed by the LAPD to deal with the gang scene in LA. Then these marines went back to Al Anbar Province in Iraq and deployed the same tactics that they had learned with the LAPD. So LAPD has its fingers and its footprint on military tactics around the world. Of course when we refer to the militarization of the LAPD we must expose the equipment and weaponry of the LAPD, which knows no bounds. The LAPD has one of the largest helicopter squads, around twenty-one or so on last count, and a huge array of light and heavy weaponry. They acquired drones about two and a half years ago adding to the massive architecture of surveillance, but we've been able to keep them grounded with our "Drone Free LAPD! No drones LA" campaign. The LAPD became the base for two very key information and intelligence gathering programs. The first one was the Suspicious Activity Reporting (SAR) program, which came on the heels of the 9/11 Commission. And the way they define suspicious activity is, and I quote: "observed behavior, reasonably indicative of pre-operational planning of terrorist and/or criminal activity." And what you get are these absolutely bogus reports being led for benign activities. For example, a group of young female students from an art school were out on field study using cameras and the next thing you know they get stopped, they get harassed, and their information goes into SAR, which is then uploaded to

Spreads from the Center for Research on Criminal Justice's report *The Iron Fist and the Velvet Glove: An Analysis of the US Police* (Berkeley, CA: Center for Research on Criminal Justice, 1975).

a joint terrorism database. One of the key theses that arose from 9/11 Commission report was that it happened due to lack of information sharing because the security agencies were not speaking to each other. Subsequently Congress passed a law in 2004 called the Intelligence Reform and Terrorism Prevention Act (IRTPA). One key feature of that law was that it gave the president the mandate to create an information-sharing environment, with new shared databases that can be accessed by every law enforcement agency, campus police, tribal police, every federal agency, every local and regional government agency, private contractors, private businesses and individuals. And these structures are called Fusion Centers. This gives the LAPD the remit to increasingly codify counterterrorism and counterinsurgency methodologies into the police. This gives them a lot of leeway, secrecy, and, by extension, immunity from prosecution. The new rhetoric of national security is being tough on crime, tough on national security, and tough on terrorism, and linking them all together. There are about eighty-five of these Fusion Centers around the country. One of the largest ones is in Southern California.

When thinking about militarization, we also have to look at these tactics because militarization is not limited to the use of weaponry. A report that came out last year shows that close to about 65–70 percent of the SWAT teams are now being used for low-level crimes. This shows how the stated intent of a particular program over time expands into other aspects of our lives. These programs started as counterterrorism and counterinsurgency programs and are now deployed in everyday local policing.

NSH

Alongside the Fusion Centers and the increase in SWAT teams, using drones to control neighborhoods seems to introduce a new dimension of control and surveillance. With the Stop LAPD Spying Coalition campaign so far, have you managed to keep these drones grounded in Los Angeles?

HK

Yes. The Seattle Police Department in late May 2014 delivered the drones to the LAPD. We at the Stop LAPD Spying Coalition found out and we launched a campaign immediately for "Drone Free LAPD." People came together as a coalition of different groups and up until now the LAPD swears they have not used the drones. Our demand is for them to be dismantled or to be given back to the manufacturer.

NSH

Connecting counterterrorism with new techniques of surveillance was also the main focus of a recent European Police Congress in Berlin. There the police claim they are tackling the threat posed by the influx of undocumented people from wartime regions where the so-called Islamic State or Daesh, or other groups are active. The preemptive measures they propose are based on the suspicion that these new populations bring an uncontrollable danger of terrorism with them.

● These are tools of social control promoting a culture of suspicion and fear. ●

HK

Let me tell you about the LAPD's "architecture of surveillance." Are you familiar with TrapWire? TrapWire is a street-based technology that is faster than facial recognition. It collects your body image, which is then immediately sent to the Fusion Centers in real time and it is put up against an existing body image of you to see if it matches. This is happening even when you're walking down the street. A similar more powerful technology known as Digital Receiver Technology (DRT) is used by the LAPD and the FBI. It can simultaneously jam phone calls for example. There is also an interesting memo by the department of Homeland Security from July 2013 basically claiming that people who are against gentrification should be classified as so called "anarchist extremists." This definition could therefore be applied to people involved in housing rights. So anybody who is, for example, doing anti-gentrification work could now be labeled as a so-called "anarchist extremist." At

the end of the memo it says that you need to create a
Suspicious Activity Report on these people to put them
on the central list to be sent to the Fusion Centers.

NSH
The Department of Homeland Security defined anti-gentrification
activity as anarchist extremist?

HK
Yes. And the Fusion Centers are collecting this data and
profiling people most of the time without us realizing.
Speculative and hunch based policing is becoming
legitimized publicly and it's just a matter of time
before reasonable indication gets adopted as a legal
standard. So it is really, really messed up where all
this shit is going.

When in 2003 the Department of Homeland Security was
created it was given extraordinary power and money. Within
that, the Office of Director of National Intelligence
was created, which then oversaw all the eighteen major
intelligence agencies including the Defense Intelligence
Agency (DIA) and other different intelligence agencies.
So the Fusion Centers and the information-sharing
environment fall under the larger purview of the director
of National Intelligence and there is a program manager
that oversees it. Since 2003 the Department of Homeland
Security has allocated money to Urban Area Security for
what it calls "emergency preparedness programs." All of
this is funneled through the Federal Emergency Management
Agency (FEMA). They have given over 40 billion dollars
to various municipalities from which a stream known as
Urban Area Security Initiative (UASI) goes directly to
local law enforcement.

NSH
So policing is more and more based on predictive methods and
speculation and connected to surveillance. The definitions of the
SAR program, of suspicious behaviors that indicate preoperational
planning of criminal or terrorist activity sound so open and vague
that it could actually include anything.

HK
Right. They have a whole list of behaviors. For example,
when somebody is taking photographs in public, using
video cameras, drawing diagrams, taking notes, driving
evasively, changing appearances, walking into an office
building, or asking about hours of operation. Their
point is that by surveilling somebody's behavior who
is engaging in such activities we may be able to tell
that they may be planning on doing something wrong. And
it was the LAPD that became the first law enforcement

agency in the country to launch the SAR program. They set it up in a way that when the police observe a certain behavior, or stop you or just make a note of some particular characteristic, they log it. The log containing your information, many times including your race, name, and gender, immediately goes to the LAPD Counter-Terrorism and Special Operations Bureau. There it is checked to see whether there is any "nexus" to terrorism or criminal activity and then passed to these Fusion Centers. There the information is supposedly vetted again and uploaded and made accessible to everyone with access to this system, which includes the 18 thousand local law enforcement and federal agents across the country. In October 2009 the LAPD launched a companion program called iWATCH: See Something, Say Something. This program actively recruits community members as informants for the police. What this did was in effect legitimize speculative, preemptive policing.

NSH

How would you possibly be able to separate this kind of speculative policing from racial profiling?

HK

The results clearly show that you cannot. Since the start of this program in LA, the LAPD Inspector General has released three audits. The first was in March 2013 in which his office took a four month sample of the Suspicious Activity Reports, which also included race, gender, and everything else, and the samples showed that 82 percent of these reports were individuals identified as nonwhite and the majority of them were Black. The second audit came out in January 2015 showing that from all the reports that went to the Fusion Centers, 30 percent were opened on the Black community in Los Angeles, which is proportionally only around 9.4 percent of the total LA population, and when you look at the gender configuration 50 percent of the women were Black women. Over 70 percent in the second audit were people of colour. The most recent audit was released in September 2016 and that once again showed an overwhelming majority of people of color. What is also very alarming is that each of the three audits show that very high percentages of these reported SARs are coming through iWATCH: See Something, Say Something. In essence these programs are a license for racial profiling, not only by police but also private individuals.

NSH

So these algorithms are working 24/7?

HK

Exactly! In essence the policing is increasingly now being led through artificial intelligence where information is gathered, analyzed, stored, and shared. It is bogus because the information is data-driven, machine-driven, and these diagnoses are increasingly incorporated into sentences and paroles. Before the war on terror there was the war on crime, the war on gangs, and the war on drugs that created mass incarceration.

NSH

Does Stop and Frisk also lead to an increase in the statistical numbers of criminal offenses?

HK

Absolutely! It is called Stop in Los Angeles. Although every twelve hours the crime data goes in, but the stop data, even if it doesn't show criminal activity, is going into one of the many data bases LAPD has created. This is happening right now in the real-time crime analysis section in the LAPD. The crime data information goes in and through algorithms it searches out locations. They create these 500 × 500 "hot spots" in particular neighborhoods. They then launch squad cars as a preemptive policing methodology. Fifteen out of the twenty-one divisions in the LAPD are using this preemptive method which is completely speculative policing and it puts communities under siege. The National Academy of Science came out with a 300 hundred page report in 2008 where they looked at two key features of intelligence gathering: surveillance and data mining. They expressed a lot of skepticism about this speculative policing methodology saying there was not much consensus that behavioral surveillance was very relevant to counterterrorism. It is interesting how law enforcement agencies and our political establishments choose to neglect such analysis and do not engage in the mass education of the communities impacted by these programs. Because they know that people would look at them and see that these are tools of social control promoting a culture of suspicion and fear even though the narrative behind these programs is counterterrorism.

NSH

The US police are also exporting their military and predictive policing experience right?

HK

Yes. Both home and abroad. The head of counterterrorism goes to places like Abu Dhabi, Singapore and elsewhere. With the concept of militarization we need to broaden our understanding of what this really means as now we have this huge military industrial complex.

NSH

So SWAT policing is just the tip of the iceberg as it can become public more easily when for example somebody gets killed or shot. But it's important to see the whole picture of what the militarization of policing does and what social control is and how all of that relates to a strategic racist policy of segregation and colonization.

HK

Sure. The creation, the development and the structure of the police itself is an expression of extreme right-wing racist ideology and is fundamentally awed by design. It is a systemic legalized form of social control and enforcement of white supremacy. We have to look at the legacy of white privilege. When we look at white privilege we also look at the funding and the foundations that are covertly supporting the police authorities. We also have to look at the role of nonprofits within our movements and their complicity in the development and strengthening of the national security police state. Last year we exposed the collusion of the American Civil Liberties Union (ACLU) with LAPD's counterterrorism. For us it is really critical what community accountability means. We called out the ACLU of Southern California on the basis of their communications with the LAPD counterterrorism division, which were revealed through our filings for public records. We had a community meeting. We told them that this is really unacceptable and it has to stop. The point I am trying to make is that in these places these are people, including white folks, who are primarily lawyers or academics, who are not on the street and are not bringing real experience to the conversation. The change has to come from the bottom up and from those of us who have the eyes of the people. And we are the ones who are often the first suspects in society. We start from how it impacts a suspicious person on the street because, for example, nobody is more suspicious than a Black homeless person or a queer transgender person or an undocumented person. The "sex worker" status is attached to a homeless woman as well. And we can't have this conversation without talking about the control of private money and profiteering.

Now body cameras are being seen as this magic bullet. The manufacturers of body cameras stand to reap massive profits. Their stocks are going through the roof. The LAPD was also under a federal consent decree from 2001 until 2013. This came after the Department of Justice (DOJ) threatened to sue the city of Los Angeles, the LAPD, and the LA Police Commission after it investigated massive violations of peoples' civil rights and constitutional violations. This was in the late 1990s after the Rampart scandal, where there was a police station called Rampart with a long history of violence, torturing, killing and planting false evidence. This was happening everywhere, but Rampart just got busted for it. The DOJ reasoned that the LAPD was incapable of self-governance. The city decided to come into an agreement. This was called the Consent Decree. The city finally voted on the agreement and a federal judge was appointed as a monitor. As a result of all this, one of the many agreements was to install video cameras in the police cars. The city spent millions of dollars to install these cameras. By 2011 they had about 300 squad cars equipped with cameras. The judge lifted the consent agreement in May 2013. In April 2014 it was revealed publicly that the LAPD officers had intentionally tampered with the antennae of ninety out of 300 patrol cameras. And so while these body cameras are looked at as a remedy, we are utterly against the use of body cameras as they are another tool of surveillance and that's exactly how it played out. First, the policy that they have crafted requires the LAPD officers to review the footage before filing their first reports. Second, they say that everything in the background is evidence as well. This is an issue of facial recognition and that is another major program they have. Third, they will retain the footage as long as they want. A lot is going on with these body cameras and it has become more about liability than anything else.

NSH

You have mentioned that the LAPD cannot be reformed and that it actually needs to be abolished.

HK

When you start looking at the whole apparatus you start seeing different things that are all messed up and you know that it's been tried before and it cannot be reformed. These are structures and systems of power that have been created that are fundamentally awed and they keep on maintaining a systemic and institutionalized structure of racism and white supremacy ideology and colonization. For us the abolition of policing is a long-term goal and the first point of entry is demanding mass education and awareness. For example, on March 19, 2016, we pushed the city's Human Relations Commission to hold a public meeting on the LAPD SAR program. The commission lost its subpoena power and it can't change anything. But at least we managed to do one of the things that we wanted to do, which was have a city agency host an open community meeting to discuss and challenge the LAPD counterterrorism program. Looking through records there are many things not only about militarization, but about drawing parallels with the power and use of the US military. The issue of mission creep is real

What Really Happened In Los Angeles

PRESS RELEASE

The attempted overt act of massacre against the Black Panther Party and genocide against Black people generally that took place this past December 8th in L.A. has never been completely exposed by the running dogs of the pigs, the Press--News Media. The Los Angeles Southern California Chapter of the Black Panther Party suffered attack at three places: Our home at 334 W. 55th Street, our Community Center at 1100 1/2 W. Exposition Blvd, and the main office of the Southern California Chapter at 4115 S. Central Ave. Al-

though the people of those areas witnessed everything that went down, here is a brief report for all the people who were not there:

334 W. 55th Street: At about 5:00 a.m., a band of fascist nightriders slipped up to the house. Inside were the Deputy Minister of Defense, Geronimo; brother Long John, sisters Kathy Kimbrough and Saundra Pratt; and Evon Carter, Chapter Communications Secretary and her two children, Michelle--4 years old and Osceola (the young revolutionary child of Bunch Carter)-- 8 months old. They were sleeping, as were most people at that ridiculous hour.

Without warning, knock, request or invitation, the Murder-Inc. fascists kicked down the door in the same manner the murderers did in Chicago four days before when they out-right and in cold blood brutally murdered the Deputy Chairman of

our Illinois Chapter, Fred Hampton and Defense Captain, Mark Clark. The pigs then opened fire on each bedroom. In looking through the house anybody with common sense can see there was no "exchange of shots" (even though "G" is charged with conspiracy to assault with the intent to commit murder and assault with a deadly weapon, as is Saundra Pratt.) You don't have to be a balistics expert to see that the shooting was done over and near all the beds ONLY. In one of the beds was Evon and her two children. Shots are over that bed too.

After the cowardly, forced entry was made, the pigs forced everyone to lie down at gun point with handcuffs locking their hands behind them. The "arrest" was over. No warrant was ever seen by the brothers and sisters in the house. Everyone including Michelle (8 years old) and Osceola (8 months old) were taken to the pig pen.

1100 1/2 W. Exposition Blvd.: At the appointed time for the entire massacre, 5:00 a.m., another battalion of SS troops secretly crept up on the Walter "Toure" Pope Community Center. Asleep inside were three brothers and one sister: Ike Houston, Al Armour, Craig Williams, and Sharon Williams. They were awakened by the sound of rapid fire weapons. They were being attacked by the occupying troops. These four young warriors did all they could to save the People's Breakfast--Community Cen-

ter.

Finally, after over and hour, they were forced out of the house--one by one. Each of them was thrown down the stairs and off the porch, kicked particularly in the ribs and face, handcuffed, thrown into the pig cars, taken to the pig pen and booked--for what?--Possession of a Bomb (?). (see Interview with two sisters from the community.)

4115 South Central Ave.: Again at the same designated time, over 450 troops of the gestapo forces of the LAPD, Metro Squad, SWAT (Special Weapons and Tactical Squad), FBI, with National Guard "standing by" with Army personnel carriers (tanks) and several 60 caliber machine guns mounted on tripods, calling themselves serving a "warrant", viciously and with the intent to destroy all life, attacked the Southern California Chapter's Central Headquarters.

The brothers and sisters inside were asleep, after a long day of serving the people. They were awakened with the sound of tear-gas cannisters breaking through the windows and the sound of gun shots. (See report on each prisoner.) Those inside were our Youth--who were there because they've dedicated their lives to serving the people: Bernard Smith--17 years old; Gil Parker-- 19 years old; Wayne Pharr--19 years old; Will Safford--19 years old; Renee "Peaches" Moore--19 years old; Tommie Williams--19 years old; Paul Redd--19 years old; Jackie Johnson--20 years old; Robert Bryan--23 years old; Melvin "Cotton" Smith--41 years old; Roland Freeman--22 years old; and Lloyd Mims--18 years old.

These beautiful brothers and sisters suffered one of the most outlandish and vicious attacks ever laid upon people not engaged in declared war. They held the People's office for 5 long hours, in an attempt to make sure these mad-dog attackers did not totally destroy what belongs to the people. They survived an attack as heavy as any in Vietnam. They protected the People's office and to many people's amazement--survived.

As they came out around 10:10 a.m.--one by one--tear-gassed, wounded and tired, the masses of people--who had been able to get through the cordon---cheered them. There was no question in anyone's mind as to what had happened there. The people had seen in practice what our Minister of Defense, Huey P. Newton, has always said, "The Spirit of the People is Greater than the Man's Technology". And it is.

When we talked with Robert Bryan later, he told us that everyone inside kept looking at the pictures on the walls; of Bunchy, and John, of Huey, of Bobby, of Eldridge --and what struck him most and helped all of them survive were the last lines of Bunchy's poem, BLACK MOTHER, which were printed on the wall: "I'd rather be without the shame---a bullet lodged within my brain..."

ALL POWER TO THE PEOPLE! and to the Vanguard of the People's Revolution!

For Immediate Release
December 17, 1969

We as health workers have long been appalled at the second rate health care provided for Black, Brown and other oppressed people. We have spoken out against the bad working conditions, low wages and extreme oppression of health workers--mostly Black and Brown and unorganized. Now we must make a statement about the obvious genocidal attack on the Black community as a target where the Black Panther Party is the bull's eye. This murderous assault comes off the same planning board as the mass murders of Vietnamese villagers in My Lai. We will not stand for such atrocities.

The Black Panther Party has stood up and confronted the wrongs in this system and because of this has become the first victim in this repressive attack on the Black community. On Dec. 4, 1969 Fred Hampton, a leading Black Panther in Chicago, and Mark Clark, a Black Panther member in Peoria, were murdered while asleep in bed. In order to prevent such a murder in Los Angeles, 11 members of the Black Panther Party had to protect themselves for six hours to assure that surrender would not mean immediate slaughter at the hands of the 450 man LAPD armed attack on the Panther headquarters at 4:30 a.m. on December 8, 1969. During this attack, the health and safety of

the community were ignored as ammunition was fired into homes without warning and tear gas was thrown around indiscriminately, resulting in hospitalization of one baby and continued ill effects for several families.

The day before this attack, Dec. 7, 1969, several doctors and nurses went to the central LAPD jail to see that George "Duck" Smith, shot at and knocked unconscious outside the Panther office and then arrested on minor charges the night prior, was receiving proper medical attention. We were refused permission to see him even though he asked to see one physician among us by name. He never did receive skull x-rays or careful observation that such a head injury requires.

Several doctors and nurses have been to prisons and the prison ward at Los Angeles County General Hospital since the attack on the Panther office on Dec. 8, 1969. We have been generally stalled and denied admission to see the prisoners and their medical records. When we did finally get to see several prisoners, we discovered the following:

Several prisoners including

exam in the p... guards (Bruises ... thighs where ... forced apart wer... an outside doctor... get a chance to se... 3. Several prison... seen by prison do... the specialized ... needed--Al Armor... ledge, never saw ... even though he h... on the eye.

4. People arreste... tal club swinging a... ful demonstration ... one in front on th... quarters on Dec. ... beaten after arre... no medical attenti... (These are just ... of the atrocious r... beatings the pri... during th past wee...

The Black Pan... recognized that ... seriously underm... the community to fi... and needs. We as... join with the Blac... in the following ac...

1. We demand t... nurses chosen b... be allowed to see ... arrested and sen... to assure proper ... tion and to help ... rest beatings. Ev... doctors do treat ... we insist that ou... allowed in to insp...

appropriate care... working for the ... less than indiff... needs of the pris... 2. We will mobi... to have medical ... observers prese... more such viciou... 3. The Black P... planning to file ... Los Angeles Po... (This is just one ... suits being filed ... try.) for denial ... and beatings of p... 4. We ask all t... join with us an... to open the A... Carter Free C... Central Ave., wh... people and sup... needs. Come Sun... from Noon - 4:0... the "finishing"... building into sha... following Saturda... be open every ... after.

The health ca... serve the people ... community must ... make sure it do... test the repress... government and ... Police Departme...

and it's going to continue. People's distrust of the police force is deep and then there is the force's history of violence and corruption. And further afield this pre-emptive policing is influencing other countries' policing. For example, the UK started a program called "Prevent" to deal with homegrown radicalization. In the United States they looked at it as violent extremism so this program got launched with a summit at the White House in January 2015. Los Angeles, Boston, and Minneapolis became part of the program. The idea behind it was to observe suspicious behavior particularly by young Muslim men and women and high school students, observing whether they were getting radicalized or showing signs of anger. This January the FBI issued guidelines on countrywide extremism and homegrown radicalization for all high schools in the United States. It's targeting the youth who can be seen as potential for radicalization. And now, of course, these young people and the immigrant community that I'm a part of have become highly politicized. Who knows where this will all go.

NSH
Is being politicized now becoming a crime?

HK
Acting out of one's politicization is considered potential suspicious behavior that could lead to tracing, tracking, monitoring, and possible arrest. The idea of the program is to have an early intervention. So teachers, psychologists, and social workers are now being brought in to play a role in observing them.

NSH
So it's become part of the teachers' job to observe the kids?

HK
It's part of the guidelines, yes. They claim they are the "eyes and ears" and on the front line for authorities to prevent so-called radicalization and future acts of terror.

[...]

It's broken. Since a long time ago. And every time a new crack occurs, it merges with older cracks. Every time a new piece breaks, it joins collateral broken fragments. Every time a new part is consumed by fire, it falls onto the charred remains of the prior blazes. We are not here to fix it but to study the wreckage, to seek a different way of collectivity and life.

Three years ago, in 2013, Husby was burning; Kista, Tensta, Rinkeby were burning; Vällingby, Skärholmen, Arsta, Norsborg, Farsta, Flemingsberg, Södertälje, Älvsjö, and Jordbro were burning. Before that, London was burning, Paris was burning, and, before, Los Angeles was burning. And now Charlotte is burning, and Birzeit has been burning for a long time.

But this is not what is broken.

What is broken is the very foundation on which these places are built.

● What is broken is the violent conflation of reason and terror in sovereign power, the violent conflation of war and politics. ●

So let's talk about violence.

Voices emerge from the piles of brokenness: the wreckage of sovereignty. Exercising sovereignty is first of all the capacity and the power to "exercise control over mortality," according to Achille Mbembe. The "necropower" that can kill and grant life, that decides who lives and who dies. But it also includes what Michel Foucault called biopower, the domain of life over which power has taken control, the organization, deployment, and subjugation of life. Mbembe says that "the state of exception and the relation of enmity have become the normative basis of the right to kill." The sovereign power perpetually evokes a fictionalized enemy and emergency. racism is the ultimate technique of sovereign rule, and, according to Foucault, it is "the condition for the acceptability of putting to death."

We're asking you:

● How can anything other than the repetition of that bio/necro power emerge out of achieving sovereign status? ●

Or anything other than adding more surface to the embodiments of border and control regimes? Fred Moten questions the achievements that lie in seeking or striving for executive, legislative, or jurist embodiment, the very embodiment that grants sovereign power. He makes a plea for "insovereignty," an insovereignty that would reject peace or even truce with the subjugation of life and death. This "untruce" would not only include the traditional accounts of sovereign power within the boundaries of the nation-state, its institutions, or groups of people. Insovereignty makes a plea with and for the single body, the individual, politics, and poetry, and we suggest extending the plea to art.

It rejects active participation in the delusion that what is broken can be fixed. Fred Moten says it can't be.

● That we need to seek new economies of being with and for, and that we need to study with others what it means to be unsovereign. ●

RUTH WILSON GILMORE AND CRAIG GILMORE, "Beyond Bratton," in *Policing the Planet: Why the Policing Crisis Led to Black Lives Matter*, ed. Jordan T. Camp and Christina Heatherton (New York: Verso, 2016), 173–199.

TONY PLATT ET AL., *The Iron Fist and the Velvet Glove: An Analysis of the US Police* (Berkeley, CA: Center for Research on Criminal Justice, 1975), 23, 54, and 57.

TONI NEGRI, "The Crisis of the Crisis-State," in *Revolution Retrieved: Writings on Marx, Keynes, Capitalist Crisis, and New Social Subjects 1967–1983* (London: Red Notes, 1988), 181–182.

TOM KEENAN, "Evidence and its 'Failures': Filming the Police," Image Controversy VI: Art, Aesthetics, Politics, part of Regarding Objects: A Survey of the Forensic Turn (lecture, KW Institute of Contemporary Art and the University of Potsdam Research Training Center, May 27, 2015).

JAMES BALDWIN, "A Report from Occupied Territory," *The Nation*, July 11, 1966.

ACHILLE MBEMBE, "Necropolitics," *Public Culture* 15, no. 1 (Winter 2003): 11–40.

MICHEL FOUCAULT, *Society Must Be Defended: Lectures at the Collège de France 1975–1976* (Paris: Seuil, 1997), 228.

FRED MOTEN, "History Does Not Repeat Itself, but It Does Rhyme," in *After Year Zero: Geographies of Collaboration* (Chicago: university of Chicago Press, 2015).

STEFANO HARNEY AND FRED MOTEN, *The Undercommons: Fugitive Planning and Black Study* (New York: Minor Compositions, 2013).

THE BLACK PANTHER
Black Community News Service

25 cents

VOL. IV NO. 8 — SATURDAY, JANUARY 31, 1970

PUBLISHED WEEKLY — **THE BLACK PANTHER PARTY** — MINISTRY OF INFORMATION BOX 2967, CUSTOM HOUSE SAN FRANCISCO, CA 94126

FREE BREAKFAST FOR SCHOOL CHILDREN

INSIDE: THE INVINCIBLE THOUGHTS OF THE BLACK PANTHER PARTY CAN NEVER BE DESTROYED BY FIRE NOR WATER — PAGE 10

Cover of The Black Panther: Black Community News Service 1, no. 8, January 31, 1970, published by Black Panther Party, Ministry of Information, San Francisco. Courtesy of the Southern California Library.

Built to Be Torn Down, Fed to Be Starved, Resurrected to Be Disposed Of: Capitalism Is a Riot, a Riot from Above

Gal Kirn and Niloufar Tajeri

A blind spot, discomfort, and dissonance arise concerning collective memory on riots.[1] How come such highly mediatized and disputed political events evaporate from public remembrance as quickly as they seem to have appeared? When we analyze specific case studies from different time periods and geographic contexts, similar patterns of exclusion, domination, and exploitation begin to emerge. These patterns not only frame and trigger riotous uprisings but continue in their aftermath, now in the form of a lack of broad, public investigation, debate, and memorial practices. It seems that even in the wake of uprising, the public oblivion, the blind spot, not only remains intact but also strengthened.

The Challenge of Remembering "Riots"
The dictionary defines a riot as "a violent public disorder" and "a tumultuous disturbance of the public peace."[2] Such a definition is an expression of a deeply negative image of riots: on the one side, a violent "crowd" and "disorder"; on the other side, an assumed desire for "public peace" and "order." Such a definition is based on a legalistic idea of "public peace," an idea that neutralizes a deeper logic of class, race, and gender divisions in neoliberal capitalism that is vital to the causes of riots that we want to discuss here.

Our initial research into riots joined the chorus of voices challenging the very term "riot": when is a riot really a riot, and when is it called a "riot" to delegitimize political actions and the voices of dispossessed communities? Who remembers Los Angeles in 1992, France in 2005, the United Kingdom in 2011, and Stockholm in 2013 as "riots" and why? Why do many scholars and activists prefer to define these events as resistance, uprisings, or revolt? Why do some participants in "riots" and residents of marginalized urban communities address these political events as mere intensifications of their everyday lives? The moment we enter the discourse around "riots," we find ourselves in the middle of an ideological battleground that leaves little space to maneuver: how can we move beyond a merely objectifying frame (criminalization vs. structural conditions) and ask if and how the ways we remember riotous uprisings could flip the idea upside down and point toward a different future for affected communities within the larger society? Riotous uprisings are most popularly remembered as mere violent disturbances or violent "riots" of "mobs"—not as political events.

1. This text is a result of the project "Thinking Monument to Suburban Riots," which we started at the Akademie Schloss Solitude (2015–2016) and which was further explored in a series of workshops, exhibitions, and an online "Archive of Suburban Dissent" (Gal Kirn and Niloufar Tajeri, "Archive of Suburban Dissent: Introduction," *Pages,* September 23, 2017, https://www.pagesmagazine.net/en/articles/archive-of-suburban-dissent-1-introduction), a public program within the ifa Gallery exhibition *Riots: Slow Cancellation of the Future* (curated by Natasha Ginwala), and our text "Notes on the Archive of Dissent: Monument to Sub/Urban Riots," in *Performing Museum,* ed. Aleksandra Sekulic and Dusan Grlja (Novi Sad: Museum of Contemporary Art Vojvodina, 2016).

2. *Merriam-Webster,* s.v. "riot *(n.),*" https://www.merriam-webster.com/dictionary/riot#h2.

The question of memory, memorial practice, and how to conceptualize a monument to suburban riots was pivotal for our research on riotous actions in the United States (especially Watts in 1965 and 1992), in the French *banlieues* in 2005, and in the United Kingdom in 2011.[3] Why would one want to remember, even commemorate, irrational violence and disturbance of the peaceful order? Given that the conventional definition of riots is deeply problematic—since it calls only for moralizing and disciplinary action toward affected communities—it comes as no surprise that any sort of collective effort to remember riots as a broad, complex phenomenon, demonstrating the agency of affected communities and their concerns and grievances, is swept under the rug of oblivion.

Departing from the critique of the conventional definition of riots, we would like to suggest an alternative term: *riotous uprisings.* "Riotous" because they are accompanied by an outbreak of violence with elements that are not all emancipatory or progressive, and "uprising" because it speaks of the specific political rationality of the insurgents.[4] The violence and opaque rationality of riotous subjectivity is not set against peaceful and just conditions; rather, riotous uprisings rise against social, economic, and political inequalities and the objective and subjective violence of the police and the state. The uprisings predominantly target the planes of institutionalized racism and capitalist dispossession. While uprisings develop different degrees of consciousness and organization, they always relate to present and past struggles against asymmetries in the economic, social, and spatial contexts.

But why do riotous uprisings start? What are their immediate causes? Uprising starts as an act of refusal and indignation over injuries and injustices located either in the immediate experience of police violence or in blatant everyday racism. Furthermore, uprisings reject capitalist systems that impose enclosure, segregation, and destruction of the physical and social fabric of the neighborhoods of dispossessed communities. These physical separations carry ideological effects/affects that enforce a division between "us" (what the dominant society perceives as a "civilized" majority of respectful citizens following the rule of law, etc.) and "them" (those perceived as "barbaric," uneducated, or unemployed, or from different religious and cultural backgrounds). Its most emblematic division is described by Frantz Fanon when he defines colonized space as a world that is "cut in two, where the dividing lines are shown by barracks and police stations."[5] Visible spatial exclusion changes not just the way society perceives certain people but also, in turn, how they perceive themselves.[6]

3. In our text, we offer a detailed analysis of the causes, similarities, and divergences between the cases of riotous uprisings in the United Kingdom/London, Paris and Lyon, and Los Angeles/Watts. Kirn and Tajeri, "Archive of Suburban Dissent: Introduction."

4. For details, see Margit Mayer, "Riots as Contestations of Neoliberal Urbanism," starting on page 145 in this volume.

5. Frantz Fanon, *The Wretched of the Earth* (New York: Grove, 1991), 38.

6. In the specific case of London, we can speak of socioeconomic segregation rather than spatial segregation, since different social groups sometimes occupy the same area. See Owen Hatherley, "Look at England's Urban Spaces: The Riots Were Inevitable," *openDemocracy*, August 17, 2011, https://www.opendemocracy.net/en/opendemocracyuk/look-at-englands-urban-spaces-

These uprisings, then, openly challenge and negate the organization of space and time and reject the everyday (mis)management with/of the residents and their means of (re)production. The common denominator of the riots under question is *negational*, tendentially striving to abolish the existing state of affairs.

Who are the agents of the uprisings? As Dilip Gaonkar nicely shows in this volume, there is a long history of the negative image of crowds, and other racial and classist terms work to disqualify collective agency: scum, rabble, *racaille, Pöbel*. For Alain Badiou, uprisings are led by a riotous section of the population, "a tumultuous assembly of the young, virtually always in response to a misdemeanor, actual or alleged, by a despotic state."[7] Furthermore, rioters are seen as agents that produce structural injustices at the same time that they are seen as a threat that can develop into a larger insurrection, even revolution. The urban poor and, more generally, the dispossessed have long been seen only as a "social problem" to be dealt with. Previously they were handled by social services, but now they are being made invisible: externalized to the growing prison industry where they are perversely sent back to market as forced labor.[8] The ideological battle thus confirms "riots" as negative and irrational events in the form of an even stronger spiral of police violence, surveillance, and dispossession. This dispossession can be seen in cuts to social services, but also in urban regeneration projects that supposedly "revitalize"—that is, gentrify and demolish—liminal urban spaces, part of the ongoing policy and logic that we describe as "riots from above." There can be, then, no surprise why such rage and riots erupt continuously. There is, however, a visual-political paradox that while these communities are under severe surveillance and scrutiny by the police and the state, they remain virtually invisible within the larger society. Moreover, the conventional account of riots deems the events as anti-political. This ideological operation strips rioters of political rationality—it robs them of their indignation over legitimate causes and, even more importantly, of their agency. There is a long history of colonial apparatuses and practices that sustain the image of a barbaric, irrational "other" not capable of governing themselves. Colonialism not only enslaved and exploited the bodies of these "others" but also managed and controlled their bodies in space.[9] The suppression of riots involves not only the immediate quelling of unrest but also the covering up of structural asymmetries and antagonisms that are made tangible during the riotous uprising.

riots-were-inevitable; Jeremy Till, "The Broken Middle: The Space of the London Riots," *Cities* 34 (2013): 71–74.

- 7. Alain Badiou, *Rebirth of History* (New York: Verso, 2012), 23.
- 8. Ruth Wilson Gilmore, *Golden Gulag: Prisons, Surplus, Crisis, and Opposition in Globalizing California* (Berkeley: University of California Press, 2007).
- 9. Fanon, *Wretched of the Earth*; Hacène Belmessous, "French Banlieues: Neighborhoods in a State of Exception," Suburban Geographies, *Funambulist* 2 (November–December 2015), https://thefunambulist.net/articles/french-banlieues-state-exception-neighborhoods-hacene-belmessous.

Such tremendous ideological energy and unified repressive responses to resisting subjects and their respective urban spaces point to the central symptom that haunts any society host to riotous uprisings. In the context of riots, social trauma is related to the "fear of the masses" and the ultimate fear of social disintegration. This chain of traumatic and irrational thinking sees urban riots and insurrections as the early stages of civil war, destruction, and finally a lapse into a sort of "state of nature." This is an old fear, and it is strengthened by three central characteristics of riotous uprisings: their unpredictability, their uncontrollability, and their destructive power.

These characteristics point to the fundamental quandary of any political philosophy that deals with entities and notions that are *seemingly* more stable and rational. *Seemingly,* because it is the neoliberal nexus of state and economy that is deeply unstable and irrational. *Seemingly,* because there is a civil war going on against the poor and racialized communities, with urban demolition programs ripping apart entire communities and relentlessly advancing social disintegration on a large scale. This is part of what Marx taught us: the logic of capital is based on a "permanent revolution" with a ruling class profiting from crisis and chaos.[10] What remains deeply unsettling for the dominant class is the fact that riotous uprisings continue to hit at the core of the modern capitalist state by showing no respect for either private or public property, and also by denying the state monopoly over violence. Riotous actions and assemblies can be instances of emancipation and empowerment and as such ought to be acknowledged as a source of political power.

In juxtaposition to riotous excess, rioters encounter a very different excess of force that reaffirms the existing asymmetries: police responses and capitalist dispossession intensify the structural conditions that reproduce immiseration and create the conditions for future riots. The barricade looks very different from the perspective of police officers with real munitions, armed vehicles, and whole ideological and repressive state apparatuses at their backs. We claim *that the actual riot takes place from above.*

Riot from Above: Built to Be Torn Down

Capital necessarily creates a physical landscape in its own image at one point in time only to have to destroy it at some later point in time as it pursues geographical expansions and temporal displacements as solutions to the crisis of overaccumulation to which it is regularly prone. This is the history of creative destruction... written into the evolution of the physical and social landscape of capitalism.
— David Harvey[11]

●   10. Marshall Berman, *All That Is Solid Melts into Air: The Experience of Modernity* (New York: Penguin Books, 1982), 95.
●   11. David Harvey, "The 'New' Imperialism: Accumulation by Dispossession," *Socialist Register* 40 (2004): 66.

To solve its inner contradictions—that is, too much accumulation generates surplus that needs to be absorbed, which generates too much accumulation that generates surplus that needs to be absorbed, and so on—capital destroys the very environments it creates, just to start all over again. And it does so by means of dispossession. It dispossesses people of their pensions and homes, for example. This is why we propose that, instead of speaking about riots and rioters exemplifying irrationality and violence, what is actually irrational and violent is the immanent force of destruction and demolition within the capitalist urban logic. What society would plan and build mass housing only to demolish it a few decades later? A society whose driving force is evidently more profit. However, the price that is paid by poorer sections and by the environment for this constant exploitation of human and natural resources is high. The word "riot" much more appropriately describes the logic of capital demolishing houses, neighborhoods, and collective identities on a mass scale. The loss of home and community is brutal—it is a form of slow violence, and, as Loretta Lees and Hannah White have shown, it is "stressful and destabilizing" at the level of individuals, of families, of neighborhoods.[12] We are speaking of loss of identity and memory, the loss of belonging in neighborhoods where people were, where people are, and where people will be displaced and dispossessed again and again. For the dispossessed, "public peace" never existed and will never exist. For, as Marshall Berman has written:

> If we look behind the sober scenes that the members of our bourgeoisie create, and see the way they really work and act, we see that these solid citizens would tear down the world if it paid. Even as they frighten everyone with fantasies of proletarian rapacity and revenge, they themselves, through their inexhaustible dealing and developing, hurtle masses of men, materials and money up and down the earth, and erode or explode the foundations of everyone's lives as they go. Their secret—a secret they have managed to keep even from themselves—is that, behind their facades, they are the most violently destructive ruling class in history.[13]

While liberal-conservative critiques of "riots" portray them as merely acts of violence and looting, we should rather think and ask: what is a brick in the shop window compared to mass destruction of social housing and communities by public demolition programs like the National Program for Urban Renovation (PNRU) in France, the Estate Regeneration Programme in the United Kingdom, the systematic privatization of public property and social housing in Germany, or the systematic demolition of public housing in the United States starting as early as the 1970s? These are the true representatives and agents of riots from above. Acts of violence (stigmatizing and displacing tenants), vandalism (demolition of housing estates and of social and physical

---

● 12. Loretta Lees and Hannah White, "The Social Cleansing of London Council Estates: Everyday Experiences of 'Accumulative Dispossession,'" *Housing Studies* 35, no. 10 (2019): 1709.

● 13. Berman, *All That Is Solid Melts into Air*, 100.

infrastructures), and looting (privatizing public property, dispossession of tenants) are manifold in these programs and come as no surprise when we look at the modes of Fordist housing production in Western postwar welfare capitalism and the paradigm of what David Harvey termed a "spatial fix": the production of new spaces and/or spatial displacement to fix the problem of overaccumulation.

In the first phase (from the 1950s to the early 1970s), Western production of mass housing was a project of absorbing labor surpluses and capital through the expansion of physical infrastructures for production, reproduction, and consumption, oftentimes succeeding in the demolition of older residential buildings. The mass production of housing for workers took place side by side with growing construction industries, production of machines, development of materials, and technological innovation.[14] In the second phase (from the 1970s to the 1990s), the destruction and devaluation of physical infrastructure started when capital abandoned these sites—when capital flees to more profitable branches and territories ("spatial fix") and leaves behind surplus populations and surplus housing.[15] The second phase is marked by occasional riots; one can remember the first instances in the United Kingdom and France in the 1980s, when the racialized population from the former colonies, together with urban poor, rose up against the state. In the third phase (from 2000 to the present), we can observe the revaluation—in the form of gentrification and "social mixing"—that comes along with large-scale demolition and privatization programs—that is, when capital moves back in. This phase is marked by repeated nationwide riots against the backdrop of neoliberal restructuring of urban spaces.

The neoliberalization of the urban has been key to the formation of recent urban uprisings, as German political scientist Margit Mayer argues.[16] Spaces and housing that primarily serve to absorb surplus capital and surplus labor are *surplus spaces* and *surplus housing*. These are sites that can be reactivated anytime for the absorption of surplus capital, thanks to neoliberal urbanism. The extent of demolition and devaluation of the spaces in which surplus populations/the urban poor live, as well as the imminent threat of destruction, displacement, and dispersal, is central to understanding why and how riotous uprisings occur.

Through analysis of the current state of postwar housing estates, it is clear that we have entered a cycle of "creative destruction." Economic analysis alone, however, cannot adequately explain what is happening in these spaces. The question of class needs to be coupled with the question of race and knowledge of the postcolonial condition, both of which

---

14. A detailed account of Fordist modes of production in the postwar era can be found in David Harvey, *The Condition of Postmodernity: An Enquiry into the Origins of Cultural Change* (New York: Blackwell, 2015).

15. The concept of "spatial fix" described here is outlined in more depth in David Harvey, "Globalization and the 'Spatial Fix,'" *Geographische Revue* 3 (2001): 23–30.

16. See her contribution in this volume, or, for a more detailed description, see also Margit Mayer, Catharina Thörn, and Håkan Thörn, eds., *Urban Uprisings: Challenging Neoliberal Urbanism in Europe* (London: Palgrave Macmillan, 2016).

are pivotal for understanding the notion of "social mixing" so present in the demolition programs as well as for understanding urban uprisings themselves. The questions of race and class come together when we speak of the racialization of the pauperized, of migrant workers, and of those dispossessed: racialized paupers are first "accommodated," after that abandoned, then displaced, and finally "mixed" as a generative value in the gentrification process.

> Capitalism requires inequality, and racism enshrines it.
> —Ruth Wilson Gilmore[17]

The economic and social inequality that the capitalist urban logic produces and reproduces has been widely discussed. That this logic is supported and maintained by structural racism can be seen just by recognizing for a moment the openly racist discourse around the quarters, districts, estates, and neighborhoods most dramatically affected by destruction. These places are described as dangerous, full of crime, scary, dark, ugly, barren, dirty, messy. No sources needed—every big city can offer an example of a place that is inhabited by mainly Black people and/or people of color that is commonly characterized in at least one of these ways. The stigmatization of poor and racialized people has a spatial equivalent: the ugly, dubious neighborhood. In the United States it's the inner city, in France the *banlieue*, in Germany the *Sozialer Brennpunkt*, in the United Kingdom the council estates: every place has its "problem area." And the discourse around it creates a general agreement within the dominant society that some kind of change has to happen, that whatever is done there would be an improvement. Social mixing has been a buzzword for a while—underpinned by the racist assumption that if it becomes whiter, it becomes better. It is no surprise that the paradigm of social mixing is one of the major pillars of the Estate Regeneration Programme in the United Kingdom, as well as the demolition program PNRU in France.

The riot from above is a riot against poor and racialized people, cloaked in laws and deals and processes, veiled in the language of urban regeneration, and enforced by police and other state authorities. Affected people experience such a riot as violence—slow violence, structural violence—and as dispossession of space, identity, and sense of place. There is an emotional aspect to it, without which it is impossible to gather the depth of it. A violence that is deep and tough and old, and against which the broken glass on the streets after a riotous uprising seems a rather noble gesture. The riot from above destroys the homes of the most vulnerable.

17. Ruth Wilson Gilmore, foreword to Bobby M. Wilson, *America's Johannesburg: Industrialization and Racial Transformation in Birmingham* (Athens: University of Georgia Press, 2019), ix.

Riot from Above, Pruitt-Igoe, 1972:
"One day we woke up and it was all gone"

Built on the ground of demolished slum dwellings, the housing project Pruitt-Igoe, designed by Minoru Yamasaki, in St. Louis, was built in 1954 and demolished less than twenty years later. While the image of the complex's demolition came to symbolize the failure of modernism in postmodern architectural discourse, the history of Pruitt-Igoe has since been revisited by scholars like Sabine Horlitz, Elizabeth Birmingham, and Katharine G. Bristol.[18] Now we can see that Pruitt-Igoe tells a story of racism, dispossession, and the institutional and structural deconstruction of public housing programs in the context of global capitalist restructuring in the early 1970s.[19] It was not a single, extraordinary case but the start of a process of US-wide demolitions—a process of "riots from above."[20] When asked what happened in 1971, Ruby Russell, former resident and representative of the Tenants Affairs Board of Pruitt-Igoe, answered: "Well, one day we woke up and it was all gone."[21]

Her words resonate with the last sentences in John Akomfrah's film *Handsworth Songs*: "Those who live among the abandoned aspirations which were the metropolis." The people who moved in with high hopes in 1954, seeking justice and a share of the wealth created on their backs, then saw everything deteriorate as capital moved away, leaving them dependent and unemployed. What happens when there is no possibility or freedom to "move out with the capital," when one is fixed to the "surplus space"? In Pruitt-Igoe people were left with few choices: bare survival or resistance. The noise of 1965 Watts and the 1968 riots echoed in Pruitt-Igoe—as the riot from above, or as what historian Alice O'Connor has described as the "conservative counterrevolution" in the form of policies against public housing during

18   Charles Jencks, *The Language of Post-Modern Architecture* (London: Academy Editions, 1991), 23.

19.   See Sabine Horlitz, "The Construction of a Blast: The 1970s Urban Crisis and the Demolition of the Pruitt-Igoe Public Housing Complex," in *Crisis, Rupture and Anxiety: An Interdisciplinary Examination of Contemporary and Historical Human Challenges*, ed. Will Jackson, Bob Jeffery, Mattia Marino, and Tom Sykes (Newcastle upon Tyne: Cambridge Scholars Publishing, 2012), 17–38; Elizabeth Birmingham, "Refraining the Ruins: Pruitt-Igoe, Structural Racism, and African American Rhetoric as a Space for Cultural Critique," *Positionen 2*, no. 2 (1998): 291–309; and Katharine G. Bristol, "The Pruitt-Igoe Myth," *Journal of Architectural Education* 44 (1991): 163–171.

20.   Alicia Olushola Ajayi, "Public Housing in the United States: Saint Louis and the National Destruction of Poor Black Homes," Designed Destructions, *Funambulist* 11 (May–June 2017), https://thefunambulist.net/articles/public-housing-united-states-saint-louis-national-destruction-poor-black-homes-alicia-olushola-ajayi.

21.   Chad Freidrichs, dir., *The Pruitt-Igoe Myth* (2011), film.

"One day we woke up and it was all gone," says Ruby Russell, the representative of Pruitt-Igoe's Tenants Affairs Board. Still from the documentary *The Pruitt-Igoe Myth*, directed by Chad Freidrichs (2011).

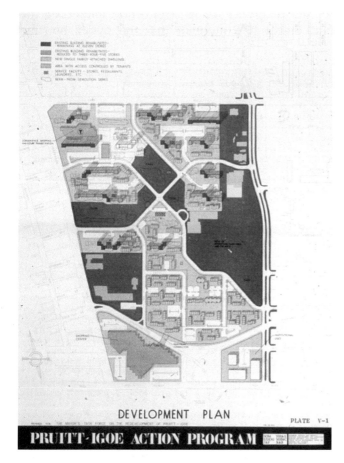

Rather than demolish Pruitt-Igoe, Skidmore, Owings & Merrill developed an alternative scheme to remodel and adapt the housing complex in 1972.

the Nixon administration.[22] Step by step, funds were withdrawn, which made life in Pruitt-Igoe intolerable. On the one hand, rent-striking tenants formed assemblies (like the Pruitt-Igoe Tenants Affairs Board) and negotiated with councils and the St. Louis Housing Association, and studies on how to adapt and remodel the housing complex—for example, the Pruitt-Igoe Action Program by Skidmore, Owings & Merrill.[23] On the other hand, media, housing officials, and politicians encouraged a racist discourse, criminalization and stigmatization included. The only solution in "racial capitalism" to "resolve" the issue—without fundamentally challenging its own logic—was demolition. Ruby Russell again: the housing officials "haven't solved any problems by deciding to tear this place down. They're just sweeping dirt under the rug. The real problem is that nobody wants to spend millions of dollars just so poor people, and especially poor people in large families, can have decent housing."[24]

Sabine Horlitz shows that one of the many reasons for the pauperization of Pruitt-Igoe tenants is the fact that in the moment that the public housing

22. Alice O'Connor, "The Privatized City: The Manhattan Institute, the Urban Crisis, and the Conservative Counterrevolution in New York," *Journal of Urban History* 34, no. 2 (2008): 333–353; Richard Nixon, "Special Message to the Congress Proposing Legislation and Outlining Administration Actions to Deal with Federal Housing (September 1973)," in *The American Presidency Project*, ed. John T. Woolley and Gerhard Peters, University of California, Santa Barbara, https://www.presidency.ucsb.edu/documents/special-message-the-congress-proposing-legislation-and-outlining-administration-actions; Richard Nixon, "Radio Address about the State of the Union Message on Community Development (March 1973)," in *American Presidency Project*, https://www.presidency.ucsb.edu/documents/radio-address-about-the-state-the-union-message-community-development.

23. Sabine Horlitz describes in depth how the famous image of the building's detonation in 1972 was part of the demolition tests of the Pruitt-Igoe Action Program, which planned "to reduce the number of buildings and convert those that remained," a fact that Charles Jencks failed to mention. In fact, the image represents an attempt to save the complex. The decision to abandon the rescue plans and demolish the complex was made in autumn 1973; final demolition work was not completed before 1976. Skidmore, Owings & Merrill had set up an on-site office in the community center, residents were interviewed, participatory workshops were implemented, and residents were employed on the project. "This plan might not only have prevented the demolition of Pruitt-Igoe, but might have once again turned the housing complex into a pilot project nationwide: this time for the re-modeling and programmatic redefinition of large-scale public housing." Sabine Horlitz, "The Case of Pruitt-Igoe: On the Demolition of the US Public Housing Complex in St. Louis, 1972," *Candide* 10 (2016): 66–88. "[The plan] suggested shops within the apartment areas, a small shopping center on the north side and a large one on additional land to the south, both tied to Pruitt-Igoe with pleasant walks and streets. The buildings would be clustered in six 'villages,' still using the street-aligned utilities but not following the street patterns... The plan calls for leaving the debris in place, to be compacted and mounded for landscaping, and in some cases to be piled against buildings to convert present ground floors into subfloors... The new scheme, prepared from painstaking and well-aimed research in both design and social implications, shows promise of making Pruitt-Igoe a neighborhood instead of a project, and of involving it in surrounding Model Cities activities as an ongoing community." George McCue, "$57,000,000 Later, an Interdisciplinary Effort Is Being Made to Put Pruitt-Igoe Together Again," *Architectural Forum* (May 1973): 42–45.

24. Horlitz, "The Case of Pruitt-Igoe," 82.

settlement was built, the economy was being fundamentally restructured: factories moved to the outskirts, the usage and ownership of the automobile dramatically altered urban planning, and suburban housing emerged—for white people—all of which simultaneously created racial segregation based on wealth, the ability to buy a car, and the accessibility of credit from banks.[25] Pruitt-Igoe was "red-lined" and distanced from sites of labor, which forced tenants into dependency on social aid. The moment capital moved away, when the housing association had its funds taken away by HUD, the actual abandonment became visible. Criminalization and racialization, combined with a discourse that suggested modernist design encouraged antisocial behavior, began shifting attention away from structural problems and from the violent, traumatic experience of losing one's own home. "It's almost like losing a child," another resident says in *The Pruitt-Igoe Myth*, trying to grasp the deep feeling of this loss.[26]

Riot from Above, Les Minguettes, 1983: "J'ai peiné"

In response to the riotous uprising "L'été chaud des Minguettes" in 1981, the first tower to be detonated in the housing project Les Minguettes in Vénissieux/ Lyon happened exactly fifteen years after it was built by architects Eugène Beaudoin and Franck Grimal. In October 1994, ten more towers with an estimated 600 housing units were razed. Between 2005 and 2015, within the national demolition program PNRU (Programme nationale pour la rénovation urbaine) in France, a total of 1,671 units were demolished. These were demolitions on the grand scale, shock therapy for poor(er) neighborhoods.

Watching the ten towers in Les Minguettes being dynamited in the early 1990s, a resident commented: "Personally, I am troubled. Maybe others can adjust, but not me..."[27] Some people cheered, many were distressed. Feelings of pain and sadness were expressed, as well as a sense of hopelessness and helplessness. There was an intuition—a memory of a colonial past—that something bigger, even more

- 25. Sabine Horlitz, "Der Fall Pruitt-Igoe: Planungsparadigmen, Lenkungsmodelle und Rezeption des US-amerikanischen Sozialwohnungsprojekts" (PhD diss., Freie Universität Berlin, 2015).
- 26. Freidrichs, dir., *The Pruitt-Igoe-Myth*.
- 27. "Personellement j'ai peiné. D'autres peut-être s'arrangent, pas moi…" See the report "Destruction du quartier des Minguettes," Institut National de l'Audiovisuel (October 11, 1994), https://www.youtube.com/watch?v=Xk-Je1eQ5po.

The demolition of the first tower of Les Minguettes in Vénissieux in June 1983. Courtesy of the Bibliothèque municipale de Lyon.

unjust, was about to happen. For demolition and destruction have been inscribed in the history and memory of people of color in France, experiences from a colonial past translated easily into the French version of accumulation by dispossession since 2004: the PNRU. The €45 billion program rampaged through social housing between 2003 and 2013: 140,000 housing units were demolished in this period.[28] People lost their homes, their neighborhoods, and their social networks, nominally distracted by community outreach programs and workshops.[29]

Riot from Above, Cité de Balzac, 2012:
"Il y a tous nous souvenirs d'enfance dedans"

28. "Rapport de l'ONZUS: Dix ans de PNRU," Agence nationale de la rénovation urbaine, May 13, 2013, https://www.anru.fr/fre/Actualites/Evenements/Rapport-de-1-ONZUS-dix-ans-de-PNRU.
29. David Giband, "Housing the Banlieue in Global Times: French Public Housing and Spaces between Neo-Liberalization and Hybridization," in *The Routledge Handbook on Spaces of Urban Politics*, ed. Kevin Ward, Andrew E. G. Jonas, Byron Miller, and David Wilson (New York: Routledge, 2018).

"Personally, I am troubled. Maybe others can adjust, but not me…" Watching the demolition of buildings in Les Minguettes, a resident voices her feelings of pain. Still from the Institut National de l'Audiovisuel's report "Destruction du quartier des Minguettes," October 11, 1994. Courtesy of the Institut National de l'Audiovisuel.

"It hurts, it really hurts. Because there are all our memories of childhood in there… and now everything fell down like all of a sudden." Still from the news report "La cité Balzac fait peau neuve," September 5, 2012, by Alejandra Magnasco and Elena Brunet.

Cité de Balzac, near Paris, was inaugurated in 1967. The first slab, ABC, was demolished in 2007; the second, DEF, followed in 2010, and the last one, GHJ, in 2012. Five hundred and four homes were lost within five years. Watching the last slab fall, many inhabitants were torn between excitement over the spectacle of violence and the feeling of loss. After soothing her crying sister, a teenage girl says, smiling, "It hurts, it really hurts. Because there are all our memories of childhood in there… and now everything fell down like all of a sudden."[30] David Giband has described the implementation of PNRU as "silent violence" against tenants by forcing them to move and leave their personal and social networks.[31]

Riot from Above, Heygate Estate, 2011–2014: "It's breaking us up"

The Heygate Estate, in South London, was designed by Tim Tinker and completed in 1974. Its demolition was decided already in the late 1990s, but its

"It's breaking us up." Former resident Liz Joseph revisits the Heygate Estate shortly before its demolition. Still from the film *Revisiting the Heygate* (July 2013).

- 30. "Ça fait mal, très mal. Parce qu'il y a tous nos souvenirs d'enfance dedans… tout est tombé comme ça d'un coup." Alejandra Magnasco and Elena Brunet, "La cité Balzac fait peau neuve," *Nouvel Observateur* (September 5, 2012), https://alejandramagnasco.com/cite-balzac-vitry-veut-faire-peau-neuve.
- 31. Giband, "Housing the Banlieue in Global Times."

residents were left in the dark about the future of the estate for more than a decade before the demolition actually started. At the Heygate Estate, a total of 1,194 council flats were demolished in different phases, with the last residents evicted in 2013. Liz Joseph, a former leaseholder, revisited the abandoned estate shortly before its demolition. Troubled by the loss of her social contacts and friends, she sums up the experience: "It's breaking us up," she said, and "I would come back tomorrow, if I could. That's all I can say. It's very sad to see it like this."[32]

Loretta Lees and Hannah White speak of this violence in their study of the everyday experience of dispossession by council tenants and leaseholders in London's Heygate and Aylesbury Estates. They found that, since 1997, 54,263 housing units were demolished in London, with a conservative estimate of 135,658 households displaced within the UK Estate Regeneration Programme.[33] "Social cleansing can be understood as a geographical project made up of processes, practices, and policies designed to remove council tenants from space and place."[34] They trace the slow violence and accumulative processes of dispossession and show the many assaults on the urban poor by different political administrations starting in the early 1970s. Focusing on the actual experience of this kind of assault, they document feelings of loss, withdrawal of tenants' sense of place, suffering, and unsafety. As the term "accumulated dispossession," coined by Lees and White, suggests, "the state... plays an active role in coordinating new forms of dispossession and diminishing the power of the poor in favor of the rich."[35] What happens when one's home and social network are taken away by the state on a mass scale? When "I have no alternative!" is the only response to questions about surviving the severest chain of experiences—one of which is gas poisoning from the demolition of blocks around one's home.[36] What happens when the level of dispossession reaches the level of health and safety? When it goes beyond the home and assaults the body? Is that the moment when the "silent violence," the "slow violence," the invisible violence becomes visible—despite remaining unseen to the law and to the state? What does it mean when the state is the rioter?

32. *Revisiting the Heygate* (July 2013), https://www.youtube.com/watch?v=zffKMFTbrBk&feature=emb_logo.
33. The units are either demolished or slated for demolition. Lees and White, "The Social Cleansing of London Council Estates," 1701.
34. Lees and White, "The Social Cleansing of London Council Estates," 1702.
35. Lees and White, "The Social Cleansing of London Council Estates," 1718.
36. Lees and White, "The Social Cleansing of London Council Estates," 1711.

"Riots from above" is our speculative thesis that understands the riot *first* as a set of continuous urban policies and programs that respond both to the challenge of riots/uprisings and to the logic of capital, which together adjust urban planning to neoliberal urbanity and deregulation. Furthermore, with an evacuation of social services and stronger policing and surveillance, the grounds for future riots and uprisings are prepared. The neoliberal city—that is, a "market-driven urbanity" (see Asef Bayat's contribution to this volume)—not only does not consider the needs of inhabitants but systematically destroys and demolishes the very infrastructures, social and physical, that inhabitants need in order to lead a decent life. A kind of "urban mining" of corporate and public cooperation seeks to eliminate the remaining public goods in order to privatize and restructure them according to corporate interests. The last resources of public property—social housing—are being demolished at a pace unseen in times of peace. Skillfully designated as "regeneration," the urban renewal programs in Western neoliberal states begin with the destruction of communities and social housing that has been associated with high levels of crime, unemployment, and the fear of people who are stigmatized/racialized. In the liminal urban zones, a permanent modality of "riot from above" is at work.

"Riots from above" then operate with their own form of excess. If the excess of riotous uprisings wants to—even if unconsciously—undo and destroy such brutal conditions of social life and experimental techniques, then the excess of riots from above worsen the system of injustices at the expense of its most marginalized parts. This process is accompanied by a continual eradication of historical memory, of the political and cultural emancipation that riots from below bring with them, and offers another reason for collective efforts to take the riotous uprisings seriously.

A Supplementary Note on the Subjectivity
of Riotous Uprising

The riotous uprising points precisely to the gravest injustices and asymmetries in society but also succeeds—even if only shortly—in collectivizing the feeling of injustice in the affected communities. It triggers new, or radicalizes the old, organizational, communal forms of resistance. The literature on riots and uprisings has not arrived at any consensus on what kind of political agency/subjectivity the rioters (per) form. Broadly speaking, there are two major standpoints of analysis: sociological and political-theoretical.

First, for more critically inflected sociologists/social theorists, the agents of uprisings would comprise the urban poor, the marginalized or generally dispossessed and racialized subjects. Once their relationship to capitalist modes of production has been evaluated, one could call the rioters an integral part of the "surplus population" (in Marx's terms). Marx spoke about the "reserve industrial army" of labor, which for capital comprises the most disposable section of the population. Marx analyzes surplus population from the standpoint of capital that fluctuates between being and nonbeing, appearing and disappearing. As an excess to the otherwise criticized statistical concept of "population," the surplus is both part and not part of the working class. This is implied by the resurrection of dead labor into capital. Such definitions remain "sociological" or structural, since they primarily describe the objective position of rioters in capitalist society in terms of exclusion, poverty, and space vis-à-vis capital.

Second, in political theory we encounter first of all crowds (see Dilip Parameshwar Gaonkar's contribution to this volume for details) and also "parts without part"/the uncounted (Rancière), the multitude (Negri), the "tumultuous assembly of the young" (Badiou), the *Lumpenproletariat* (Marx, Fanon), and Clover's politicized take on "surplus population." What these authors agree on is the modality of the riots and that any political forms it might develop are precarious and unstable.

The idea of the *Lumpenproletariat* points to a political excess similar to how "surplus population" points to a specific excess in the labor market. Here the *Lumpen* work as excess over Marx's own emancipatory agent of social change: the proletariat. We would suggest that riotous subjectivity cannot be read in the solely pessimistic terms of Marx's *Lumpenproletariat,* as a political subjectivity that will necessarily support more authoritarian tendencies and lack class consciousness. Despite his pessimistic tone, Marx shows the structural fractures within the working class that can provide important lessons for future political organization. If Marx was overly pessimistic after the events of 1848, Fanon, writing in the context of liberation struggles, offered a more optimistic perspective on the idea of the *Lumpen*. For Fanon, *Lumpenproletariat* are formed by the newcomers to the urban slums that he calls a "mass of humanity" that "will spearhead the new rebellions."[37]

Both sociological and political-theoretical approaches nevertheless have some major epistemological limitations: in the case of a sociological analysis, they run the risk of falling into an "objectivism" (sociologism) that denies riotous agents any transformative potential, while in the case of political analysis, "voluntarism" can romanticize riotous subjects as some pure politics unaffected by form/mediation. A critical dialectical approach, then, has to think through the tension between the structural position of the urban marginalized poor and their (im)possible political subjectivation—that is, to think through the transformation of the urban poor through riotous actions, from the preceding political experiences to those following the riotous uprisings. Riotous uprisings are by default preceded by a wave of political actions and protests within the affected communities that is predominantly ignored by the general public and the police.

Riotous uprisings change something not only in their immediate surroundings, policies, policing, and discourse but also in the agents of uprising themselves. To paraphrase Joshua Clover, the way that surplus activates in political action is riot. It is poignant that many participants in riots describe their sense of empowerment and feelings of unity with

● 37. Fanon, *The Wretched of the Earth*, 81.

many (un)likely neighbors and even neighboring/conflicting gangs. That sense of empowerment, however short and precarious, speaks of "politicization" on the part of the urban poor. It also illuminates the suggestion that it is *only through the struggle itself,* through riotous uprisings and the violent response against them, that political agency appears and changes the urban poor themselves. Riotous subjectivity carries a deep awareness of social injustice—be it directed against police or against corporations in a sort of "moral economy of the poor."[38] This does not mean that after a riot, riotous subjectivity shall enlist in a leftist party, a trade union, or a revolutionary movement. But it also does not mean that the rioters simply go back to their everyday lives and continue in the same circumstances forever. In other words, if objective analysis and its most prominent categories of race and class give us a solid understanding of social processes that cause misery, such analysis might not be very useful for rethinking the transformative potential of uprisings. Rather, they might even contribute to a more general despair that limits sections of the population to the same space without hope for exit.

There is no historical necessity that conditions the urban poor to eternal hell on earth, which means that there is neither a riotous messiah to be awaited nor a political recipe that can solve the situation in an instant. It is only through the laborious political work involved in decolonizing and transforming such dire social circumstances and in building coalitions and solidarities that go beyond strict corporatist-identitarian alignments that one can expect a veritable social transformation. The categories of class, race, and, in the context of riots, too often also gender, need to be weaponized against the permanent riot from above.[39] In this, riotous subjectivity has already played an important role historically, since every major revolution started with riots of the dispossessed, and we predict that they will play a vital role in our future.

Finally, to take seriously the emancipatory potentiality of riotous subjectivity, one can speak of its transformative dimension: uprising is directed toward abolition of the existing oppressive state of affairs. That said, we are not interested in the immediate objective outcomes of many particular riots—which often even worsen the conditions that sparked the riot in the first place—but are much more interested in the feeling of empowerment and the building of solidarity in the most unfavorable circumstances. Despite circumstances of despair, riotous uprisings have arisen and will rise again. Riotous subjectivity acquires its own legacy; as John Akomfrah powerfully states, it is crowded with the ghosts of many other stories of (past) oppressions while also nurturing fragments of an emancipatory future. Could we not say that riotous subjectivity offers a space where we can weave back together the critique of political economy (the most extreme logic of riots from above), the awakening of new revolutionary beginnings, and a constant reminder of the irreconcilable split of society? Against the (post)colonial monumentality and

38. Cf. E. P. Thompson, *Customs in Common* (New York: New Press, 1991).
39. Riots have often been associated with the predominantly male figure of militancy.

its remainders, Fanon focuses on a completely new society that will not be developed from the standardized image of development in Europe. Riotous subjectivity and memorial iconoclasm—seen in today's anti-racist Black Lives Matter (BLM) movement—are best expressed in the words of Fanon, for whom *Lumpenproletariat* dreams are,

> muscular dreams, dreams of action, dreams of aggressive vitality... against the colonizers, against the world compart-mentalized, Manichaean and petrified, a world of statues: the statue of the general who led the conquest, the statue of the engineer who built the bridge. A world cocksure of itself, crushing with its stoniness the backbones of those scarred by the whip. That is the colonial world.[40]

Once we recognize riotous uprisings as expressions of the deepest symptoms of the unjust world, we can see in what way they—riots them-selves—are already becoming monuments commemorating the triply traumatic genesis of modern capitalist society: protection of property (capital), protection of life (monopoly of violence), and protection of order (surveillance state). Riots from above are a constitutive part of the logic of capital, of the regimented demolition in everyday life, of the class and racial divisions imposed on the minds and lives of people. While riotous subjectivity, against all odds, perhaps one day in the near future may become a trigger for revising oppressive memories, repair-ing injustices, and triggering solidarities among the oppressed instead of furthering their internal division. Against the lost futures and past/present perpetuation of the (post)colonial condition, the uprising can tear down the devastating legacy of riots from above.

● 40. Fanon, *Wretched of the Earth*, 15.

Revolving Anger &
The Tarot Bansky

Zena Edwards

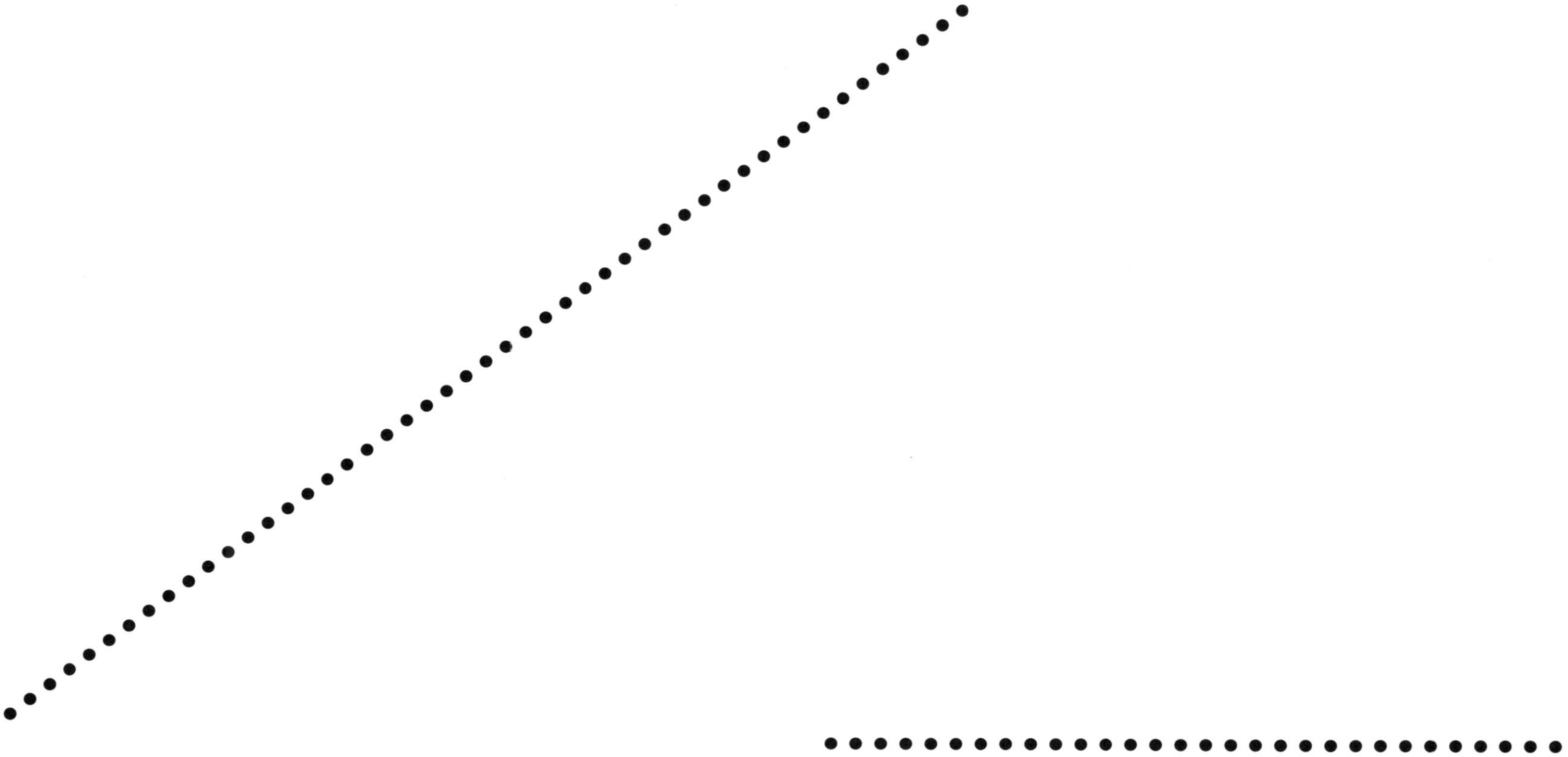

O

A human need indeed,
whose revolving anger like a frenemy,
a flowered tourniquet
throttling its own future.

"This morning I woke up in a curfew
O God, I was a prisoner, too, yeah!
Could not recognize the faces standing over me
They were all dressed in uniforms of brutality."
"How many rivers do we have to cross
Before we can talk to the boss?
Them belly full but we hungry
A hungry mob is an angry mob
The rain fall but the dirt too tough."

It's just Them and us
Them and us
Them versus us

five of brushes, "if you win the rat race you are
still a rat," + the sister of brushes

If you don't give a fuck in 2019, then you're stuck. You're trapped, thinking you are victorious in a climate of austerity. A righteous messy pride holds your hand at night when you are cold, trying to decide whether to pay for your heat or to eat. The humanity in a dying empire's veins has dried up, its subjects thrown into a delirium of hunger, into the stupor of consumerism that binds people together when they, too, close their thinking eye in bliss and ignore the detail of politricks, strangely proud of their own oppression, surrounded by others that think the same, dressed in colors of the void. And they will wake you up in their dream, your nightmare, and you will not recognize yourself. You will be wearing a uniform. The uniform is black, and you move as a shadow, think as a shadow, under a rib of your own starvation.

Them belly full but we hungry

The hungry mob is Elders and the youth learning agency, embodied wisdom. Both competing for the same social home allocation and housing rights, for safe streets to walk on, for equal access to benefits and welfare, and for health care that is slowly diminishing due to the aggressive privatizing David Cameron swore he would not ignite. Yet, he lines his pockets with smiles from closed deals behind closed doors. Nurses and junior doctors are striking to protest how profit-over-people is making their jobs triple hard. They fall asleep at their posts, snatching some quick shut-eye between shifts, while shameless politicians blame them for failing the people whom they themselves have impoverished. The lolling towns of Big Pharma and private, outsourced administration and maintenance companies salivate over the fracturing of the National Health Service. Cameron began the flow. Boris will maintain it. Meanwhile, the hungry mob grows more agitated.

Observe the psychology of the oppressed,
the Pathology of Privilege
speeding their humanity to the edge

three of buckets + two of buckets + Death

What is left for them to do? Both young and old form orderly British queues in the same benefits office, while in private they seethe, stuck in grief, wanting to reach out in hope to partner in resistance. The problem is this state-installed fracturing. The medicine is intergenerational dialogue to bridge the gulf between us. Our words, free from finger pointing and shame. However, common ground is found behind the cock of a loaded gun named patriotism.

Let them blame the immigrants. Let them blame the muslims and the gays, the blacks, the hipsters and the toffs. Let them blame the single moms and the women who want equal pay because utopia is not found on a designer label or in the lottery tickets, or

while scrolling through eBay. Nationalism sits like a comfortable bulldog in a steel clip, aimed at their own heads, waiting for the right time to liberate themselves through the barrel, and rebellious Brexit Leaver dreamers will share memories although they are generations apart.

the Moon + the Lovers

This is the climate of the subconscious standing in the light of the silvery moon; the silvery moon who cannot even see her reflection because of the floodlights from the football grounds, whose tribal chanting is heard for miles around—there is comfort in group activities.

So bodies are riddled with anger that weaves between their teeth, like barbed-wire braces that straighten their common English into correct Britishness; and anger flows over their tongues like an ocean of plastic forks and plates at cheap summer weddings—anger at promises made about employment policy, maybe even a universal basic wage, and social housing that would be affordable, and increases in state services, even though the housing crisis is the worst it's been since the 1940s. World War II was a valid excuse.

Everybody believed that Margaret Thatcher had done them a favor by opening up the possibility of becoming a homeowner, of being upwardly mobile, of having your own castle. It didn't matter how punk you were, you could own the council flat you were born in. The idea of two classes set to meet—the working and middle classes, pawns in a forbidden merger, in a housing crisis thirty-five years later.

What was Cinderella's dream became her nightmare. A romance, two alien entities coming together, a Tory opportunity to win Labour votes. But in the end, it was charity with strings. It was charity with chains. Some working-class communities found themselves with properties that they could no longer maintain. Structural damage, leakages, and disrepair because of the lack of council care. State neglect. Resident debt by default.

The rumble of deep property development, regeneration, the veil of gentrification. Worse still, the buying of surrounding land, and properties stand empty. Less space for renters; they have to use the back door, exiled from their own Estates. They might be rat runs, but they were theirs. Security and policing reaches another level. This used to be a tight community. Now the price of British soil is set for international investors from South Korea, Saudi Arabia, and China.

> "UK's renting millennials face homelessness crisis when they retire."
> —*Guardian*, July 17, 2019

> "2018 saw record levels of overseas investment into London with Asian investors accounting for the largest share with £3.6bn."
> —Linklaters, 2019

> callous, you build a society made to suit your measure
> Stitch up the logic, the fix, the equation of pressure
> —Lies (multiplied by) corruption (multiplied by) "every breath is daylight robbery"
> string up (lynch) Robin, reward the sheriff
> let them riot (times) looting (squared) for a media frenzy
>
> Criminalizing the youth
> The media machine is monstrous
> gorging on the overwhelmed, shaken to paralysis
> The machine calls this "apathy"
> Time to be wide awake to the master's voice—
> an illusion of power
> they are ostracized, reclaiming the streets with blood
> while politicians continue to lie.

What was learned from these cons, these political dupes and bamboozlements, was that government could not be trusted when it came to social policy and the environment. Local councils—north, south, east, and west—have proven themselves to be shady, nepotistic, self-interested, with only a few employees within them who understand the laws and loopholes that can actually help some of the most vulnerable people in impoverished areas: those who need access to services and green spaces, places where their mental health and well-being can be exercised, monitored, maintained, and can thrive.

Tension in "da Endz" intensified. Police stop-and-search laws returning to the draconian era of the 1970s, when your humanity did not count. Vicious banter. Violent jibes and man-handling, searching pockets, the Queen's "bully boy" hands all over the bodies of boys from the age of twelve to men of fifty-two, their personhood belonging to the state. Racist ep-ithets spat unto their manhood—this is only one of the ugliest faces of the British constabulary. Accounts of misbehavior and harassment by the UK police force is rarely reported in the mainstream; it is expected that these kids of color deserve even less.

Laws applied discriminatorily target those of African descent and Muslim Asians—who already feel disenfranchised by the school system, by the employment sector, and by higher ed-ucation. That is the status quo. The law protects those who protect the status quo.

> "he who controls the media, controls the public."
> the TV "guide" disguised as adult content
> pushing key stage 2 sound bites with intent
> to turn the cogs in the machine in the age of apathy
> injecting inflammatory blatancy
> gone are the days of "PC"
> an inferno of a cancer, fanning the dis-ease
> till resistance to explode is low
> the lack of belonging dealt the final blow
> and all the neighborhood got robbed that day,
> the papers blared "London's burning!"
> but this is the Frankenstein of your creating

> ten of brushes + the ace of spray cans | the
> Sun + the sister of buckets

The people were tired of being told what they could and could not be angry about. The writing was on the wall. The state and its enforcers do not see human beings at all. It's made plain. They are denied their humanity, their emotion, imagi-nation. Watched on CCTV thirty-seven times a day, streaming their activities like reality TV. And how miraculously security footage went missing after the murder of an IC3, with military weaponry: "We're at war, yes!" the boys will say.[1] Another

---

● 1. "IC3" is the police classification used to describe a Black male.

ZENA EDWARDS

dead Black Male, a son, Family, who can no longer speak for himself, so the others cannot look away. His Ancestors took him by the hand and told him, "not in vain." It took the death of yet another, Mark Duggan, to finally cause the lion to roar, for the "Manz Dem," the people, to show their teeth.

> Duggan's story is buried under a BBC
> whitewash blackout, it needs to be told
> on August 6th (2011)
> on a Tottenham side road
> i bumped into his wife-to-be, Simone,
> i asked what was happening,
> she told me, "they killed him"
> the street's patience was waning,
> 5 days later and still
> no explanation,
> she hung limp, boneless, mourning
> in the arms of loved ones: refuge,
> a cloned woman withering under the shadow
> of the death of her children's father, his body still cooling

They called the rioting mindless. However, mindless food is a staple diet—mindless television, mindless education that does not ask them to think, that does not represent them, only regurgitates programmed mind states of "know your place"—that of factory fodder and jailbait.

Intimacy is extinct. Sex education is Snapchat, WhatsApp, and Periscope livestreamed, sharing bodily fluids with the death of their innocence. Celebrities mindlessly celebrate the selves Hollywood made them. A million decadent "likes" for a lifestyle stitched by tiny hands and hungry mothers, in Bangladesh or China, whose husbands fight or fall under the indignity of their own cold governments who've sold them out to European corporations. This is the backdrop upon which the flames flew across thirteen cities in the United Kingdom; the pretext and prison mentality that flew its flag across the colonized waves in tyranny and terrorism of its empire desire to rule.

> All this talk and talk about criminality, opportunism, material-
> ism turned nihilistic
> Balk at the "have and have-not" polemic
> when it's human beings on the ground
> living the hard reality of it
>
> compassion is the missing link,
> the "them and us" instinct prevails
> the "haves" find contemptuous anger,
> when the "have-nots" trespass and jump the rails
> The sport is now in the sentencing and terms in jail
> Clean up the gentrified streets for those Olympic ticket sales
>
> See that youth // repeatedly, ferociously,
> punching Ladbrokes, the betting shop's reinforced glass,

with raw fists,
this is rage from a page
not yet written in history books
check how his rage bubbled then hissed
then roared, the steam released
"easy bredrin, calm down blud, come on,"
his mate said and pulled him away,
camaraderie in the fury

let's talk about the anger,
cos the stakes are high
straight to the camel's back
and wonder why
a need ignored turns so ugly

five of brushes

This is anger revolving. This is/was fury hurtling along the streets, along cobblestones concreted over. Day two on the 6 o'clock news, I saw the resistance army, when all gangs across London city called a truce. #DeadthePostcodeWar hashtagged a moment of truth—clarity about who the enemy was.

Born in the eighties, these are Thatcher's children. This is/must be what she had wanted. This is what she and Reagan conceived, as he ravaged Black and Latino communities with floods of crack cocaine from corrupt police departments. Then radical hip-hop—Public Enemy, KRS1, Wu Tang, Dead Prez—would be a UK import. This rebel music emboldened the lyrics and rhymes of young minds on British soil, making their own beats and bars, a street symbiosis to absorb their oppression, transmute it, reflect it back as redemptive fire; to chop the long arm of colonial feudalism short.

The riots were needed. They are insurrections that scored the land with a rebel's mark, a momentous shift to the makeup of the country's history of policy and lawmaking. They remind us of the privileged class who believed that poverty was a eugenic inheritance that could literally be identified by facial and physical features. Only a century ago, child labor was lawful; only a century ago, impoverished families, mothers, would prefer to die on those damn streets than go to the workhouse to be indentured laborers, separated from the children. The men were paid in beer, rooting the drink culture we know now, to drown out the noise of injustice and of an immoral class system.

This is the bed of the Riots/Insurrections of 2011; the crescendo of the main act of a thousand-year-long theater piece. The ruling classes, intoxicated with greed and privilege, needed this scene to play out to give themselves meaning, to shuffle through policy masquerading as sobriety, to set skewed moral standards that we are all forced to live by, imagine ourselves rubber-stamped and approved by.

they kettle children here, for real?
For real. the absurdity, let alone the outcry,

so tantrums are inevitable as
children will test boundaries before they fly

your rationale? Bring out old water cannons,
rubber bullets then bullshit sentencing
replace the fashion of a hoodie to a time Dickensian
no Caps in court unless the style is Oliver Twist's
"Please sir, can you fuck me up some more?"
and we see the age in which this judicial system exists
the ink of law on dusty pages, Victorian ages still persists

ten of buckets | mamma of buckets + 2nd Hierophant
as Marilyn Monroe + the Tower
So who has learned what about themselves today? Don't all rush to
put your hands up at once. It is understandable, the/a system relies on
complicit cogs and wheels. A game of chess requires players, gambling
requires those who take risks—including the house.

The gamble of the Brexit campaign attempted to ensure there would
be one language of conformity spoken on British shores. That would
be true if it were not for England's sordid immigration debate, rooted
in the debt owed to its ex-colonies. Refugees and asylum seekers bear
the brunt of Brexit expletives, reduced to a number, a stat, a monster
who remains quiet in the corner, kneeling in prayer, tolerating the same
disrepair as UK citizens, ignored and undermined till their makeshift
home is engulfed in a hail of cover-ups and payoffs, buck-passing and
nonaccountability, a flare in the night named Grenfell.

Grenfell: nothing is more indicative of disgruntled privilege's contempt
for the ethnically diverse and working class.

Then there are those who are tempted to find healing in what we have
become addicted to. A despondency and apathy of being so overwhelmed. The disappointment after the storm can feel more keen, more
cutting, more numbing... We have to look more closely and see where
we are being cheated on, where the emperor's new clothes are really
only the lifted skirts of a dark lord who listens to the sound of his own
voice that we swallow. We must vomit it out and find the love that comes
behind the poison and rhetoric—before the world is flushed down the
drain, only knowing itself to be a resource for consumption and empire.

the Hangman + the Hermit + the eight of pockets
+ the world

But when we action our passion to defend something that feels beyond our reach, an understanding must be made clear. Our calling will not become an irritant hum that they will become accustomed to, propping up the program of the populist press and politics that fuel the turning wheel of anger. It is we who are responsible for our own destinies. When riots calm.

The images that accompany this piece are courtesy of Shiloh Lewis.

A Night of the Dispossessed: The Imaginable Violence of the Grenfell Tower Fire

Nadine El-Enany

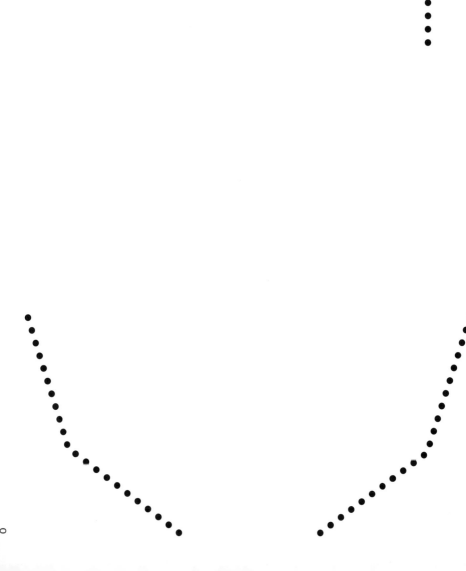

I'm angry and I'm frustrated and believe you me it's hard to contain that anger… Those responsible for ruining our lives walk free like nothing has happened… I have nightmares when I see and think of my friend who lost his wife and two kids… The system wasn't built in a way where it's now broken. The system was built this way. It was made this way to keep the rich up here and the poor down here… Don't think that along the lines something's gone wrong. No, no, no. They have perfected this over the years. And only now, only now, the light is starting to shine. I promise you, and trust me this is a promise that will not be broken, the light will shine and these scumbags will be held to account and our loved ones will not be remembered this way.
—Karim Mussilhy, whose uncle died in the Grenfell Tower fire, speaking on the second anniversary of the fire

The summer of 2019 saw the second anniversary of the Grenfell Tower fire. Seventy-two people were killed in the social housing block fire, which broke out on the night of June 14, 2017. The fire spread rapidly because of Grenfell Tower's highly flammable exterior cladding—which had been installed primarily to enhance the building's aesthetics for the predominantly white, wealthy people living in the surrounding area. There was only one stairwell, and no sprinkler or alarm system. Survivors and family members of those killed have seen no justice, neither in the narrow legal sense of the word nor of the transformative, meaningful kind. Buildings across the country remain fitted with the same cladding that caused the fire to spread so quickly.[1] Those who knew the risks walk free.[2] The public inquiry drags on as families go to bed fearful of another night like that one.[3] As Karim Mussilhy, whose uncle died in the fire, made clear in his speech at a rally on the second anniversary, systemic issues lie at the heart of both why the fire happened and why there has been no justice more than three years later, why those in power have escaped accountability and why families continue to sleep in unsafe buildings night after night.

The violence of Grenfell is a slow or structural violence and thus is not legible to the legal system, which is interested only in the immediate causes of the fire. As Britain is a colonially configured space in which the presence of poor, racialized people is constantly called into question, the colonial and racial dimensions of the fire cannot be ignored. The racialized poor are

1. Graeme Demianyk, "Grenfell-Style Cladding Still on More Than 300 Tower Blocks Two Years after Disaster," *Huffington Post*, June 14, 2019, https://www.huffingtonpost.co.uk/entry/grenfell-cladding-two-year-anniversary_uk_5d02494ee4b0985c4198eace.
2. Peter Apps, "The Lost Lessons of Lakanal: How Politicians Missed the Chance to Stop Grenfell," *Inside Housing*, July 3, 2019, https://www.insidehousing.co.uk/insight/insight/special-investigation--the-lost-lessons-of-lakanal-how-politicians-missed-the-chance-to-stop-grenfell-61834.
3. Robert Booth, "Grenfell Fire Inquiry Admits It Will Not Report until October," *Guardian*, May 17, 2019, https://www.theguardian.com/uk-news/2019/may/17/grenfell-fire-inquiry-admits-it-will-not-report-until-october.

disproportionately vulnerable to police harassment and violence and confinement to unsafe housing. In such a context, riots must be understood as anticolonial revolts. But in that case, why have we not seen a riot or an official response in the wake of the Grenfell fire? The racialization of the majority of the victims as Muslim meant that the violence they endured did not compute as unacceptable violence—as the emergency that it was—to the wider British public. Britain's colonial history, the war on terror, and recent imperial invasions have created a context in which violence against Muslims is normalized. As such, the violence suffered by the Grenfell victims, was imaginable and therefore seemingly acceptable, failing to galvanize the wider British public.

The Slow and Uninterrogable Violence of Grenfell

The Grenfell Tower fire embodies the double meaning of atrocity. Not only was it a sudden, horrifying occurrence, but its origins are in slow violence. Slow violence is that of "calamities that patiently dispense their devastation while remaining outside our flickering attention spans."[4] Slow, or structural, violence is harder to identify than sudden violent spectacle. Yet, in the case of the Grenfell fire, the violence and degeneration that preceded the horror of the fire was perceptible. It was perceptible to its eventual victims and survivors, but they and their calls for help to make their homes safe were dismissed by the state authorities responsible for the building until it was too late. They had the answers then, and their families, friends, and wider community have the answers now, and, still, nobody is listening. The system, as Karim Mussilhy argued, has been "perfected" in such a way that the worst can happen and business can go on as usual.

Systemic causes—including questions of racism, stigmatization, and wider social issues affecting social housing communities—have been left outside the scope of official investigations into the fire. The Grenfell Tower inquiry, which began in May 2018, is focused on the immediate causes of the fire. Legal challenges to the narrow scope of the public inquiry were met with the argument that systemic issues are nonjusticiable. Sir Martin Moore-Bick, chair of the public inquiry, stated that "the inclusion of such broad questions within the scope of the Inquiry would raise questions of a social, economic, and political nature which in my view are not suitable for a judge-led inquiry."[5] Not apparent to the system are the causes of death that lie beyond the realm of the immediate. Such official investigatory processes are, as Sherene Razack has argued, "structured to have little time for the past."[6]

4. Rob Nixon, *Slow Violence and the Environmentalism of the Poor* (Cambridge, MA: Harvard University Press, 2011), 6.
5. *R (on the application of Daniels) v May* [2018], para: 11.
6. Sherene Razack, *Dying from Improvement: Inquests and Inquiries into Indigenous Deaths in Custody* (Toronto: University of Toronto Press, 2015), 6.

Patricia Tuitt has argued that the inquiry's effectiveness will be stunted as long as it fails to "reflect the diversity of the Grenfell Tower community, in terms of both race and faith."[7] The majority of those who died in the fire were racialized, many of them Muslim.[8] Each time we are faced with the names of those who died or with assembled images of their faces, the fact that the vast majority of them are Muslim is inescapable. Although official inquiry documentation is available in Arabic and Farsi alongside English, indicative of the victims' racialization, racial discrimination is not an issue under investigation.[9] Thus, Tuitt writes, "Grenfell Tower residents, particularly its black and brown communities, have become inured to the spectacle of British judges holding just beyond their reach the powerful weapons of the law."[10]

The delay and denial of justice for victims of racial state violence is commonplace in Britain. One need only look at the tireless campaigning of the families of victims—disproportionately young black men—who have died at the hands of the police. Despite thousands of deaths, there has never been a successful conviction of a police officer.[11] Custody deaths are at the sharp end of racial state violence. Inquest juries have yielded verdicts of unlawful killing in twelve death-in-custody cases in Britain. Yet even in these cases, the officers involved have not been held criminally responsible. In a context in which colonial legacies of racism mean that the personhood of some people is denied, racial state violence becomes part of the work of the state. The violence of the legal system thus manifests in its inability to recognize the violence of its agents. The stories we hear (and see) internationally of police shooting unarmed black men, women, and children bring home the reality that racialized people are disproportionately at risk of the most brutal forms of state violence as they move around white hegemonic spaces. Furthermore, as the Grenfell Tower fire demonstrates, racialized people are also

7. Patricia Tuitt, "Law, Justice and the Public Inquiry into the Grenfell Tower Fire," in *After Grenfell: Violence, Resistance and Response*, ed. Dan Bulley, Jenny Edkins, and Nadine El-Enany (London: Pluto, 2019), 119.
8. M. Rice-Oxley, "Grenfell: The 72 Victims, Their Lives, Loves and Losses" *Guardian*, May 14, 2018, https://www.theguardian.com/uk-news/2018/may/14/grenfell-the-71-victims-their-lives-loves-and-losses; and https://www.theguardian.com/uk-news/ng-interactive/2018/may/14/lives-of-grenfell-tower-victims-fire.
9. In acknowledgment of Britain as a white supremacist context, I use the term "racialized" to refer to people who are nonwhite. Following Cheryl Harris, I adopt the definition of white supremacy posited by Frances Lee Ansley: "By 'white supremacy' I do not mean to allude only to the self-conscious racism of white supremacist hate groups. I refer instead to a political, economic, and cultural system in which whites overwhelmingly control power and material resources, conscious and unconscious ideas of white superiority and entitlement are widespread, and relations of white dominance and non-white subordination are daily reenacted across a broad array of institutions and social settings," in Frances L. Ansley, "Stirring the Ashes: Race, Class and the Future of Civil Rights Scholarship," *Cornell Law Review* 74 (1989): 993, 1024, cited in Cheryl I. Harris, "Whiteness as Property," *Harvard Law Review* 106, no. 8 (1993): 1714; Nadine El-Enany, "Before Grenfell: British Immigration Law and the Production of Colonial Spaces," in *After Grenfell*, ed. Bulley, Edkins, and El-Enany, 50–61.
10. Tuitt, "Law, Justice and the Public Inquiry," 121.
11. See Harmit Athwal and Jenny Bourne, eds., *Dying for Justice* (London: Institute of Race Relations, 2015).

acutely at risk of state violence in their own homes, as a result of austerity and deregulation policies as well as of abandonment by state authorities.

Britain as a Colonial Space

I have written previously about why we cannot ignore the colonial and racial dimensions of the Grenfell Tower fire, arguing that the victims were haunted by histories of colonialism that made them acutely and disproportionately vulnerable to abuse, neglect, violence, and death.[12] Histories of colonial dispossession thus continue to structure our present. Meanwhile, the ignorance of Britain's colonial history and of its ongoing effects is profound. Colonial ideas of race and racial inferiority continue to have disastrous and ongoing consequences for people with ancestral or geographical histories of slavery and colonization. Many of the Grenfell victims and their ancestors suffered the dispossessing effects of colonialism. They lived and fled not only the lasting material consequences of colonization but also the economic decline caused by global trade and debt arrangements that maintain a colonially structured world.

Britain remains colonially configured, its immigration laws functioning to keep its former subjects out while, within its borders, the racialized poor find themselves cordoned off, overpoliced, and the subjects of a discourse that presents them as unjustly enriched and undeserving.[13] The statistic that children who live above the fourth floor of high-rise blocks in England are more likely to be black or Asian is striking in a country that is 87 percent white.[14] This is a reflection of the fact that racialized people are disproportionately represented in Britain's working class and are victims of "discrimination—tacit or outright—when allocated housing."[15] High-rise living in England is traditionally associated with social housing, and half of the United Kingdom's black population lives in poverty. Two-fifths of racialized people live in a household earning below average income.[16] Akwugo Emejulu and Leah Bassel have demonstrated the differential impact of austerity policies, which disadvantage minority women disproportionately and exacerbate existing inequalities.[17]

12. El-Enany, "Before Grenfell"; see also Nadine El-Enany, "The Colonial Logic of Grenfell," *Verso* (blog), July 3, 2017, https://www.versobooks.com/blogs/3306-the-colonial-logic-of-grenfell.

13. See Nadine El-Enany, *(B)ordering Britain: Law, Race and Empire* (Manchester: Manchester University Press, 2020).

14. Danny Dorling, *So You Think You Know About Britain* (London: Constable, 2011).

15. Lynsey Hanley, "Look at Grenfell Tower and See the Terrible Price of Britain's Inequality," *Guardian*, June 16, 2017, https://www.theguardian.com/commentisfree/2017/jun/16/grenfell-tower-price-britain-inequality-high-rise.

16. Further, 30 percent of the Bangladeshi population live in overcrowded housing compared with 2 percent of the white population; 15 percent of the black population and 16 percent of the Pakistani population live in overcrowded housing. Office of National Statistics, 2018.

17. Leah Bassel and Akwugo Emejulu, *Minority Women and Austerity: Survival and Resistance in France and Britain* (Bristol: Policy Press, 2017).

As the British Empire was in decline, successive British governments introduced immigration controls withdrawing the rights of racialized Commonwealth citizens and British colonial subjects to enter the British mainland. Via immigration and nationality law, the British Empire thus created itself anew as a nation-state. Importantly, it did so via the legal concept of patriality, introduced by the 1971 Immigration Act, which stipulated that only those born in Britain or with a parent born in Britain had the right to enter and stay. The act thus prevented the vast majority of racialized colonial and former colonial subjects from traveling to and settling in Britain. Following the passage of the 1981 British Nationality Act, a concept of British citizenship was elaborated, and eligibility was also contingent on patriality.[18]

Britain has long projected a notion of itself as being under siege by racialized Commonwealth citizens. Paul Gilroy writes, "black settlement has been continually described in military metaphors which offer war and conquest as the central analogies for immigration."[19] Such descriptors of Commonwealth immigration have included "the unarmed invasion, alien encampments, alien territory, and the new commonwealth occupation."[20] As Gurminder Bhambra and John Holmwood note, "it was precisely the idea of an 'immigrant-descended,' non-white, population that came to be regarded as a threat to national identity."[21] The idea that racialized people posed a threat to Britain carried consequences for Commonwealth citizens and colonial subjects (and their descendants) already living in Britain. Once "alien cultures" came to "embody a threat, which, in turn, invited the conclusion that national decline and weakness have been precipitated by the arrival of blacks," deportation became possible, as did the enactment of internal forms of racial exclusion for those who could not easily be removed.[22] Internal bordering became a new mode of colonialism, producing and sustaining the postimperial project of a white Britain. Such internal bordering has occurred in part through the institution of policy and legal regimes that effectively construct "a border in every street."[23] Borders "follow people and surround them as they try to access paid labour, welfare benefits, health, labour protections, education, civil associations, and justice."[24] This process has been described as "everyday 'bordering and ordering,'" which produces "new

---

18. See El-Enany, (B)ordering Britain.
19. Paul Gilroy, There Ain't No Black in the Union Jack (London: Routledge, 1987), 44.
20. Gilroy, There Ain't No Black in the Union Jack, 44–45.
21. Gurminder K. Bhambra and John Holmwood, "Colonialism, Postcolonialism and the Liberal Welfare State," New Political Economy 23, no. 5 (2018): 582.
22. Gilroy, There Ain't No Black in the Union Jack, 46.
23. Church of England, cited in Rachel Robinson, "A Border in Every Street," Liberty, April 3, 2014, https://www.libertyhumanrights.org.uk/news/blog/border-every-street.
24. Bridget Anderson, Nandita Sharma, and Cynthia Wright, "Why No Borders?," Refuge 26, no. 2 (2009): 6.

social cultural boundaries."[25] These boundaries are policed by "anyone anywhere—government agencies, private companies, and individual citizens."[26] In Britain, a hostile environment policy was introduced in the Immigration Acts of 2014 and 2016 and ensuing amendments, and has resulted in racialized people experiencing "nation-state borders no matter their physical location."[27] In 2018 it came to light that the heightened scrutiny of immigration status led to thousands of people being detained, deported, and denied access to housing, healthcare, education, and financial services.[28] In this way, internal bordering is on a continuum with external bordering, whereby colonial resources, broadly conceived, are withheld from racialized populations both in and outside Britain.

Racial exclusion has thus manifested not only at the external border but also internally, as racialized people are confined to sites of extreme deprivation, predominantly in the inner cities, where British police forces brutally enforce Britain's newly articulated white nationalist boundaries. Gilroy has shown how young black men have been demonized and constructed as criminals, as well as how police violence and harassment is enacted with impunity in racialized neighborhoods.[29] These areas were the sites where the fascist, white nationalist political party the National Front demonstrated while the police looked on.[30] Section 4 of the 1824 Vagrancy Act, known today as "stop and search" and previously dubbed the "sus" laws, was used disproportionately by the police against former colonial subjects and their children resident in Britain. For Nicole M. Jackson, this "postimperial" assertion is crucial to understanding the meaning of police harassment of racialized people: "when police officers, as representatives of the State, harassed Black youth with sus arrests, they reinforced the idea that Black people did not belong in England. To be English was to be white. Without a claim to residence or the hope of full assimilation, Black Britons were cast as the perpetual other within the nation—a colony within the metropole."[31] The Vagrancy Act had fallen into disuse since its introduction with the Napoleonic War. It was widely considered among black parents to have been brought back into use specifically to

25. Nira Yuval-Davis, Georgie Wemyss, and Kathryn Cassidy, "Everyday Bordering, Belonging, and the Reorientation of British Immigration Legislation," *Sociology* 52, no. 2 (2017): 229–230.

26. Yuval-Davis, Wemyss, and Cassidy, "Everyday Bordering, Belonging, and the Reorientation of British Immigration Legislation."

27. Sarah Keenan, "A Prison around Your Ankle and a Border in Every Street: Theorising Law, Space, and the Subject," in *Handbook of Law and Theory*, ed. Andreas Philippopoulos-Mihalopoulos (New York: Routledge, 2018), 76.

28. See, for example, Amelia Gentleman, "'My Life Is in Ruins': Wrongly Deported Windrush People Facing Fresh Indignity," *Guardian*, September 10, 2018, https://www.theguardian.com/uk-news/2018/sep/10/windrush-people-wrongly-deported-jamaica-criminal-offence.

29. Gilroy, *There Ain't No Black in the Union Jack*.

30. Nicole M. Jackson, "Imperial Suspect: Policing Colonies Within 'Post'-Imperial England," *Callaloo* 39, no. 1 (2016): 203–215, 204.

31. Jackson, "Imperial Suspect," 213.

"harass Black youth in public spaces."[32] Jackson argues that the use of "sus" laws "demonstrated a redrawing of the boundaries of the nation and legitimate versus illegitimate citizenry. Because the ordinance was disproportionately used against Black people, it aided in their marginalization in society and they were recast as an internal colony within the nation."[33] Two years before the 1981 Brixton riots, Metropolitan Police statistics showed that of 1,894 "sus" arrests made in 1979, 797 (42 percent) were Afro-Caribbean or Asian, even though these groups comprised only 4.2 percent of London's population.[34]

The police targeting of racialized people has reinforced Britain's postcolonial articulation of its borders. As Jackson has argued, by seeking to control young racialized people, the British police made it "clear that Black people did not belong in, or to, the English nation."[35] The colonialism that brought "these youngsters' parents to the metropole" could be ignored while the police served to "reinscribe the separation of the Empire (or the global empire) from English shores."[36] Yet police harassment of racialized people must also be understood as "lingering expressions of empire."[37] Through racially targeted violence, the police reasserted colonial power over racialized subjects on the British mainland. Ashley Dawson has argued that police deployment of "draconian Victorian-era 'sus' laws" produced "black British communities in particular as a target of forms of oppression linked directly to colonial practices of racial violence."[38] Within and at the borders of the supposedly postcolonial state, racialized persons continue to be profiled, policed, halted, searched, brutalized, killed, and examined postmortem.

Riots as Anticolonial Revolts

If racialized subjects living in Britain are "colonies within the nation," riots must be understood as "anticolonial revolts."[39] Colony and Commonwealth citizens who arrived in postwar Britain received little assistance from the British authorities and relied on community networks for support and sustenance. British government ministers argued that legislation outlawing racial discrimination would be "unworkable and unenforceable."[40] The Cabinet Committee on Commonwealth Immigration feared that providing housing and other support and advice services to new arrivals would encourage more racialized people to travel to Britain. It stated that "as long as

32. Jackson, "Imperial Suspect," 205.
33. Jackson, "Imperial Suspect," 203.
34. Jackson, "Imperial Suspect," 205, 207–208.
35. Jackson, "Imperial Suspect," 205.
36. Jackson, "Imperial Suspect."
37. Jackson, "Imperial Suspect."
38. Ashley Dawson, The Routledge Concise History of Twentieth-Century British Literature (New York: Routledge, 2013), 151.
39. Jackson, "Imperial Suspect," 203.
40. D. Dean, "The Conservative Government and the 1961 Commonwealth Immigrants Act: The Inside Story," Race and Class 35, no. 2 (1993): 58.

immigration remained unrestricted, the use of public funds for that purpose could only serve as an added attraction to prospective immigrants and would frustrate the efforts we were encouraging Commonwealth and Colonial governments to make to reduce the rate of emigration from their territories to the United Kingdom."[41]

In 1981, Brixton, London, was the scene of an anticolonial uprising led by young black residents resisting Metropolitan Police harassment. At the time, a police stop and search operation code-named "Operation Swamp" was ongoing.[42] The evocation of wild and unkempt land barely concealed the operation's materially and symbolically imperial ambitions. Brixton was flooded with officers, some reported to have been wearing National Front badges.[43] A report into police and community relations in Lambeth, commissioned by Lambeth Borough Council and published in 1981, described the police presence there as an "Army of Occupation."[44] The 1981 rioters made clear political demands, criticizing the way they were policed and setting conditions for the police's dispersal: "They wanted the police to withdraw, they wanted an end to police harassment, and they wanted those arrested to be released." They also "wanted to put their case to the media."[45] The crowd attacked businesses with a reputation for refusing service to racialized people and other minority communities.[46]

The Scarman Report, the outcome of the official inquiry into the riots, provides a picture of Britain as a space of domestic colonialism in the 1970s and 1980s. The report betrays the colonial mindset prevalent in British society in several respects. Reflecting on the presence of racialized people in British inner cities, Lord Scarman refers to "our new society," suggesting a claim to ownership reserved for white Britons who must now come to terms with the presence of racialized people in Britain.[47] Such possessive language appears throughout the report: "*Their* lives are led largely in the poorer and more deprived areas of *our* great cities."[48] Scarman describes black people living in Britain as "immigrants to a strange country," indicative of how racialized people were not considered to belong in Britain.[49] He writes that "ethnic minority groups" experience "the same deprivations as the 'host community' (the

41. Dean, "Conservative Government and the 1961 Commonwealth Immigrants Act," 59.
42. Lord Scarman, *The Scarman Report: The Brixton Disorders 1–12 April 1981* (Pelican Books, London, 1982), 46.
43. Scarman, *Scarman Report*, 51.
44. *Final Report of the Working Party into Community/Police Relations in Lambeth* (Public Relations Division, London Borough of Lambeth, Brixton Hill, London SW2, January 1981).
45. Scarman, *Scarman Report*, 58.
46. Scarman, *Scarman Report*, 75.
47. Scarman, *Scarman Report*, 209.
48. Scarman, *Scarman Report*, 35.
49. Scarman, *Scarman Report*, 24.

white British population), but much more acutely," implying that Britain's racialized population occupies a guest status.[50] In its evidence to the inquiry, even the Commission for Racial Equality distinguished racialized people in Britain from the "local population."[51]

In a remarkable colonialist faux pas, Scarman likens the officers policing the riots to "Aunt Sallies," stating that "lines of police officers behind shields effectively become 'Aunt Sallies' for the crowd to aim at."[52] The traditional English game of Old Aunt Sally has been described as follows: "Aunt Sally is a big black doll on a stick, with a pipe in her mouth, and an orange or some toy for a prize, which you win by hitting her with a stick if you are lucky."[53] The blackface doll is thought to have derived from "a low-life character named Black Sal who had been created by Pierce Egan in his series Life In London of 1821."[54] The game of Aunt Sally was also played in France, where it was known as "jeu de massacre," meaning "wholesale slaughter."[55] Scarman's unquestioning use of the metaphor betrays the complex combination of colonial nostalgia and amnesia that pervades British society.[56]

Although Lord Scarman's report on the Brixton riots acknowledged the social disadvantage disproportionately experienced by "ethnic minorities" in Britain, the analysis failed to engage with the imperial dimension of the causes of the riots and the anticolonial character of the uprisings.[57] Instead, the riots were understood in a law and order framework, as the criminal venting of anger at the police and as a product of poor parenting on the part of black mothers.[58] The black youth who participated in the riots were also blamed for their own social disadvantage. The reasons Scarman offers for their higher levels of unemployment serve to propagate racial stereotypes, including "lack of qualifications, difficulties arising from unrealistic expectations, bad time-keeping, unwillingness to travel and, most important of all, trouble with the English language."[59] The establishment's colonial mindset is further revealed when Scarman inadvertently and inappropriately evokes Britain's long history of exploitation of racialized

50. Scarman, *Scarman Report*, 35.
51. Scarman, *Scarman Report*, 137.
52. Scarman, *Scarman Report*, 153.
53. The *New York Times* of April 16, 1866, cited in "Aunt Sally," *World Wide Words*, 2000, http://www.worldwidewords.org/qa/qa-aun1.htm. See also Tony Collins, John Martin, and Wray Vamplew, eds., *Encyclopedia of Traditional British Rural Sport* (London: Routledge, 2005).
54. James Redding Ware, *Passing English of the Victorian Era, A Dictionary of Heterodox English, Slang, and Phrase* (London: G. Routledge & Sons, 1909), cited in "Aunt Sally," *World Wide Words*.
55. Collins, Martin, and Vamplew, eds. *Encyclopedia of Traditional British Rural Sport*.
56. The game of Aunt Sally continues to be played in Britain, but without a racialized doll as the target.
57. Scarman, *Scarman Report*, 194–195.
58. Scarman, *Scarman Report*, 25, 196.
59. Scarman, *Scarman Report*, 28.

labor when he suggests putting "idle" black labor to use by encouraging participation "in projects to clean up and regenerate the inner city."[60] The expectation in the report is that more disorder will follow and that this is something intrinsic to a "multi-racial" society.[61] Once again, rather than understand racism as a product of centuries of British colonialism, the British establishment deems its cause to be the presence of racialized people in Britain.

Scarman's description of the Brixton riots as young black people "demonstrating to millions of their fellow citizens the fragile basis of the Queen's peace" is evocative of the anticolonial content of the riots. Scarman reports that in the course of the riots, petrol bombs were "used for the first time on the streets of Britain" and surmises that this tactic was "copied from the disturbances in Northern Ireland"—not coincidentally a British colony.[62]

The Absence of a Riot and Imaginable Violence
Notwithstanding potential danger in the form of domestic violence, particularly for women and children, people expect their homes to be safe places, removed from some of the risks associated with the public sphere. However, it is often state neglect that makes people's homes—places that are supposed to be sanctuaries—unsafe. State institutions in the United Kingdom are oriented toward the protection of the white population and are violently disposed toward racialized populations. Although the Grenfell Tower fire affected social housing, the context in which it took place is one in which the safety of tenants, whether private or public, is not prioritized. A year before the fire, Conservative MPs voted against a Labour amendment to the Housing and Planning bill that would have required landlords to ensure that all rented accommodation was safe for human habitation.[63] Meanwhile, as part of the government's effort to create a "hostile environment" for irregularized migrants, the Immigration Act of 2016 made it illegal for landlords to rent to people without an immigration status. This legislation is thus productive of internal borders, which in turn enable the exploitation of irregularized renters along with those presumed to be irregularized as a result of their racialization. As Sarah Keenan has written, "while a subject's visa status has traditionally been checked at the territorial entrance point the [2016] Act introduces a range of 'in-country' immigration status checks, meaning that those who provide not only housing but also banking services, drivers' licenses

60. Scarman, *Scarman Report*, 169.
61. See, for example, Scarman, *Scarman Report*, 132–133.
62. Scarman, *Scarman Report*, 13.
63. Frances Perraudin, "Tories Reject Move to Ensure Rented Homes Fit for Human Habitation," *Guardian*, January 12, 2016, https://www.theguardian.com/society/2016/jan/12/tories-reject-move-to-ensure-rented-homes-fit-for-human-habitation.

and marriage certificates are required to check the immigration status of applicants before providing them with the relevant service."[64]

It is important to see this hostile environment not as a new set of policies but as a continuation of colonial control as enacted in the metropole. A combination of official neglect and targeted discrimination has characterized the response of British authorities to the arrival of former colonial subjects and Commonwealth citizens since the postwar era.[65] In the 1960s the Cabinet Committee on Commonwealth Immigration refused to provide housing trusts with the necessary resources to improve accommodation in places such as Notting Hill, close to where Grenfell Tower was to be built in 1972. Nigel de Noronha has pointed out that "the roots of state investment in social housing for the working classes are in the campaign to build 'homes fit for heroes' after World War I. However, as Robbie Shilliam has shown, there is historically a selective signification of who rightfully comprises the working class, despite the fact that, 'race is class… there is no politics of class that is not already racialized.'"[66]

There is no doubt that those who have been campaigning for racial and housing justice for some time thought that the Grenfell Tower fire would have a galvanizing effect. How could people let the sun set on a day that took the lives of seventy-two people in a fire in a tower block that was not safe for human habitation? There is also no doubt that the authorities feared a riot. Police arrived at the fire dressed in riot gear; there were rumors that the real death toll was not being announced in order to quell potential riots.[67] That the authorities feared a riot suggests that even they knew the conditions demanded an uprising. After all, London is no stranger to riots. In 2011 the death of Mark Duggan, an unarmed black man, at the hands of the London Metropolitan Police—a killing later rubber-stamped by an inquest jury as "lawful"—sparked riots across the country.

The absence of a riot in the traditional sense, according to rapper and activist Lowkey, can be explained in significant part by the fact that the majority of the victims of the fire were Muslim.[68] One implication of the counterterror discourse, legislation, police harassment, and media portrayal of people racialized as Muslim

64. Sarah Keenan, "A Border in Every Street: Grenfell and the Hostile Environment," in After Grenfell, ed. Bulley, Edkins, and El-Enany, 83.
65. See El-Enany, (B)ordering Britain.
66. Robbie Shilliam, Race and the Undeserving Poor (Agenda, Newcastle upon Tyne, 2018), 180.
67. Caroline Davies et al., "How the Grenfell Tower Disaster Unfolded," Guardian, June 14, 2017, https://www.theguardian.com/uk-news/2017/jun/14/how-the-grenfell-tower-disaster-unfolded.
68. See Monique Charles, "ComeUnity and Community in the Face of Impunity," in After Grenfell, ed. Bulley, Edkins, and El-Enany, 185.

as a threat to national security has been the impossibility of their organizing against their oppression, in solidarity with others, without being constructed as terrorists. Muslims in Britain are surveilled as part of a McCarthyist system called Prevent, which co-opts the wider community and public institutions (ranging from hospitals to schools and universities) and legally obliges them to report people suspected of being "drawn into terrorism."[69] In such a context, it becomes difficult for Muslims to organize themselves politically in a manner that would be considered a legitimate form of dissent. Further, collective action puts them at risk of accusation, criminalization, and state violence.

As mentioned above, the absence of official timeliness in making Grenfell Tower safe can in part be explained by the racialization of its residents. Some Grenfell survivors reported that "they felt the implicit message from everyone they contacted before the fire for help with the building was 'you are a guest in this borough, and a guest in this country, you have no right to complain.'"[70] If we cannot ignore the colonialist and racial logics at play in the causes of the fire and the absence of a riot, we cannot ignore them in seeking to understand why, three years after the fire, there has been so little action from the authorities to make homes safe and to address the systemic issues affecting social housing.

The lack of official action combined with an absence of galvanization of the general public suggests that the violence of the Grenfell fire has not registered either with the responsible authorities or with significant parts of the spectating public. The violence that occurred on the night of the fire was, for the majority of Britons and for those in power, an imaginable sort of violence. It happened in the main to victims against whom violence is normalized. Since the war on terror, Muslims have become expected and acceptable victims of violence. They were killed in the millions in the US- and UK-led invasion of Iraq, and they continue to die in the hundreds of thousands in conflict situations and as a result of drone strikes.[71]

What did people see when they looked at pictures of the faces of the people whose lives were taken in the Grenfell Tower fire? They saw women in hijabs, the brown faces of men and young children. They saw the faces of people described daily

69. Counter-Terrorism and Security Act 2015.
70. Dawn Foster, "Would a White British Community Have Burned in Grenfell Tower?" New York Times, June 20, 2017, https://www.nytimes.com/2017/06/20/opinion/london-tower-grenfell-fire.html.
71. Medea Benjamin and Nicolas J. S. Davies, "The Iraq Death Toll 15 Years After the US Invasion," Common Dreams, March 15, 2018, https://www.commondreams.org/views/2018/03/15/iraq-death-toll-15-years-after-us-invasion; "Syria Death Toll: UN Envoy Estimates 400,000 Killed," Al Jazeera, April 23, 2016, https://www.aljazeera.com/news/2016/04/staffan-de-mistura-400000-killed-syria-civil-war-160423055735629.html; "Counting Drone Strike Deaths," Columbia Law School Human Rights Clinic, 2012, https://www.law.columbia.edu/sites/default/files/microsites/human-rights-institute/files/COLUMBIACountingDronesFinal.pdf.

by mainstream officials and media outlets as either terrorists or the unfortunate—even deserving—victims of geopolitical violence. Violence against Muslims is so normalized that it passes as unremarkable, even when it occurs in the form of a fire in a twenty-four-story tower block in the London borough of Chelsea and Kensington, one of the richest places in the world. Research has shown that the extent to which white people feel empathy and humanize others correlates with implicit racial biases, where negative stereotyping of those with darker skin corresponds to a lower level of empathy shown to them.[72] Feelings of empathy are known to encourage cooperation and assistance between human beings, while an absence of identification with the suffering of others can lead to violence and abuse.[73] Thus, while it is true that there are similarly clad, unsafe tower blocks up and down the country occupied by people who are white, it is significant that the fire did not happen in one of those blocks. Had the victims of the fire been people against whom violence on such a scale is considered exceptional and unacceptable, the response, the preventative action, the justice daily demanded, may have been delivered by now.

United in Silence

In contrast with the inaction of the authorities, both before and after the fire, there has been unyielding action from survivors, families, and members of the wider Grenfell community. Authorities not only failed to respond to the calls of residents to make their homes safe, they also failed to respond in an adequate or timely manner after the fire. Residents and their loved ones were abandoned. The community came up with its own response, organizing rescue, aid, food, and shelter. The organization Grenfell United was created by survivors and the bereaved to campaign for safe homes, justice, and change.[74] As Karim Mussilhy has said, "we have united and we have formed true friendships and become activists to demand change... pain unites us and pain also changes us... Two years on and we're still neglected, abandoned by the government and other authorities that should have been there from day one but I guess had they have been there, there would be no Grenfell United."[75]

72. Matteo Forgiarini, Marcello Gallucci, and Angelo Maravita, "Racism and the Empathy for Pain on Our Skin," *Frontiers in Psychology* 108 (2011): 2.
73. Forgiarini, Gallucci, and Maravita, "Racism and the Empathy for Pain on Our Skin."
74. See https://www.grenfellunited.org.uk.
75. Karim Mussilhy speaking on the second anniversary of the Grenfell Tower fire.

Courtesy of Guilhem Baker/LNP.

North Kensington specifically, as Lowkey has said, has "a history of turning tragedy into triumph."[76] Notting Hill Carnival was the African-Caribbean community's reaction to attacks on it by the far right in 1958 and to the murder of Kelso Cochrane, a young black carpenter, in 1959.[77] Monique Charles has written of how the carnival has become "a way, along racial and cultural lines, to assert one's right to space and place and celebrate culture."[78] Since the Grenfell Tower fire, a monthly silent march has taken place in the streets of North Kensington. The community comes together on the 14th of every month to walk in silence, winding their way to the location of the fire. Daniel Renwick has described the Grenfell community as "organizing on mute." For him, it is "a poignant form of protest."[79] A community with a voice but nevertheless "unheard," coming together in their thousands, resisting in silence.[80] It is not a riot, but it is a silence that resonates. How is hard to say, but one can hear it. For Gabriela Jimenez, resistance against systemic injustice requires listening "to and for" the "elsewhere in the voices performing decolonial efforts" in the course of struggle.[81] While resistance can include "shouting" or "chanting" and rioting, it can also include silence.[82]

Addendum

This contribution was completed before the Black Lives Matter uprisings of the summer of 2020, which were sparked by the killing of George Floyd by police in Minneapolis on May 25, 2020. While this means I cannot address in detail the implications of this particular moment for organizing around the Grenfell Tower fire, it is nevertheless important to mention some developments. As discussed, until now it has been difficult for the families of Grenfell Tower victims to politically organize around racism as a causal factor in the fire—due to their racialization as Muslim, the challenges that come with political mobilization in the context of the war on terror, and the Grenfell Tower inquiry's exclusion of race from its terms of investigation. In the course of the Black Lives Matter uprising, Grenfell survivors have made the crucial connection between what happened to their loved ones and racial state violence in the form of police killings by making the point that their loved ones couldn't breathe either. Hisam

76. Anu Shukla, "We Have a History of Turning Tragedy into Triumph," *Red Pepper*, March 7, 2018, https://www.redpepper.org.uk/we-have-a-history-of-turning-tragedy-into-triumph.

77. Gordon Rayner, "After 50 Years Kelso Cochrane's 'Killer' Is Named in Book on Notorious Notting Hill Race Murder," *Telegraph*, September 7, 2011, https://www.telegraph.co.uk/news/uknews/crime/8747963/After-50-years-Kelso-Cochranes-killer-is-named-in-book-on-notorious-Notting-Hill-race-murder.html.

78. Charles, "ComeUnity and Community in the Face of Impunity," 169.

79. Daniel Renwick, "Organizing on Mute," in *After Grenfell*, ed. Bulley, Edkins, and El-Enany, 40.

80. Renwick, "Organizing on Mute."

81. Gabriela Jimenez, "(T)racing Mother Listening: W. E. B. Du Bois & Sigmund Freud," *Sound Studies* (blog), October 1, 2018, https://soundstudiesblog.com/tag/christina-sharpe.

82. Jimenez, "(T)racing Mother Listening."

Choucair, who lost six family members in the fire, drew parallels between the killing of George Floyd and the fire. He said, "When my sister rang the fire brigade she said, 'We cannot breathe.' This is a similar phrase used in America at the moment."[83]

On Monday, July 6, 2020, the words "We can't breathe" were projected onto Grenfell Tower. This powerful action made visible the fact that the violence the victims suffered is in fact racial state violence. This development marks a clear and necessary embrace of a coalitional anti-racist politics and ac-knowledges the limitations and depoliticizing effect of formal channels, such as that of the inquiry. At the same time, it sent a vivid message to the Grenfell Tower inquiry to recognize the role of racism in the fire. Indeed, the projection took place as the work of the inquiry resumed following the pandemic. Leslie Thomas QC, who is representing a group of bereaved families, stated in his opening submission that,

The Grenfell fire did not happen in a vacuum... A majority of the Grenfell residents who died were people of color. Grenfell is inextricably linked with race. It is the elephant in the room. This disaster happened in a pocket of one of the smallest yet richest boroughs in London. Yet the com-munity affected was predominantly working class. That is the stark reality that cannot be ignored. The impact of race and poverty on this disaster this inquiry must not ignore.[84]

Thomas, too, drew a link with the killing of George Floyd, whose last words, "I can't breathe," were the same as many of those who died in the Grenfell Tower fire.[85]

83. Fatima Manji, "Grenfell Tower Relatives Call For Inquiry to Investigate Role of Racism in Fire Tragedy," *Channel 4*, June 11, 2020, https://www.channel4.com/news/grenfell-tower-relatives-call-for-inquiry-to-investigate-role-of-racism-in-fire-tragedy.

84. Joe Roberts, "'We Can't Breathe' Projected on Grenfell in Stark Reminder of Victim's Final 999 Calls," *Metro*, July 7, 2020, https://metro.co.uk/2020/07/07/cant-breathe-projected-grenfell-stark-reminder-victims-final-999-calls-12956452/?ito=cbshare.

85. Peter Apps (@PeteApps), twitter post, July 7, 2020, 10:16 a.m., https://twitter.com/PeteApps/status/1280430557306982400.

Chrono-Cartography of the October 17, 1961, Massacre of Algerians in Paris

Léopold Lambert

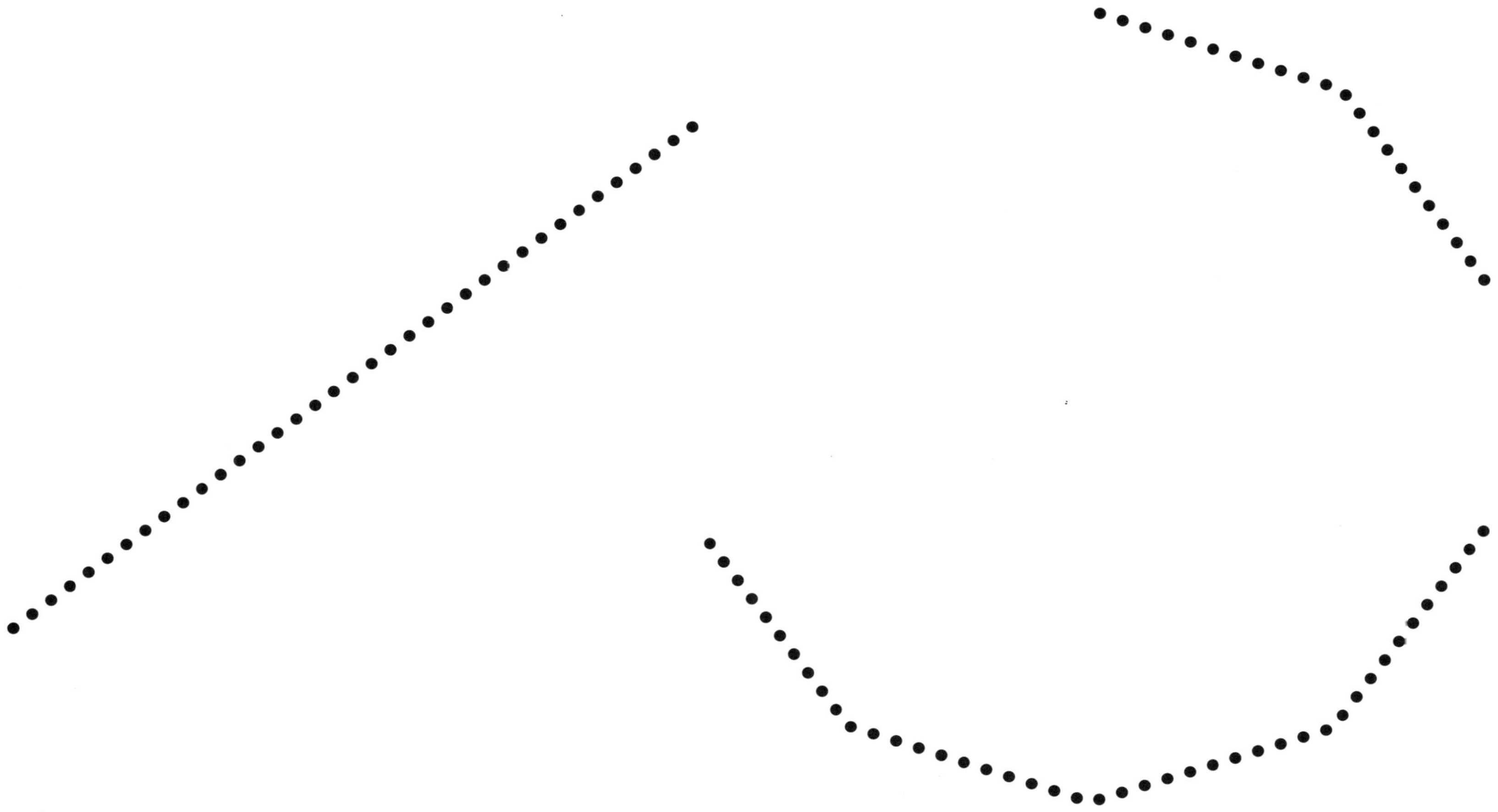

French colonialism ended in 1962 with the independence of Algeria. Or so goes the national myth of a postcolonial France, which nonetheless still flatters itself to have "a presence" across three oceans through its so-called "overseas territories." One piece of legislation illustrates how the counterrevolution led by France against the Algerian Revolution between 1954 and 1962 was the beginning of something much more than an end. The state of emergency, drafted, voted, and immediately applied in April 1955, at the beginning of the Algerian Revolution, reveals a geography and a history of the French colonial continuum. Declared three times during the Algerian Revolution (1955, 1958, 1961–1962), it was then applied in the 1980s in the three overseas colonies of Kanaky (i.e., New Caledonia), the Wallis and Futuna Polynesian archipelagos, and Tahiti-Nui (i.e., French Polynesia), and again in 2005 in the French *banlieues* (suburbs) against youth in revolt, the majority of whose parents and grandparents were colonial subjects in Africa and the Caribbean. The most recent state of emergency, from 2015 and 2017, applied to France and the overseas colonies and particularly targeted Muslim individuals and families. This targeting continues today through the 2017 law that made permanent the vast majority of measures allowed by the state of emergency (police searches, house arrests, mosque closures, perimeters of security, etc.). In March 2020, the French government drafted a new law in response to the global COVID-19 pandemic, entitled "state of sanitary emergency" in a deliberate link to the "regular" state of emergency already in place.

The history of the Algerian Revolution is therefore crucial for what it can teach us about today's structural racism in France. One particularly critical event in this history was the massive demonstration of Algerians organized by the Front de Libération Nationale (FLN) in the streets of Paris on October 17, 1961, which was met by the French police with murderous violence. It took about forty years for this massacre to be somewhat recognized as such, and its memorialization by the French authorities remains timid today. One thing is striking in the official acknowledgment as well as in the memorialization of this event every year: the idea that the massacre could have happened only in one very specific place at a very specific time.

According to the central narrative, the extremely violent scenes of French police officers throwing Algerians into the Seine in the center of Paris manifested the "hot-blooded" moment of suppression of massive demonstrations. What further research reveals, on the contrary, is that this massacre occurred in a multiplicity of spatialities and temporalities.

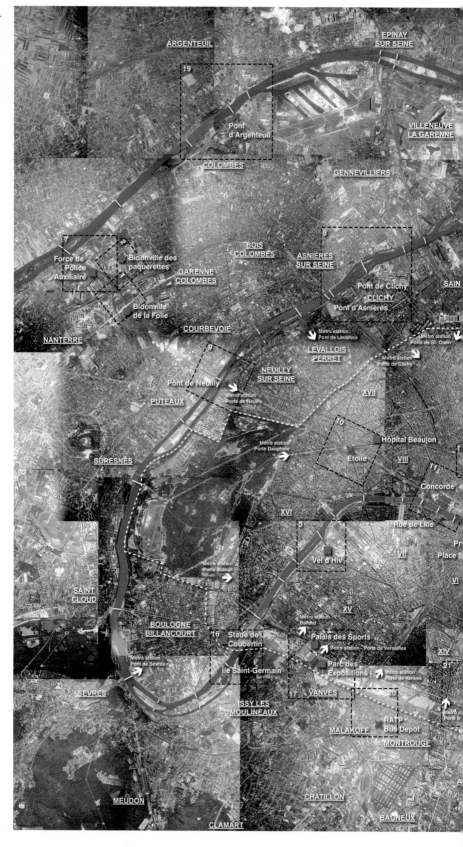

Map of the events on October 17, 1961, Paris. Each numbered square corresponds to one of a series of maps, some of which are included in this essay. The series of maps—using aerial imagery from the time—illustrates the many spatialities and temporalities of French police violence during the October 17, 1961, massacre in Paris. Courtesy of Léopold Lambert.

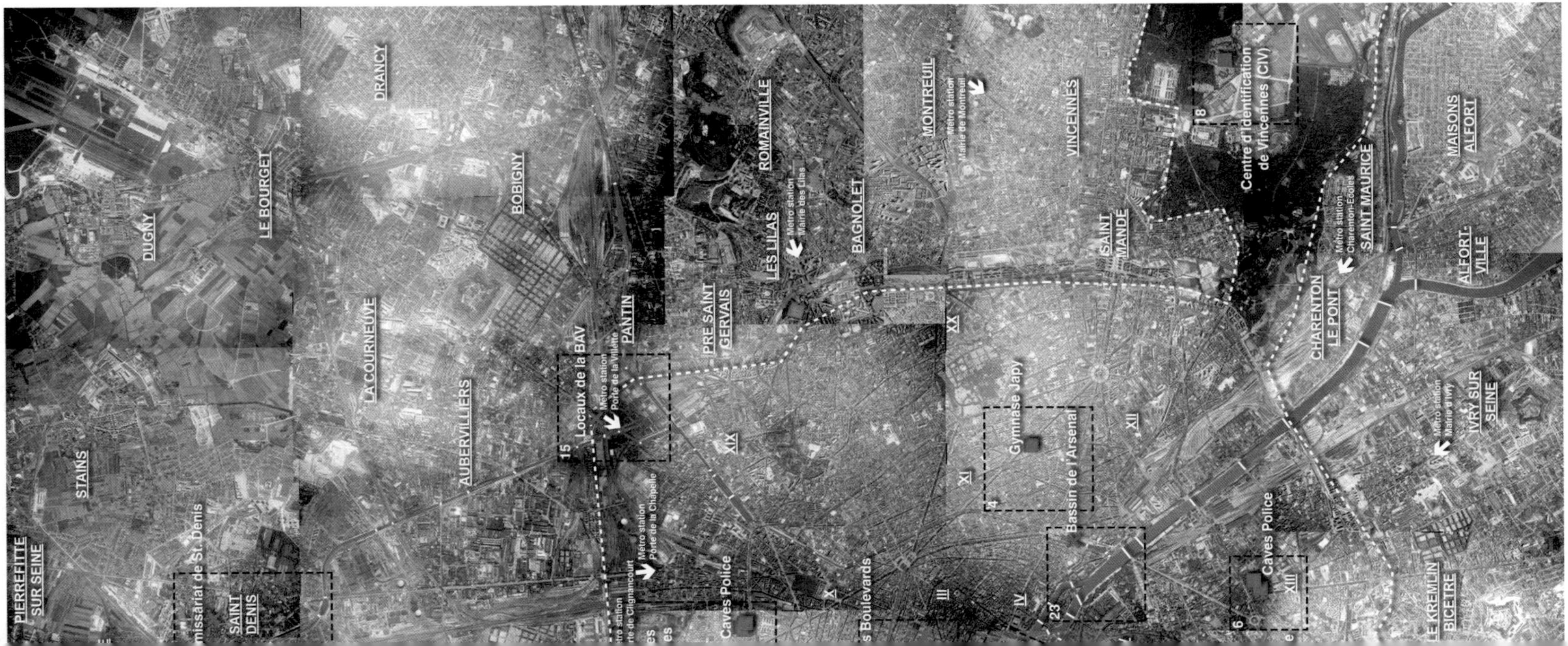

PIERREFITTE SUR SEINE

STAINS

DUGNY

LE BOURGET

missariat de St. Denis

SAINT DENIS

LA COURNEUVE

DRANCY

AUBERVILLIERS

BOBIGNY

15 Locaux de la BAV

Métro station Porte de la Villette

PANTIN

tro station rte de Clignancourt

Métro station Porte de la Chapelle

es

es

Caves Police

PRE SAINT GERVAIS

XIX

LES LILAS

ROMAINVILLE

Métro station Mairie des Lilas

X

BAGNOLET

s Boulevards

III

MONTREUIL

Métro station Mairie de Montreuil

XI

XX

4 Gymnase Japy

IV

Bassin de l'Arsenal

23

VINCENNES

XII

SAINT MANDÉ

6

18

Caves Police

Centre d'Identification de Vincennes (CIV)

XIII

e

CHARENTON LE PONT

Métro station Charenton-Écoles

SAINT MAURICE

LE KREMLIN BICETRE

Métro station Mairie d'Ivry

IVRY SUR SEINE

ALFORT-VILLE

MAISONS ALFORT

BIDONVILLE DES PAQUERETTES
Nanterre in 1961 is remarkable for the vision it offers of a paradigm transition when it comes to segregated housing. The remote "bidon-villes" are progressively evicted, destroyed, and replaced by high-density social housing in low-density urbanism. This new paradigm forms what still constitutes today a common form of housing for postcolonial residents in general, and Algerians in particular.

Map of Bidonville des Paquerettes, Paris, 1961. Courtesy of Léopold Lambert.

In order to understand this event, some historical context is necessary: In 1961 the revolution led by the FLN that aimed to decolonize Algeria was already seven years old.[1] Initiated in rural Algeria, the decolonial movement spread to the country's cities, as well as into large French cities, where a significant number of Algerians lived (about 350,000 in 1962). Although several administrative institutions dedicated specifically to North Africans residing and working in France had been created by this time by the French state, Algerians in France were not administratively considered colonial subjects and were entitled to virtually the same rights as any other French citizen, Algeria being considered a part of France. In reality, job and housing segregation was rampant, and the police, particularly in Paris, practiced racial profiling on a daily basis.[2]

1. For a detailed description of the way architecture was used as colonial counterrevolutionary weapon, see Samia Henni, *Architecture of the Counterrevolution: The French Army in Northern Algeria* (Zurich: gta Verlag, 2017).

2. See Clifford Rosenberg, *Policing Paris: The Origins of Modern Immigration Control Between the Wars* (Ithaca, NY: Cornell University Press, 2006), for an account of the 1920s and the 1930s, in particular.

The Brigade des Nord-Africains (BNA), which explicitly targeted North Africans and had provided auxiliary officers to the
Gestapo during the occupation by Nazi Germany (1940–1944),
was dissolved in 1945, but in 1953, a new branch of the Paris
police was created according to the same logic: the Brigade
des Agressions et Violences (BAV).[3] Racial profiling as a colonial and counterinsurrection tactic was never made more
explicit than when, on October 5, 1961, a curfew solely for
Algerians was declared by the Seine Préfecture de Police, in
the Paris metropolitan area.

One particular character is central not only to the October 17,
1961, massacre but more generally to the French state's history
of violence from the 1940s to the 1980s: Maurice Papon. During
the Nazi occupation of France, Papon was secretary general
of the prefecture in Bordeaux and, as such, he facilitated the
deportation of 1,600 Jews from the South of France to the camp
of Drancy (in a Paris *banlieue*), before they were eventually
deported to and murdered in Auschwitz. Only in 1998 was
he tried for his participation
in the Holocaust, and after
France's liberation in 1945,
Papon was given numerous
executive responsibilities, all
connected to French colonialism and counterinsurgency.
In fact, in the postwar years,
he was appointed to increasingly important positions in
Morocco and in Algeria. In
1956, for example, he was
named Inspecteur Général de
l'Administration en Mission
Extraordinaire (IGAME) to
lead the counterinsurrection
against decolonial move-
ments in the northeastern
part of Algeria. In 1956 and
1957, records attest to the
killing of 18,316 so-called
"rebels" by the French colonial police and army, as well
as to 117,000 people being
"regrouped" into camps.[4]

One of Nanterre's *bidonvilles* in Jacques
Panijel's film *Octobre à Paris* (1962). Courtesy
of Les Films de l'Atalante.

●   3.   See the works of authors Mathieu Rigouste and Emmanuel Blanchard for a
more detailed genealogy.
● 4.   See Fabien Sacriste's text "Aurès, Algeria: Regroupement Camps During
the Algerian War for Independence," in "Architecture and Colonialism,"
Funambulist 10 (March–April 2017: 14–17).

CONCORDE
Police officers filter, search, arrest, and beat Algerians directly on the subway platforms. A journalist succeeds in taking a few pictures of the carnage.

Rue Royale

1st ARRONDISSEMENT

Rue de Rivoli

Métro station - Concorde

Jardin des Tuilleries

Quai d'Orsay

RUE DE LILLE
Algerians fleeing from the Concorde subway station and the massacre near the Préfecture de Police (see frame 12) are held back by the police who beat them in the street.

Boulevard Saint-Germain

Rue de Lille

7th ARRONDISSEMENT

Map of Concorde and Rue de Lille, Paris, 1963. Courtesy of Léopold Lambert.

In 1958 the FLN in Paris was particularly active in its clandestine political organizing, raising and transferring funds—with the occasional help of French "suitcase carriers"—and regularly assassinating its opponents: Algerians they considered "traitors" and French police officers. On March 13, 1958, police officers demonstrated in front of the French Parliament to demand more latitude and immunity in their jobs; the next day, Papon was named prefect of the Seine and was charged with annihilating the FLN in the Paris metropolitan area, taking advantage of his previous colonial training in counter-insurrectional tactics. On August 28, 1958, Papon organized massive roundups of Algerians, detaining 5,000—including at the infamous indoor velodrome, the Vel d'Hiv, where, on July 17, 1942, 12,884 Jews had been rounded up before being deported to Auschwitz. In January 1959, Papon created the Centre d'Identification de Vincennes (CIV), where Algerians could be legally put under house arrest without trial. In March 1961, he created a new branch of the police under his direct orders: the Force de Police Auxiliaire, composed of *harkis*

(Algerian volunteers in the French police and army in France and Algeria). These officers were given the widest latitude in their suppression of the FLN, and any Algerians suspected of having ties with the decolonial organization—and, given that the FLN was known for intimidating recalcitrant Algerians into paying the revolutionary tax, this meant almost all Algerians—were arbitrarily arrested and tortured in police stations and nearby basements. Some of those tortured were thrown into the Seine months before the October 17, 1961, massacre now associated with this atrocious practice.

As mentioned above, one particular measure taken by Papon was the establishment of a curfew specific to Algerians, which began on October 5, 1961. This measure motivated the FLN in France to organize massive demonstrations in Paris on October 17. All Algerian men were asked to join the demonstrations unarmed—any person found with even a knife risked being severely punished by the FLN—in the center of Paris that evening in order to protest the curfew and French colonialism more generally. Some women joined the march, but most of them formed their own protest on October 20 that also suffered severe repression. What the maps included here attempt to demonstrate is the difficulty for Algerians living and working in Paris's *banlieues* to access the center of the city in order to join these demonstrations—and here a broader point can be made about the segregation in Paris still operative today. Bridges and subway stations were particular sites of violence during the massacre, as their narrowness allowed for tight and systematic control by the police.

The police systematically arrested and beat protesters on the subway platforms in the Concorde metro station—providing the occasion for tragically ironic photographs, as "concorde" translates to "harmony." Courtesy of La Contemporaine.

PRÉFECTURE DE POLICE
Maurice Papon is giving his orders from the command room. The technological level of its monitoring is high enough to understand that everything that is happening that night is either directly ordered or tolerated by the Prefect. At 10pm, the large courtyard of the Prefecture is full of arrested Algerians being beaten by officers. The wounded are dragged into a police truck to be "brought to the hospital." The Hôtel Dieu hospital, across the street however only receives 29 wounded that night. The others are instead thrown into the river and killed.

CHATELET
Many of the Algerians arrested across Paris are first gathered at Chatelet before being transferred to the various detention facilities. Arrestees are systematically beaten.

4th ARRONDISSEMENT

Boulevard de Sébastopol

Rue de Rivoli

Hôtel de Ville

Pont Neuf

Pont au Change

Pont Notre Dame

Pont d'Arcole

QUARTIER SAINT-SÉVERIN
This neighborhood counts many hotels where Algerian workers live. Between 1958 and 1962, they are regularly raided.

Hôpital Hôtel Dieu

Boulevard du Palais

PLACE SAINT-MICHEL
The front of the left-bank demonstration towards the Préfecture de Police is blocked by police officers. Many Algerians are arrested and systematically beaten. Others are thrown over the bridge into the river.

Quai Saint-Michel

Notre Dame

6th ARRONDISSEMENT

12

Map of the Préfecture de Police, Paris, 1963. Courtesy of Léopold Lambert.

Two of the few photographs taken the night of the massacre. Top photograph by Elie Kagan. Courtesy of AFP. Bottom photograph by Daniele Darolle. Courtesy of Getty Images.

On many bridges, Algerians were arrested, beaten with batons, and even sometimes shot and thrown into the Seine. Although it has not been proven that Papon gave direct orders for the massacre, he was present in the command room of the Préfecture de Police, only meters away from the bloodbath of Saint-Michel, and the lack of any order to prevent the violence and killings, as well as the false rumors on police radio that some officers had been killed by Algerians, effectively leaves him the commander responsible for the massacre—a crime for which he was never prosecuted.

This systematic dimension of the crime can be found when one looks beyond the supposedly "hot-blooded," murderous suppression of the demonstrations. Later that night and in the following days, systematic beatings and even killings continued in improvised detention centers of various sizes—the largest of which were the indoor Stade de Coubertin (1,800 detained), the Parc des Expositions (6,600 detained), and the CIV itself (860 detained)—at the police-regulated bridges at the gates of Paris, and at the FLN's demonstrations for Algerian women and children on October 20.

GRAND REX
4,500 people march peacefully on the Grands Boulevards as part of the right-bank demonstration between République and Opéra. At 9:47pm, the police fire on the Algerian crowd at the level of the popular theater, Le Grand Rex. Several Algerians are killed.

RUE RÉAUMUR
The second right-bank demonstration from Opera to Republique counts less demonstrators for reasons explained in frame 14.

10th ARRONDISSEMENT

2nd ARRONDISSEMENT

1st ARRONDISSEMENT

Grands Boulevards

Boulevard de Sébastopol

Rue Réaumur

Rue de Turbigo

Les Halles

Map of the Grands Boulevards, Paris, 1964. Courtesy of Léopold Lambert.

13

The number of Algerians killed or injured during this dreadful week in October 1961 remains unclear, in particular because of the way the police archives have been manipulated to reflect a much lower number of casualties—some people who had been killed were also on the list of people deported to Algeria—but it is estimated that between 200 and 300 Algerians were detained and/or shot to death and that 70 to 84 additional people were killed after having been thrown into the Seine. These deaths took years to be acknowledged, in contrast to the nine victims of the February 8, 1962, massacre, who were killed by Papon's police at the Charonne subway station during large demonstrations of French people against the Organisation de l'Armée Secrète (OAS) and the suppression of Algerians. These nine French people were members of the main workers' union, the Confédération Générale du Travail (CGT), and of the Communist Party, and they were commemorated by 500,000 people in the streets of Paris four days later, a sharp contrast to the absence of significant protests following the massacre of the Algerians.

Photograph of the demonstration on the right bank. Courtesy of Jacques Boissay/Roger Viollet.

Finally, in 2001, a plaque was arranged in Saint-Michel to commemorate the "memory of the numerous Algerians killed in the bloody suppression of the peaceful demonstration of October 17, 1961." As is often the case when it comes to the memorialization of colonial crimes in France, those responsible are not directly cited, making it a crime with no criminals. As explained at the beginning of this essay, such a narrative also significantly reduces the spatial and temporal scope of the massacre itself. In case the plaque was still too explicit, Paris mayor Bertrand Delanoë declared to the press: "This plaque is not meant to be against anyone." For these reasons, one might give precedence to another official plaque set up in Saint-Denis (a Paris *banlieue*) in 2007:

> On October 17, 1961, during the Algerian War, thirty thousand Algerian men and women of the Paris region demonstrated against the curfew that was imposed on them. This movement was brutally suppressed on the order of the Prefect of Paris. Demonstrators were killed by bullets, hundreds of men and women were thrown into the Seine River, and thousands were beaten and imprisoned. Dead bodies were found in the Canal Saint-Denis. Against racism and forgetting, for democracy and human rights, this plaque has been inaugurated by Mayor of Saint-Denis Didier Paillard on March 21, 2007.

14

OPÉRA

The FLN in France planned two demonstrations for the right-bank. For Algerians living in the East and North-East banlieues, from République to Opéra, and another, for Algerians living in the North and North-West banlieues following the opposite path on a parallel street. This second demonstration is less succesful as many Algerians arriving at Opéra are arrested by the police as soon as they exit the subway station.

9th ARRONDISSEMENT

Rue Saint-Lazare
Rue de Châteaudun
Rue Lafayette
Boulevard Haussmann
Opéra
Boulevard des Italiens
Démonstration path
Métro station - Opéra
2nd ARRONDISSEMENT
Démonstration path

Map of Opéra, Paris, 1956. Courtesy of Léopold Lambert.

Photograph of the demonstration on the right bank. Courtesy of Getty Images.

Nevertheless, here again, the broader context of colonialism remains unspoken, illustrating once more that France has never fully engaged with the structurally racist and colonial violence of its past—let alone of its present, which operates in direct continuity with this violence.

More than 27 percent of France's current population was alive in 1961, and many actors in the October 17 massacre, both Algerian demonstrators and French police officers, still carry its memory—its traumatic wounds (for the former) and its immunity to responsibility (for the latter). History often forgets to mention the way perpetrators and victims have to live together in societies indifferent to (if not in denial of) the violence of their relationship. In this regard, the genealogy of this violence is perpetuated not solely through familial generations but also through the racialization of a French society ruled and controlled by an overwhelmingly white political class and police— the Brigade Anti-Criminalité (BAC), created in 1971 following the colonial logics of the BNA and the BAV, and particularly

AÉROPORT D'ORLY
Starting Oct. 19, 400 arrested Algerians are deported to the South of Algeria in an engineered televised spectacle. 1,100 other Algerians will be deported this way. Some names on the lists of deportees are however suspected to dissimulate their actual death in the police hands.

WISSOUS

ORLY

PARAY-VIEILLE-POSTE

Map of Parc des Expositions and Palais des Sports, Paris, 1960. Courtesy of Léopold Lambert.

active in the *banlieues*, is the most obvious example—and, at the other end of the spectrum, racialized subjects whose lives are often territorially, socially, and economically segregated from their more privileged counterparts. In Paris, a city that has not changed much structurally since the second part of the nineteenth century, the weaponized spatiality shown on the maps here remains fully operative today.

Arrested Algerians deported to Algeria in front of journalists. Top photograph courtesy of Keystone France/Getty Images. Bottom photograph courtesy of AGIP/Bridgeman Images.

"We are the descendants of the Algerians you have not drowned." Graffiti by anticolonial activists for the 2019 anniversary of the October 17, 1961, massacre. Courtesy of Léopold Lambert.

References used in the making of the maps: Amiri, Linda. *La bataille de France*. Paris: Laffont, 2004; Einaudi, Jean-Luc. *La bataille de Paris*. Paris: Seuil, 1991. In 1999, Einaudi was sued by Papon for defamation. After presenting his extensive research to the court, Einaudi won his case; Maffre, Laurent and Monique Hervo. *Demain, Demain*. Paris: Actes Sud BD, 2012; Panijel, Jacques, dir., *Octobre à Paris*. Film, 1962; Rigouste, Mathieu, "The Colonial Genealogy of the French Police." In "Police," *Funambulist* 8 (November–December 2016): 42–49.

15 Years after 2005: Anticolonial Reflections on the Concept of "Riots" in the French Context

Dariouche Tehrani

0

Fifteen years ago, on October 27, 2005, Zyed Benna and Bouna Traoré, two young Arab and Black (respectively) inhabitants of an immigrant neighborhood called Les Bosquets, in the *banlieue* Clichy-sous-Bois, near Paris, were killed by the police during a pursuit following a racial profiling.[1] The news spread quickly through the neighborhood, and inhabitants confronted the police. The feeling of revolt then spread through the entire country—especially through other *banlieues*—and intense clashes between the police and inhabitants arose repeatedly over the next month. This popular resistance of *banlieue* dwellers against the racist French state and its armed forces has come to be remembered as the "2005 riots." While this episode could have been called a revolt, a resistance, a rebellion, an uprising, or even a war of liberation, the term that has maintained itself as the exclusive and indelible name of this and similar episodes is "riot."

Why this name? More profoundly, what does this language perform in terms of the political perception of the event? What structures of thought, explicit or very much implicit, make the concept of "riot" appealing to those who use it to name popular resistance, be they journalists, politicians, simple citizens, or—above all, and as far as I will be concerned here—police and leftist activists or theorists. In a word, then, the goal here is to question the descriptive neutrality of the concept of "riots" and to show how, far from being neutral, the concept of "riots" is a tool to neutralize the event of revolt. Such a reflection, in the context of the 2005 revolts and, more generally, of the history of popular resistance in French *banlieues*, is closely related to what has already been denounced by *banlieue* activists as early as the 1970s as "colonial management"—that is, what happens in the *banlieues* today and has been happening since the 1950s is an internal process of colonization within the imperial metropole against the formerly colonized subjects of the French Empire and their descendants. It is from this anti-colonial perspective that it becomes clear that the events of 2005 are best described as "revolts," not "riots."

In both theoretical debates and political circles, most of the discussions around "riots" tend to focus on the question of whether they are political. The answers given then offer a value judgment on the event at hand and its participants. The concept of "the political" is therefore held as the key to legitimacy. Analyzing the discourse of anti-"riot" and

1. While they were being chased by the police, who wanted to check their identities, Zyed Benna and Bouna Traoré sought shelter in a power plant and were electrocuted. Although journalists and police officials called their deaths an "accident" to absolve the police, *banlieue* inhabitants and anti-racist activists denounced their deaths as a police killing because the manhunt that led to their deaths was a result of racial profiling. I will therefore write about their deaths as people speak about the incident, as a police killing and not an accident, in order to avoid reproducing the legal/journalistic version of events. I wish to speak from the situated perspective of the common imaginary of people who face police violence.

DARIOUCHE TEHRANI

pro-"riot" actors around the 2005 events and other occasions allows us to see how they disagree, but, more importantly, the analysis can also show how they might share a colonial perspective on the *banlieues* and its inhabitants.

"Riots" as Anti-Politics: Politicization and the Civilizing Mission

On the one hand, opponents argue that "riots" are not political. They characterize "riots" as spontaneous, misled forms of action and their participants as impulsive, irrational, "feral," "scum"—or even *"racaille,"* in the words of former French president Nicolas Sarkozy. But this portrayal (and the value judgments it implies) is made only to enable a program: for the necessary "politicization" of these so-called "rioters." This "politicization" is deemed necessary by the Right and the institutional Left, but one might even hear anarchists speak in these terms.

In the context of revolts in the French *banlieues*, the idea of "politicizing" "rioters" is deeply structured by racism. Indeed, "politicization" in this context is a code word for "civilization." The "rioters," in order to be legitimate political actors, must be integrated into "civil society." As the term "civil society" already implies, this necessitates their being civilized—that is, converted to the mainstream, predominantly white, Christian-centric conception of what legitimate politics is, be it party politics or revolutionary politics. In other words, believers in the necessary "politicization" of "rioters"—whatever their affiliation on the political spectrum might be—are agents of French imperialism and its "civilizing" mission. In the French context, being political means being assimilated into the legitimated French political society.

From the point of view of the *banlieue*, there is no real difference between, on the one hand, a blatantly racist right-winger arguing that "rioters" are terrorists who need to be deradicalized and recivilized (we should not forget, in the context of anti-Muslim racism, that some of these "terrorists" are or are perceived as Muslims) and, on the other hand, anarchists who describe themselves as anti-fascist and anti-racist but argue that "rioters" are blindly violent and need to be taught "politics." It is in this context of anti-riot ideology that, after the 2005 revolts, both the Right and the institutional Left called for more security in the *banlieues*, deployed thousands of police officers and unanimously declared a state of emergency—an act under French law that was created in and for its colonies.[2]

After 2005 efforts were made by the state precisely to "politicize" *banlieue* inhabitants: calling on them to vote and to

2. For more on the history of the state of emergency in France, see Léopold Lambert's essay "Chrono-Cartography of the October 17, 1961, Massacre of Algerians in Paris" on pages 235–250 in this volume.

cease their chronic abstention, recruiting local associations to promote integration, creating new community organizations, and selecting more so-called diverse (i.e., Black or Arab, and more often women than men) ministers and candidates for local elections and city councils. In fact, the period after the 2005 revolts witnessed a boom in community associations in the *banlieues*. These associations were funded by the government and supported by municipalities in order to offer pre-structured frameworks for inhabitants to channel their frustrations, to become more "rational" and hence more "civilized."

The associations themselves range from simple entertainment clubs to more directly political collectives, such as NGOs that oppose racial profiling or seek civic education for the youth. These associations are led by inhabitants of the *banlieues*, but their recruitment follows the classic paths of clientelism and vote-securing strategies—techniques that have historically been developed by the institutional Left and particularly by municipalities managed by the French Communist Party and the Parti Socialiste (a center-left liberal party). The idea is to integrate *banlieue* inhabitants into the realm of legitimate politics, insisting that if they want to be heard, they need to speak the same political language as the colonial state. In this situation, the state kidnaps and appropriates the spirit of the revolt and mutates it into controlled structures and behaviors.

This technique was elaborated in 1983 when, after a series of racist and security-motivated murders in the *banlieues*, a national march that crossed France from south to north and gathered thousands of people—the March for Equality and Against Racism—was created. While the march was organized autonomously by *banlieue* inhabitants, the then center-left government led by the Parti Socialiste created a parallel organization, SOS Racism, immediately after the march to signal its recognition of racism as a problem and to publicize the fight against it. However, SOS Racism's anti-racism excluded questions of state racism, class, access to education, employment, anti-Muslim racism, anti-Zionism, et cetera. SOS Racism, which still exists, was part of a strategy of containment in the *banlieues*, but this containment took the form of "politicization." The association aimed to convert people from the *banlieue* to a form of state-sanctioned anti-racism while at the same time the state was criminalizing all other forms of autonomous resistance, whether it was violent or not.

Attempts to politicize the *banlieues* have also pushed some institutional actors to face their own limits. In 2010, the radical-leftist New Anticapitalist Party tried to recruit people from the *banlieues* into local political office to lure more *banlieue* voters. In one region, it chose a woman who happens to wear a hijab to lead the list. After a huge media controversy led by defenders of anti-Muslim racism, the party decided to remove the woman from the ballot, effectively submitting to the anti-Muslim, racist consensus that has been in place in France since early colonial times. Here, we see how racism structures even the most leftist parties. But more importantly, we can see how the civic religion of secularism pushes politics in France to be defined by racist standards of "civilization." Hence, *hijabi* women become a symbol of supposed non-civilization and as such are not accepted as agents of party politics because their politicization would oppose the colonial/Christian-centric definition of Western civilization. "Politicization" therefore is an instance of "civilization" that either converts its actors into "good citizens" or excludes those who are perceived as being incapable of civilization.

Besides the allocation of state budget to police and politicization, the state civilization project also occurs by means of the spatial reorganization of the *banlieues*. Right before the 2005 revolts, in 2004, the French state launched the National Agency for Urban Renovation (Agence Nationale pour la Rénovation Urbaine, or ANRU), aiming to radically restructure housing in the *banlieues* to create "social diversity." In practice, this meant the widespread demolition of housing estates and, consequently, a massive forced displacement of the *banlieue* population. As Stefan Kipfer has shown, the ideology and techniques of "urban renovation" in France were pioneered by colonial administrators on the basis of their experience in colonial counterinsurgency strategies, making urban renovation itself a neocolonial policy.[3] The reorganization of space is vital to its social and military control, a point that the French state has learned through its colonial experience. For some *banlieue* inhabitants, the demolition of their homes, especially the sound of demolition, recalled memories of the Algerian War. Hence, housing policies in the *banlieues* might be considered as both the background and the effect of the 2005 revolts. Inhabitants were reacting to the violence of urban renovation, and urban renovation was one of the tools that the state used to fight the revolt.

More than a mechanical reaction to the killing of Bouna Traoré and Zyed Benna, the 2005 revolts therefore resisted the deep structure of "colonial management" in the *banlieues*, a structure that supported police violence, racism, class domination, urbanism, and every aspect of daily life. The 2005 revolts, then, are one instance of anticolonial resistance that has been going on in the French metropole for decades.

In 2008 Nicolas Sarkozy, who had been minister of the interior (effectively head of the police forces) in 2005 and was now

3. Stefan Kipfer, "Neocolonial Urbanism?: *La Rénovation Urbaine* in Paris," *Antipode* 48, no. 3 (2016): 614.

president, launched the "Grand Paris" plan, an investment project that aimed to organize Paris as a modern, dynamic, investment-friendly metropolis. The *banlieue* would be better integrated into Paris as a form of spatial desegregation. The goal was to "open" the *banlieue* through new subway lines, to decentralize power and move some government institutions into the *banlieue*, to push Parisians to live in the peripheries to create racial and social diversity, et cetera. This project was a way to "civilize" the *banlieue* through space: opening, diversifying, and integrating this dark, anarchic, closed space where crime (supposedly) proliferates. But this civilizing move also went hand in hand with militarization. In fact, the police play an active role in the process of redesigning the *banlieues*: public space and roads are designed to enable more control and easy intervention by the police, fences and surveillance cameras are installed in public and semipublic spaces, and there is increased police presence—and in the case of state of emergency, military presence.[4] And as is well known, the new housing aimed at middle-class white Parisians is a form of gentrification that also goes hand in hand with the militarization of space.

When we look at the companies that have been commissioned to build the new housing estates, the neocolonial politics behind the Grand Paris project become even more apparent. One of them is Bouygues, a telecommunications company that now is also a leading player in the construction market. Bouygues is also a main contractor for prison building and management in the new public-private system. Bouygues is "civilizing" the *banlieue* by "opening" it to white middle-class families while managing the prison-industrial complex where the criminalized *banlieue* inhabitants will be jailed and exploited.[5] This is a perfect example of how the state, with its capitalist allies, is leading a colonial counterinsurgency war against *banlieue* inhabitants.

At the same time, the minister of urban development and the minister of youth and sports were spending a lot of money to "politicize" *banlieue* inhabitants through the aforementioned

- 4. According to the Decree n°2007-1177 of the French Urbanism Code, the police are given an active role of advising in projects of urban renovation. Any urban project is dependent on a "security study" to be carried out by the police. In practice, this means the presence of police agents in local councils for urban renovation planning.
- 5. For further information, see the company's website, www.bouygues-construction.com. On Bouygues and the prison-industrial complex, see http://www.francetvinfo.fr/economie/bouygues-va-construire-et-gerer-trois-prisons_1613589.html. On the company and its link to urban renovation, notably in the Grand Paris project, see http://www.bouygues-construction.com/blog/en/en-direct-des-chantiers/grand-paris-express-ca-creuse-bouygues-travaux-publics. Bouygues is also a sponsor of "Commit to neighborhoods," an event organized by ANRU to praise the "social innovation" that represents urban renovation; see www.anru.fr/fre/Actualites/Evenements/Troisieme-edition-du-Concours-S-engager-pour-les-quartiers.

community programs and subsidies to politically moderate local associations, which encourage integration into French political society and assimilation to the colonial mechanisms structuring French politics. Politicization and militarization then are complementary; they are both ways to "civilize."

Riot Idolatry: Savagery and the Racialization
of Political Violence
At the other end of the political spectrum are sympathizers with "rioters." The sympathizer argues that "riots" are the epitome of the political. We can observe here an apology for "riots," or some kind of fascination and mythologization. The figure of the rioter is usually linked to the "dangerous classes," which are incarnated by different groups at different times. Historically, it was peasants sabotaging their crops to threaten the landlord; the figure then became the urban proletariat—the Communard of 1871 building barricades in Paris, for example. Nowadays, the figure of the rioter is incarnated by the *banlieusard*, the formerly colonized subject of empire living in racially segregated neighborhoods. This figure of the *banlieusard* as rioter cannot be separated from racist structures of thought, given our colonial context. While the *banlieusard*-as-rioter is sanctified by pro-"riot" actors, this sanctification does not escape logics of racialization. In some cases, if *banlieusards* are valued, it is because of their supposed savagery—a stereotype that obviously originates in racism.

For example, the protests in France in 2016–2017 against neoliberal labor laws saw the emergence of new techniques of resistance; people met and shared a certain spirit of autonomy, which gave birth to cultural creation. Lots of different slogans were written on public walls as a form of radical urban poetry. One of them read, "Agir en primitif, prévoir en stratège" ("Act as a primitive, plan as a strategist"). This phrase has become one of the mottoes of the autonomous movement and, indeed, is a verse by René Char, a French poet who fought against the Nazis (although most people ignore this fact). Regardless, the centrality of the figure of "the primitive" here is striking, especially as it is opposed, although in a complementary way, with that of the "strategist." In this very moment of political innovation, the movement feels itself obligated to appeal to the traditional ethnological, colonial, and racist figure of the primitive. In our colonial context, and given the genealogy of the figure of the primitive, the primitive *is* the *banlieue* rioter. The primitive as a figure is associated with pure feeling, fearlessness, action, simplicity, et cetera—or, rather, everything that the Modern Man thinks he lacks. Through a series of binary associations, one cannot but think of the opposition between rational and irrational, brute force and fine intellect, riot and politics, or, for us, *banlieue* and the Left. Therefore, in this apology for "riots" and "rioters," we find a mirror of the racism of conservatives. Not a paternalistic racism (as in the case of the institutional Left) but a more subtle process of radical exoticization of the *banlieusard*-as-rioter. The *banlieusard*-as-rioter is a bestial body, to be imitated for its savagery and fearlessness. Here, the racist colonial imaginary is inverted, and savagery is valued to maintain and extend colonial structures of thought. While conservatives and the institutional Left conceive of *banlieusards* as primitives to be civilized, the far Left tends to portray *banlieusards* as savages to be maintained in their savagery for political benefit.

This representation of the savage is materialized in situations of encounter between leftist circles and people from the *banlieue*. In February 2017, at the peak of leftist mobilization against the labor law, Théo Luhaka, a twenty-two-year-old Black inhabitant of the *banlieue* Aulnay-sous-Bois, was raped by police officers during his arrest. The sexual nature of the attack elicited a sense of moral outrage that made it more important in some ways than other cases of police violence, like the murder of Adama Traoré, a young Black man killed by police the year before and whose death inspired important mobilizations. Luhaka's rape and the moral outrage that followed, added to the fact that the rape happened during the peak of the anti-labor law movement, set the stage for an encounter between leftist protesters fighting the labor laws and *banlieue* inhabitants fighting the colonial management of their lives in their own neighborhoods. There is a popular idea that revolution in France will happen when these two forces are able to cross the class, racial, religious, and existential borders separating them. In terms of political theology, this meeting between the two forces was seen as some kind of redemptive end-time.

This meeting indeed happened. After the rape, more than three thousand people, from both leftist circles and the *banlieues*, gathered near the courthouse of Bobigny, a city near Aulnay-sous-Bois. The presence of hundreds of police officers wearing full riot gear exacerbated tensions, and leftist activists and *banlieue* inhabitants necessarily cooperated to fight the police. Remembered as the Battle of Bobigny, this episode came, in the leftist mind, to materialize the myth of the final meeting between the two forces. However, this meeting brings us back to the motto "Act as a primitive, plan as a strategist," and the racialization of political violence. While in the political imaginary, "primitive" and "strategist" represent two parts of the same person—the perfect revolutionary—in this particular situation, each part in this duality is assigned to one of the two groups. As we can imagine, the primitive force is assigned to *banlieue* dwellers, and the strategist part is given to the leftists. I remember going to Bobigny for another gathering against police violence later that year after a leftist protest in Paris. A few people from the autonomous front block came too. Once there, they declared, "If the others from the block"—that is, the "front block"—"are not here, we're not staying. Last time was great because the block was here, if it isn't then it's all disorganized and useless." And then they spent a few minutes explaining how *banlieue* rioters were pure force that needed to be channeled and driven by "the block," by which they meant by themselves, four white men from Paris, four self-proclaimed "strategists."

A quick detour through history shows the colonial origin of such a conception of politics and war. Here, the *banlieusard*-as-rioter is the contemporary equivalent of the *tirailleur sénégalais*, a special company of the French imperial army made up of people from Senegal and other colonies in sub-Saharan Africa. This force was nicknamed the La Force Noire by General Charles Mangin, who sent them to the forefront of each battle because their Black skin was supposed to frighten the Nazi enemy before the skilled white soldiers came to do the "real job." The similarity between the two cases is striking. One should also not forget that after World War II, the *tirailleurs sénégalais* who survived were often killed in battle against French officers themselves, or at best were left unpaid and were never recognized as participants in the victory of the so-called anti-Nazi "Free France" that continued to colonize their land and dehumanize them—a point that might push us to be careful about the ways in which we imagine the "sacred meeting" between certain leftists and people from the *banlieues* in the future.

The concept of "riot," then, is set in a political framework in which the colonized can be considered an agent in one of two equally racist ways: either to be "politicized"—that is, "civilized" and assimilated—or to be mystified as a primitive savage. In either case, the *banlieusard*, as a figure out of *The Wretched of the Earth* in contemporary metropolitan France, is seen as a member of some kind of *lumpenproletariat*, an abstract surplus population deprived of any political history, memory, specific tradition of struggle, or autonomy, a person who should either be civilized through politics or be used as an avant-garde army (i.e., cannon fodder) in "riots."

In more political terms, and even in terms of strategy, the structure of thought that uses "riots" as a central concept hides an event-driven conception of the political that considers struggle an accumulation of punctual confrontations rather than a continuity of spirit, tradition, and practices of struggle. Mogniss Abdallah, a *banlieue* activist working on the ground since the 1970s, perfectly sums up this point when he recalls the critique of leftist attitudes toward the *banlieue* formulated by the Arab Workers Movement (Mouvement des Travailleurs Arabes, or MTA):

Spectacular but ephemeral apparitions in the media, "short-term work of political agitation without long-term view," analyses that are overdetermined by the incantatory denunciation of "systematic racist policies" without giving credit to the complex reality as it is lived by "the masses" in the everyday.[6]

Political Violence Beyond the Concept of "Riots"

Doing justice to popular mobilizations in French *banlieues*, then, requires decentering the event of spectacular confrontation and ceasing the use of the term "riot" as a central analytical tool. Instead, the struggle in the *banlieues* should be approached from a long-term perspective anchored in the long history of anticolonial struggle within the French Empire. We need to reinsert the 2005 events—as well as every other moment of intense and massive anticolonial mobilization—in a narrative that stretches back to anticolonial resistance in French and other Western colonies, to the great anticolonial mobilization in the shantytowns of Nanterre and other metropolitan French cities during the Algerian Revolution, and to later movements of resistance in the *banlieues*. There is a tradition of struggle, a spirit and practice of resistance that, often implicitly, shapes any contemporary movement of so-called "post"-colonial descendants of colonized subjects of the French Empire. It is precisely this long history of struggle that is erased by the event-driven analysis implied by common use of the concept of "riots" in many contemporary discussions of protest in the *banlieues*.

These anticolonial reflections on revolts should not be reduced to the struggle of immigrants and their descendants. The very same structures reemerged concerning the Gilets Jaunes (Yellow Vests) movement, the most intense revolt in France since 2005. Indeed, one should never forget that in a colonial context, class cannot be understood outside of race—that class is always already racialized in one way or another.[7] Gilets Jaunes were depicted as "dangerous classes," and in a similar way to rebel *banlieue* inhabitants, they were also animalized as savage rioters by the state and the media. They were racialized too, but as white trash, marking the return of the medieval figure of the peasant rioter. In the same way, institutional parties tried to kidnap their revolt through "politicization." The racialization of their political violence was accompanied by their characterization as anti-Semitic, sexist homophobes—and as racists. One should also remark that

6. Mogniss H. Abdallah, *Rengainez on arrive! Chroniques des luttes contre les crimes racistes ou sécuritaires, contre la hagra policière et judiciaire des années 1970 à aujourd'hui* (Paris: Libertalia, 2012), 41. Translation by the author.

7. For more on this, see Joshua Clover's essay "Ideologies of Riot and Strike" on pages 83–96 in this volume.

aside from the leftists, many anti-racist, pseudo-anticolonial activists refused at first to take part in the movement, giving the very same arguments offered by the state and the media—despite the fact that they should have been the very first to understand the counterrevolutionary process of racialization of political violence and the dehumanization of its actors that were at play here.

Thinking of "riots" in anticolonial terms pushes us to radically rethink political violence outside colonial and racist structures of thought. It is a necessary step to develop concrete tools of self-defense and ways to organize outside and against the realm of state categories, to oppose the counterinsurgency strategies of those who mislabel revolts as "riots" precisely in order to make them stop.

Cities of Dissent

Asef Bayat

Revolutions are not just about extraordinary rebels, astute leaders, or strategic visions, however indispensable they may be. Nothing promising is likely to transpire without the mass of ordinary people, those subaltern subjects struggling to make ends meet; their engagement is vital to bring revolts into the social mainstream. Urban life can push subalterns to engage in extraordinary politics not only by cultivating dissent but also by providing space for its expression. In the past three decades, many large cities in the Middle East have experienced a neoliberal transformation, a kind of restructuring that added new depth and dimensions to urban dissent. Not only did this new urbanity furnish extensive marginalization; it also fostered new dynamics of publicness and extended the possibilities for popular dissent and insurrection.

Neoliberal Urbanity

The neoliberal city is a market-driven urbanity; it is a city shaped more by the logic of the market than the needs of its inhabitants, responding more to individual or corporate interests than public concerns.[1] It is marked by an increasing deregulation and privatization of production, collective consumption, and urban space. Public amenities become subject to outsourcing while the logic of private business is brought into urban governance. In this logic, the urban space becomes the function of what David Harvey calls "surplus-capital absorption," in that the city becomes the site of capitalist operation in pursuit of profitability rather than one that serves public needs.[2] This restructuring has in practice caused much change in the domains of work/production, collective provisions, and the lifeworld (the way in which people subsist and operate in their daily existence), all with far-reaching implications for configuring urban space and politics.[3]

With the gradual implementation of the structural adjustment in the Middle East since the 1990s, the ex-populist or socialist states increasingly retreated from public provision and collective welfare; public-sector firms have been rationalized, private enterprises increased, and urban employment structure experienced a dramatic shift. With neoliberal rationalization, employment in the public sector shrank; workers were laid off, transferred, or retrained for different jobs, while their perks, security, and welfare diminished or disappeared. Continuing rationalization further brought about unemployment, casual work, and an expanding informalization, which altogether has resulted in the fragmentation of urban labor.[4]

● 1. This essay is a shortened version of the chapter "Cities of Dissent" in the volume *Revolution without Revolutionaries: Making Sense of the Arab Spring*, by Asef Bayat (Stanford, CA: Stanford University Press, 2017). It is also reproduced here with permission of the American Anthropological Association, *City & Society* 24, no. 2 (August 2012): 110–128.
● 2. David Harvey, *Rebel Cities: From the Right to the City to the Urban Revolution* (London: Verso, 2012), 22
● 3. For an exploration of the neoliberal city in advanced industrialized countries, see Jason Hackworth, *The Neoliberal City: Governance, Ideology, and Development in American Urbanism* (Ithaca, NY: Cornell University Press, 2006).
● 4. See Asef Bayat, "Activism and Social Development in the Middle East," *International Journal of Middle East Studies* 34, no. 1 (February 2002): 1–28.

Currently, a pervasive sector of dispersed informal and casual jobs and services marks the economic destiny of neoliberal cities.[5] An estimated 180 million Arabs subsist in this sector.[6]

The partial retreat of public authorities from the provision of collective consumption like urban services, health, and education left people's everyday necessities to either the whim of private capital, the reach of the NGOs, or the mercy of religious charities, which are increasingly informed by neoliberal ideas. Not only were essential subsidies on basic staples like bread, oil, and gas reduced; the removal of rent control subjected scores of vulnerable households (in particular, the newly married and young families) to the dictates of the land market.[7] The predominance of private capital in urban operations meant that fundamental goods, services, and spaces—such as drinking water, electricity, transportation, garbage collection, green spaces, clean air, schools, clinics, and policing or security—were subject to privatization or were, at best, provided by a three-tier (state-private-NGO) system in which the affordable state provision was decreasing because of low investment or by "backdoor privatization."[8]

Today, the deterioration of working-class public housing, with its dilapidated structures and profound neglect, is essentially an extension of slum life.[9] Egypt's public housing, a vestige of President Gamal Abdel Nasser's distributionist socialism, differs little from the substandard informal settlements in their dereliction and disregard and are less flexible for expansion and innovation. In what Harvey calls "accumulation by dispossession," the states assist in pushing the poor, who have insecure tenure rights, out of the city center so they can grab high-quality land to hand over to the corporations in pursuit of megaprojects such as shopping malls, leisure sites, or office buildings.[10] This is an extension of the age-old policy of gentrification, where dispossession takes place de facto by the invisible force of high prices and inhospitable social ecology. Thus, in place of public housing or the amenities of the welfare state era, we see today the development of megaprojects that cater largely to local and foreign elites.

5. Alejandro Portes, Manuel Castells, and Lauren Benton, eds., *The Informal Economy: Studies in Advanced and Less Developed Countries* (Baltimore: Johns Hopkins University Press, 1989); Alan Gilbert, "Love in the Time of Enhanced Capital Flows: Reflections in the Links between Liberalization and Informality," in *Urban Informality: Transnational Perspectives from the Middle East, Latin America, and South Asia,* ed. Ananya Roy and Nezar Alsayyad (Lanham, MD: Lexington Books, 2004), 33–66.

6. Hernando de Soto, "The Free Market Secret of the Arab Revolutions," *Financial Times,* November 8, 2011.

7. An early meticulous analysis can be found in Marsh Posusney, *Labor and the State in Egypt: Workers, Unions, and Economic Restructuring* (New York: Columbia University Press, 1997); see also Iliya Harik and Dennis Sullivan, eds., *Privatization and Liberalization in the Middle East* (Bloomington: Indiana University Press, 1992).

8. In this "backdoor privatization," patients, for instance, have to bring their own medicine to public hospitals, or pupils have to have private lessons in public schools to compensate for the deterioration of public education. For the negative impact of this new economic restructuring social policy in the Middle East, see Massoud Karshenas and Valentine Moghadam, eds., *Social Policy in the Middle East: Economic, Political, and Gender Dynamics* (London: Palgrave Macmillan, 2006).

9. Mike Davis, *Planet of Slums* (London: Verso, 2006).

10. Harvey, *Rebel Cities,* 18–19.

Of course, these processes are not totally new; rather, they have been accentuated and intensified by neoliberal policies, which, in the mean-time, herald decentralization, democracy, and citizen participation. Even though civil society is unequal, and primarily the more privileged institutions are able to influence governance, some opportunities for subaltern mobilization may also open up. What did these remarkable processes mean to urban space and its inhabitants? More specifically, how are the politics of the urban subaltern population articulated in these neoliberal times? Existing literature on informality has strikingly little to say about the spatial implications of informal life and even less on the effects of the neoliberal city and the kind of politics it engenders. These are crucial, for they have significant bearing on the formation of dissent, the raw material for the Arab uprisings.

The City Inside Out

The neoliberal city is in part a city inside out, where a massive portion of the urban population, the subalterns, become compelled to operate, subsist, or simply live in public spaces—in the streets, in a substan-tial "outdoor economy." Here, public space becomes an indispens-able asset, capital, for people to survive, operate, and reproduce life. Strolling in the streets of Cairo, Tehran, Tunis, or Istanbul in the middle of a working day, one cannot help noticing the astonishing presence of so many people operating outdoors in the streets—working, running errands, standing, sitting, playing, negotiating, or driving. One wonders why there are such inconceivable traffic jams at this time of day when people are supposed to be in enclosed spaces.

The increasing layoffs and unemployment (the Middle East–North Africa region had the highest, 26 percent, youth unemployment rate in the world in the 1990s and 2000s), which resulted from restructur-ing the public sector, removing job guarantees, and transferring from manufacturing to services and high-tech capital-intensive industries, boosted both casual and durable informal work.[11] This work is embod-ied in street vendors, messengers, drivers, and carriers, those laboring in the street, and the spectacular pavement restaurants. Tens of thou-sands of motorcyclists make a living by illegally working on the streets of Tehran, transferring mail, money, documents, goods, and people in constant contention with the police. Some 100,000 such cyclists move around the Tehran bazaar area alone every hour. In 2009 the police con-fiscated over 78,000 motorcycles and fined some 292,000 individuals in this same area.[12] Diminishing income and social protections (such as food subsidies and rent control) have compelled many poor families to deploy more family members, like women and children, to earn a living, who often end up in the outdoor economy.

11. According to an ILO report cited in Jumana Al Tamim, "Youth Unemployment in MENA Region Disturbingly High," *Gulf News*, February 7, 2012; and Masood Ahmed, Dominique Guillaume, and Davide Furceri, "Youth Unemployment in the Mena Region," IMF, June 13, 2012, https://www.imf.org/external/np/vc/2012/061312.htm.

12. Alireza Sadeghi, "Everyday Life of the Subsistence Motor Cyclists," unpublished paper, Tehran, 2016.

Slum dwelling, casual work, under-the-table payment, and street hawking are no longer characteristics of the traditional poor; they have spread also among educated young people with higher status, aspirations, and social skills—government employees, teachers, and professionals. Informal life and precarity have thus become a facet of educated middle-class existence, forming a new middle-class poor. By 2011, 30 percent of college graduates in Egypt, Tunisia, and Jordan were out of work. It is not uncommon to discover that taxi drivers, street petition writers, or various kinds of traders are actually teachers, low-income bureaucrats, army personnel, or even professionals such as lawyers. I recall in Tunis in the spring of 2011 that a young man who offered to guide me to an address in exchange for two dinars was a college graduate who had studied literature.

Now that men tend to work multiple jobs, with the result that they are never home, women and housewives have to take on many of the tasks traditionally assigned to men—paying bills, attending to bank business, dealing with car mechanics, daily shopping, taking children to and from school, or going to government offices. Thus, women too, whether working outdoors or running errands, have increasingly been present in public spaces. Even though the rise in the expression of public piety has placed greater pressure on unveiled women in public places, it has allowed greater freedom for women from traditional families to be active in outdoor public places. In 2011 some 2,000 veiled women worked as taxi drivers along with their male counterparts in Tehran under the Islamic Republic. This kind of compelled and desired publicness stands in sharp contrast to André Gorz's notion of domestic or "home work" as the "sphere of freedom" and self-regulation in contrast to the discipline of social economy (or the sphere of necessity), where people have to work to survive.[13] In today's Middle Eastern neoliberal cities, the outdoor economy and public presence are both a necessity and (for some women) a space for self-expression.

The city inside out is not limited to the spatial features of working life; it resonates even more powerfully in the everyday lifeworld. Simply, neoliberal logic expands and deepens the informalization of lifeworlds, of which outdoor life is a key attribute. Thus, the gentrification of city centers to accommodate global enterprises tends to push scores of low-income and middle-class families to live in the expanding slums and squatter areas where outdoor life constitutes an underlying feature. Not only does informal subsistence heavily rest on the outdoor economy; the informal communities, slums, and squatter settlements rely greatly on outdoor public space that inhabitants utilize as places of work, sociability, entertainment, and recreation.

Strolling through the back streets of Cairo, Tunis, or Aleppo, one could not miss the spread of vast markets, mechanic shops, or pavement restaurants in packed neighborhoods; there might be the sound of

---

13. André Gorz, *Paths to Paradise: On the Liberation from Work* (London: Pluto Press, 1985), and *Farewell to the Working Class* (London: Pluto Press, 1982).

happy music from colorful tents filled with families, friends, and neighbors attending a wedding ceremony; or the somber sound of Quran recitation signaling a death in the neighborhood; or the energetic commotion of teenage boys playing soccer. The poor people's cramped shelters, as in Cairo's Dar El Salam settlement, for instance, are simply too small and insufficient to accommodate their spatial needs. With no courtyard, no adequate rooms, and no spacious kitchen (if there is one at all), the poor inhabitants are compelled to extend their daily existence into public outdoor spaces—to the alleyways, streets, open spaces, or rooftops. It is in such places where the poor engage in cultural reproduction, in organizing public events—weddings, festivals, and funerals. Here, outdoor spaces serve as indispensable assets to both the economic livelihood and social/cultural lives of much of the urban population.[14]

In a striking contrast to the spreading out of the poor, there has been a simultaneous process of enclosure that represents one of the most glaring features of neoliberal urbanity. Along with the expansion of slums, with their real and imagined dangers of crime and extremism, has come the historic flight of the rich into the safe havens of gated communities—the Beverly Hills, the Utopias, the Dream Lands, and Sidi Bou Said of the large cities of the Middle East.[15] As the lower classes were increasing their presence in public spaces, where it seemed "they were everywhere," the rich, now apprehensive of the physical presence and "social dangers" of the dispossessed, sought their own enclosed and exclusive zones—private beaches, exclusive neighborhoods, gated communities, and securely guarded bars, restaurants, and places of sociability, work, and even locations of worship and prayer. It is not just in Rio de Janeiro or Johannesburg that the elites' sense of security has been ensured by bodyguards, checkpoints, electronic monitoring systems, and barbed wire; the elites of Tehran, Tunis, and Istanbul also expressed profound anxiety about "urban dangers." Even their automobiles have not been spared formidable locks, bolts, and alarms.[16]

Subaltern Politics in the Neoliberal City
What are the implications of neoliberal urbanity in the Middle East for the politics of urban subalterns—particularly those who operate under authoritarian states and repressive regimes? The prevailing view on the Left seems to suggest that a neoliberal city is a lost city—where capital rules, the affluent enjoy, and the subalterns are entrapped. It is a city

14. See Asef Bayat, *Street Politics: Poor People's Movements in Iran* (New York: Columbia University Press, 1997); See also Asef Bayat, "Cairo's Poor: Dilemma of Survival and Solidarity," *Middle East Report* 202 (1996): 7–12; Asef Bayat and Eric Denis, "Who Is Afraid of Ashwaiyyat? Urban Change and Politics in Egypt," *Environment and Urbanization* 12, no. 2 (2000): 185–199.
15. Ayfer Bartu and Biray Kolluoglu, "Emerging Spaces of Neoliberalism: A Gated Town and Public Housing in Istanbul," *New Perspectives on Turkey* 39 (2008): 5–46; Khaled Adham, "Globalization, Neoliberalism, and the New Spaces of Capital in Cairo," *Traditional Dwellings and Settlements Review* 17, no. 1 (2005), http://iaste.berkeley.edu/pdfs/17.1c-Fall05adham-sml.pdf.
16. See Karina Landman and Martin Schönteich, "Urban Fortress: Gated Communities as a Reaction to Crime," *African Security Review* 11, no. 4 (2002): 71–85. Various practices of securitization of modern megacities are fully discussed in Stephen Graham, *Cities under Siege: Military Urbanism* (London: Verso, 2010).

of glaring inequality and imbalance, where the ideal of the "right to the city," the ability of inhabitants to collectively restructure the urban, has all but vanished.[17] Evidence in a number of cities in the Global South, including the Middle East, seems to give some plausibility to this claim.[18] For instance, Mona Fawaz's studies on Beirut document how neoliberal policies have in the past three decades disempowered the "informal people," because urban land prices have increased (as a result of the presence of expats, foreign capital, and companies), police control on their encroachments has expanded, provision of social services has been delegated to nonstate agencies such as NGOs and political parties, and there is now greater competition for such meager services because their clientele now includes the impoverished middle classes.[19] This is in line with Harvey's argument that the poor are structurally entrapped in the logic of capital from which they have little chance to escape unless something is done to change the way that capitalism as a whole operates.[20] For instance, how can the poor deal with the deteriorating environment that affects their lives in a city where leisure, green spaces, and clean air are becoming privatized? In short, the neoliberal city is the victim of "urbicide" by global elites who kill cities, such as Managua, by disembedding and fragmenting them through zoning and expressways that connect the elites' work and leisure to their gated communities, leaving the rest to decay in the poverty, crime, and violence of slums.[21]

Quite distinct from this position are those of other thinkers like Mike Davis, who seem to actually sense a strong resistance on the part of the dispossessed in the "planet of slums." Indeed, for Davis, slums are like "volcanoes waiting to erupt," and their explosion might herald the emergence of "some new, unexpected historical subject" carrying a "global emancipatory" project. Even though slum dwellers do not constitute a Marxian proletariat, they are believed to have the potential to carry out radical actions.[22] Indeed, slums already constitute the highly volatile collective where the "gods of chaos," the dispossessed, the "outcasts," deploy their remarkable strategy of chaos—suicide bombing and "eloquent explosions"—to counter the "Orwellian

- 17. The idea of the "right to the city" seems to be more complex than what the current usages suggest. According to Mark Purcell, Lefebvre's original idea is perhaps its most comprehensive formulation: "Lefebvre's right to the city is an argument for profoundly reworking both the social relations of capitalism and the current structure of liberal-democratic citizenship. His right to the city is not a suggestion for reform, nor does it envision a fragmented, tactical, or piecemeal resistance. His idea is instead a call for a radical restructuring of social, political, and economic relations, both in the city and beyond." Mark Purcell, "Excavating Lefebvre: The Right to the City and Its Urban Politics of the Inhabitants," Geo Journal 58 (2002): 101. This seems to be in line with David Harvey's understanding of Lefebvre. See David Harvey, "The Right to the City," New Left Review 53 (2008): 23–40.
- 18. For a number of case studies, see Asef Bayat and Kees Biekart, eds., "Cities of Extremes," special issue, Development and Change 40, no. 5 (2009).
- 19. Mona Fawaz, "Neoliberal Urbanity and the Right to the City: A View from Beirut's Periphery," in Bayat and Biekart, "Cities of Extremes," 827–852.
- 20. Harvey, "The Right to the City."
- 21. For such conclusions, see Dennis Rodgers, "Slum Wars of the 21st Century: Gangs, Mano Dura, and the New Urban Geography of Conflict in Central America," in Bayat and Biekart, "Cities of Extremes," 949–976.
- 22. Mike Davis, "Planet of Slums: Urban Involution and Informal Proletariat," New Left Review 26 (March–April 2004): 28.

technologies of repression."[23] Slums, in short, herald the "urban wars of the twenty-first century," similar to Eric Wolf's "peasant wars of the twentieth century."[24] Since the violence affects both rich and poor, Dennis Rodgers concludes that the subalterns have basically lost this war to the neoliberal political economy and its henchmen.[25]

While these analyses offer valuable insights into our understanding of the predicament of the ordinary urbanites in these new liberal times, they also raise important questions. For instance, if, in Harvey's view, the solution to counter the process of dispossession lies in forging large-scale global social movements to undo or stop the neoliberal onslaught, how are the poor to carry this responsibility? If the dispossessed are to wait for a social revolution to reverse the course of capitalist encroachment, what are they to do in the meantime; what strategy should they pursue in their daily lives? In other words, for the foreseeable future, the urban disenfranchised are trapped in the structural web of the current capitalist system and the states that uphold it. Mike Davis, however, appears to be more optimistic. He seems to believe that a formidable resistance is already taking place, one couched in the rapid spread of Pentecostalism in African and Latin American slums and the language and violent practices of radical Islam in the Middle East—suicide bombing and spectacular explosions.

This, however, is a difficult argument to sustain. As I have suggested elsewhere, radical Islam is hardly the ideology of the urban dispossessed; rather, it builds on the attitudes and expectations of the broadly educated middle classes who feel marginalized in the prevailing economic, political, and international domains.[26] When Davis speaks of spectacular violence emanating from slums, he seems to refer to the exceptional cases of Baghdad and Palestinian Gaza, where poverty and exclusion were mixed with a blatant foreign occupation (the United States in Iraq and Israel in Palestinian territories). Almost nowhere else in the Global South, including the Middle East, do we observe the same type of violence as developed at times in Baghdad's Sadr City or the Gaza Strip in the mid-2000s.

In fact, an exclusive focus on such post-conflict social violence as gangs or on conventional large-scale mobilization and social movements may distract us from paying adequate attention to the intricate processes of "life as politics" among subalterns in the cities of the Global South. An exclusive preoccupation with such categorical dichotomies as passive-active or win-lose can entrap our conceptual imagination,

23. Davis, "Planet of Slums," 206.
24. Eric Wolf, *Peasant Wars of the Twentieth Century* (Norman: University of Oklahoma Press, 1999).
25. Rodgers, "Slum Wars of the 21st Century." See also Jo Beall, "Cities, Terrorism and Urban Wars in the 21st Century," (working paper no. 9, Crisis States Research Centre, London School of Economics, London, 2007).
26. For a detailed analysis, see Asef Bayat, "Radical Religion and the Habitus of the Dispossessed: Does Islamic Militancy Have an Urban Ecology?," *International Journal of Urban and Regional Research* 31, no. 3 (September 2007): 579–590; Asef Bayat, *Revolution without Revolutionaries: Making Sense of the Arab Spring* (Stanford, CA: Stanford University Press, 2017).

preventing us from exploring further and discovering the intricate ingenuity that subalterns may discreetly use to assert and defend themselves. This new urbanity, the city inside out, generates new dynamics of publicness that can have important implications for social and political mobilization—what I have described as "street politics" and the "political street."[27] While the subaltern groups may lose much of their traditional claims to the city, they tend in response to discover and generate new places to escape where they recover their claims in a different fashion and, in some cases, compel the elites to retreat. The social dimensions of the neoliberal city inside out in the context of the authoritarian state engender the type of grassroots mobilization that I have called "social nonmovements," which reinforce and deepen both street politics and the political street.[28]

Politics on the Street
When people are deprived of or do not trust electoral power to change things, they tend to resort to their own institutional power to exert pressure on adversaries to meet their demands—like workers or university students going on strike. But for those who lack such institutional power or settings (such as the unemployed, housewives, and broadly the "informal people"), streets become a crucial arena to express discontent. For such subaltern groups, however, the centrality of streets goes beyond merely the expression of contention. Rather, streets may actually serve as an indispensable asset or capital for them to subsist and reproduce economic and cultural life. In other words, not only do they resort to streets to organize rallies or protest actions; they also encroach on street space to conduct business, operate workshops, sell merchandise, prepare and serve food, organize funerals, entertain, and socialize. In all of these arenas, the actors are involved in a relation of power over the control of public space and public order. They are involved in street politics, which describes a set of conflicts and the attendant implications between certain groups or individuals and the authorities that are shaped and expressed in the physical and social space of streets—from back alleys to the main avenues, from invisible places to escape the city to main squares. The attendant conflict arises because the subjects engage in active use of public spaces, which under the modern state they are supposed to use only passively in the ways that the state approves. So the street vendors who carry out their business on the pavement, the poor people who extend their lives onto the sidewalks, the squatters who take over public lands, lower-class youths who appropriate street corners, or protesters who march in the streets are all involved in some way in street politics.[29] Daily tensions, if not physical confrontations with the authorities, mark the social world of the urban subalterns, keeping them in a constant state of insecurity and mobilization.

27. See Asef Bayat, *Life as Politics: How Ordinary People Change the Middle East* (Stanford, CA: Stanford University Press, 2013), chap. 1.
28. Bayat, *Life as Politics*, chap. 1.
29. For details, see Bayat, *Street Politics*.

But streets are not just places where conflicts are shaped and/or expressed. They are also venues where people forge collective identities and extend their solidarities beyond their immediate familiar circles to include the unknown, the stranger. What facilitates this extension of solidarity is the operation of some latent or passive network between individuals who may be unknown to one another even though they share common attributes. Passive networks are instantaneous communications between atomized individuals that are established by tacit recognition of their commonalities and are mediated through real or virtual space. Thus, street vendors, who might not know each other, can still recognize their common position by noticing each others' pushcarts, vending tables, or chants. Similarly, young people who are strangers to each other, such as soccer fans, who have similar hairstyles, wear blue jeans, or act in a certain way, connect to one another and recognize their shared identities without necessarily establishing an active or deliberate communication and without being part of an organization. The unlawful motorcyclists in Tehran go further by informing one another of police crackdowns by hand gestures, blinking lights, or shouting "police."

Aside from shaping, expressing, or extending discontent and serving as an asset or capital for livelihood, streets signify a powerful symbolic utterance, one that goes beyond the physicality of streets. This is the "political street," as in "Arab street" or "Muslim street," by which I mean the collective sentiments, shared feelings, and public opinions of ordinary people in their day-to-day utterances and practices that are expressed broadly and casually in urban public spaces—in taxis, buses, shops, sidewalks, or mass demonstrations.[30] For instance, the undeliberate practice of public nagging in most of the Middle East where ordinary citizens speak out, vent, and exchange grievances in public, appears to be a salient feature of public culture in the region, serving as a crucial element in the making of public opinion and a component of the political street. The political street then signifies the cognitive, intellectual, and affective domain of the city inside out—a domain wherein sentiments are expressed, emotions shared, and collective opinions formed informally in urban spaces. This has been important in Arab societies because when authoritarian regimes disallow institutional mechanisms of conveying public opinion, the urban street comes to serve as a measure of the public sphere and locus of political expression.

Reclamation of public space by poor people through encroachment, functioning, and subsisting constitutes an expression of street politics, while simultaneously feeding into and accentuating political street. In other words, through this encroachment, dispossessed are constantly engaged in struggles in and about urban space; they become a party in the contest over shaping urban form and molding urban texture, the domains of the social, the cultural, and the sensory—noise, smell, and sight. This life-driven and constant nature of spatial politics among

30. Bayat, *Life as Politics*, chap. 1.

the Middle Eastern poor distinguishes it from that engendered by the Occupy movements, whose presence in the public space, the streets, was essentially deliberate and transitory rather than structural and enduring.

How do these contestations in and about urban texture take place when authoritarian Middle Eastern states curtail the organized and sustained challenges to the political and economic elites? I have proposed that the political constraint under authoritarian rule compels the urban disenfranchised to resort to a particular form of mobilization, the unorganized and unassuming nonmovements. Nonmovements, or the collective actions of noncollective actors, are the shared contentious practices of a large number of fragmented people whose similar but disconnected claims produce important social change in their own lives and society at large, even though such practices are rarely guided by an ideology, recognizable leadership, or organization.[31] For instance, in Riyadh, Saudi Arabia, women challenge certain gender norms through the practice of what they call "pushing normal."[32] Groups of women stroll, frequent, and mix with men in the sex-segregated street cafés; ride bicycles in public places; or establish and visit art galleries that host both men and women. In prerevolutionary Egypt, lower-class youths and soccer fans (ultras) who gathered and asserted presence in hostile urban locations operated as nonmovements, as did educated unemployed people in Tunisia in their pursuit of sustenance. In broad terms, the nonmovements reflect how such marginalized groups as Muslim women, youth, or the urban disenfranchised in the Middle East may succeed in making their respective claims for gender equality, citizenship, and the right to the city, despite their being dispersed, unorganized, and atomized. But the notion of nonmovement is particularly pertinent to the way in which the urban dispossessed become engaged in street politics and the political street.

The Dispossessed in Street Politics

Nonmovements represent perhaps the most salient features of activism by the urban dispossessed in the Middle East. I refer to the quiet, pervasive, and enduring encroachment of poor people on the propertied, the powerful, and the public in their quest for survival and bettering their lives. Lacking a clear leadership, articulated ideology, or structured organization, these dispersed efforts represent the largely individual, everyday, and lifelong mobilizations that often involve collective action when the gains are threatened.[33] In the primary cities of the Middle East, the encroachment has been expressed by millions of rural migrants embarking on long migratory journeys to escape misfortunes and search for better livelihoods and new lives. They begin their new existence by grabbing plots of land to put up shelters in the seemingly abandoned, unnoticed, and opaque urban escapes—in the back streets, under bridges, on rooftops, or somewhere in the outer spaces of the megacities.

- 31. Bayat, *Life as Politics*.
- 32. Amelie Le Renard, *Society of Young Women: Opportunities of Power, Place, and Reform in Saudi Arabia* (Stanford, CA: Stanford University Press, 2014).
- 33. I have already referred to these nonmovements of the urban poor in terms of the "quiet encroachment of the ordinary." See Bayat, *Street Politics*, 1.

Once the families are settled in, they acquire electricity by connecting their homes to the nearby power poles and then secure running water, often ingeniously, by installing underground pipes or using makeshift hoses to run water from a neighbor's supply or public pipes in the vicinity. Phone lines are obtained more or less in a similar fashion. As more neighbors gather, they build roads and places of worship and manage garbage—efforts that out of necessity become collective.[34] By 2011 over 65 percent in Cairo, 40 percent in Aleppo, and 25 percent of all Moroccans had crafted an informal life of this sort.[35] Some 180 million Arab breadwinners in such habitats, mostly without regular work and urban skills, strive to earn a living by encroaching by the thousands on the main streets, sidewalks, and squares as hawkers, vendors, or street workshop workers who then take advantage of favorable business opportunities that shopkeepers and rich traders created. In their lifeworlds, these disenfranchised groups manage their daily collective lives by co-existing, resolving disputes, and handling the outlaws and criminals who tend to inhabit such spaces. Yet they have not been able to escape constant insecurities of debt, illegal existence, and uncertain destinies.[36]

Such daily encroachments by multitudes of people have virtually transformed the cities of the Middle East and by extension the developing world. Over time, they have created massive communities with millions of inhabitants with complex lifeworlds, economic arrangements, cultural practices, and lifestyles.[37] By 2011 more than 46 percent of urban settlers in the Middle East were living in such a world. In these largely undefined urban spaces, the poor tried to live relatively autonomous lives, basing their relationships more on self-reliance, reciprocity, flexibility, and negotiation, traits that stood against yet negotiated with modern notions and institutions of bureaucracy, fixed contracts, and discipline. They carved off, claimed, and even pushed back the elites from sizable areas of the urban universe. By doing so, they posed the question of who owned, managed, and exerted power over the cities and who the players were in the urban governance.

I do not wish to depict a romantic vision of a resisting subaltern population, even though I realize that there is, as seen in the New Urbanism perspective, a temptation to idealize street and sidewalk life or to see in informality a panacea for urban ills.[38] It is certainly valuable to recognize the agency of the dispossessed in distributing social goods and opportunities and in creating their vibrant communities. But who can

34. These observations draw on my studies of the urban poor in Iran and Egypt. See Bayat, *Street Politics*; and Bayat and Denis, "Who Is Afraid of Ashwaiyyat?," 185–199.

35. David Sims, "The Arab Housing Paradox," *Cairo Review* (Fall 2013), https://www.thecairoreview.com/essays/the-arab-housing-paradox.

36. Asef Bayat, "Cairo's Poor: Dilemmas of Survival and Solidarity," *Middle East Report 202* (January–February 1997): 7–12.

37. David Sims, *Understanding Cairo: The Logic of a City Out of Control* (Cairo: American University in Cairo Press, 2011); Ayse Yonder, *Informal Settlements in Istanbul, Turkey: From Shacks to High-Rises* (Salzburg: Pratt Institute, 2006); Asef Bayat, "Tehran: Paradox City," *New Left Review* 66 (November 2010): 99–122.

38. See, for instance, Mitchell Duneier, *Sidewalk* (New York: Farrar, Straus and Giroux, 1999).

deny that the neoliberal onslaught has brought much slum demolition, gentrification, and removal of street markets? How can one dispute the fact that the logic of control in the modern state conditions the political authorities to turn any opaque space—the slums, informal markets, underground lives, or even unregistered humans—into transparent, quantifiable entities? Indeed, demolishing spontaneous settlements, deliberately burning street markets, and carrying out programs of slum upgrading can establish transparency and knowledge that can ensure social control.[39] Yet the truth is that the very logic of neoliberal urbanity carries in itself the force behind generating such parallel, unknowable, and opaque lifeworlds. It renders both dispossession and repossession simultaneously parallel processes, thus turning urban physical and social space into the site of a protracted battle for hegemony. The poor respond to structural dispossession by not letting go easily—they often resist slum clearance and demolition or make these measures politically costly. In Cairo during the early 2000s, selective demolition caused the furious settlers to wage street protests and demand resettlement; in Tehran the poor in the early 1990s agreed to vacate only after being compensated, and in Tunisia urban riots forced the government to embark on serious upgrading. In general, slum clearance and demolition do happen, but people still move to different, more remote, less visible, and less strategic locations to reclaim what they have lost and begin life again. In this long war of attrition, power reveals its limitations. It is therefore simplistic to claim that the nonmovements serve as safety valves for the regimes of oppression. This claim not only ignores the complexity of the state-nonmovement relation but, more importantly, overlooks the norm-changing outcome and structural incremental dynamics of its encroachment—winning a position, reinforcing it, and then moving forward to capture a new one. For instance, the squatters do not stop after securing a shelter but continue demands for running water, electricity, phone lines, garbage collection, paved roads, security, and official recognition.

Such modes of living in the cities of the Middle East are similar to how illegal migrants manage their movement and lives at the international level. There exist now massive border controls, barriers, fences, walls, and police patrols. Yet migrants keep flooding in—by air, sea, and road; hidden in the back of trucks and trains; or simply on foot. Indeed, the anxiety and panic that subaltern groups have caused among the elites at national and international levels is remarkably similar. The Cairo elite lament about the "invasion" of peasants from the Upper Egyptian countryside; and the Istanbul elite warn of the encroachment of the "black Turks," meaning rural poor migrants from Anatolia. In a strikingly similar tone, white European elites express profound anxiety about the "invasion of foreigners"—Africans, Asians, and in particular Muslims—whom they see as having overwhelmed Europe's social habitat, distorting the European way of life by their physical presence and cultural habits—their behavior, dress, mosques, and minarets.[40] These subjects are

●   39. See Bayat and Biekart, "Cities of Extremes."
●   40. Steven Erlanger, "Amid Rise of Multiculturalism, Dutch Confront Their Questions of Identity," *New York Times*, August 13, 2011.

involved in appropriating opportunities and social goods, asserting the right to the city. They are engaged, in other words, in a struggle for citizenship—a process similar to what Partha Chatterjee describes for India in his *Politics of the Governed*.[41] Thus, while the neoliberal city deprives many of its inhabitants of urban citizenship, it is also true that the disenfranchised do force the elites into socio-spatial retreat and enclosure—to the gated communities, private security guards, locked vehicles, partial governance, and parcelized hegemony. So in response to the neoliberal strategy of "accumulation by dispossession," the subaltern subject may resort to survival by repossession.

The Logic of Repossession

Why and how can survival by repossession happen? Two factors are crucial. The first has to do with the particular characteristics of the nonmovements and the second with the nature of the political settings (state forms) within which nonmovements operate. Nonmovements represent the collective action of noncollective actors, who are oriented more toward action than by being ideologically driven, concerned more with practice than protest.[42] Unlike conventional forms of activism, which by definition are extraordinary practices, nonmovements merge into and are part and parcel with the ordinary practices of everyday life. Thus, poor people's resolve to migrate, build shelters, or work, live, function, and stroll in streets all represent instances of the ordinary practices of daily life, which unlike extraordinary acts such as attending meetings, marching, or demonstrating, remain mostly immune from repression. What grants power to these nonmovements is not the unity of actors, but the many (even though dispersed) people simultaneously doing similar, albeit encroaching, things.

This, however, cannot happen under just any circumstances and state forms. Nonmovements usually work under the state forms that cannot, do not, or are perceived not to meet the social and material needs of the disenfranchised, who are then compelled to resort to direct action. Instead of forming collective protests to demand jobs or housing, poor people may simply acquire them through direct action. Poor people succeed in doing so largely because the states under which they operate are "soft": despite their often authoritarian disposition and political omnipresence, they lack the necessary capacity, hegemony, and technological efficacy to impose full control over society. So there remain many uncontrolled spaces that the innovative subaltern groups can utilize to their advantage. Even though these states produce many strict rules of governance, the laws are often easily broken; or even though bureaucrats treat the poor harshly, they are often not difficult to bribe. Consequently, despite its seeming omnipresence, the reach (let alone the hegemony and legitimacy) of the state remains acutely limited, which leaves many free zones that the nonmovements can utilize to thrive.[43]

- 41. Partha Chatterjee, *The Politics of the Governed* (New York: Columbia University Press, 2004).
- 42. For the full elaboration of the concept of nonmovements, see Bayat, *Life as Politics*, chap. 1.
- 43. For details, see Bayat, *Life as Politics*, chap. 1.

Equally crucial are the actors' civic virtues, their perseverance and innovative ability to assert their presence in society: that is, the subalterns' capacity to recognize their limitations while discovering new opportunities and deploying inventive methods of practice to take advantage of the available spaces to resist and move forward. I am pointing to the art of presence, the ability of subaltern subjects to assert their collective will in spite of all odds, to circumvent the constraints, utilizing what is possible, and discover new spaces within which to make themselves heard, seen, felt, and realized. In normal times, this politics of presence serves as a mechanism through which subalterns strive to subvert their status of dispossession and make the best of what is perceived to be possible. But revolutionary times facilitate the grassroots journey toward more audible encroachment and organized mobilization. By definition, nonmovements imply already-active individuals who may emerge from their backstreets to join in the broader revolts and uprisings; they navigate between the everyday encroachments and revolutionary protests that take shape in the spatial expanse of the neoliberal city, the main squares. The squares represent the spatial locus and political form of subaltern struggles in the Arab revolutions.

1984

Gauri Gill

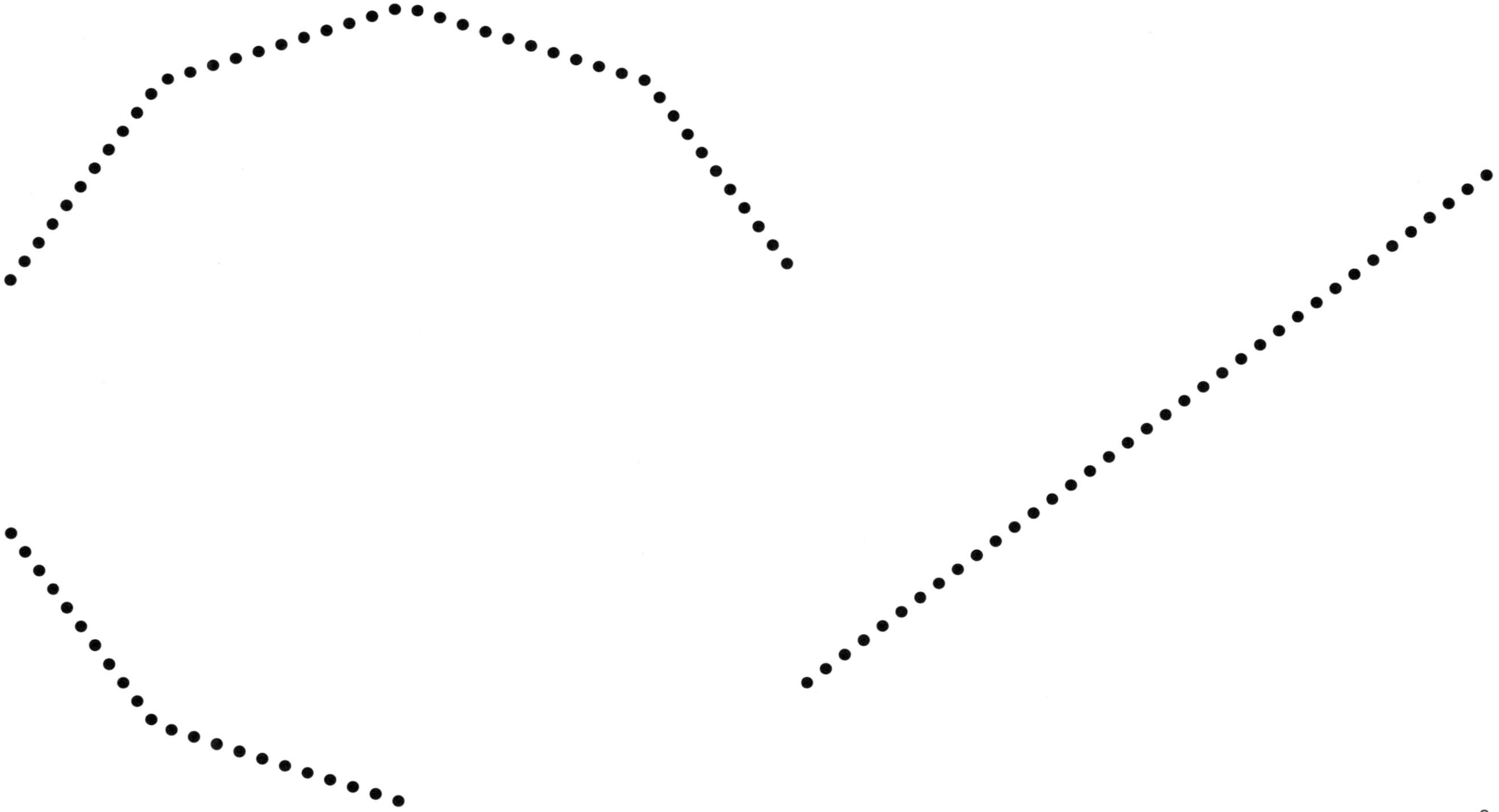

gauri gill 1984

Trilokpuri Block-32

artition capital
no food, no water
87 - married 4 children
works in a factory, electrical socket
god hasn't written happiness
in our destines
poor people - earning & eating.
want justice
005 11th August Parliament Protest
18th August promises
no compensation employment, hanging
they're living happily.
what good are we?

we won't get justice
nobody else well.
precedence
me will keep fighting
our children will fight our
battle.
we'll never forget
blot on Congress
will never get washed.
Rajiv Gandhi had blown us to
bits, so he was too.
what goes around, comes
around.
→ Not my mother,
everyone else's mother

This is an excerpt from the project *1984* by Gauri Gill. Originally released on Kafila.org in April 2013, rereleased in November 2014, November 2017, November 2019, and June 2020. The original document included texts on the 1984 anti-Sikh pogrom in India and their aftermath by a range of contributors paired with various artworks. Some of those contributions have been reproduced here, alongside the artist's own ongoing bibliography. All photographs and captions are by Gauri Gill.

In 2005, when I heard Nirpreet Kaur relate her 1984 story, she had to have a psychologist present in the room. Even for us mere listeners, it was too much to fully absorb. I did not know what to do with the weight of her words.

Among the tragic events of recent days in India, 1984 has been invoked repeatedly in various contexts—state complicity against minorities; using violence to mobilize majoritarian populations electorally; breakdown of institutions including the police and administration; false equivalences that convert one-sided pogroms into two-sided riots; justice denied. My father often said to us after the 1984 pogrom, "What happened may appear to be only about Sikhs, but if India does not address it, if justice is not served, this precedent will come back to haunt the country again and again. And we will never know whose turn will come next."

Yet, for a very long time, there was a silence around 1984, even a lack of much-needed solidarity. At the time, there were no twenty-four-hour television channels, cell phones, internet or social media; what we have are only eyewitness accounts, notes and sparse photographs. Photographers who documented the massacre that November were terrified that their photographs would be made to disappear from photo-labs in New Delhi by the Central Government. Images did disappear. Those that survived may now be used as evidence, or to relive the emotion. At a street exhibition of photographs organized in 2012 by the activist lawyer H. S. Phoolka at Jantar Mantar, many of the visitors wept even as they used their cell phone cameras to rephotograph the images on display. Others spontaneously started to do the Ardās, or Sikh prayers. This made some friends uncomfortable. A prominent activist friend said to me that day, "Sikhs should adopt more secular means, many might feel uncomfortable with non-secular ways of protesting." Yet, members of the sadly almost exclusively Sikh gathering that day were protesting using familiar means, ways that provided comfort. The Ardās contains the historical memory of the oppression and suffering of the Sikhs, how they bore it, as well as their aspirations. Someday, perhaps the 1984 pogrom will find place within it too. In any case, being targeted specifically for their religious identity, they were perhaps justified in using the very same means to express themselves. In the words of Hannah Arendt, "If one is attacked as a Jew, one must defend oneself as a Jew. Not as a German, not as a world-citizen, not as an upholder of the Rights of Man."

In 2005, after the release of the Justice Nanavati Commission Report on November 1984, and later in 2009, to mark the twenty-fifth anniversary of the pogrom, I visited Delhi's resettlement colonies, and took photographs in Trilokpuri, Tilak

Vihar, and Garhi, as well as at protest rallies in the city. These photographs appeared in prominent Indian print media publications then. Mediated by the mainstream, they formed a kind of artifact, and had a certain relevance embedded in that particular context. I wondered how the images would be read and understood when circulated more intimately. I also wished to use them to trigger a conversation about 1984 with other citizens of Delhi, specifically my community of fellow artists. In early 2013, I asked several friends, those who were present in Delhi that November, or have lived here since or prior, or who see themselves in some essential way as part of this city, to write something for each image. It could be a direct response to the photograph, or a more general observation related to the event; it could be tangential, poetic, personal, fictional, factual or nonsensically true in the way that were Toba Tek Singh's seminal words on the partition.

In September 2014, I returned to Tilak Vihar. I met with Darshan Kaur and other widow witnesses, saw children from "impacted" families play and recite at the Guru Harkishan Public School, and went into the Shaheedi (Martyrs) Memorial Museum—where the only visitors were the family members of those in the photographs. In August 2019, I visited the new SGPC memorial at Gurudwara Rakab Ganj. It was hard to locate inside the Gurudwara complex, made of concrete and steel, and deserted. The unending lists of victims' names stared at me.

"Jis tann lāgé soee jāné," a Punjabi saying goes. Only she whose body is hurt, knows. But it is also for those of us who are not direct victims, to try and articulate, to remember and retell, the history of our shared city—and universe. A world without conversations and fellowship; without the stories, experiential accounts, personal interpretations, diaries, secrets and myriad truths of ordinary individuals; one in which the narrative is entirely subsumed and controlled by the all-powerful State and its willing henchmen, or by a dominant majority, would indeed form 1984 in the Orwellian sense.

The photographs from 2005 first appeared in *Tehelka* (with Hartosh Bal); and from 2009 in *Outlook* (with Shreevatsa Nevatia). The corresponding captions are roughly as they were inscribed in the published reports.

Text responses are by Amitabha Bagchi, Jeebesh Bagchi, Meenal Baghel, Sarnath Bannerjee, Hartosh Bal, Amarjit Chandan, Arpana Caur, Rana Dasgupta, Manmeet Devgun, Anita Dube, Mahmood Farouqui, Iram Ghufran, Ruchir Joshi, Rashmi Kaleka, Ranbir Kaleka, Sonia Khurana, Saleem Kidwai, Pradip Kishen, Subasri Krishnan, Lawrence Liang, Zarina Muhammed, Veer Munshi, Vivek Narayanan, Monica Narula, Teenaa Kaur Pasricha, Ajmer Rode, Arundhati Roy, Anusha Rizvi, Nilanjana Roy, Inder Salim, Hemant Sareen, Priya Sen, Shuddhabrata Sengupta, Ghulam Mohammed Sheikh, Nilima Sheikh, Gurvinder Singh, Jaspreet Singh, Madan Gopal Singh, and Paromita Vohra.

Suite of drawings by Gagan Singh. Endpiece drawings by Venkat Singh Shyam.

Released on Kafila.org in April 2013, rereleased in November 2014, November 2017, November 2019, and June 2020; 22.86 × 17.78 cm; 116 pages, 45 black-and-white photographs; 24 drawings; free to download, print out, staple, and distribute.

To: gauri.gill@gmail.com
Subject: 1984

The other day on the metro to Shadipur, I watched
this girl who was standing near the door, facing the
corner and listening to her headphones with her eyes
tightly shut. She would open her eyes when the song
would finish and close them again when the next one
would start. There are times when sadnesses need
to find each other, unnoticed by one or the other.
It doesn't matter that she had no idea this was
happening. [There is a monumental silence here. A
monumental crime has been committed. A monumental
history of violence has been absorbed.] The same day,
I decided to take the metro to Dwarka instead of back
to Rajiv Chowk. Winter is over. The days are clear
with incredibly short shadows at noon. People walk
around without their shadows briefly. For a moment
this city loses its soul everyday. The metro to Dwarka
was no revelation and the sun was setting and casting
all kinds of shadows. [This corner of this room of
photographs, this photograph of photographs, this
frame of absence, these people looking at us, these
garlands around a father a son a husband a saint,
this uncanny stillness, this fan that doesn't stop,
this present moment, these drawings on the wall, this
heaviness in these hands, this illegible piece, this
printed sheet, this sleeping justice, these markings
of a future, this future city, this generation, this
contained sadness, this unfathomable grief, this
corner of this room in this photograph.] I can't take
photographs on moving trains anymore. I would rather
not witness the blurs.

PRIYA SEN

The walls of Bhaggi Kaur's house covered with her grandchildren's graffiti. The scribbles and doodles stand in contrast to the framed pictures of Kaur's husband and son that hang nearby. 53-year-old Bhaggi lost her husband in 1984, while her son committed suicide by overdosing on painkillers three years ago.

Taranjeet Kaur's grandfather Jeevan Singh was killed on Nov 1, 1984. "A mob of 400–500 people followed my husband and before he could reach a safe house in Pandav Nagar, they knited him and left him to die on the rail tracks," recounts Taranjeet's grandmother Surjit, crying uncontrollably. It hasn't been easy since. "I have spent my life struggling, but I want my granddaughter to study hard," she says.

Does she usually read this way?
   Always in the same room?
   Is the tiny black object on the trunk (on the steel
cabinet) really a bird?
   Why exactly am I moved by this image?
   There are forty-eight black-and-white photographs in
my new novel, *Helium*, including this one, on an entire
page. Yesterday I showed it (without the original
caption) to my father. "Padhai ho rahi hai," he said.
"A very humble family... She is trying to locate the
past." He doesn't know yet that the photograph carries
traces of an atrocity. The caption would have disturbed
him. Among other things it would have triggered his own
memories of November 1984. Layers of cold ash. In 1984
the two cabinets in the room would have failed to hide
the victims. The phone, too, would have been equally
helpless (because the cops in Delhi were extremely busy
facilitating acts of cruelty). She was not born yet.
   When I first saw the photograph I felt its silence.
Silence filled the whole space. But, soon a detail
broke the silence. Her ear. It made me pause, and
I heard the hum of painful stories she must have
heard over and over. The same ear, I felt, would have
preserved the shape of her grandmother's voice.
   Postmemory that messy archive of trauma and its
transference. Outside the house, ironically, the same
ear must have detected ongoing shamelessness and
injustice. Collective amnesia.
   Whenever I revisit the photograph, my gaze is also
perturbed by the earring. But, is it really an earring?
Perhaps what I see is a slow t(ear). And it refuses to
fall down. I make a list of all the objects around her
bed. They, too, are listening/hearing devices. They
will outlast her.
   What book is she reading? Hope it is not a
prescribed text of "history."
   "Why should young people know about an event best
buried and forgotten?" The Indian censor board asks on
awarding an "A" rating to a film on the 1984 pogrom.
But this is not the exact reason why the picture wounds
me.
   Something within its space and accumulated time is
broken, and will always remain so.

JASPREET SINGH

I knew a young man in his twenties in November 1984. He was tall, had a loping gait, and a way of speaking that would alternate between short, staccato bursts of words, and long, perfectly formed sentences. He was studying to be a doctor, in his last years at medical school, and I thought that he was the most intelligent man I knew at the time. I was impressionable, I was sixteen.

When you are sixteen, twenty-five or twenty-seven can look very far away. You have none of the assurance that a young man in his twenties can have. When I look at pictures, I see that assurance in him, as well as its absence in me.

I idolized this man. He was my then girlfriend's elder brother. I remember that he gave me a book by D.D. Kosambi to read, and that he would sometimes take me and his sister with him on his ornithological field trips (he was an avid bird man) in the Jahanpanah forest. He taught us how to be quiet in a forest, and how to speak about things that we felt were too big for sixteen-year-olds.

He gave me a universe.

In November 1984, this young man, his sister, and his widowed mother came to live for a few days in our house in Old Rajendra Nagar after Indira Gandhi was killed. They were Sikh, and I did not want to lose the girl I thought I loved then, or her brother, to a mob. On the way home from school, I had seen a mob of men catch hold of a Sikh man, yank off his turban, throw a rubber tire around his waist and then set it on fire. A policeman watched them do this. From that day on, I have never trusted any person wearing a uniform.

I, who had barely started to take a razor to my chin, shaved the young man's full beard, so that he could "pass" as someone who would not be taken as being Sikh on the street. He had taught me many things, I taught him how to shave. There was a mess of black hair on the white tiles of our bathroom floor. His face changed. It became smaller. Much smaller. And I saw him change. I saw the brightness in his eyes dim as he saw his new, naked face in the mirror.

Something changed that day. I grew up. He lost something that he never found again. It took a few years, but eventually, he was no longer the man I knew before that November shave. He dropped out of medical school, became a recluse, stopped reading, stopped the bird walks, stopped talking to me or to his sister, became hostile and suspicious about everything.

A few years ago, I read a small item in a newspaper about a man whose body was found, months after he had died. He had been living alone, in a locked-up house, and had apparently stopped eating. A friend called me in the middle of the night, in another country, to

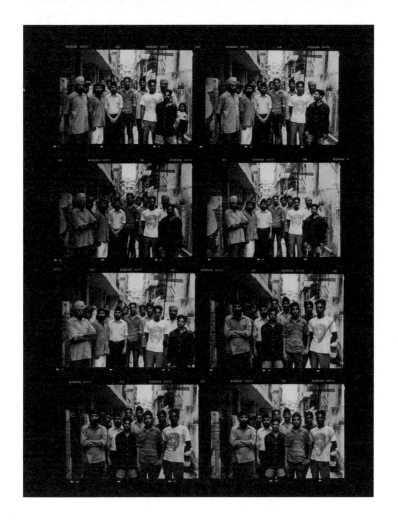

tell me what I suspected. It was the man who showed me
anatomy charts, read Thomas Hardy, and taped bird calls.

In my mind, he is the last casualty of 1984. And I
have never forgiven this city for it.

SHUDDHABRATA SENGUPTA

Sikhs protesting against the Nanavati Commission
report in New Delhi.

"How we beat those motherfuckers, I tell you. After they killed
Nndraakandhi. Each and every sisterfucking Sardar we could find. Now
they are walking around so proudly, but we taught them a lesson in
1984. We went into the shops, we went into their houses, we found them
where they were hiding, we rooted them out from cellars, from cupboards,
from the attics where they hide their business ledgers and we turned
them into chutney. Sisterfuckers." He is a thin, short, underfed man in
his late fifties, a sweaty, ratty little animal of a white-haired man,
and it's a wonder he can pedal the cycle-riksha with me sitting in it.
But the memory seems to give him energy. As he takes me from Jangpura
Extension to Lajpat Nagar Market he points to the auto repair shops, the
little dhabas, the families walking in the lanes. "You know, you how
they have beards and this hair?" While pumping ahead, he turns around to
me, grinning. He mimics a beard on to himself and he tugs it, jerking his
head upwards, nearly hitting an oncoming scooter. "They were very useful
in those two-three days, the beards and the hair! We grabbed them by the
beard, by the hair, and we let them have it!" By the time we reach the
market, he is extremely happy in the new camaraderie he has formed with
no help from me. I don't look like any kind of Sardar but I feel like
grabbing him and telling him I'm a cut-Surd and that I'm now going to
kill him. What I do is pay him his seven rupees and walk away.

LAW GARDENS, 2003

"You don't understand. They needed to be taught a lesson, these cunt-
son mias. There was no choice, it had to be done. You know we have
a whole area here at one edge of Ahmedabad where no one goes? Where
police even couldn't go earlier? We call it mini-Pakistan. Well, a
few of them got sent to the Pakistan below ground, but not enough.
What happened was just like a few small firecrackers. If we'd been
serious, it would have been much worse. We should have sent more of
them to their watan, which is under here." The fat man, who couldn't
even kill a mouse, stamps his fancy chappal on the thick lawn. I look
at the man's paunch pushing out the long, embroidered silk kurta. I
notice his churidar-type pajama has a little tear in the seam near the
ankle. A few feet away, there are people dancing marriage ras-garba and
fingering the young newlyweds. "Ei, Nitinya! Now do that Salman Khan
dance mimicry na? In front of your mother-in-law? Do, na?" The man next
to me puts his hand on my shoulder for balance, slips off his chappal
and raises his churidar leg to examine the tear. "Arre, re, re. Will
have to send that to the tailor. My good tailor was a mia but he's run
away after last year." There's no point my telling this man that I'm a
Muslim or anything like that. He's a relative by marriage and he knows
exactly who I am. He puts his leg down and slaps my back. "But the hell
with these cunt-son Pakistanis you love so much. Tell me! We haven't
met since way before that Eden Gardens test in 2001! Were you at the
stadium when Harbhajan fucked the Australians with that hat trick?"

RUCHIR JOSHI

I look at this horror, this heartbreak, these shards of
memory that broken people carry around with them stitched
into their skins, these portraits of fragile lives that
continue to be lived long after the hammer has fallen
and smashed everything, and I ask myself—why, in our
country, do the architects of genocide always return to
power with a thumping majority?

Why?

What is it about us?

Why are we so ugly?

ARUNDHATI ROY

1984 Sikh Genocide Memorial, Gurudwara Rakaab Ganj Complex, New Delhi.

SHO sheena - He had started
flirtaqat - rand on lips.
friends had become enem
Army had saved us
Nanavati - give justice.
Darshan Kaur
State is silent, as if
nothing happened!
guilty have been made
guilters
children haven't ever been
given father's love.

widows
2

Pappi Kaur, 15 years old.
Police sent the mob
cut people open
burnt people alive.
look now sardars are dancing
cut their eyes, doctor took the
eyes out
"spent 3days, 3nights in corpses"
torches, beautiful women
get out of here
nobody was ready to help.
they were all ready to kill
took us into camps

family saved - wish
25 yrs., nobody has come back

● A

Adam Jones, *Genocide: A Comprehensive Introduction*, Routledge Press (ISBN 9781317533856), 2016

Aatish Taseer, *The Way Things Were*, Pan Macmillan (ISBN 9789382616337), 2014

A.G. Noorani, *CIVIL LIBERTIES: Supreme Court and Punjab Crisis*, EPW magazine, September 22, 1984

A.G. Noorani, *CIVIL LIBERTIES: Rule of Law and Terrorism in Punjab and Northern Ireland*, EPW magazine, October 20, 1984

A.G. Noorani, *CIVIL LIBERTIES: Ill-Treatment of Political Detenus*, EPW magazine, April 20, 1985

A.G. Noorani, *CIVIL LIBERTIES: The Terrorist Act*, EPW magazine, June 1, 1985

A.G. Noorani, *Misra commission under fire*, Sikh Review, 35 (401), May 1987

A.G. Noorani, *CIVIL LIBERTIES: Repressive Laws in Punjab*, EPW magazine, September 12, 1987

A.G. Noorani, *CIVIL LIBERTIES: Ill-Treatment of Political Detenus*, EPW magazine, January 23, 1988

A.G. Noorani, *Crisis in Judiciary*, Frontline, May 11, 2018

Ajaz Ashraf, *1984 revisited: The guilty men of Delhi*, Sikh Review, 41 (11), November 1993

Ajeet Caur, *November Churasi* (short story collection), Navyug Publishers, 1995

Ajmer Singh, Etmad A. Khan, *Carnage 84, The Ambushing Of Witnesses*, Tehelka magazine, Special Issue, October 8, 2005

Amandeep Sandhu, *Roll of Honour*, Rupa Publications (ISBN 9788129120236), 2013

Amarjit Chandan, *Jugni* (essay), Likhat Parhat, Navyug Publishers, 2013

Amarjit Chandan, *Punjab de QatilāN' nu* and *O jo huNdey sann* (poems), *JarhāN*, 1995, 1999, 2005

Amarjit Chandan, *The Camera and 1984*, https://sikhchic.com/1984/the_camera_1984, 2012

Amitav Ghosh, *The Ghosts of Mrs Gandhi*, The New Yorker magazine, July 1995

Amiya Rao, *When Delhi Burnt*, EPW magazine, December 8, 1984

Amiya Rao, *The Delhi massacre and censoring the Sikhs*. Index Censorship, 14 (4), 1985

Amiya Rao, Aurobindo Ghose, N.D. Pancholi, *Truth about Delhi violence*, Report to the Nation, Citizens for Democracy (India), 1985

Ammtoje Mann, *Hawayein* (feature film), 2003

Amnesty International, *India, Break the Cycle of Impunity and Torture in Punjab*, January 2003

Amnesty International, *31 years and Waiting, An Era of Injustice for the 1984 Sikh Massacre* https://www.amnesty.org.in/images/uploads/articles/Campaign_Digest_W.pdf, 2016

Anshu Saluja, *Engaging with Women's Words and their Silences, Mapping 1984 and its aftermath*, Sikh Formations, Volume 11, Issue 3, 2015

Anurag Singh, *Giani Kirpal Singh's Eye-Witness Account of Operation Bluestar*, Published by B. Chattar Singh, Jiwan Singh (ISBN 978-8176013185), 1999

Arpana Caur, *Wounds of 1984* (painting), 2000

Arvind-Pal S. Mandair, *After 1984? Violence, Politics and Survivor Memories*, Sikh Formations, Volume 11, Issue 3, 2015

Avtar Singh, *Returning to 1984*, Timeout magazine Delhi, April 26, 2013

● B

Balbinder Bhogal, *Monopolizing violence before and after 1984, Government law and the people's passion*, Sikh Formations, Volume 7, Issue 1, 2011

Baljit Malik, *The cry for justice (or innocent Sikh victims of the carnage that followed Mrs. Gandhi's death)*, Illustrated Weekly of India magazine, February 16, 1986

Baljit Malik, *Can political expediency be allowed to interfere with the due process of law? How long will the innocent Sikh victims of the carnage that followed Mrs. Gandhi death wait for justice?*, Spokesman Weekly, March 3, 1986

Basharat Peer with Khushwant Singh, *Anti-Sikh riots a pogrom*, Rediff.com news site, May 9, 2001

● C

Citizen's Commission, Delhi, *31 October to 4 November, 1984, Report of the Citizen's Commission, Delhi*, Tata Press, 1984

Cynthia Keppley Mahmood, *Fighting for Faith and Nation, Dialogues With Sikh Militants*, University of Pennsylvania Press (ISBN 978-0-8122-1592-2), 1996

Cynthia Keppley Mahmood, *A Sea Of Orange, Writings on the Sikhs and India*, Xlibris Corporation (ISBN 978-1-4010-2857-2), 2002

● D

Darshan Singh Tatla, *The Third Ghallughara: On the Sikh Dilemna Since 1984*, Sikh Formations, Volume 11, Issue 3, 2015

● E

Ensaaf.org (Ensaaf is a nonprofit organization working to end impunity and achieve justice for mass state crimes in India, with a focus on Punjab, by documenting abuses, bringing perpetrators to justice, and organizing survivors), ongoing

Ensaaf, *The Punjab Mass Cremations Case, India burning the Rule of Law*, January 2007

Ensaaf, *Punjab Police, Fabricating Terrorism Through Illegal Detention and Torture*, October 2005

EPW magazine editorial, *Mishra Commission, Rewriting History*, March 7, 1987

EPW correspondents, *Who Are the Guilty? Causes and Impact of the Delhi Riots*, November 24, 1984

● F

Forum Gazette, *Minorities not for burning*, 1 (5), August 15, 1986

● G

Gagan Singh, *1984* (drawings), 2019

Gauri Gill, *1984* (notebook for free download and distribution, www.gaurigill.com), 2014–ongoing

Gurmukh Singh, *Representations of the 1984 Tragedy in Punjabi Cinema: Ideology and Cultural Politics*, Sikh Formations, Volume 11, Issue 3, 2015

Gurcharan Singh Babbar, Ed. *Government-organised carnage, November 1984*. Babbar Publications, New Delhi, 1998

Gurvinder Singh Dimpy, *Remembering November 1984 killings: Was it a riot, massacre or pogrom?*, Understanding Sikhism–The Research Journal, 5 (2), July–December 2003

Gurvinder Singh, *Chauthi Koot* (feature film), 2016

● H

Harbhajan Singh, *Meri Kāv Yatra* (collected poems), Navyug Publishers, 1989

Harbhajan Singh, *Unee Sau Churasi* (poems and essays), compiled, edited and introduced by Amarjit Chandan, Chetna Parkashan Publishers, Punjabi Bhawan, Ludhiana (ISBN 978-93-5112-249-4), 2017

Harjit Malik, *A Punjab Report*, EPW magazine, September 15, 1984

Harjit Malik, *Misra Commission Report, Salt on Raw Wounds*, EPW magazine, April 25, 1987

Harjinder Singh Dilgeer and Awtar Singh Sekhon, *India kills the Sikhs*, Sikh Educational Trust, Edmonton, 1994

Harinder Baweja, *Two commissions go wrong*, Sunday Observer newspaper, February 8, 1987

Harinder Baweja, *Police Used Political Clout To Stop My Probe*, Tehelka magazine, April 25, 2009

Harinder Baweja, *When A Big Tree Falls, The Earth Shakes*, Tehelka magazine, April 25, 2009

Harinder Baweja, *1984 victim brings alive Sajjan's riot act*, Hindustan Times newspaper, April 29, 2012

Harminder Kaur, *Blue Star over Amritsar*, Ajanta Publications, New Delhi, (ISBN 9788120202573), 1990

Harnik Deol, *Religion and Nationalism in India, The Case of the Punjab*, Routledge Press, London (ISBN 978-0-415-20108-7), 2000

Harpreet Kaur, *The Widow Colony* (feature film), 2006

Hartosh S. Bal, *Minorities and the Mob*, Open magazine, October 31, 2009

Hartosh S. Bal, *Always Forget*, New York Times newspaper, November 20, 2012

Hartosh S. Bal, *Secular Nonsense on 1984*, Open magazine, September 4, 2013

Hartosh S. Bal, *The Shattered Dome*, Caravan magazine, May 1, 2014

Hartosh S. Bal, *Sins of Commission*, Caravan magazine, October 1, 2014

Harveen Sachdeva Mann, *'Our periodic table of Hate': The archive of 1984 Punjab in Jaspreet Singh's Helium*, Sikh Formations, Volume 14, Issue 1, 2018

H.S. Phoolka interviewed by Chander Suta Dogra, The Hindu newspaper, September 11, 2013

H.S. Phoolka, R.S. Chhatwal, N.S. Bawa and J.M.S Sood, consultant editor Manoj Mitta with Delhi Sikh Gurudwara Management Committee, (CD), *Carnage*

84, Massacre of 4000 Sikhs in Delhi, includes area wise details of the violence linked to a map of Delhi, 1000 affidavits of victims and witnesses, official and non-official inquiry reports and other source material, 2016

Himadri Banerjee, 1984 Punjab Tragedy in Hindi Literary Archives: Images Beyond Punjab in India, Sikh Formations, Volume 11, Issue 3, 2015

The Hindu newspaper (Madras), Who was responsible for the Delhi riots?, February 25, 1987

● I

Inderjit Badhwar, Mishra commission: Serious setbacks, India Today magazine, April 30, 1986

Inderjit Singh Jaijee, Politics of Genocide Punjab 1984–1998, Ajanta Publications (ISBN 8120204158, 9788120204157), 1999

Iqbal Singh, Punjab Under Siege, A Critical Analysis, Allen, McMillan and Enderson publishers, New York (ISBN 978-0-934-83904-4), 1986

● J

Jaideep Singh Mander, More Mass Graves & Burnt Down Gurdwaras Identified in India, Punjab Newsline, April 13, 2011

Jagjit Singh Aurora, 1984: Justice denied to victims of massacre, Sikh Review, 51 (8), August 2003

Jarnail Singh, I Accuse... Penguin Books India (ISBN 978-0-670-08394-7), 2009

Jasdev Rai, KHALISTAN IS DEAD! LONG LIVE KHALISTAN! Sikh Formations, Volume 7, Issue 1, 2011

Jaskaran Kaur, Barbara Crossette, Twenty years of impunity, the November 1984 pogroms of Sikhs in India, A Report by Ensaaf (ISBN 978-0-97870-730-9), second ed. 2006

Jaskaran Kaur, Dhami Sukhman, Protecting the Killers, A Policy of Impunity in Punjab, India, Human Rights Watch, New York, October 2007

Jaspal Naveel Singh 'HOW MANY OF US REMEMBER 1984?': NARRATING MASCULINITY AND MILITANCY IN THE KHALISTANI RAP BRICOLAGE, Sikh Formations, Volume 9, Issue 3, 2013

Jaspreet Singh, Carbon, Open magazine, November 9, 2013

Jaspreet Singh, Helium, Bloomsbury USA (ISBN 978-1608199563), 2013

Jaspreet Singh, Thomas Bernhard in New Delhi, New York Times newspaper, July 22, 2013

Jaspreet Singh, NOVEMBER: POEMS, Bayeux Arts, Canada (ISBN 978-1988440125), 2017

Joyce Pettigrew, The Sikhs of the Punjab, Unheard Voices of State and Guerrilla Violence, Zed Books Ltd. (ISBN 978-1856493567), 1995

Jyoti Grewal, Betrayed by the state, the anti-Sikh pogrom of 1984, Penguin Books India (ISBN 978-0-14-306303-2), 2007

● K

Khalsa Aid Canada and Abhishek Madhukar, Lapata. And the Left Behind, Canada, UK and USA tour, 2019

Khushwant Singh, Fifteen fateful years: 1984–99 (Delhi riots), Seminar magazine 476, 14–16, April 1999 https://lapata-exhibition.com/?fbclid =IwAR2tYwFgJlt77U7xJW87Or-9B51U23- 50_4qWyy_Xyky_lTfJzvyp8K3WEY

● L

Lionel Baixas, The Anti-Sikh Pogrom of October 31 to November 4, 1984, in New Delhi, http://www.massviolence.org/ The-1984-Anti-Sikhs-pogroms-in-New-Dehli?artpage=8

Loveleen Kaur, THE TEAR IN THE FABRIC OF MULTICULTURALISM, The recurring image of the Sikh extremist, Sikh Formations, Volume 10, Issue 1, 2014

1984 Living History Project, 1984livinghistory.org, online archive of videos about 1984

● M

Madhu Kishwar, Gangster rule: The Massacre of the Sikhs, in Religion at the service of nationalism and other essays, Oxford University Press, New Delhi, 1998

Mahmood Awan, Khalistan, anti-sikh Pogrom, and poetry of 1984, The News, Pakistan (http://tns.thenews. com.pk/khalistan-anti-sikh-pogrom-poetry-1984/#.We25jBOCxsN), 2017

Maloy Krishna Dhar, Bitter Harvest: A Saga of the Punjab, Ajanta Publications, Punjab (ISBN 9788120204539), 1996

Manjit Bawa, Mapping the Conscience, 1984-2004 (paintings, body of work about 1984, curated by Ina Puri), Jehangir Art Gallery and Palette Art Gallery, 2004

Manjit Bawa, My Punjab, Illustrated Weekly of India magazine, October 14, 1990

Maninder Singh Kang, Bhaar (short story), from Bhet Waali Gall, Lokgeet Prakashan, Chandigarh, 2009 OR South Asian Ensemble, Spring 2011

GAURI GILL

Manoj Mitta & H.S. Phoolka, *When a Tree Shook Delhi*, Roli Books (ISBN 978-81-7436-598-9), 2007

Mark Tully and Satish Jacob, *Amritsar: Mrs Gandhi's Last Battle*, Jonathan Cape 1986, Rupa Publications (ISBN 978-81-291-0917-0), 2006

Mie Lewis, Jaskaran Kaur, *Punjab Police, Fabricating Terrorism Through Illegal Detention and Torture*, Ensaaf, October 2005

● N

Nandita Haskar, *Mishra commission: A hoax*, Sikh Review, 34 (389), June 1986

Nanavati Commission Report, http://www.carnage84.com/homepage/nancom.htm, 2005

● O

● P

Paash, *Dharmdeekhsha laee Vinaypatra* and *Bedakhli laee Vinaypatr* (poems in Punjabi), *LaRhāN ge Sathi*, eds. Gursharan Singh & Narbhinder, Balraj Sahni Prakashan, 1988

Paash, *Blog on the Revolutionary Indian Poet* (http://paas.wordpress.com/category/paash-in-english/), ongoing

Pal Ahluwalia, *The Politics of Intimacy, (Re) thinking 1984*, Sikh Formations, Volume 6, Issue 2, 2010

P.C Alexander, *1984: Assassination and massacre of Sikhs*, Sikh Review, 48 (11), November 2000

Parvinder Mehta, *Repressive Whispers of History Lessons and Legacies of 1984*, Sikh Formations, Volume 11, Issue 3, 2015

Parvinder Singh, *1984, Sikhs Kristallnacht*, Ensaaf, May 2009

Pav Singh *1984: INDIA'S GUILTY SECRET*, Kashi House, Britain (ISBN 978-1911271086), 2017

Patwant Singh, *Needed salves for the Sikh's wounds*, Sunday Mail newspaper, April 5, 1986

Patwant Singh, *The Sikhs*, New York, Alfred Knopf (ISBN 978-0-307-42933-9 and 0-307-42933-4), 2000

Paul Brass, *Language, Religion and Politics in North India*, Cambridge University Press, Cambridge (ISBN 978-0521203241), 1974

Paul Brass (ed.), *Riots and Pogroms*, Macmillan Press, London (ISBN 978-0-333-66976-1), 1996

Payal Singh Mohanka, *Koi Sardar Hai*, first-person account, Illustrated Weekly of India magazine, December 23, 1984

People's Union for Democratic Rights and People's Union for Civil Liberties, *Who are the Guilty? Report of a Joint Inquiry into the Causes and Impact of the Riots in Delhi from 31 October to 10 November, 1984*, New Delhi, http://www.pucl.org/Topics/Religion-communalism/2003/who-are-guilty.htm, PUCL 2003

People's Union for Democratic Rights, *1984 Carnage in Delhi, A Report on the Aftermath*, Delhi, November 1992

Prem Parkash, *Ih oh Jasbir nahin* and *Kanhi* (short stories in his collected *Katha Anant*), Navyug Publishers, 1995

Pritam Singh, *Government Media and Punjab*, EPW magazine, January 12, 1985

Punjab Disappeared, *Punjab Disappeared* (documentary), 2019, www.punjabdisappeared.org

● Q

● R

Radhika Chopra, *1984-Disinterred Memories*, Sikh Formations, Volume 11, Issue 3, 2015

Rahul Bedi, *A Darkness Unforgotten*, Tehelka magazine, April 29, 2009

Raj Thapar, *How do you do it (Delhi riots)*? Forum Gazette 5, August 15, 1986

Rajni Kothari, *Carnage: The how & why of it all*, Sikh Review, 42 (11), November 1994

Ram Narayan Kumar, et al, *Reduced to Ashes, The Insurgency and Human Rights in Punjab*, South Asia Forum for Human Rights, 2003

Ram Rahman, *Never Forget*, Open magazine, November 17, 2012

Ranbir Kaleka, *Smoke, Fire and Glass* (painting), 1984

Ranbir Kaleka, *Boy without Reflection* (painting), 2004

Ranbir Singh Sandhu, *Struggle for Justice, Speeches and Conversations of Sant Jarnail Singh Khalsa Bhindranwale*, Sikh Educational and Religious Foundation (ISBN 978-0967287416), 2000

Reema Anand, *Scorched White Lilies of 84*, Rupa India Publications (ISBN 8129115416), 2010

Richard D. Mann, *Media framing and the myth of religious violence: The othering of Sikhs in* The Times of India, Volume 12, Issue 2–3, 2016

Rita Verma, *Making Meaning of 1984 in Cyberspace: Youth Answering Back to Reclaim Sikh Identity and Nationhood*, Sikh Formations, Volume 7, Issue 1, 2011

Ritu Sarin and Nirmal Mitra, *White washing the crimes of 1984*, Sunday Magazine, March 14, 1987

Romesh Silva, Jasmine Marwaha, Jeff Klingner, *Violent Deaths and Enforced Disappearances During the Counterinsurgency in Punjab, India, A Preliminary Quantitative Analysis*, Palo Alto, Ensaaf and the Benetech Human Rights Data Analysis Group–HRDAG, January 26, 2009

R. S Chhatwal, *Victims of November 1984 denied justice*, Sikh Review, 51 (3), March 2003

● S

S. Balwant, *Ithasik Vishvasghat* (An Historic Betrayal) *Delhi 1984*, 50-page memoir, published in several publications – Hun - 31, Dec 2015; republished the same year in *Des Pardes* (UK) and *Punjabi Tribune* (Chandigarh)

Safina Uberoi, *My Mother India* (documentary film), 2009

Sanjay Suri, *1984: The Anti-Sikh Violence and After*, Harper Collins (ISBN 9351770710, 9789351770718), 2015

Saroj Vasishth, *Kala November, The Carnage of 1984*, Rupa Publications (ISBN 8171673287), 1995

Schona Jolly, *No Justice for India's Sikhs*, The Guardian newspaper, UK, October 31, 2009

Shashi Kumar, *Kaya Taran* (feature film), 2004

Shobhita Naithani, *I Don't Think Justice Will Come*, Tehelka magazine, April 25, 2009

Shonali Bose, *Amu* (feature film), 2005

Shruti Devgan, *From the 'crevices in dominant memories': virtual commemoration and the 1984 anti-Sikh violence*, Identities>Global Studies in Culture and Power, Volume 20, 2013

Shubhashish Bhutania, *Kush* (short film), 2013

Sidharth Bhatia, *A Journey to a Past that Will Not Pass*, The Wire, online news site, November 1, 2016

Siddharth Varadarajan, *Moral indifference as the form of modern evil*, The Hindu newspaper, August 12, 2005

Sikhchic.com (website with compilation of articles related to Sikh history and contemporary affairs, ongoing), http://sikhdigitallibrary.blogspot.in/ (website with compilation of articles), ongoing

Singh Twins, *Nineteen Eighty-Four (The Storming of 'The Golden Temple')* (painting), 1998

Smitu Kothari, Harsh Sethi, eds. *Voices from a Scarred City, The Delhi Carnage in Perspective* Lokayan, Delhi, 1985

Sondeep Joshi, *Wounds of '84 riots still fresh for them*, Times of India newspaper (New Delhi), November 1, 2003

S. Muglaokar, *Flawed inquiry's flawed report*, Indian Express newspaper (New Delhi), February 28, 1987

Spokesman Weekly, *Mishra Commission report: The thin divide between myth and reality*, March 16, 1987

S.S. Abraham, *Mishra report: An exercise in evasion*, The Times of India newspaper (New Delhi), February 28, 1987

Steven I. Wilkinson, ed., *Religious Politics and Communal Violence*, Oxford University Press, New Delhi (ISBN 9780195672374), 2005

Sunday Mail newspaper, *Mishra Commission. Fuelling scepticism*, March 7, 1987

Sunday Observer newspaper, *Mishra report a complete let down: It was expected that nothing would come of it*, March 1, 1987

Surjit Brar, *Lahu Bolda Hai*, Balraj Sahni Yadgar Prakashan, 1984

Surjit Patar: 24 poems in *Birkh Arz karey*, Shabdalok, 1992, and 9 poems in *Hanyrey vich Sulaghdi varanmala*, Shabhadlok, 1992. New rendering of *udo varis shah nun vandal si, hunh shiv kumar di vari e*: http://www.giss.org/media/Udo_Warus_Sha_Nu_CD.wav

● T

Teenaa Kaur Pasricha, *1984 WHEN THE SUN DIDN'T RISE* (documentary film), 2017

Tusha Mittal, *When He Sees A Cop He Wets His Pants*, Tehelka magazine, April 25, 2009

Tusha Mittal, *I Had To Dress My Boys In Frocks*, Tehelka magazine, April 25, 2009

Tusha Mittal, *A Pack Of Wolves in Khaki Clothing*, Tehelka magazine, April 25, 2009

GAURI GILL

Two Path Productions, *Kultar's Mime*,
http://www.indiegogo.com/projects/
kultar-s-mime

• U

Uma Chakravarti and Nandita Haksar, *The
Delhi Riots, Three Days in the Life
of a Nation* (ISBN 978-8170620204),
December 1987

Uma Chakravarti, *Victims, 'Neighbours',
and 'Watan', Survivors of Anti-Sikh
Carnage of 1984*, EPW magazine, October
15, 1994

Uma Chakravarti, *Long Road to Nowhere,
Justice Nanavati on 1984*, EPW
magazine, August 27, 2005

Upamanyu Chatterjee, *The Assassination
of Indira Gandhi*, London magazine,
June 1985

• V

Veena Das, *Anthropological Knowledge
and Collective Violence: The Riots in
Delhi, November 1984*, Anthropology
Today, published by the Royal
Anthropological Institute of Great
Britain and Ireland, Volume 1, Number
3, 4–6, June 1985

Veena Das, *Life and Words, Violence
and the Descent into the Ordinary*,
University of California Press (ISBN
978-0520247451), 2006

Veena Das, *Mirrors of Violence,
Communities, Riots and Survivors in
South Asia*, Oxford University Press,
India (ISBN 978-0195632217), new ed.
June 1983

Venkat Singh Shyam, *1984* (drawings), 2019

Vikram Kapur, *Time Is A Fire* (novel),
Srishti Publishers and Distributors
(ISBN 81-87075-79-1), 2002 (ISBN 81-
87075-79-1), 2003

Vikram Kapur, *1984 In memory and
imagination, Personal Essays and
Stories on the 1984 Anti-Sikh Riots*,
Amaryllis (ISBN: 978-93-81506-91-2),
2016

Vikram Kapur, *The Assassinations: A Novel
of 1984*, Speaking Tiger Books (ISBN
978-93-86702-33-3), November 2017

• W

Waryam Singh Sandhu, *Chauthi Koot* (short
story collection), Sangam Publications
Samana (ISBN: 9789382804468), 2013

Wikileaks

• X

• Y

• Z

O

Figuration/Disfiguration: Racial Logic and Representation

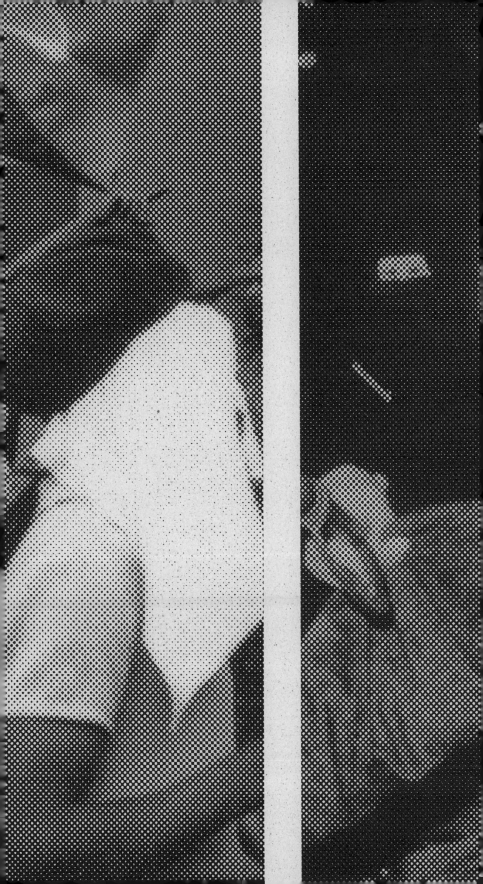

Introduction
Natasha Ginwala

"What struck me most about those who rioted was how long they waited. The restraint they showed. Not the spontaneity, the restraint. They waited and waited for justice and it didn't come. No one talks about that…," notes Toni Morrison on the Los Angeles Riots of 1992. Morrison points to how superficial explorations of riots see them in terms of speed, defiance (a loss of sensibility), and a muddy event horizon that blurs facticity: visceral stuff brims over with "burnin' and lootin'" (as Bob Marley and the Wailers called out in their 1973 album). But when we see the cumulative patterns of riots, we have to ask anew: Where did they begin? What has changed in the system as the cycle of waiting, systemic injustice, and rage repeats itself?

The third section of this anthology, "Figuration/Disfiguration: Racial Logic and Representation," collects contributions from artists and writers who endeavor toward testimonial production. Specific riots—such as the Tunisian Dignity Revolution, the St. Pauls Riot, the Durban Riots, and recurring ethnic riots in Sri Lanka—are read against the grain by practitioners who have directly experienced these events and have closely examined their unresolved legacy. In what follows, Josh Kun adds a revelatory unpacking of the sonic dynamics and improvisatory edit of Santiago Álvarez's short film *Now!* as "a militant art of audiovisual recycling" while treating montage as a figuration of the alliance building against global racism and unjust death. Spending time in the city archives of Bristol and among community groups, Louis Henderson navigates the 1980 riots through the "Bristol sound" and St. Pauls Carnival, entwining the timelines of the colonial plantation system and the "sus laws" implemented during the Thatcher regime while listening to images as well as found footage for echo and reverb, infusing the address of dub poets such as Linton Kwesi Johnson and the sirens of sound systems and police cars.

Poetry is a compelling witness to the wounds and the gains of rebellion. In "The Manifesto Unwritten" (on page 18 of this volume), Satch Hoyt composes these lines:

> Let's huddle close this morning breakfast,
> count our limbs, pick scabs off sores,
> Pay respect to the ancestors,
> place offerings at secret shrines.

In narrating the Durban Riots and their fragments through the dramaturgy of looking, Vivek Narayanan's essay in this volume problematizes the framing of active participation and passive observation. Those included in the riots are not merely those in the streets: voyeurism implicates European protagonists, Indian and African communities, and inevitably newspaper readers with their greedy eyes—even the writer himself as he analyzes a photograph.

NATASHA GINWALA

Guy Debord's "The Rise and Fall of the Spectacular Commodity-Economy" was published in *Internationale Situationniste* (Situationist International) as an analysis of the Watts Rebellion in Los Angeles during the summer of 1965, when the city's Black population rose against law enforcement—the police and the National Guard. He notes:

> Even those prepared to acknowledge apparent justifications for the black anger in Los Angeles (though not, of course, any real ones)—all the theorists and spokesmen of the international Left (or, rather, its nothingness)—deplored the irresponsibility and disorder; the looting—especially the fact that liquor and weapons were the first targets of plunder; and above all; the estimated 2,000 fires started by the Watts petrol-throwers to light up their battle and their celebration. Who has defended the rioters of Los Angeles in the terms they deserve? Well, we shall... The task of a revolutionary journal is not only to endorse the Los Angeles insurgents, but also to help supply them with their reasons: to offer a theoretical account of the truth sought implicitly by their practical action.[1]

Left movements and establishment forces' apologies for rioters' actions and demands have an enduring history. There is a broken promise here: fundamentally, that rioters and protestors must recognize a discriminatory politico-legal system while striving to live on equitable terms. While the state apparatus and segments of Left leadership come to the defense of bourgeois property rights, the systemic flaws and fault lines of class and race continue to persist and play against marginalized communities.

Oana Pârvan's thesis on Tunisia's Dignity Revolution of 2011, stirred by Mohamed Bouazizi's self-immolation and led by the suburban unemployed, students, and a unionized workforce, examines how those designated as "surplus life" by the neo-imperial economy are pushed toward "unruly" practices and strategies of necro-resistance (see Pârvan's piece in this volume).

In many cases, the aftermath of rioting has brought on even more repressive policing measures and drawn-out court disputes. Riots occur when there has been a profound breach of trust, as the social contract becomes worn down by systemic abuse and profiling of minority groups. The voices gathered in this book respond to communal grief and transitional justice; they mourn for those missing bodies, false arrests, and the many generations that live with the traumas that arise from the frictions and histories of riots. In his contribution to this book, Chandraguptha Thenuwara considers the memorialization of the Black July Riots in Sri Lanka as a circuit of gestures and artistic strategies that show how state forces institute forced forgetting, transformation of the enemy image, and state-led postwar urban beautification, and how the "ghost images" of violence replay in riots that ignite with renewed intensity. "Figuration/Disfiguration" examines the blurred lines and fragments: the sonic, visual, and social registers of riotous encounters as a meshwork rather than as totalizing image or narration.

● 1. Guy Debord, *A Sick Planet* (London: Seagull Books, 2008), 5.

In Search of 1949

Vivek Narayanan

Dis poem will not change things:
dis poem *needs* to be changed.
—Mutabaruka

Chronicle of Deaths Not Foretold: A Narration of the Durban Riots
(Quotations taken from the testimony of Major George Bestford, District Commandant of Durban, to the Riot Commission)

Rushing into Indian area

The scene in Pine Street, Durban at about 12.30 p.m. to-day, when hundreds of Natives sought fresh trouble. Crowds of Europeans thronged the streets to watch the rioting and made the police's job of controlling the rioters far more difficult.

...ces such as occurred

...and is a growing resentment among Natives towards Indians,

This piece was originally presented in 1999 at the African History Seminar at the University of Kwazulu-Natal Durban, and was subsequently uploaded to Abahlali.org. Many sources cited in this essay have since been lost or could not be updated due to the lack of access to libraries and archives during the COVID-19 pandemic.

VIVEK NARAYANAN

Thursday, January 13, 1949

Approximately 5:15 p.m.: Harilal Basanth, a forty-year-old Indian shop owner, smashes fourteen-year-old George Madondo's head into a shop window. A "minor disturbance" breaks out. The police send a van to investigate.

5:25 p.m.: In the busy Victoria Street bus rank, the fight has begun to escalate; Africans want to "hit the Indians whom they alleged had either seriously assaulted or killed a Native youth." A large crowd of Indians gathers in Victoria Street, but they are prevented from marching to the market by the police. The police send reinforcements.

6:00 p.m.: Indian men and women throw bricks and other objects at Africans on the street.

6:30 p.m.: Some shop windows have been smashed; there are "large numbers of both Europeans and non-Europeans about." The rioters on the street are mainly African but include some Indians and Europeans. There is not yet much damage to property.

7:00 p.m.: Accounts of the event have been carried home to barracks and residential areas; in Cato Manor, buses are stoned.

8:30 p.m.: In Clairwood and the southern part of central Durban, Indian-owned buses are stoned.

11:00 p.m.: A rain shower breaks out; fighting begins to quell.

Friday, January 14

Morning: News of a general attack against Indians at 5:00 p.m. reaches the police.

Midday: An Indian is assaulted by a group of Africans at the Victoria Street Market's Queen Street entrance; in the street, young Africans chase Indians, hitting them with sticks and stones. "Indians retaliated by throwing bricks and bottles from balconies not only at the youngsters but also at working Natives who break for lunch at noon."

12:30 p.m.: Police reinforcements arrive.

1:00 p.m.: Groups of up to 200 Africans begin to congregate near the markets.

2:00 p.m.: Large groups of Africans march along Berea and Bellair Roads, throwing stones at Indian shops, dwellings, and "everything 'Indian.'" A group of about 400 gathers at the Somtseu Road Native Barracks and begins to arm itself. Smaller groups form in Victoria Street, Greyville, and along Umgeni Road. In Victoria Street, one interview subject personally sees an "impi" followed from behind by a European with his face blackened by shoe polish.[1] Unarmed militant Africans assemble in the Stamford Hill and Overport areas. In Clairwood, large groups of armed Indians congregate and begin to clash with groups of Africans. At this point, both groups seem to be fighting mostly with sticks. Groups of Indians begin to attack Africans (some of them innocent) around the city.

3:00 p.m.: Groups of Africans march along Maydon Road, West Street, and Point Road toward town. Some of the armed groups (occasionally dispersed or disarmed by the police) begin to march toward Cato Manor. In Cato Manor, African women and children throw stones at Indians and their transport.

3:15 p.m.: About 1,000 residents of the Somtseu Road barracks rush the neighboring (Indian) Magazine Barracks, but are stopped at the gate, which was generally locked at night.

3:45 p.m.: Large numbers of Indian stores are smashed and looted in the Point police area. A militant group from the Somtseu Road barracks begins the first clash with police, who fire upon them.

4:00 p.m.: With the arrival of militant male impis from the barracks and compounds around the city, the fighting in Cato Manor intensifies; there is large-scale destruction of property, assault, and looting.

Shortly before 5:00 p.m.: The police hear that an Indian has fired on Africans with a revolver. African accounts tell of many more Indians shooting with revolvers.

6:00 p.m.: Fighting spreads as far as Pinetown, ten miles west of Durban. In Cato Manor, the situation becomes very serious: Indians are being dragged out of their homes. In the area toward Booth Road,

---

●   1.   The word "impi" is often used to refer to a regiment of Zulu soldiers, although the actual technical term for that is "ibutho."

Indian men are killed and Indian women raped. Indian refugees begin to stream into camps around the city. Police have begun to fire indiscriminately at groups of Africans, whether they are directly involved in the rioting or not.

7:00 p.m.: Situation in Cato Manor reaches its peak; houses are looted and set on fire.

9:00 p.m.: Army and naval regiments arrive in Cato Manor.

11:00 p.m.: Fighting in most areas begins to quell. In Cato Manor, it continues through the night.

Saturday, January 15

6:00 a.m.: Fighting in Cato Manor has died down; the dead and the wounded are being collected. Further police and military regiments arrive from all over South Africa. All bars and beer halls are closed. A number of arrests have been made.

Sunday, January 16

Isolated rioting. Police begin to receive "numerous reports of assaults by Indians on Natives."

Enter the Puppeteer
My narrative grows to explain this existence
amidst the harbour lights that remain in the distance.
—Black Star, "Respiration"

Where else can I begin, but here—with these very words, with the brown fingers that type them by the computer's fluorescent light late one night in my office, in a university that (they tell us) has transformed irrevocably, a simple—but never taken—night walk away from the unlit expanse of Cato Manor, in this city sprawled out around me, determined, it seems, to keep its secrets? The cultural historian in me still obstinately wants to believe that he can know, that he can enter the foreign country of the past through excavation and begin to live there, that he can see the world through the eyes of that past's natives on their own terms, and that he can present that past, exposed or uncovered, an object already there and waiting to be seen, to those that inhabit his world fifty years later. The reality, however, is that the process of scholarship is never innocent. To pursue an event for years, to become obsessed with it as I have, one must have a very serious stake in the meaning of that event. I grew up an Indian boy in Zambia, at the boundaries of cultures and nations, not knowing at all (until I learned to narrate myself) that I was standing at such an intersection. I confess: like many of the foreigners who came to South Africa in the wake of 1994, I, too, was here to taste "the dream," the fruit of years of struggle. For me, this meant the hope—nurtured by stories of Gandhi and, later, how Indians and Africans came to participate in a joint struggle—that I could once again recover a childhood of effortless border crossings. Yes, the struggle did happen; but the reality of struggle, I was to learn, is never as sexy as its narrated counterpart.

Nineteen forty-nine. I sound out the date as I write this, and hear the numbers echo in my head. Historians are perhaps, by definition, numerologists. The number 1949 seems to carry a kind of *muti* on its own, the way it seems so easy to remember, the way it stops just short of the half-century, containing everything that came before it, the way it seems to wait for the months to pass and for the nine to roll back into a zero, a beginning as well as an end. For many Indian South Africans, still uncertain of whether they truly belong to this country or to another imagined one, it is one of the few dates that have survived in widespread popular memory—along with "1820 settlers" (a slippage by which they replace the dates of their own arrival with that of Europeans in Natal), "1948," and "1994." It is one of a handful of dates that, for them, ironically, marks their presence in this land.

Ladies and gentlemen of the jury, fellow commissioners of inquiry, I need to tell you first that I am not innocent. I have before me, on my desk, a crude photocopy of a photograph, taken from the front page of the *Natal Daily News* on January 14, 1949, which shows "crowds of Europeans" "rushing" to the Indian areas to watch the rioting. There is some proof that Europeans were involved in the riots, both as rioters and as calculating inciters, but now I want to suggest that this photograph points to one very different kind of involvement.

From the photograph, we could say that the Europeans were not participating but looking, perhaps with a kind of morbid curiosity, for what would be a glimpse into closed worlds at the point of their eruption, what—to them—would be a glimpse into an exotic, primal scene. But looking, as the physicists tell us, is never a merely passive activity. The photograph and the guarded tone of its caption demonstrates to us that by their very presence as spectators, the European crowds could begin to shape the events as they unfolded, that the story would necessarily have to unfold in the context of the colonial gaze. It is because of the shaping quality of this gaze that many Indians and Africans involved in a joint struggle would hesitate to discuss their differences before a European audience today. Looking, in fact, carries with it a tremendous responsibility and, if the voyeurism of those in the photograph troubles us, then we must think very carefully about our own voyeurism as scholars. Many times over the course of my research I have wondered if I myself was looking too far into things, that I might shape the story through that looking and through the process of allowing others to look. There is no riot apart from its telling, and there is no telling that is not structured by ideology. If the story that I'm about to tell is a story of how the riot is created through multiple readings of its significance—its moral, if you will—then the story that I tell will also be a parable, an allegory. Whatever you see here is refracted through my gaze, and if I am to live up to that responsibility, then I must try to write my parable from a new vantage point, one that trumps and interrogates the ethnic fragmentation of the riot and, indeed, much of South African historiography to date. I must try and lift the upheavals out of their place in "Indian history" and try—given the limitations of who I am—to read against it in a larger context. I pause to wish myself good luck.

The Spark

The various accounts of the 1949 riots that I consider in this essay have to begin somewhere. In the vast range of narratives (both oral and written) that I have been trying to plumb, they begin—almost universally—with what the Riot Commission Report called "the spark": the altercation between George Madondo and Harilal Basanth on a chaotic, muggy, and cloudy Thursday afternoon. In interviews, I have painfully tried to guide people through life histories until the point of the riot to see if I can get them to arrive at the riot at a different point (that of personal experience), but there seems to be a continual need on the part of the interviewees to return to this "spark."

Academic accounts to date inevitably begin with the altercation as well—perhaps because it offers the hard residue of names and facts—but then move anxiously, like most popular accounts, to explanations of a larger order such as the old saws of class conflict, political differences, and so forth. I don't dispute, of course, that a course of events involving thousands of people would necessarily involve macro-level "causes." Yet there is a strange tension in this narration, and a very real problem: how does such a small, everyday event transmute into something so much larger? And why did not one of the numerous fights and arguments that broke out between Indians and Africans throughout the course of the 1930s and 1940s suffer the same fate? I can't pretend to answer such questions completely, but the first set of clues must likely be found by piecing together what might have happened in that encounter.

Luckily for us, Harilal Basanth was brought to trial for his assault on February 1 , 1949. It was a remarkably short trial, and the judge in charge could hardly, at that stage, not convict him— he was fined £1 or seven days' imprisonment, and justice was served. In the trial, we learn from both parties that Madondo knew the shop well and often went there to buy cigarettes. Earlier that Thursday, Danragh, Basanth's sixteen-year-old shop assistant, had been sent to the "Native" market on an errand and had been stopped by Madondo, who asked him for a cigarette. We cannot know from the self-serving court testimonies what exactly Danragh's reply was, but it resulted in him being slapped twice by Madondo. It was as a reply to these slaps that Basanth later accosted Madondo and, without exchanging too many words, ended up pushing him into a shop window.

Madondo denied being a member of a gang in Basanth's trial, but either way he certainly had well-wishers at the scene of his assault. He suffered head wounds from the glass and did not, it would appear, tell them the prehistory of the event. Tunywa Dlamini, perhaps the only rioter to have been interviewed in detail, acknowledged the irony of this when he spoke of Madondo years later. It turns out that Madondo grew up to be something of a gangster, a "cynical" and "unpleasant" man. Dlamini referred to Madondo as the one who ruined the country (*owaqeda izwe*): "...he tells you quite calmly because he knows it was by the anger of God that though he was injured it ought to have been intervened in and checked, instead of which much damage was done to the country." It must have been a shock, especially not knowing the prehistory, to see a large forty-year-old Indian man suddenly come and push a fairly slight fourteen-year-old African boy against a shop window. For many Africans at the scene, it may have echoed what they narrated—in their depositions to the commission—as a longer history of *physical* (not just economic) intimidation by Indians, such as the beatings that Africans sometimes received at the hands of bus conductors and their cronies. At any rate, the encounter, which was as much about age and masculinity as it was about race, came to be read in an instant as *senselessly* racial. This seems to have been the most common reading and was—within minutes—written back into many of the African male onlookers' practice. They wanted, as they told the police, to set things right.

If the majority of accounts of 1949 refer back to "the spark" as a founding event, what is striking is how they diverge from there. Many Indian accounts of the spark are often vague about the details, and they generally submerge the disturbingly violent nature of Basanth's action—often reducing it to a beating or to "a couple of slaps"; in these accounts, the spark serves as a parable of how irrational and "tribal" Africans are. The commission report, which considered the detailed list of African grievances as essentially fictional or irrelevant, said, in its typical sardonic style, that "the spark which caused this tragic explosion was almost ludicrous in its insignificance." African accounts, in interviews and in depositions to the commission, recover some of the event's violence but also retell it as parable. In most of these accounts, the main action takes place inside the shop, not outside it, where Madondo is engaged in buying or selling—variously, zinc, or scent, or newspapers (as in Dlamini's account). Furthermore, the shop assistant frequently disappears from these accounts, and the encounter is reduced to the classic trope of shopkeeper versus customer, or shopkeeper versus rival street vendor. In this simplified version, the story becomes an easier emblem of the treatment of Africans at the hands of the "arrogant Indian," marked, paradigmatically, as a shopkeeper.

The accounts of "what really happened" had already begun to splinter irrevocably by 5:15 p.m. on Thursday. What should be evident here is that this very divergence of readings, the process by which the fight between Basanth, Danragh, and Madondo comes to have very different kinds of symbolic and ideological freight for people of different communities, is *itself* crucial to the process of how the riots come into being. As these accounts spread through the divided spaces of the city and begin to diverge and consolidate, the stakes involved in what was happening and what should happen next also began to increase. The riot became irrevocably "racial," and it could increasingly resolve itself only through a violent encounter between divergent epistemologies. This is precisely why, as those who study similar kinds of events around the world have found, riots can be truly understood only in the terms of their fragments (as Gyan Pandey has argued).[2]

At 5:15 p.m. on Thursday, however, I would contend that this process was still quite incomplete. None of the parties

2. Gyan Pandey, *Routine Violence: Nations, Fragments, Histories* (Stanford, CA: Stanford University Press, 2005).

involved could predict what would unfold over the course of the weekend. In order to gain real force, the riot had to enter a few more cycles of (mis)reading and practice. A crowd of Indians marching toward the market who were increasingly predisposed to understand the gathering crowd of Africans as intrinsically violent and an arriving police force that saw the event as a "public disturbance" and not an occasion for conflict resolution both become essential, as do the rioters, to the escalation of the fight. The targets of the rioters in Victoria Street on Thursday the 13, we must remember, were, specifically, Indian *shops*. Thus, at this stage, a grievance against Basanth translated itself into anger against Indian shopkeepers in general.

Indian store owners had a reputation for black-marketeering. Whether this was true or not is, of course, a difficult question to answer when it is framed in purely racial terms. What we know is that between 1946 and 1948, 257 Indians were convicted on violations of price control regulations, as opposed to 78 Europeans and 27 Africans. Black-marketeering was not a purely Indian preserve, but it is certainly possible that the tenuous, breaking-even nature of many Indian businesses (whose owners were also far more generous with credit than their European counterparts) meant that a large number of them *did* resort to such practices.

Working-class Indians were also incensed, at different points, about the black-marketeering of Indian merchants. In a clear but perhaps unintentional echo of Thursday the 13, a "large crowd" of poor Indians marched to and laid siege to the store of an Indian merchant who was stockpiling rice and selling it at inflated prices as soon as the Tuesday (January 18) after the weekend of the riots, as press reports tell us. They forced themselves into the store and began serving themselves but then paid the controlled prices for the goods.

It makes sense, then, that on the first evening of the riots, there were a few Indian looters and rioters as well. Yet the possibility of the riot evolving into pure class conflict was restricted, quite literally, by the fact that Indians did not and could not follow African men back to the barracks and compounds on that Thursday evening.

The future course of the riots, in fact, was to be determined not in Victoria Street, by those rioters who continued to wage their battle until late on Thursday night, but in the all-male spaces of the various compounds and barracks in which the majority of young African men lived. An irreversibly racial reading of the riots consolidated itself in those spaces that evening. Various stories of the riot were related and, through the "subversive trigger" of rumor, the riot was remade to carry new levels of symbolic freight. In one famous account mentioned in the commission report, for instance, Madondo had been killed by the Indians, and his head had been placed in a mosque. Thus, in this tale, the image of the Indian as a cruel shopkeeper was grafted onto another Orientalist image, prevalent at least since the 1930s, of the Indians as "amatagata," mystical black-magic men (Indians I have interviewed remember the chant, during the riots, of "Bulala matagata").[3] If the commission reports and newspapers such as Indian Opinion narrate this story as a thinly disguised parable of African ignorance and gullibility, we must see this perspective as a reminder of the closed spaces (religious and otherwise) to which Africans were not admitted, spaces in which Indians, no doubt, consolidated equally ignorant accounts of their "others." If we are to understand what happened the next day, we must now turn our less-than-innocent gaze toward the closed circuits of those African male dormitories.

The Tsotsi and the Coolie

The Indian has nimbler wits than the Native… [who] is inclined to assess merit in terms of physical strength… The Zulu is by tradition a warrior… The Native is hostile to strangers merely because they are different… [Such] racial characteristics… played an important part in the riots.
—Report from the Riot Commission, 1949

To begin to see how the rioters were constructed by the media (Indian as well as European) of the time and by the commission report, we might consider the famous photograph that first appeared on the front page of the Natal Daily News's on Friday, January 14, 1949, and was then reprinted the following Friday in Indian Opinion. The Daily News's initial caption for the photograph was fairly neutral; Indian Opinion, however, spoke to a more restricted audience and made explicit what the photograph already suggests through its ways of seeing. This was supposed to be the "typical" rioter or, indeed, for some, the "typical" African. We are told that he is young, muscular, and barefoot. As his left arm prepares to hurl a missile, there is a grin on his face and a strange, possessed light in his eyes. He is unpredictable, spontaneous, and gleefully violent.

This was the mythical subject known widely to South Africans of all hues as "the tsotsi." If that handful of European liberals and not-so-liberals who gained their cultural capital by promoting themselves as having "an intimate knowledge of native affairs and the native mind" were crucial in cultivating this mythical subject and distinguishing it from that of the "law-abiding Christian native," they could also, when in a more generous mood, suggest the distant possibility of rehabilitation for the

---

● 3. "Bulala matagata" translates to "kill the black-magic men."

A'&i ;t :/ the Riots
r\in: r i ;: ;ᴚʹ!!

tsotsi by using the term "loafer." The tsotsi and the loafer were one, but while the tsotsi was beyond redemption, the loafer's problem was that he did not share the Protestant ethic and consequently had little to do with his time but get drunk and look for trouble.

Furthermore, if we look at verdicts in cases before the Durban Magistrate's Court through the course of the 1930s and 1940s, we find that "loafers" can be European, Indian, or African. Generally speaking, the tsotsi, or loafer, was also defined by the spaces that he was seen to inhabit—the dangerously liminal and uncontrollable spaces of shack settlements in Cato Manor or Booth Road, or the interracial working-class rooms and backyards of central Durban. In the testimonies to the Riot Commission of 1949, the riots are blamed—by Indian, European, and African witnesses alike—on the unruly and spontaneous tsotsi, or loafer.

It seems logical that since the rioting reached its most violent stage in the Cato Manor and Booth Road areas that the rioters must have lived in those spaces. To this end, much of the commission's time was devoted to the question of high rents and exploitation in Cato Manor. But is that where the core of rioters really came from? This is a difficult question because, as I have already suggested, the riot unfolded in expanding circles, drawing more and more groups of people into its emerging narrative. We can begin to answer it, however, by looking at the statistical charts compiled by the police on the 93 Africans serving terms of imprisonment in the Durban Central Prison for offenses linked to the riots. These were presumably the worst offenders, and an illustrative sample of the 357 Africans convicted in the wake of the events of January 1949.

What emerges from police interviews is that only 15 of these 93 prisoners lived in Indian residential areas or on Indian farms, while 14 lived in *European* residential areas and on European farms. Of those living under Indian landlords, 11 told the police that they were at least satisfied with their accommodation, and 4 complained of excessive rent and lack of water or sanitary provisions. Only 2 of the prisoners lived in Indian-owned rooms in Cato Manor, of whom one was "satisfied" and one not. The majority, 52 prisoners, lived in Durban's various all-male compounds or barracks and so were not jobless at all but were part of the city's incipient working class.

The intricacies of cultural and political organization among these men were, as far as we can tell, very decentralized, negotiated through oral networks and located in fluid *practices* as opposed to clearly bounded and stable institutions. This is probably why, despite the various mechanisms of discipline and surveillance in place in the barracks, these men were able to keep the nuances of their political discussions away from the colonial gaze. Nevertheless, thanks to the work of scholars such as Veit Erlmann, David Hemson, Paul la Hausse, Iain Edwards, and Tim Nuttall, and through the process of reading the testimonials to the Riot Commission report, we can begin to imagine the worlds in which they lived.[4]

The men who lived in the barracks were, in theory at least, migrant laborers. They maintained strong links to the rural countryside and a strong respect and admiration for Zulu royalty. It was for this reason that the authorities arranged, in the wake of the riots, for Chief Cyprian and his uncle Prince Regent Mshiyeni to tour the Corporation Barracks and "locations" and encourage racial harmony. Their impending arrival, a native commissioner was to tell the *Daily News*, "brought a remarkable change in Natives' hearts." Indeed, Wellington Masuku, the supervisor of the compound of the Coronation Brick and Tile Company, spoke of this excitement and the "great disappointment" those in the compound felt when they learned that he was only going to tour the Durban Corporation's compounds and not their own.

4. See, for instance, Iain Edwards and Paul Maylam, *The People's City: African Life in Twentieth-Century Durban* (Pietermaritzburg: University of Natal Press, 1996); Veit Erlmann, "'The Past Is Far and the Future Io Far': Power and Performance among Zulu Migrant Workers," *American Ethnologist* 19 (1992): 688–709; David Hemson, *Class Consciousness and Migrant Workers: Dock Workers of Durban* (PhD diss., University of Warwick, 1979); Paul la Hausse, "'The Cows of Nongoloza': Youth, Crime and Amalaita Gangs in Durban, 1900–1936," *Journal of Southern African Studies* 16, no. 1 (1990): 79–111; and Tim Nuttall, *Class, Race, and Nation: African Politics in Durban, 1929–1949* (PhD diss., University of Oxford, 1991).

The martial traditions and networks of the countryside had also been carried into town and preserved in the "ngoma" dances on the streets during the course of the riots. (The Durban branch of the Bantu Ministers Association told the commission in its list of "remedies" that African women especially wanted to see the dances stopped.) At the same time, these rural traditions, beliefs, and practices were constantly being reworked and reimagined in a specifically urban context.[5]

Warfare in the countryside (decimated by colonial policies and natural disasters) played itself out in fierce battles between clans. Before and after the Durban riots, newspapers carried reports of a battle between the Mncunu and Mthembu clans that had resulted in several deaths. In the city, however, the migrants in the barracks and compounds had long begun to understand their solidarities and conceive of their struggles on much larger levels. In the 1929 riots, it was this same group that had taken on the state as well as Europeans, and African witnesses to the commission did speak of 1949 as the direct successor to 1929. In fact, for them, and for many other Africans, January 1949 was not a "riot" but a war, part of the long struggle of Africans for rights in the city.

The state had its own reasons for intervening in the riots and brutally demonstrating its military capabilities; it knew that the attacks on Indians might well have been a prelude to direct challenges to the state or lay Europeans on a region-wide or even countrywide level.

If the networks of political and military organization in the barracks and compounds were informal and decentralized, they certainly were not—as many accounts try to suggest—chaotic or undisciplined. On the evening of January 13 and through the weekend, "runners" were sent to most of the compounds in Durban, definitely across Natal, and perhaps even beyond to mobilize the troops for the war. Two instances where they failed are telling: on the Natal Estates, where the local chief, Ngcobo, intervened at the behest of the estate manager, and the Coronation Brick and Tile barracks, where Masuku intervened. Nevertheless, in many compounds, the fact that the runners were able to make a connection and mobilize residents so quickly suggests strong evidence of *prior* networks.

The impis from the barracks did not see their problem in class terms and attacked any Indian, whether poor or rich. It is likely, as I have suggested, that they saw themselves involved in battle and were willing to do whatever seemed necessary. In this way, the 1949 riots were an odd echo of the anti-German riots in Durban during the World War I, where Europeans

● 5. Erlmann, "'The Past Is Far.'"

attacked what they perceived as German shops and citizens as part of their contribution to the war effort. At the same time, the first wave of the Zulu rioters, as we learn from interviews and testimonials, often did not engage in what might be seen as "undignified" activities such as looting; they smashed shop windows, for instance, but were followed by *another* group that looted the shops.

The looters, who are perhaps a little more deserving of the title "tsotsi," could well have included those habitual offenders from central Durban who appeared before the Durban magistrate's court on repeated occasions, and they could have been central to the rioting on Thursday evening. This criminal world, which both transgressed racial boundaries and was tangled in them (with, for example, one Indian hiring an African to take revenge on another Indian and so on), explains how a handful of working-class Europeans and even one or two Indians, far removed from the ideologies of the barracks, also came to participate in the riots.

Why, then, did the disciplined front of rioters proceed so deliberately toward Cato Manor on Friday? While most of them did not live in Cato Manor, they probably knew the area well if they went there for their weekend fun. Cato Manor held currency as a symbol: it remained one of the last spaces in the city where Africans owned land. In the testimonies to the Riot Commission, many witnesses express anger at the way—and this is how they see it—zoning regulations had divided the city into Indian and European areas, leaving nothing for Africans.

It was not the segregation they opposed, but the fact that they were not given their own segregated area within municipal limits. It makes sense that the rioters were specifically concerned with driving Indians out of Cato Manor so that, at the very least, this area could be zoned for Africans, and so that they could capture their own legitimate place within the "Durban system." As Iain Edwards has shown, they were successful to a limited extent, but they paid a very high price.[6] The riot was soon to be suppressed brutally, in a case of police and army action never before seen in Durban, where crowds of Africans were fired upon almost indiscriminately.

The fury of the attack in Cato Manor, however, meant that Indians there were largely victims, and a stream of thousands of Indian refugees began to pour into emergency camps, where some would remain, homeless, for several months. This was not entirely true elsewhere. The dominant parable of the riots depended on not only the unruly "tsotsi" but also the

---

6. See Iain Edwards's chapter on Cato Manor in Edwards and Maylam, *The People's City*.

submissive and weak "coolie," who had caused the riot through his cunning exploitativeness but could now only lie in wait for the European state to come and save him. This account, perpetuated as much by Indian leaders as by Europeans, is one that still has not met an adequate challenge.

In fact, if we look, at least, at the official statistics (which, of course, by the city officials' own admission may not have been accurate) on who died in the riots and how, some strange discrepancies arise. More Africans than Indians died by the end of the riots—87 (including 6 women) as opposed to 46 Indians. Accounts of police and army action invariably involve the use of revolvers, but only 33 of the 87 deaths are from gunshot wounds. The rest are from head wounds and stab wounds, which also account for most of the Indian deaths. Is it possible that Indians claimed as many lives as they lost?

In Victoria Street, Indians would continue to throw missiles at Africans regardless of whether they were involved in the riots or not. In Clairwood, however, Indian reprisals took a decidedly more violent turn. I have found in my interviews that many Clairwood Indians speak proudly of their "fighting back," and the riots have inspired a whole mythology of those who fought, such as the man nicknamed "Long Jack." In these attacks, spearheaded by Clairwood's own informal networks of gangs, Indians used their own "traditional" weapons, such as the machete used for cutting cane, and a few were in possession of guns. It is not clear who their targets were, but it is likely that it included a number of Africans who had never intended to become part of the events.

By the time the riots had been declared officially "over" by the authorities, they had pulled into their vortex a whole range of actors who had come to impose an irreversibly "pure" racial reading of the events and had enacted this reading directly into their practice. Apart from the core of rioters from the barracks and compounds, a whole range of other Africans had written themselves into the narrative. There were those who threw stones, those who looted shops, those who hurled insults, or those who made threats and chased Indians. The riots had come to be imagined as a primal racial conflict and, through this imaginary, had become just that.

These readings, and the various stories they engendered, were structured and splintered by the various closed spaces in which they moved. By the time the riot was over, and well after, Indians, Europeans, and Africans had derived completely different meanings from the events. This divergence of meaning had itself been the motor by which the riot unfolded, and it ensured that, in a sense, the riot would not actually end on Sunday but would expand underground through memory and telling, multiplying endlessly in the decades that followed. Yet perhaps the greatest irony was the strange symmetry between the most divergent accounts. The Indians who lived in Clairwood will today, driven by that special nostalgia that only the Group Areas Act could foster, speak of how the 1949 riots showed that "the Indians in Clairwood were different... they had real unity."[7] In 1949 Wellington Masuku had echoed this very same idea in his statement to the Riot Commission when he said, "In a way this fight was like many others between the two sections. The only difference was that, on this occasion, the Africans showed unity and determination."[8]

The Reading and Writing Continue

After much deliberation over its "terms of reference," the government appointed a Commission of Enquiry, with F. D. van der Heever as its chair, to begin hearings a few weeks after the riot had ended. Scholars around the world are learning the hard way how such commissions are always more about trying to engineer catharsis and reestablish the state's monopoly over truth than anything else. This commission was no different, except that it was frustrated in these ambitions by the boycott of, among other groups, the African National Congress (ANC), the Natal Indian Conference (NIC), and the South African Communist Party (SACP) because they were not allowed the right of cross-examination. Nevertheless, it sat through more than a month of hearings and promptly produced a report that would honestly not have needed most of the testimonials it heard. As Kenneth Kirkwood of the South African Institute of Race Relations commented in his report on the events, "the Commission set aside virtually the whole of the evidence that submitted the riots to social analysis."[9]

Meanwhile, groups of Indians began to plan and carry out isolated attacks on Africans, some of which were intercepted by the police. Out of the fear of such reprisals, a new crisis was created: about 2,000 African refugees, mostly women and children, were made homeless by the riots and began to stream into a new set of camps. Africans began a general boycott of Indian buses that was to last through the year, and P. R. Pather of the Natal Indian Organization (NIO), who argued that the riots proved that non-European unity could not work, met with the defense minister to ask that Indians in isolated farm areas be issued guns.

Over the next year, a number of almost-riots, such as one in Booth Road in June, began to break out and, on Dingaan's Day 1949, rumors of a fresh set of attacks kept the police busy. The

7. From personal interviews conducted by the author.
8. *Report of the Commission of Enquiry into Riots in Durban*, 1949, https://www.sahistory.org.za/sites/default/files/archive-files3/report_of_the_commission_of_enquiry_into_riots_in_durban.pdf.
9. Maurice Webb and Kenneth Kirkwood, *The Durban Riots and After* (Johannesburg: South African Institute of Race Relations, 1949).

riot had already, in January, moved onto a new, international level of multiple readings. It made the front page of newspapers in England, India, and the United States, where it was seen as the fruits of apartheid policy. For the South African government, the riot demonstrated the opposite—that segregation was the only way to solve the problem of racial conflict.

Today, accounts of the 1949 riots have been submerged back into the closed spaces in which they were born. For almost all Indians in Natal, stories of the riot have been fashioned into object lessons learned in youth from elders, and form a bedrock of folktales rarely broached in interracial spaces. What strikes me, though, is how and why there continues to be an overwhelming silence about the events of January 1949 in the shared South African public space. For an event in which more than 2,000 people were killed or injured at a pivotal point in South African history, it has produced little more than a few articles and an honors thesis or two. Where does this overwhelming silence come from, and what is it hiding? I must end by trying to negotiate this rather knotty question.

Speaking in Space, 1949–1999

There is a strange and disturbing resonance between the silences we keep today and the divergent narratives withheld from the public in and before 1949. How did 1949 happen, and can it happen again? If we look for a moment not at where the various accounts that emerge within and around the Riot Commission diverge, but at what they share, we may begin to find an answer.

What almost all the witnesses agree on, truth be told, is the idea of separate development, the idea that too much intermixing between races is a dangerous thing. Today, the history of apartheid makes it hard to defend a discourse of segregation, but if we consider how the idea of segregation becomes reinvented in the discourse of multiculturalism (as opposed to cross-culturalism), we might get an idea of how people at the time perceived its liberating possibilities. People turn to the idea of multiculturalism because they want to preserve the possibilities inherent in difference. For the apartheid government, segregation had to take place in the context of hierarchy. For the African witnesses to the commission, however, segregation implied the chance to have their own space in the city, to run and purchase from their own businesses. For the NIO and even the NIC, segregation allowed Indians to preserve a sense of cultural purity and pride. Thus, like the tale of the 1949 riots, the meaning of segregation comes to have radically different possibilities for different actors, and I would argue that the majority of Durbanites had come to accept the essential, if not the corollary, premises of segregation well before the advent of apartheid.

The problems, however, for a nonhierarchical discourse of segregation are threefold: first, the very notion of segregation presumes the presence of others; second, in order to make cultural segregation work, one has to police various boundaries, the most important of which is the sexual one; and third, in order for segregated cultures to share a common geographical and political space, one needs a mediating center. Thus, a solution was found in the organization of psychic, if not necessarily physical, space.

At the center of this psychic space, we have the shared public sphere à la Habermas, although its boundaries are nebulous, and the journey into private spaces becomes more of a gradual slide than a jump. In the Durban of 1949, this public sphere is mediated by strictly European institutions, but non-Europeans are allowed in as long as what they say remains within the limits of what can be said in the context of colonial logic. As we move slowly toward more private, racialized spaces, a range of accounts emerge that are not admitted into the public space. Importantly in the South African context, the boundaries are always mediated through language. To enter fully into the shared central public space, one needs to speak and write English well; in order to enter fully into the African private space in Natal, one needs at least to speak Zulu. When I looked for statements about Indians made by Africans prior to the riots, for instance, I never found them in English. Yet, as the town clerk John MacIntyre pointed out, a number of letters to the editor (an in-between space between the oral and the printed word?) had appeared in *Ilanga Lase Natal* before 1949 expressing just the kinds of grievances later aired in the commission report and elsewhere. And, as we move further into private spaces, there are things one can never hear unless one is a cultural insider.

The year 1949, I have suggested, can be read as a parable of the flow and divergence of information through these restricted colonial spaces; apartheid was to complete the process of mapping these spaces onto the geography of the city. Yet, in the post-apartheid city, the integrity of these spatial boundaries is still very much preserved. Consider, for instance, the recent incident where Amos Maphumulo, the editor of *Ilanga*, was brought to book for making anti-Indian statements in an editorial. In order for this to happen, his statements first had to appear in translation. When this happened, there was a massive outcry by public authorities and an immediate crackdown, without consideration for the nuances of the sentiment he was trying to express. As I was to learn from friends, a later show of support for Maphumulo in *Ilanga*'s letters to the editor never made it to the English press, and the issue was laid to rest.

In 1949 there were individuals who transgressed the racialized spaces of the colonial city, such as, for instance, Indian communists. Yet, as Goolam Vahed has shown, Indian communists were able to reconcile their cultural identities as Indians in closed racial spaces and as communists in a shared, multiracial space, and I would argue that they did this by splitting their selves and preserving a set of silences in the shared space.[10] The situation in 1999 remains, I want to suggest, much the same, with the possible difference that we are more multiply positioned than ever before. We need to begin to make better use of our multiple positions and to transgress spaces and silences—carefully—if we want to build and imagine a truly cross-cultural world.

It's difficult for me to narrate a parable without the possibility of redemption, and, in that spirit, I want to end with an extended quote. The events of 1949 did offer redemption when they forced an emergency meeting between the South African Indian Congress (SAIC) and the ANC. If the issue of non-European unity had continued, despite attempts to the contrary, to be a vexed one, it may also, paradoxically, have been the event that made necessary a new era of more intense collaboration. George Singh, the veteran activist, told the story for the oral history archive project of the South African Institute of Race Relations. It may be a suspiciously rosy story, but it remains a good parable for the possibility of transgressed spaces:

> "Those were the 1949 riots... early 1949. (Pause.) The thing lasted for a whole week, the tension was there for a good week, the whole of Durban was involved. Then there was a joint big meeting of the SAIC [and the ANC]... at the International club in Pine street, Durban.
>
> The meeting started off—this is rather important— on a sort of discordant note—they had been called by the Indian leaders to try and just merely pacify things in Durban and of one thing and the other but...
>
> I remember there was heated discussion right to the lunch and after lunch some of the members came back and said, 'Now I think the question of the Cato Manor riots is merely a temporary issue. There are many other issues facing our communities jointly. We'll have to get together from time to time to establish a common platform for our joint activity.' More or less along those lines. Anyway that view seems to have held the day.
>
> Then—after the meeting I remember this little incident... Dr. Dadoo and Champion. It was like a truce meeting in wartime... [They] marched right to the edge of the so-called African line. When they reached

● 10. Goolam Vahed, "Race or Class? Community and Conflict Amongst Indian Municipal Employees in Durban, 1914–1949," Journal of Southern African Studies 27, no. 1 (2001): 105–125.

the other side they were given a rousing reception and welcome in spite of all the anti-Indian tensions. It was a great victory... for the joint leadership."

Unruly Life: Subverting "Surplus" Existence in Tunisia

Oana Pârvan

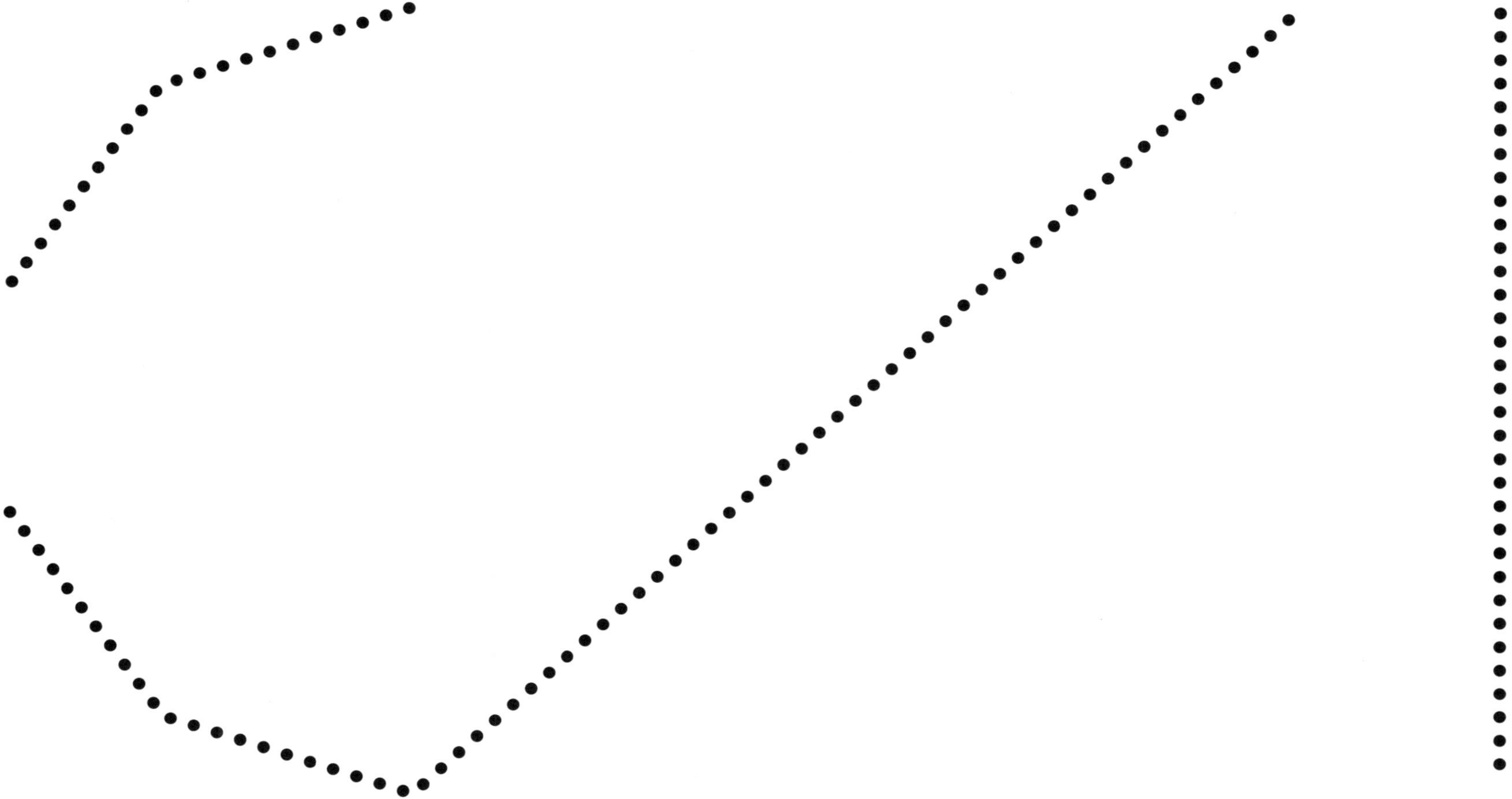

OANA PÂRVAN

T

The Tunisian Dignity Revolution of 2011 can be seen as a popular response to an ongoing economic restructuring. The revolution corresponds to a progressive dispossession of the most vulnerable categories of the country's population: mainly suburban (and also rural) unemployed and underemployed people. This revolutionary event, generated by a network of related riots, contested the way certain spaces—mostly in the south and center of the country, alongside the urban *hwem* (deprived peripheries)—were marked by a historical exclusion and disposability. The mobilizations became a mass movement thanks to an alliance between the suburban unemployed, students, and a unionized workforce that brought Ben Ali's police state (backed by Western nations) to a standstill.

The Tunisian revolutionaries started off by putting their lives on the line to fight the local police. At the same time, they exposed the internal colonialism and the damaging consequences of the "structural adjustments" with their demand of "Bread, Freedom, Dignity!"[1] But once they crossed the borders and reached Europe, where they became "undocumented migrants," their fight for dignity continued. And the tactics of protest—tactics that traveled from Sidi Bouzid all the way to Lampedusa—were sometimes the same (demonstrations, occupations, acts of self-harm, rioting, and arson).

Those who initiated the unrest after Mohamed Bouazizi's self-immolation in December 2010 had already been struggling with precarious informal work and persistent state abuse for years. But what is the significance of the fact that the century's first revolution was pioneered by the unemployed? And what was that revolution a sign of? This essay interrogates the global subjects of struggle, their mobility practices, and the motivations that drive them, both within and against the constituted order. The Tunisian Dignity Revolution offers a privileged standpoint from which to identify the interweaving of colonialist and capitalist logics, while also representing an extensive archive of resistance strategies, across East/West borders.

As the Tunisian Revolution shows, the riot is a privileged tactic of collective action for surplus populations expelled from formal labor and destined to "informal economies, often semi- or extralegal"—that is, for a "portion of humanity that earns

---

● 1. Structural adjustments programs (SAPs) set conditions for loans granted by international financial organizations such as the International Monetary Fund and the World Bank. Despite their declared goal of reducing poverty, these conditions subject countries in economic crisis to a massive contraction of public spending and force deregulation for the private sector.

less than subsistence amounts," often at great risk.[2] In today's riots, there is an immediate connection with this growing category of labor without access to a formal wage and subject to state violence. The connection between the disenfranchised and the practice of rioting arises not only because many states' answer to the surplus population is a carceral one, but also because, as Joshua Clover accounts, "as increasing portions of population are rendered surplus to the economy in turn, the state turns more and more to coercion as a management style: the social wage of Keynesian compromise is withdrawn in favor of police occupation of excluded communities."[3] This is how "surplus life" becomes "the subject of politics and the object of ongoing state violence" while "the public of surplus [is] treated as riot at all times—incipient, in progress, in exhaustion—not out of error but out of recognition."[4]

Clover identifies a connection between the variable access to productivity (as formally waged employees) and the way collective action shifts the focus of these "surplus populations" from struggles of production (strike) to struggles of circulation (riot). More specifically, and more relevant to the Tunisian situation:

> When the material substrate of daily life is the pooling of populations in circulation, in informal economies—*a collective population* rendered surplus and forced to confront the problem of reproduction in the marketplace rather than in the formal wage—in this situation, any gathering on the corner, in the street, in the square can be understood as a riot. Unlike the strike, it is hard to tell when and where the riot starts and ends. This is part of what allows the riot to function both as a particular event and as a kind of holographic miniature of an entire situation, a world-picture.[5]

While this analysis develops along the lines of Clover's work on contemporary struggles unfolding in the "overdeveloped West," Tunisia is arguably different. Its difference can be put down to its colonial past, the development of a neopatrimonial state (concentrated on the northern coast), and the way its territory has been impacted by neoliberal policies. Last but not least, the Tunisian population is marked by a different articulation of race and class divisions.

- 2. Joshua Clover, *Riot. Strike. Riot: The New Era of Uprisings* (New York: Verso, 2016), 156.
- 3. Clover, *Riot. Strike. Riot*, 47.
- 4. Clover, *Riot. Strike. Riot*, 170.
- 5. Clover, *Riot. Strike. Riot*, 123 (emphasis added).

I have chosen Clover's understanding of "surplus life" because it resists attempts to strip unintegrated labor power of its dignity. Through the state abandonment, abuse, and criminalization of disenfranchised rural and suburban Tunisians (also targeted as "undocumented" migrants, "Salafists," "terrorists," and *houmani,* or "inhabitants of the deprived suburbs"), those in power are clear about which lives they believe deserve to be nurtured. In this sense, when certain acts of public self-harm (such as self-immolation) spark mass unrest, they interrupt the "business as usual" exclusion game, which keeps the majority of the population in a state of intermittent survival despite being engaged in an informal economy worth the equivalent of 50 percent of the country's GDP.[6]

I understand the term "surplus life" as a double articulation: of the way life is being produced and of what it produces. On the one hand, the idea of "surplus life" indicates a horrific condition of life, resulting from the fact that certain groups of people (especially impoverished rural and suburban communities) are *produced as surplus* and therefore deemed dangerous, indecorous, disposable. Beyond the Marxist understanding of surplus (the labor of the reserve army), these categories occupy the place of the excess, of the abject, and their lives are affected by the way the state abandons and/or disciplines them. On the other hand, the idea of "surplus life" is also a reminder of how people can reject their production as surplus; as political subjects, they work from within a level of disposability and bareness that is forced upon them. In this sense, surplus life is different from bare life in that it regards doing politics within a state of bareness as a starting point. By claiming dignity while weaponizing one's own biological life (through acts of self-harm), what is played out is a sort of affirmative thanatopolitics.[7]

Lineages of Resistance: *Fellaga, Houmani, Harraga*

When the French colonists occupied the Tunisian territory in 1881, the survival of the peoples who inhabited the area relied on a symbiotic relationship between nomadic and sedentary groups, centered around the oases for agriculture and the desert for breeding animals (such as the camel).[8] This relationship was based on the collective ownership of lands and on the occasional exchange of crops and animal-derived products or tools, as well as on the protection tax (*saliab*) that

6. Aziz Krichen, "L'affaire de Jemna: Question paysanne et revolution democratique," October 31, 2016, https://habibayeb.wordpress.com/2016/10/31/laffaire-de-jemna-question-paysanne-et-revolution-democratique.
7. Roberto Esposito, "Biological Life, Political Life," lecture at Goldsmiths, University of London, October 1, 2015.
8. The majority of the Tunisian territory is characterized by an arid or even desert climate, with the exception of the oases. Only the north benefits from a more fertile climate, and this is precisely where all the main urban centers have developed.

sedentary groups paid to the warrior nomadic tribes (mainly Berbers). The French colonists prohibited the *saliab* tax (which had supported the nomadic groups), imposed their own taxes, and forced nomads to become sedentary, while also subjecting them to taxes and initiating a process of land privatization. Progressively dispossessed through debt, thousands of former *fellaga* (peasants) and animal breeders, together with the poor European settlers, headed toward the cities for their livelihood as *corteges de déracinés*, "cohorts of uprooted people." "The climatic and capitalist calamities push[ed] entire sections of the rural society into becoming a sub-proletariat."[9] The cohorts of dispossessed occupied the space around the urban capital, Tunis.

According to the official numbers, the precarious *bidonvilles* (or *gourbi-villes*) at the outskirts of the capital grew from a population of two thousand people in 1935 to ten thousand in 1941.[10] The inhabitants of the *bidonvilles* got by on petty scams, reselling objects and food they found in the garbage, committing small robberies, begging, or practicing sex work.[11] The local beylical authority tried to hinder their settlement in numerous ways: by limiting inhabitants' movement with detailed mobility permits (for both humans and animals) and by repeatedly deporting, fining, and detaining them.[12] By 1946 the *bidonvilles* were inhabited by fifty thousand people. In the 1970s the main peripheral neighborhoods of the capital were converted from illegal settlements to officially administered zones. These are today's *hwem*.

Before 2011, according to one report,
the security apparatus also performed a social function, which was reinforced following the introduction of the structural adjustment policies. The security apparatus maintained social order by keeping disadvantaged neighborhoods on a tight police leash. Using raids, and the later Law 52-1992 [criminalizing cannabis use], the security forces used combating youth crime and drug abuse as a cover for stepping up their containment of the "dangerous classes" and physically hemming them in.[13]

9. Claude Liauzu, "Un Aspect de la crise en Tunisie: La naissance des bidonvilles," *Revue française d'histoire d'outre-mer* 63, no. 3 (1976): 607–621.

10. Significantly, *gourbi* has an Amazigh (Berber) etymologic origin and starts being used in the French colonial period to indicate a shack or a precarious dwelling made of earth and sticks.

11. Liauzu, "Un Aspect de la crise," 615.

12. Before the colonial period began in 1881, Tunisia was a *beylic*—that is, a province of the Ottoman Empire with some autonomy as it was ruled by a local governor, called a *bey*.

13. Olfa Lamloum, *Politics on the Margins in Tunisia: Vulnerable Young People in Douar Hicher and Ettadhamen*, International Alert, March 2016, https://www.international-alert.org/sites/default/files/Tunisia_PoliticsOnTheMargins_EN_2016.pdf.

Most of the inhabitants of the *hwem*, the *houmani*, had in fact moved to the suburban peripheries in search of livelihood and a chance to support their families in rural Tunisia. Meanwhile, under pressure from international financial organizations, the Tunisian government initiated a process of public divestment and liberalization of resources (such as land and water) in the rural areas (which comprise the majority of the Tunisian territory), and in doing so crippled the subsistence lifestyle of most of the population—especially given much of the country's desert-like climate and the centrality of family farming.

This public divestment, alongside the privatization of land and water, increased the national divide: between the rich Tunisia (the capital, the north, and the coast, with pioneer cities like Sfax and Sousse) and the "Tunisia of rich resources." As Amel Rahbi from the League of Human Rights explains, "Ever since the colonial period, the country has been built upon the illusion of a useful Tunisia concentrated on the coast. This model continued after independence. The rest of the country is therefore abandoned, impoverished, discriminated against."[14] On the one side, the rich Tunisia is the financial center, profiting from the agricultural, mining, textile, and tourism industries. On the other side, the rest of the country is subject to a constant extraction of its natural resources, such as "water, agricultural lands, oases, ores (like phosphate, iron), gas, and oil," while, at the same time, being pushed into a "spiral of exclusion."[15] In other words, southern Tunisia and central Tunisia are main sites of resource extraction, while their population is underprivileged by state policies and the politics of the central government—policies and politics that are more focused on addressing the interests of the economic groups of the north.

The bigger the gap between the north and the rest of the country grew, the more these areas required a series of ever-changing survival strategies, an everyday anxious and precarious *course à l'hkobza*, literally the "race for bread."[16] A good example of these "bread race" strategies has been provided by Walid, an unemployed bricklayer from Kasserine (in the northwest), condemned to "get by, selling scrap iron one day, fruits another day, and then maybe oil smuggled from Algeria."[17]

14. Quoted in Rosa Moussaoui, "Les vies brulées des jounes chomeures de Kasserine," *L'Humanité*, February 10, 2016.

15. Habib Ayeb, "Social and Political Geography of the Tunisian Revolution: The Alfa Grass Revolution," *Review of African Political Economy* 38, no. 129 (2011): 467–479; Mohamed Elloumi, "Capacité de resilience de l'agriculture familiale tunisienne et politique agricole post révolution," in *Accaparement, action publique, stratégies individuelles et ressources naturelles: Regards croisés sur la course aux terres et à l'eau en contextes méditerranéens*, ed. G. Vianey, M. Requier-Desjardins, and J. C. Paoli (Montpellier: Centre International de Hautes Études Agronomiques Méditerranéennes, 2015).

16. Hamza Meddeb, "L'ambivalence de la course à 'el khobza': Obéir et se révolter en Tunisie," *Politique Africaine* 121 (2011): 35–54.

17. Najeh Missaoui and Oussama Khalfaoui, *Dégage, dégage, dégage: Ils ont dit dégage!* (Tunis: Editions Franco-Berbères, 2011).

The Tunisian spaces of exclusion, the heritage of colonial zoning, and dispossession practices are concentrated around the rural south and the overcrowded *hwem* of Tunis (such as Ettadhamen, Douar Hicher, and Ariana), where time oscillates between a suffocating immobility and the anxious pursuit of an everyday livelihood, as described in the popular song "Houmani," released by Hamzaoui Med Amine and KAFON in 2013:

> We live like trash inside a bin
> Poor, without a dime
> We wake up late; we never see the time passing
> I don't even have a clock
> Here the atmosphere is suffocating.
>
> With my head down, we go ahead
> One dime doesn't stay long in my pocket
> I passed too quickly from youth to old age, my brain weakened
> [by substances].[18]

In a region with "the highest rates of unemployment in the world across recent decades," as Gilbert Achcar describes, the "spatial, economic, social, and political marginalization of one part of the country and society in favor of another" was the "direct cause of the revolutionary process that ended the mafia dictatorship of Ben Ali-Trabelsi."[19]

Riot: How to Destabilize a Police State
The most significant precedent for the 2010 Tunisian Dignity Revolution took place in 2008 in the city of Gafsa, headquarters of the Gafsa Phosphate Company. A massive rebellion, which became known as the Gafsa Intifada, was triggered by the announcement, on January 5, 2008, of 380 workers, technicians, and managerial staff newly hired by the company.[20] Thousands had applied for these positions, and the selection reeked of nepotism. The protest spread across the neighboring cities of Redeyef, Moulares, M'dilla, and Metlaoui in the form of hunger strikes, demonstrations, sit-ins, and riots. The mobilization involved seasonal workers, public sector workers, teachers, and high school students. Long-lasting sit-ins and tents were set up in strategic sites in order to slow down the economic and commercial activity of the phosphate extraction company.

18. Hamzaoui Med Amine and KAFON, "Houmani," 2013, https://www.youtube.com/watch?v=j1YZPm9TOEo. Translation my own.
19. Gilbert Achcar, "What Happened to the Arab Spring?," *Jacobin*, December 17, 2015, https://www.jacobinmag.com/2015/12/achchar-arab-spring-tunisia-egypt-isis-isil-assad-syria-revolution; Ayeb, "Social and Political Geography," 467.
20. Eric Gobe, "The Gafsa Mining Basin between Riots and a Social Movement: Meaning and Significance of a Protest Movement in Ben Ali's Tunisia," 2010, https://halshs.archives-ouvertes.fr/halshs-00557826.

The repressive response was massive: six thousand policemen were sent to besiege and occupy the cities and to raid the homes of the rebel unemployed. Hundreds of protesters were arrested and many subjected to torture.[21] Four people were killed during the clashes with the police. Hitchem Ben Jeddou El Aleimi died from electrocution while occupying the site of the electricity generator for the mine's washing plants.[22]

The 2008 Gafsa Intifada, noteworthy for its mass organization of unemployed workers and its focus on the dispossession of the poorer regions of Tunisia, represents the "general rehearsal" for the nationally transformative movement that began three years later. On December 17, 2010, local municipal agent Fadia Hamdi sanctioned Mohamed Bouazizi, confiscating his merchandise, his cart, and—some claim—slapping him in public. Desperate to get his belongings back, he set himself on fire in front of the local governor's residence. He was taken to the hospital (where he would die the next month). His act ignited a series of protests across the region. Public order brigades were called in from Kasserine, Kairouan, and Sfax to calm the unrest, but this time the turbulence spread.

The most aggressive repression occurred in the city of Kasserine, where sixty people were killed in only three days, between January 8 and 11, 2011. The city descended into massive riots. This episode marked the moment when protests across the country united against Ben Ali and his authoritarian rule. After the events in Kasserine, the most representative trade union, the UGTT, decided to support the protesters. More riots enflamed the cities of Thala and Regueb and also reached the suburbs of Tunis: "From January 9, 2011 onwards, it was through riots that hundreds of these young people entered the world of politics. That was the day when, at a roundabout opposite the line 5 terminus, at the intersection between three working-class suburbs (Ettadhamen, al-Entilaka, and el-Mnihla), the first of the anti-Ben Ali demonstrations reached greater Tunis."[23] In no time, and as an alternative to driving the police out of the suburbs, "Young people, even minors, set up self-defense committees, an embryonic form of power structure, which ended up being the only real source of authority in the two neighborhoods for over five months."[24]

On January 14, a general strike was declared by the UGTT. The police charged the strikers with tear gas, and a curfew and a state of emergency were announced. Nevertheless, Ben Ali left the country that very night, fleeing to Saudi Arabia.[25]

- 21. Missaoui and Khalfaoui, *Dégage*, 127–128.
- 22. Gobe, "Gafsa Mining Basin" 14.
- 23. Lamloum, *Politics on the Margins*, 9.
- 24. Lamloum, *Politics on the Margins* 10.
- 25. Missaoui and Khalfaoui, *Dégage*, 151–182.

That moment marked the beginning of two highly signifi-cant demonstrations: First, the initiation of the "Liberation Caravan" in Menzel Bouzaiane (the city of the first "martyrs" in the center of the country), which rallied more than four thousand people to march toward the capital demanding social justice and the resignation of the Benalist politicians. This march occupied the Kasbah (the capital's governmental center) on two occasions (January 23–28, the First Kasbah, and February 22–25, the Second Kasbah). Thousands of rev-olutionary, disenfranchised Tunisians took over the center of the capital, imposing their troublesome presence upon a po-litical establishment that had always ignored them and making themselves visible to their governors, as well as to their fellow citizens. The Kasbah was the place of class alliances, where the dispossession of the rest of the country became visible to the inhabitants of the capital.

The second major demonstration was the revolutionary inter-ruption of border control, which triggered a massive reorienta-tion of the surplus population in the region, since this "surplus" saw emigration as the only strategy to increase their margins of reproduction. This is when *harraga* started streaming out of the country. *Harraga*, in the Maghreb, is a term that indicates "those who burn," meaning both young people who "burn" frontiers as they migrate across the Mediterranean Sea and those "who are ready to burn their documents (but also their past and eventually their lives) in order to reach Europe."[26] The island of Lampedusa, south of Sicily and not far from the Tunisian coast, became the symbol of this flow. The first one hundred Tunisians reached Lampedusa only one night after the departure of Ben Ali, on January 15, 2011. According to estimates by the Italian Interior Ministry, by April 2011 more than twenty thousand people, most of whom were Tunisians, had arrived in Italy by boat.

The prospect of deportation ignited a series of riots in the Italian detention centers, accompanied by hunger strikes, self-harm, fires, and collective escapes. The riots culminated with a fire in the Sicilian detention center at Lampedusa on September 20, 2011, which resulted in violent clashes with the police and some local inhabitants.[27] Emigration had temporarily functioned as a massive relief valve, allowing the removal from Tunisia of precisely those young unemployed people who inhabited poor areas of the country and who had ignited the revolution in the first place.

●   26. Paola Gandolfi, "Spaces in Migration, Daily Life in Revolution," in *Spaces in Migration: Postcards of a Revolution*, ed. Glenda Garelli, Federica Sossi, and Martina Tazzioli (London: Pavement Books, 2013), 14.
●   27. Glenda Garelli, Federica Sossi, and Martina Tazzioli, "Postcards of a Revolution," in *Spaces in Migration*, ed. Garelli, Sossi, and Tazzioli, 199.

What Subject of Struggle? (What) Recognition in a Police State?

So far, I have taken into consideration the instances of collective action initiated from a space of exclusion, from the anticolonial *fellaga* to today's *houmani*—the (mostly) suburban young people who historically have been considered a threat to the constituted order and who ignited the revolutionary process in 2010—as a way of addressing an unbearable existential precarity. The subjects of these contemporary struggles inhabit overlapping spatialities: they are the people of the poor south and central Tunisia; the inhabitants of the metropolitan suburbs; and those among them who decide to leave the country, headed to Europe (where they start new cycles of struggle) or to eastern military fronts. As Fabio Merone has pointed out regarding the attitude of the Tunisian authorities toward these most vulnerable categories of citizens, especially in the context of the crackdown against armed political Islam, "the Interior Minister is convinced that no difference exists between *this large disenfranchised population*, Ansar al-Sharia [the Tunisian Salafi movement] and Okba Ibn Nafaa [the Quaedist brigade that has attacked the Tunisian militaries, civilians, and Western tourists]: they are all 'terrorists.'"[28]

Tunisia offers a particular example of the struggles of those designated as superfluous. First of all, the mobility patterns of impoverished Tunisians allow for reflection on the vast, global informalization of labor. In all the spaces marked by significant existential precarity—the countryside, the suburban *hwem*, European cities, and the centers of Islamic militancy—Tunisians are acting with little hope of accessing a formal wage, whether they engage in smuggling, street vending, the substance trade, the military, or care work (including sex work). In this sense, a connection can be drawn between the transnational process of the informalization of labor and the spreading of riot-related tactics of collective action, which have emerged in both Tunisia and Europe (especially against deportation in detention centers).

Surplus life is devoted to "unruly mobility" practices, maybe because those lives have very limited margins of action and movement in the first place.[29] Whether they disobey "Saturday night curfew" and leave the suburbs for the city center, or transgress European anti-migration laws, struggling Tunisians are a force of "disorganization of this controlled space."[30] Moreover,

● 28. Fabio Merone, "Explaining the Jihadi Threat in Tunisia," *OpenDemocracy*, March 21, 2015, https://www.opendemocracy.net/en/north-africa-west-asia/explaining-jihadi-threat-in-tunisia. Emphasis added.

● 29. Martina Tazzioli, "Revisiting the Omnes et Singulatim Bond: The Production of Irregular Conducts and the Biopolitics of the Governed," *Foucault Studies* 21 (2016): 98–116.

30. R. L., "Wanderings of the Slave: Black Life and Social Death," *Mute*, June 5, 2013, https://www.metamute.org/editorial/articles/wanderings-slave-black-life-and-social-death.

the violence of the riots itself is a disordering strategy. "The police now stand *in the place of* economy, the violence of the commodity made flesh."[31] Gaining temporary control over a formerly policed space, whether a neighborhood or a detention center, forces military representatives of the state to recognize the transformative agency of otherwise criminalized subjects who are constantly being dehumanized. In this, the body is "the reminder of the destroyed political bios."[32] It is "crucial in its presence to form a political space, to claim the streets in their politicality. The body is present to claim, to demand, to negotiate and to interfere. The body is there to form together with other bodies a multitude of political subjects."[33]

The claim to recognition—articulated in the suffocating atmosphere of the police state—originates from a space of alienation, a space of dispossession, and demands political transformation by disturbing the status quo's "spatial fixity" and "temporal closure."[34] Moreover, surplus life exceeds the limits of its own body by taking a stand against the distribution of life and death managed by the state.

Mohamed Bouazizi's self-immolation, alongside 160 attempted or successful self-immolations between 2010 and 2013 in Tunisia; the acts of self-harm by migrants detained at the borders of Europe; the public death of Ridha Yahyaoui; and the sewn-up lips of the hunger-striking "Kasserine 13," following Yahyaoui's death: all these practices transform the individual body "from a site of subjection to a site of insurgency, which by self-destruction presents death as a counter conduct to the administration of life."[35] In this way, "bodies deny their state-sponsored mutation into colonial subjects, obedient nationals," transforming self-inflicted death into a strategy of resistance.[36]

31. Clover, *Riot. Strike. Riot*, 125.
32. Ewa Plonowska Ziarek, "Bare Life," in *Impasses of the Post-Global: Theory in the Era of Climate Change*, vol 2., ed. H. Sussman (Ann Arbor: Open Humanities Press, 2012);
33. Ahl Al Kahf, Performative Intervention at the Academy of Fine Arts, Vienna, 2012, https://www.facebook.com/notes/اﻟﻜﻬـﻒ-اﻟ-ahl-alkahf/ahl-al-kahf-performative-intervention-jan-2012/593074547439538.
34. Brenna Bhandar, "Plasticity and Post-Colonial Recognition: 'Owning, Knowing and Being,'" *Law Critique* 22 (2011): 227–249.
35. On January 16, 2016, in the city of Kasserine, Ridha Yahyaoui protested alongside other fellow citizens against their exclusion from the employment lists as a retaliation for their activism in the students' trade union. During the protest, he climbed a light pillar and died from exposure to high-voltage electricity. His death set off regional protests, an occupation, and hunger strikes. See Banu Bargu, *Starve and Immolate: The Politics of Human Weapons* (New York: Columbia University Press, 2014).
36. Hamid Dabashi, *Corpus Anarchicum: Political Protest, Suicidal Violence and the Making of the Posthuman Body* (Hampshire, UK: Palgrave Macmillan, 2012), 9.

According to Banu Bargu, "Necro-resistance presents an embodied form of radical critique. Embodied because the biopolitical management of bodies needs resistance from the points of its application. Bodies have become sites of contestation and the vessels of a political intervention."[37] The devastated body of the necro-resistant, who has devoted their organic being to making visible the deadly action of power, "presents us with a materialist theory of being, a theory that carries with it the potential for political resistance to the violence of dispossession."[38] In this sense, extreme acts of self-harm, like Bouazizi's self-immolation (one of hundreds of similar cases), work like an affective aggregator of an all too widespread existential frustration. Within the affective/political sphere, the weaponization of one's own body (when all other political tools are inaccessible) immediately exposes the hierarchization of lives. Claiming one's right to be employed and freedom from state violence, here, stands for demanding an effective termination of existential precarity and the right to be acknowledged as a dignified member of the community. Surplus life as a subject of struggle therefore enacts practices of disobedient mobility (in the pursuit of livelihood), contests state power expropriating its monopoly on violence "both materially and symbolically" with the riot, and employs its own body as a terrain of extreme counter-conduct, articulated through practices of necro-resistance.[39]

Finally, though, the Tunisian context also allows for reflection on the transition from riot to revolution—revolution as a mass movement, animated by a vast variety of collective actions, enacted by informal and formal workers, alongside students, and able to destabilize and rearticulate the establishment. In fact, the Tunisian Revolution was the result of an alliance between suburban surplus laborers and others with a different degree of disposability, such as the unemployed, high school students, and the unionized public-sector workers able to bring the state to a standstill with their general strike. While "revolutionary movements do not spread by contamination but by resonance" dictated by the commonality of surplus lives, alliances help enforce the transformative impact of the mobilization.[40] The protests of Kasserine, at the beginning of 2016, show what happens when the alliance is no longer in place. The protesters are slowly repressed and worn down by the state, which continues to ignore their claims for economic justice, therefore directing those people toward other attempts to pursue their livelihood and dignity, such as emigration or Islamic militancy.

37. Banu Bargu, "Why Did Bouazizi Kill Himself? Fatal Politics and the Politics of Fate," conference at SOAS, September 21, 2015.
38. Bhandar, "Plasticity and Post-Colonial Recognition," 242.
39. R. L., "Wanderings of the Slave."
40. Invisible Committee, Coming Insurrection, cited in Clover, Riot. Strike. Riot, 153–154.

In this sense, the potential for an alliance, whose future form is not yet known, is one of the most significant promises articulated collectively by those who reject their production as surplus. State-driven racism, sectarianism, and segregation are only some of the techniques employed by the powers that be to prevent similar alliances. The alliance of the future can only be an abolitionist and decolonial project, as shown by the more recent mobilizations of the Standing Rock Sioux community or the Berber town of Hoceima in Morocco.[41]

From the United States to Morocco:

The global *classes dangereuses* are united not by their role as producers but by their relation to state violence. In this is to be found the basis of the surplus rebellion and of its form, which must exceed the logic of recognition and negotiation.[42]

Decolonisation, which sets out to change the order of the world, is, obviously, a programme of complete disorder.[43]

All illustrations from Oana Pârvan, *Triptych or The Riots of Whose Futures?*, collage, 2019. The collage contains reproductions of the works of calligraffiti artist eL Seed and the Tunisian street art collectives Zwewla and Molotov. The translation of these works as they appear in order are: "The morning came up from behind the peaks," verse by Aboul Qacem Echebbi, calligraffiti by eL Seed; "The dispossessed have reached the source and could not drink," graffiti by Zwewla; "The people demand rights for the dispossessed," graffiti by Zwewla; "You're owed something in this world, so stand up! Kanafani," quote by Ghassan Kanafani, graffiti by Molotov. Courtesy of Oana Pârvan.

41. I refer here to a shift from the state's focus on policing and detention as answers to the issues arising from the ongoing marginalization of large sections of the population, especially considering the importance that state violence had in triggering the initial riots leading to the 2011 mass movement.
42. Clover, *Riot. Strike. Riot*, 165.
43. Frantz Fanon, *The Wretched of the Earth* (London: Penguin, 2013), 27.

Evidence of Things Unseen But Heard

Louis Henderson

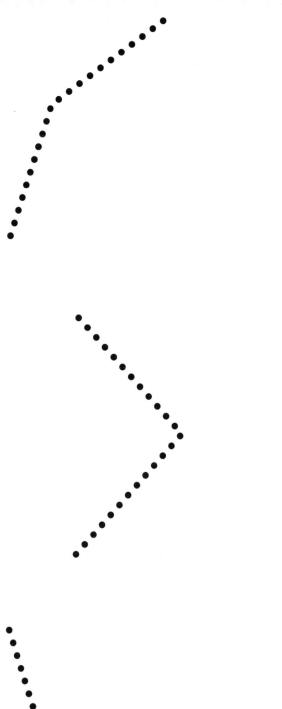

1.

"...sound and silence. What bridges the two elements is echo, the traces of creation. If sound is birth and silence death, the echo trailing into infinity can only be the experience of life, the source of narrative and a pattern for history."[1]

Bristol, August 23, 2017

A gray and pink sky dashed across with the deep blues of post-storm light. Dark rain clouds and a river the color of lead. At Portishead the boat begins to bear right, from the mouth of the Severn fed by the North Atlantic, into the River Avon, and onward toward the city of Bristol. Heading down past Clifton and into the Cumberland Basin, eventually the boat enters Bristol Harbour. On the left are the offices of Lloyds Bank, a company that grew to its powerful status from insuring enslaved people and slave ships during the Atlantic slave trade. The boat continues up St. Augustine's Reach and glides under a footbridge traversing the waterfront: Pero's Bridge, named after Pero Jones, a boy of twelve, bought as a slave for the Mountravers plantation in Nevis in 1765 by John Pinney. He was brought to Bristol as a servant to Pinney in 1783, and having never gained his freedom, here he died in 1798. On leaving the boat and walking up Cascade steps into the city, one is confronted after a few hundred meters by a tall statue celebrating the life of Sir Edward Colston (1636–1721).[2] A Bristol-born merchant, philanthropist, and member of Parliament, he is commemorated throughout the city via various landmarks, street names, three schools, and the famous Colston Hall music venue. A major part of Colston's wealth came from slave plantations producing sugar in the Caribbean, as well as from his work for the Royal African Company, an English mercantile company that transported enslaved people from Africa to the Caribbean. Bristol was the preeminent slave port in Europe during the 1730s, accounting for 18 percent of the entire British slave trade and establishing strong trade links with West Africa. Much of Bristol's wealth comes from this period, and it can still be seen in the lavish Georgian architecture that lines the streets of affluent neighborhoods. As one eighteenth-century annalist had it: "There is not a brick in the city but what is cemented with the blood of a slave. Sumptuous mansions, luxurious living, liveried menials, were the produce of the wealth made from the sufferings and groans of the slaves bought and sold by the Bristol merchants."[3]

Rain begins to pour across the pavements. People rush home from work, catching buses to the suburbs, schoolchildren flock to City Chicken, and a man leaning back on a bench, with a dog at his feet, drinks from

- 1. Louis Chude-Sokei, *Doctor Satan's Echo Chamber* (Vlaeberg, South Africa: Chimurenga, 2008), 6.
- 2. Since this essay was written, the statue of Edward Colston was pulled off its pedestal by a group of Black Lives Matter protesters on the afternoon of Sunday, June 7, 2020. They rolled the statue to Bristol Harbor and pushed it into the water. With a strong sense of poetic justice, the statue of a slave owner sunk to the bottom of the water in which slave ships were once docked.
- 3. Anonymous comment on Bristol, cited in J. F. Nicholls and John Taylor, *Bristol Past and Present,* 3 vols. (Bristol and London: Arrowsmith, 1881–1882), 3:165.

a plastic two-liter bottle of cider. Bristol, August 23, 2017. All seems so banal, so British, and then suddenly certain questions come to mind: In what ways does the afterlife of slavery still haunt the city and its recent history? What echoes or ripples from the past still resonate and drift through these city streets?

> do you, do you remember those days of slavery?
> it wasn't black man alone, who died thru bravery
> though some a dem threw dem self over board
> because dis ya slaveship overload
> it wasn't black man alone, that really really suffer as slaves
> but we suffer the hardest way until today
> [...]
> do you, do you remember those days of slavery?
> thru crooked rocks, dangerous ocean
> in ya dis ya civilisation

—Eek-A-Mouse, "Do You Remember" (Kingston, 1982)

2.

"Benign, tolerant Bristol felt betrayed; and the rest of the nation woke up in amazement. If such anger can erupt *there*, what may soon happen in more celebrated urban ghettos, like Handsworth, Birmingham, or Brixton, London?"[4]

Detail of contact sheet. Courtesy of the Bristol Archives, ref. 43129/Lib/StP/1/1/3.

The words above were printed in the *Observer* newspaper on August 6, 1980, four days after civil disturbances broke out in the St. Pauls neighborhood of Bristol. They seemed, when I read them in the Bristol Archives in 2017, to be haunted with a premonition of the divisive events that would grip the Black working-class communities through the 1980s in the United Kingdom. This newspaper clipping was a fossilized future

4. Robert Chesshyre and George Brock, "The Revolt of Britain's Lost Tribe," *Observer*, April 6, 1980, 11.

perfect, projecting what will have been, what will come to pass *(1981 Brixton riot, 1981 Chapeltown riots, 1981 Toxteth riots, 1981 Moss Side riot, 1981 Handsworth riots).* It sent me from Bristol to Handsworth, and I heard a voice that seemed to haunt the article. It said: "There are no stories in the riots, only the ghosts of other stories." The voice was an echo from the Black Audio Film Collective's *Handsworth Songs* (1986), a film that studies the riots of the 1980s from a perspective that sets them in relation to histories of British colonialism, Atlantic slavery, the Industrial Revolution, and postwar labor migration to Britain from ex-British colonies. I think it is important to listen to the songs of Handsworth, amplified by the film, as industrial ballads that lament a traumatic past that refuses to leave the present. So if what happened in St. Pauls in 1980 was a premonition of things to come, which ghosts of which stories were sung in St. Pauls?

Some people named what happened on August 2, 1980, the St. Pauls Riots. Recently I heard people refer to this episode as the St. Pauls Uprising. However we choose to describe it, the facts remain. The uprising happened because of a police raid on the Black and White Café, a local meeting point popular with young members of the Caribbean community of St. Pauls, an area that housed a large part of Bristol's Caribbean population. It was sometime late in the afternoon that the police raided the café, and a powerful backlash ensued. The first action lasted until midnight, but it never extended beyond St. Pauls. Bricks and bottles were thrown, police cars were torched, the windows of Lloyds Bank were smashed, and the police used riot shields on civilians for the first time ever on mainland Britain. Thirty-three people were injured, and 130 were arrested.

Tension had been rising between the police and the people of St. Pauls, as in many parts of the United Kingdom at that time, especially since the 1979 election of Margaret Thatcher's Conservative government and its controversial moves to invest new powers in the police. Under the Vagrancy Act of 1824, police were allowed to stop and search people in the street if they had "reasonable suspicion" that an individual had committed an offense. Informally, these laws were referred to as "sus" laws (from "suspicion"), and their social and psychological effects were tragically chronicled by the Jamaican Dub poet Linton Kwesi Johnson in his famous record "Sonny's Lettah" (1979). The lyrics are written from the perspective of an inmate in Brixton Prison awaiting trial for the murder of a policeman after trying to protect his brother from a police attack launched on the unjust (and racist and biased) grounds of suspicion of theft. The introduction of the sus laws led to outrage within certain communities in the United Kingdom as they assisted racist profiling that targeted Black, Asian, and minority ethnic people by a largely white police force. The laws were also used as a way to check people's immigration status, a violent form of surveillance that brought forth racist ideas about "Britishness" and the right to live in a country. Yet the people harassed on these grounds at that time were often second-generation immigrants, children of people from ex-British colonies such as Jamaica or India who were invited to live and work in Britain in the 1940s and 1950s. They came to a country that

Stills from *Evidence of Things Unseen But Heard*, directed by Louis Henderson (2018), 19

was economically and emotionally ruined by World War II, and they participated in the industries that brought the country back to its feet—in factories, markets, buses, hospitals, and schools, for example. Yet people from ex-British colonies had already contributed enormously to the economic and emotional development of the United Kingdom—from the wealth accrued through forced labor on slave plantations harvesting sugar, for example. So it seems, from within the present looking back through the past, that the riots, the racism, the immigration policies of the Conservative government, and the tactics of police surveillance were all haunted by the afterlife of slavery, and that the songs of St. Pauls were ballads being sung in protest.

> It woz di miggle a di rush howah
> wen evrybady jus a hosel an a bosel
> fi goh home fi dem evenin showah;
> mi an Jim stand up
> waitin pan a bus,
> nat cauzin no fus,
> wen all af a sudden
> a police van pull-up.
>
> Out jump tree policeman,
> di hole a dem carryin batan.
> Dem waak straight up to mi an Jim.
>
> One a dem hol awn to Jim
> seh him tekin him in;
> Jim tell him fi let goh a him
> far him noh dhu notn
> an him naw teef,
> nat even a butn.
> Jim start to wriggle
> di police start to giggle.
> [...]
> Mama,
> more policeman come dung,
> an beat mi to di grung;
> dem charge Jim fi sus,
> dem charge me fi murdah.
> Mama,
> don fret,
> dont get depres
> an doun-hearted.
> Be af good courage
> till I hear fram you.
>
> I remain
> your son,
> Sonny.
>
> —Linton Kwesi Johnson, "Sonny's Lettah" (London, 1979)

3.

"The photograph, which was intended to classify, measure, identify, and differentiate, offers no clue about the riot or her role in it, but I am unable to look at her face without anticipating it, without straining to hear its music."[5]

The city archives were the first place I went to in Bristol when I began the research for an essay film (of the same title as this text) reflecting on the history of the neighborhood of St. Pauls, the riots of 1980, and the music that followed in their wake. I sat there one afternoon, leafing through three scrapbooks from the 1980s that collected various newspaper clippings about the St. Pauls Uprising and its aftermath. Gradually I pieced together a picture of how the media tried to understand what happened at that time. How people blamed the problem on race, police, unemployment, drugs, and poverty. Yet none of the articles seemed concerned with looking at the history, at the many sedimented layers that built up the ground on which the riots happened. "'It came like rain out of a clear sky,' said a Black community leader. And by next day, although there were police in groups of four on every corner, and the echo of hammers as wooden boarding went up on looted windows, the clouds had gone again."[6] This seemed to be the prevalent attitude, one of utter surprise, and yet from my position in 2017, it seemed that the uprising had been waiting to happen for so many years. This could be gathered from looking through the archive, and I started to use the photographs and newspaper clippings as material evidence from which a series of speculations could unfold in the montage of my essay film. In a method akin to the critical fabulation of Saidiya Hartman, I was interested precisely in the question of whether it was "possible to exceed or negotiate the constitutive limits of the archive." I was thinking about how the archive continued to construct the discourse around these events and how it might be possible to narrate this story otherwise—as Hartman has it, by "fashioning a narrative, which is based upon archival research, and by that I mean a critical reading of the archive that mimes the figurative dimensions of history, I intended both to tell an impossible story and to amplify the impossibility of its telling."[7] This method of amplification was how I tried to fabulate this particular narrative, an amplification of the sounds that were missing from the archival material: the music of the Bristol Sound, collaged in relation to images of the riots and the streets they took place in, filmed in 2017. This is what constitutes the essay film *Evidence of Things Unseen But Heard* (2018), and it is indebted to the methods of the Black Audio Film Collective, who, it could be said, also follow the practice of critical fabulation in a work such as *Handsworth Songs*.

5. Saidiya Hartman, *Wayward Lives, Beautiful Experiments: Intimate Histories of Riotous Black Girls, Troublesome Women, and Queer Radicals* (New York: W. W. Norton, 2019), 265.
6. Chesshyre and Brock, "Revolt of Britain's Lost Tribe."
7. Saidiya Hartman, "Venus in Two Acts," *Small Axe: A Caribbean Journal of Criticism* 26, vol. 12, no. 2 (June 2008): 11.

Stills from *Evidence of Things Unseen But Heard*, directed by Louis Henderson (2018), 19 minutes and 30 seconds. Courtesy of Louis Henderson.

In the archive, I found a series of contact sheets of black-and-white photographs with "St. Pauls, 1980," written at the top. Four photographs immediately stood out: The first in the row had three policemen, each with a large Alsatian dog, standing in front of the burned-out windows of Lloyds Bank on a Bristol high street. A small crowd has gathered in front, and they are trying to look inside at the damage. Each policeman looks in a different direction. In the following three photographs, the crowd has dispersed, one of the policemen has left, and the other two look in opposite directions. The dogs are now lying down and enjoying some momentary sunshine. Further on in the contact sheets were images of overturned police cars in flames in the night, with many people crowding the streets, policemen looking in windows, looking in corners of burned-out shops, looking in notebooks. In one row of photographs is a series of close-ups of a police inspector walking through the remains of a building. First he looks down, then up, then to his left, then again to his right. In the row below, he is joined by two more inspectors in long macs. They are all looking at the charred mess.

What we have in these photographs seemed to raise an interesting question of how riots like these can or should be considered. They are images taken by someone who was looking at the police looking at the remains of the St. Pauls Uprising. The inspector's tool in this instance is his sight, and he is looking for evidence of why these people in this community decided to burn their own shops and harm the police that are apparently working to protect them. The police, through surveillance, suspicion, arrest, and incarceration, privilege sight over sound. They look, but they refuse to listen. This could be understood as the ocularcentrism of the police state and the violence it purveys. Indeed, the sus laws, and the arrests that came from them, always privileged the claims made by a member of the police according to information gathered through sight over the words or testimony of the accused. This is what *Handsworth Songs* tries to think through in regard to the riots in 1985; the public, misinformed by the media, was confused as to why the riots happened, yet nobody in the government or the police force was really prepared to listen closely to the demands of the communities that were rioting. The Black Audio Film Collective spent time in Handsworth, Brixton, and Tottenham listening to people, what they had to say, and what songs they were playing in resistance and remembrance. In the film, we have scenes of a Sikh funeral song being played to commemorate people who died in the riots, we have Rastafarian Nyabinghi drumming with singing in Amharic as the hearse of Cynthia Jarrett drives past in Tottenham, we have a scene of Jah Shaka playing reggae on a sound system in the early hours of the morning while the police wait outside. The Black Audio Film Collective manages to create images that resonate with sound, sonic-images or image-sounds. It is a different way of image-making that incorporates a generosity of *listening to* rather than *taking from* an experience of a community.

This is perhaps how "sound gives us back the visuality that ocularcentrism has repressed," a deeper and more layered form of visuality that allows for echoes from the past to resound in the present, bringing to images certain cultural, geographical, and historical specificities that might not appear at first glance, from what our eyes can gather.[8] In this sense, the echo is, as Louis Chude-Sokei remarks, "a source of narrative, a pattern for history" in that the echo allows for the continual haunting of the present by previous events and generations.[9] The body of the individual caught in the suspicious gaze of the police officer resounds with a narrative and a history that come from elsewhere. We look at the hearse of Cynthia Jarrett passing by, and we hear the music of Rastafarians from Jamaica singing in a language from Ethiopia, and it is impossible not to be moved by the association that her death, at the hands of the police in London, carries with it all of this stratified history from Africa to the Caribbean, ending up on the Broadwater Farm council estate in Tottenham burning with rage and upset on October 6, 1985.

Looking at the photographs of St. Pauls in the archive, I was interested in asking similar questions of these images. What sounds constituted the sonic space of these photographs? What could I hear as the sound of Bristol, the *Bristol Sound*? As I listened closer to the pictures of burned-out police cars in front of Lloyds Bank, I started to hear sirens, police sirens screaming through the night. The police sirens, through the powers of echo and delay from a Dub Reggae mixing desk, can eventually turn into the sirens of sound systems that flourished in the aftermath of the St. Pauls Uprising, playing rhythm and bass deep into the night, *late night blues*.

> Ok Babylon, just a riot on ok,
> I said a riot, a riot,
> No you can't deny it,
> I said a riot, a riot,
> When everyone quiet.
> [...]
> Who pay your earnin' to set Bristol burnin'?
> [...]
> Riot right here in Bristol St. Pauls England, as I would say.
> Riot throughout the world today!

—3D Production, "Riot" (Bristol, 1980)

4.
> Rock Bristol Rock,
> St. Pauls Jamming
> Can you hear the music playing?
> Fire down there!
> Wow no you can't get in there
> Fire down there!
> Wow no you can't come out there,
> Dread, wow now, well well dread.
> Over on White Ladies road, the spirit touch my soul.

8. Fred Moten, *In the Break: The Aesthetics of the Black Radical Tradition* (Durham, NC: Duke University Press, 2003), 235.
9. Chude-Sokei, *Doctor Satan's Echo Chamber*, 6.

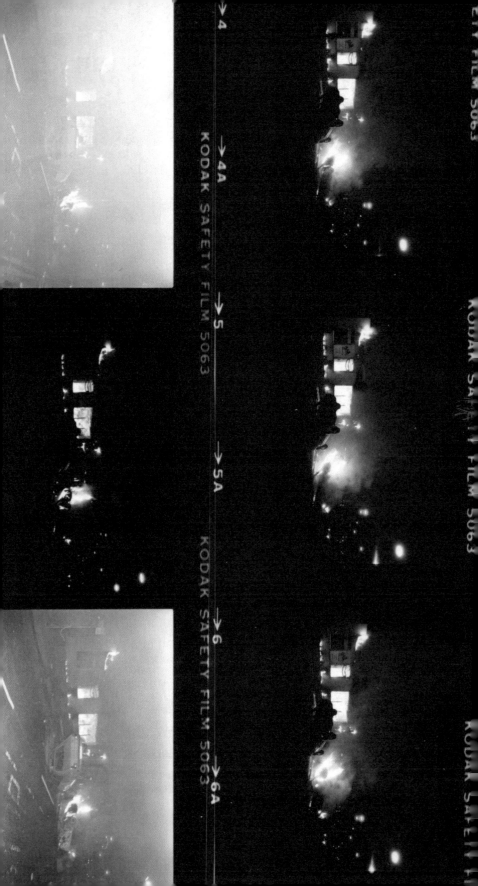

ILM 5063 ·17A KODAK S

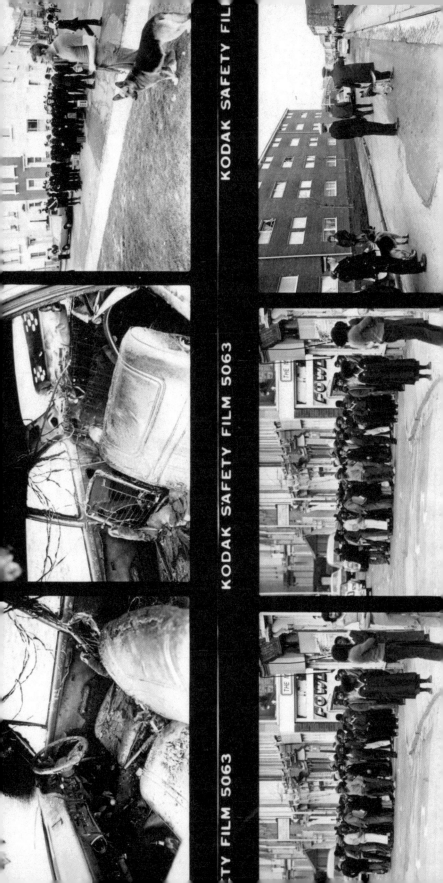

On top of Blackboy Hill, silently I make a wish
I've got to get to Henbury cemetery, read it in your history
Scipio Africanus
Scipio Africanus
Scipio Africanus
His bones are still on ya
His bones are still on ya

—Black Roots, "Bristol Rock" (Bristol, 1981)

As I continue scanning the contact sheets, the images start to change in quite a dramatic way. After three pages of burnt buildings, burning cars, broken windows, and policemen, I start to see pictures of groups of young people smiling at the camera, people seated together on walls, on cars, and on top of large speakers from a sound system in a park somewhere in St. Pauls. Listening to these pictures, I could feel the rumble of a heavy, rolling bass line and hear the words of a DJ echoing messages across the park, fragments of chatter ricocheting through space in delay. This particular succession of images, in such an order, made me think about the relation between the riots and the music of Bristol. I thought that what I was listening to within these photographs was in part the result of the uprising: from rioting against a broken system to coming together around a sound system.

After the 1980–1981 riots in the United Kingdom, the Conservative government commissioned a report by Lord Scarman to inquire into the causes and effects of the disturbances. This was an official attempt at listening, the evidence of which was largely ignored by the government and the police, however. Yet some attempts were made to create "positive" outcomes from the report as a way to stop further civil disturbances at later dates. (Of course, these attempts failed precisely because of the lack of genuine care or interest on the part of the Conservative government toward the people in question. Brixton and Handsworth rioted again in 1985, and riots continued and continues all over the country.) One outcome was the introduction of "policing by consent," as Richard King, the Bristol record shop owner and author, notes in his book *Original Rockers*: "This initiative attempted to prioritize community relations above arrest targets and for the first time sound systems were tolerated rather than targeted by the police. In St. Pauls, where sound system battles were regularly held in the newly built Malcolm X Community Centre, the community became partly defined by sound-system culture."[10] Essentially, then, as a result of the uprising, St. Pauls was somewhat left alone by the police, and the community became responsible for self-policing. The already existing sound-system culture flourished in the empty buildings of the economically restricted neighborhood, and as they were left to go on through the week and throughout the night, the parties created the space for radical experimentation and development in music. Hence Bristol became one of the most important cities in the United Kingdom for bass-heavy,

●   10. Richard King, *Original Rockers* (London: Faber and Faber, 2015), 54.

→ 12A

→ 13A

IL

sound-system-oriented music. Bristol was a purveyor of Reggae, Hip-Hop, Jungle, Drum and Bass, and, of course, the genre unique to the city itself: Trip-Hop, a music so laden with paranoia and darkness that listening to it, one can feel Bristol's bad weather, bad policing, heavy bass, and strong cannabis. A quintessentially British music.

I don't want to merely list the many names of people who emerged out of Bristol's music scene, for this is often how Bristol is spoken of. Yet I would like to focus on the culture of the sound system, how it was imported from Jamaica, what it brought to cities like Bristol, and how, through listening closely to sound-system culture in the wake of something such as the St. Pauls Uprising (of which it was such an intimate part), we can begin to hear different historical narratives around migration, colonization, and slavery in Britain.

Here we come back again to the echo, as if there is an echo echoing within this text. The echo is an aesthetic form particular to Dub Reggae, and it is frequently used as an effect in the remixed versions of songs, generally on the B side of 7-inch records (or as the extended mix on a 12-inch record). These remixed versions are often made by the producers of the original, who will take the different tracks from a recording and reorder them in various ways—cutting off the vocal track, for example, leaving only the drums and bass and backing vocals. Then, intermittently through the song, the voice of the singer may come in, fragmented through echo and delay. This style of remixing is called dubbing and is a technological process created in recording studios in Jamaica from the 1960s to the present. The echo is also an effect used on sound systems as a way to create a seamless transition from one record to another, creating a spectral, sonic web that extends from one Dub version to the next, so the echo becomes echoed and so on. One of the pioneers of Reggae production, and Dub Reggae in particular, Lee Scratch Perry, once claimed that duppies (a Jamaican term for a ghost) haunted his mixing desk in his studio, the Black Ark. I like to think, then, that Dub is a duppie music, a music created from within a ritualistic space where the dead are animated to life through echo and delay.[11] The echo is the ectoplasmic matter that allows for the voices of the dead to seep through the machines of the mixing desk and into the sound system, from Kingston to Bristol, from the 1970s to the present day. Could we then understand the sound system as a space of ritual, using dub plates as material imprints of past events that, when spiraled into motion, make a sound loud enough to awaken the dead?

Attempting to answer this question led me back to the archival material, the videos I was shooting in the present, and the conversations I was having with people who lived in St. Pauls. This was all part of a method of storytelling that attempted to offer a different understanding of why the St. Pauls Uprising took place and a way to rethink how stories could be narrated about Bristol and its history as a slave port. Through

11. For further reference, look to the work of Louis Chude-Sokei, in particular *Doctor Satan's Echo Chamber*.

the methods of critical fabulation, I wanted to treat the photographs in the archive as evidence upon which I could create an audiovisual essay about the long-lasting effects of British slavery upon certain communities in England. For me this involved a process of close listening to what was being told and how it was being told, both in image and in sound, in rhythm of speech and in beat; then, through the amplification of those sounds in and around images, I was able to piece together a proposition.

Indeed, the photographs of sound systems built after the St. Pauls Uprising, for example, were haunted by the afterlife of slavery and the violence of plantation capitalism, but they were also haunted by the echoes of uprisings against such systems of oppression. Slave revolts that had ricocheted throughout the Caribbean for centuries, from Jamaica to Guadeloupe and Cuba to Haiti. If the sounds of these images should remind us of something, it is precisely that the uprisings came from a powerful lineage of resistance. They should remind us, for example, that Jamaican independence was not granted to Jamaica by the queen of England; it was fought for through years of struggle, from maroons fighting British plantation owners in the eighteenth century to strikes and riots protesting inequalities of wealth in British Caribbean colonies in the twentieth century. There is a very important need to challenge certain British nationalist mythologies around the abolition of slavery, as they unjustly amplify the role of British parliamentarians within the process. As the voice of Paul Foot reminds us in an NTS radio show by John T. Gast from 2012, it was not people like William Wilberforce—a white, bourgeois, Conservative politician—who abolished slavery, but the enslaved people themselves.[12]

It is important to remember all of this today as these ghosts still haunt our present, they have never been laid to rest, and they continue to deal with the trauma that people are still suffering on a daily basis—from the death of Mark Duggan at the hands of the police in Tottenham in 2011 to the deportations within the Windrush scandal organized by Theresa May and the Conservative government she led in 2018.[13] I will insist on one last comment: if the present is not listened to as containing echoes from other places and other times, then there is no possibility of understanding which stories haunt the riots, and as such, they will never be heard as uprisings against the violence of racial capitalism.

All contact sheets in this piece are courtesy of the Bristol Archives, reference 43129/Lib/StP/1/1/3.

12. *RPBLC of Many Voices*, NTS Radio, broadcast May 2012. Wilberforce was, in fact, opposed to Toussaint Louverture's project of emancipation of the enslaved people of Saint Domingue (latter-day Haiti), for example, and voted to send British troops to quell the revolution.
13. The Windrush scandal is a 2018 British political scandal concerning people who were wrongly detained, denied legal rights, threatened with deportation, and, in at least 164 cases, wrongly deported from the United Kingdom by the Home Office. Many of those affected had been born British subjects and had arrived in the United Kingdom before 1973, particularly from Caribbean countries as members of the "Windrush generation" (so named after the *Empire Windrush*, the ship that brought one of the first groups of West Indian migrants to the United Kingdom in 1948).

Re-looking at Riots in Contemporary Sri Lanka

Chandraguptha Thenuwara

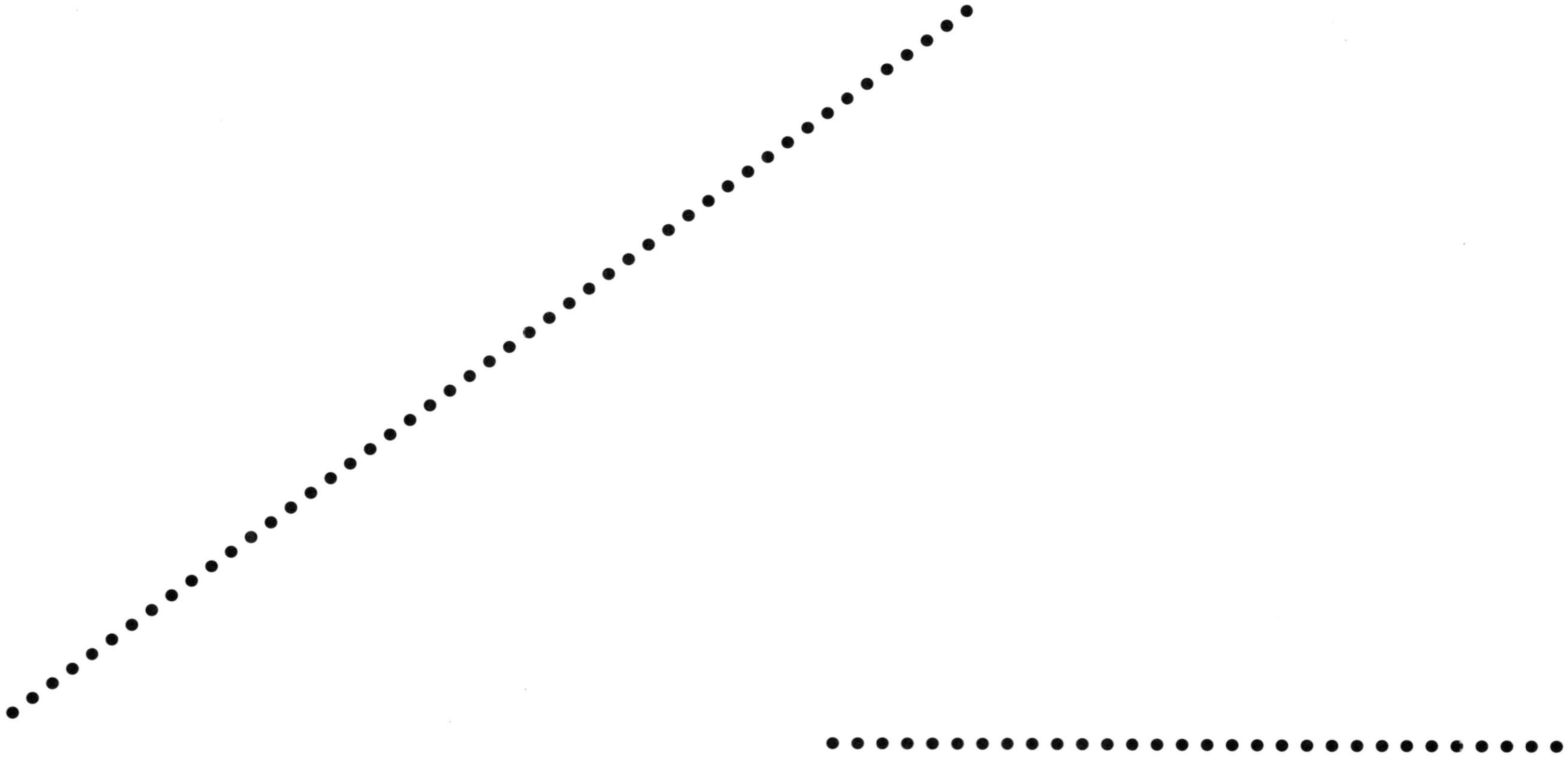

When discussing Sri Lanka, one can say that "Sri Lanka has a long and proud tradition of religious coexistence which is attested by the presence of multi-religious sacred sites throughout the island, as well as, its uniquely mixed cultural geography. Buddhists, Christians, Hindus and Muslims have historically shared public space."[1] However, this statement seems true only when there are no wars or conflicts. When we look back in time, the statement becomes a myth. In reality:

Communal violence in Sri Lanka often appears to have an ancient history. Sinhala and Tamil communities in Sri Lanka both tend to view their relationship in terms of histories which stretch back for at least 2,500 years. These histories buttress the opposing territorial claims of the two communities, and make conflict between them seem inevitable. For the Sinhalese, history justifies their claim to impose their rule over the whole island of Lanka. For Tamils, too, history is used to justify demands, in the past for a degree of autonomy for Tamil-dominated areas, and today for total separation from the Sinhala-dominated parts of the country.[2]

Then again, what about the Muslims, and what kind of history do they look back on? Similarly, this question can be posed for Sri Lankan Burghers, Malays, Veddas, and the like—what kind of history do each of these communities lay claim to?

We perceive that most of the violence in Sri Lanka is based on language, religion, and party politics. Sinhala and Tamil are the most important languages in Sri Lanka. English is the link language, inherited from British colonizers. Sri Lanka has a basic bipartite divide of majority Sinhala and multiple minority Tamil-speaking communities. Sri Lankan Tamils are the most numerous minority and are central to the country's ethnic conflict. The other two major (Tamil-speaking) minorities are Sri Lankan Muslims and the Malaiyaha, or hill-country Tamils, descendants of South Indian indentured laborers brought to the country by the British. Ethnic identities are far from primordial and, in fact, have more recent origins in the colonial state's codification of differentiation as ethnic difference.[3]

Sri Lanka was scarred by more than three decades of war fought not only over language but also over territory. The result of the conflict has been grief, loss, and silence mapped onto places of destruction and displacement. Empty houses, abandoned villages, and the rusting ruins of warfare mark the landscape, particularly in the Northern and Eastern Provinces.

1. Darini Rajasingham-Senanayake, "Dambulla Mosque Crisis: Needed a Policy for Multiculturalism and Social Integration," Island, May 5, 2012, http://www.island.lk/index.php?page_cat=article-details&page=article-details&code_title=51195.
2. Elizabeth Nissan and R. L. Stirrat, "The Generation of Communal Identities," in Sri Lanka History and the Roots of Conflict, ed. Jonathan Spencer (London: Routledge, 1990), 19.
3. Sharika Thiranagama, "Claiming the State: Postwar Reconciliation in Sri Lanka," Humanity: An International Journal of Human Rights, Humanitarianism, and Development 4, no. 1 (Spring 2013): 95.

Chandraguptha Thenuwara, *Neo-Barrelism*, 2006. Courtesy of a private collection.

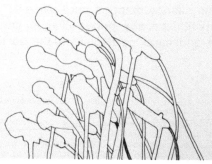

Chandraguptha Thenuwara, *Untitled II*, 2011. Courtesy of a private collection.

Rachel Seoighe further emphasizes that Sri Lanka's young generation, especially those born after 1983, grew up in a world of violence.[4] The everyday experience of warfare and state terror defined daily life for decades, impacting those lives in ways that were often dictated by ethnicity and location. The war was marked by atrocity—including torture, disappearances, and indiscriminate violence against civilians—and by efficient, orchestrated propaganda. The long war resulted in the establishment of a national security state in Sri Lanka: a militarized political culture, the rolling back of civil rights in favor of "security," and a deep state with no accountability. Nearly an entire generation of Tamils was lost to violence and migration, and a large number of Sinhalese were also killed, including civilians, politicians, and state armed forces personnel who were overwhelmingly recruited, as is so often the case, from the country's most disadvantaged communities. Not only Sinhala and Tamil but also the Muslim population suffered deep loss: war-related killings, large-scale displacement perpetrated and directed by the Liberation Tigers of Tamil Eelam (LTTE), and, most recently, postwar persecution by emergent Sinhala-Buddhist nationalist-led hate groups.[5]

But "violence is never 'senseless': it is one set of political methods among others."[6] Meredith L. Weiss, Edward Newman, and Itty Abraham discuss "assassinations and riots" as "two seemingly polar modes of political violence," noting that assassination is an age-old form of political violence that is at times an individual act and at others is carried out "by religious and secular actors, liberation movements, right- and left-wing extremists, military officers and civilian government officials alike."[7] Riots and pogroms have a similarly long history as a mode of political violence but are very different in their "methods and meanings." The two are fraught with narratives of state action and inaction—they may be directly perpetrated by the state against its citizens, or they may be condoned by the state, making it equally culpable. "Riots yield not only death, injury and destruction of property, but also a culture of terror and mistrust that influences political actions long into the future."[8]

The first political violence of recent history in Sri Lanka occurred with the armed uprising of the Janatha Vimukthi Peramuna (JVP) in 1971; it was followed by the uprising of Tamil militant youth in the mid-1970s that eventually came to be dominated by the LTTE. The LTTE came to prominence with the assassination of Jaffna mayor Alfred Duraiappah in 1975. Most of the accounts of these political uprisings are based on words. Images were rare because cameras were expensive and professional photographers were scarce. The print media and the radio were the primary sources of information. Only the eyewitness felt the brutality of

- 4. Rachel Seoighe, *War, Denial, and Nation-Building in Sri Lanka* (New York: Palgrave Macmillan, 2017).
- 5. Seoighe, *War, Denial, and Nation-Building*, 7–8.
- 6. Meredith L. Weiss, Edward Newman, and Itty Abraham, "The Politics of Violence: Modalities, Frames, and Functions," in *Political Violence in South and Southeast Asia: Critical Perspectives*, ed. Itty Abraham, Edward Newman, and Meredith L. Weiss (Tokyo: United Nations University Press, 2010), 12.
- 7. Weiss, Newman, and Abraham, "Politics of Violence," 13.
- 8. Weiss, Newman, and Abraham, "Politics of Violence," 14–15.

the political and ethnic riots that occurred from 1956 to 1958, the 1971 political insurgency, and the early struggles of Tamil liberation movements. They became stories instead. A few people knew the stories well, but only if the listener could find the proper storyteller would he or she know how terrible that story was. Publicly, what prevailed was a softened version.

After 1979 television was introduced to Sri Lanka, and everything started playing out in front of the television camera. It created a new visual culture. The image became stronger, and, with it, more image-based reportage was introduced. As the economy opened up in 1977, cameras became available in the open market and were increasingly affordable, allowing for the emergence of both professional and amateur photographers. Ella Shohat and Robert Stam, writing about "the visual," note that it never appears as "pure":

> ...it is always "contaminated" by the work of other senses (hearing, touch, smell), touched by other texts and discourses, and imbricated in a whole series of apparatuses—the museum, the academy, the art world, the publishing industry, even the nation-state—which govern the production, dissemination, and legitimation of artistic productions. It is not now a question of replacing the blindnesses of the "linguistic turn" with the "new" blindnesses of the "visual turn."[9]

While the opening of the economy created new opportunities for some, it also created political and economic upheavals that led to more violence, shrank democratic space, and allowed ethnic and religious conflict to flourish. It culminated in protracted ethnic war and conflict and offered fertile ground for the pogrom of July 1983. On July 23, 1983, amid state repression in Jaffna, a Tamil armed group attacked an army patrol, killing thirteen Sinhala soldiers. Furious, but powerless to punish those responsible, the army indulged in indiscriminate assaults, slaughtering more than seventy civilians.[10] State-instigated rioting broke out in Colombo following the government-organized public funeral for the slain soldiers. As the riots spread—lynching and destroying Tamil-owned businesses in their path—Tamils in the south of the country were forced into camps for the displaced, shipped off to Jaffna, or joined the diaspora as refugees.

When this "Black July" riot started on July 23 in the north, I was in Udispattuwa, Central Province, working as a production designer for an unrealized television film series, *Knox's Ceylon*, based on Robert Knox's life in Sri Lanka. I used to visit Colombo periodically for research and to freelance at Wijeya Publications. My boarding house was in Delkanda,

- 9. Ella Shohat and Robert Stam, "Narrativizing Visual Culture: Towards a Polycentric Aesthetics," in *The Visual Culture Reader*, ed. Nicholas Mirzoeff (London: Routledge, 1998), 45.
- 10. Social Studies Circle of the Sri Lankan Worker-Peasant Institute, "Anti-Tamil Riots and the Political Crisis in Sri Lanka," *Bulletin of Concerned Asian Scholars* 16, no. 1 (January–March 1984): 27–29, https://www.marxists.org/history/erol/sri-lanka/tamil-2.pdf.

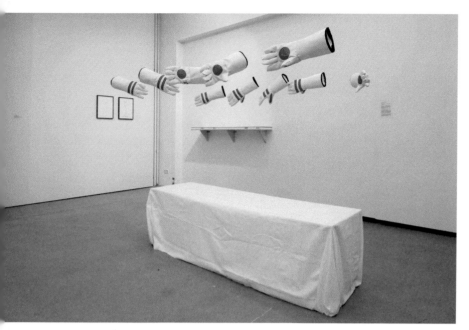

Chandraguptha Thenuwara, *VIP Convoy*, 2007, installation view of *Riots: Slow Cancellation of the Future*, ifa Gallery Stuttgart, 2018. Photograph by Henrike Hoffmann. © ifa (Institut für Auslandsbeziehungen).

Nugegoda. I arrived there on the night of July 24. Asoka Bandarage describes what happened that day and later:

> The mood of the large crowd that had gathered at the funeral of the dead soldiers at the Kanatte cemetery in Colombo on the evening of July 24 had at first been anti-government. There was growing frustration over the inequities generated by the Open Economy and the government's authoritarian policies. The crowd was already moving towards the heavily guarded house of the president in the neighborhood, but after pro-government gangs were brought in to incite anti-Tamil feelings, the anti-government cry apparently turned into an anti-Tamil cry and an outbreak of arson and murder of Tamils. The attacks on Tamils in Colombo that started on the night of July 24 continued through the next day, and for several more days.[11]

In the days that followed, as the state instigated riots against the Tamils, I witnessed the carnage before my eyes. On July 25, as I traveled by bus to Colombo, I saw a Tamil restaurant burning—I thought it might be an accident and that fire brigades would come and extinguish it. But as our bus approached the city, I saw people going hither and thither like ants. The bus continued through another part of town where I saw mobs forcibly boarding buses. I learned later that they were looking for Tamil passengers. As the bus passed through massive traffic blocks and crowds and eventually reached Thunmulla Junction, I saw that a big

●   11.   Asoka Bandarage, *The Separatist Conflict in Sri Lanka: Terrorism, Ethnicity, Political Economy* (London: Routledge, 2009), 105.

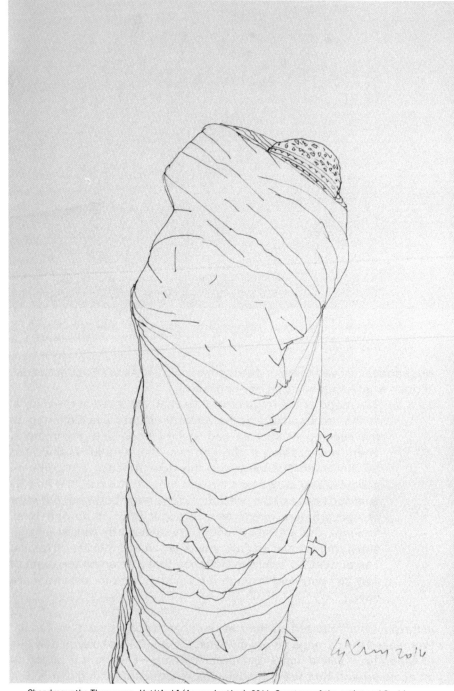

Chandraguptha Thenuwara, *Untitled I (Assassination)*, 2014. Courtesy of the artist and Saskia Fernando Gallery.

restaurant that was very popular among Jaffna Tamil food lovers was closed. On the wall, a few words were written in large letters in Sinhala: "This building belongs to a Sinhalese."

That is how the mob operated at that time, and that is why this memory stayed with me very vividly. When I went to work that day, there was no work to be done. With the massive crowds on the roads, I could find no empty buses and so started to walk to Wellawatte, where most of the Tamil inhabitants of the capital city lived. My aunt lived there too. I walked through Dharmapala Road to Colpetty Junction and from there directly to Wellawatte along Galle Road. In front of the market, there was a line of shops where I saw people looting, breaking closed doors and shop windows. A Buddhist monk was standing in front of a shop and giving orders to break the doors. I was shocked—the crowds were large and violent, there was nothing I could do. I wanted to reach Wellawatte as soon as possible. Most of the shops belonging to poor Tamil entrepreneurs were destroyed and looted. Hundreds of Tamil and Indian shops and property in the business areas of Colombo were being attacked and burned down. I found out later that mobs were using electoral lists to identify homes of Tamils, that these homes were attacked and many of their occupants killed.

As I walked, I saw how the army and the police were supporting the looters. It was much later in the day, only at about 6:00 p.m., that they started to prevent the violence, saying, "Now, enough." Until that moment, the soldiers and police allowed it to happen.

> Estimates of the number of Tamils killed in the July 1983 violence have varied widely from about 200 to about 2000 (the latter figure was given by Amirthalingam). Over 100,000 Sri Lankan Tamils were forced to enter refugee camps when several thousands of their homes, shops, factories, vehicles, and other belongings were destroyed. About 30,000 became unemployed due to the destruction of work sites, and the country experienced incalculable damage economically, politically, and morally. The Tamils were traumatized by the experience of utter helplessness and victimization in the face of Sinhala mob attacks. Many Sinhala individuals did come forward to help Tamil victims, but the Tamils' sense of insecurity, anger, and distrust of the Sinhalese generated by the terrible events of 1983 still remain.[12]

Black July happened in front of my eyes. Memories cannot be erased. They should not be erased. My memories of Black July are carved into my consciousness and still have an impact on me. It was not easy to come back to Black July creatively. I spent the next ten years studying art further, in Moscow. When I returned to Sri Lanka, for a couple of years I was busy establishing an alternative art school, Vibhavi, and teaching part time at the school I had graduated from in Colombo. It

12. Bandarage, *Separatist Conflict in Sri Lanka*, 105.

Chandraguptha Thenuwara, *Barrelscape*, 1998. Courtesy of the artist and Saskia Fernando Gallery.

took me nearly thirteen years to revisit Black July and to feature it in my art practice. I did my first sketches on camouflage at the end of 1996. Following the collapse of the peace talks between the government, led by President Chandrika Bandaranaike, and the LTTE in 1996, painted barrels appeared in Colombo as barricades. The most striking barrel barricades were around Colombo 7. In 1997 I started to make camouflage patterns and paint camouflage directly on barrels. Since then,

most of my artworks have followed the violence of the ethnic conflict in Sri Lanka and the political issues arising in those situations.

The first phase of my annual exhibition series that started in 1997 carried the title *Barrelism*. It was a direct response to the ongoing ethnic war that intensified after the Black July riots and was an expression of my critique of trying to solve the conflict with war, a war justified by the state as a "War for Peace." I believed there should be a political solution to the ethnic conflict. Such a solution was sought briefly under the

Ranil Wickeremesinghe-led ceasefire and peace talks with the LTTE in 2002–2003, but when a new government came to power in the last quarter of 2005, under the presidency of Mahinda Rajapaksa, a fresh wave of war agitation began.

Barrelism reacted to the blockade of the whole city of Colombo by these typical barrel structures. It is a Sri Lankan way to block the streets. My inspiration for *Barrelism* comes from the barricade located on Wijerama Road. Many of these blockades were installed permanently. When you see a checkpoint like this, you unconsciously check your identity card and your identity: Are you a Tamil or a Sinhalese? If there are Tamil letters on your national identity card, you instantly have problems. I know this very well as my wife is half Tamil. Once I was traveling with her in a three-wheeler, and the army stopped and asked us to show our identity cards. I always told her not to show hers—that I would show mine, and we wouldn't get into trouble. One day she showed her ID, and they asked, "Are you Tamil?" I argued with the army personnel, saying that she is my wife; it should not be their concern. My identity card was enough for the security to check us, it is in Sinhalese script, let us go. If I was humiliated near the barricades and security checkpoints, I could only imagine how it would feel to Tamils. They were treated like second-class citizens all the time, even though we had been living together for 2,500 years.

My work *Barrelism Tourist Map* was produced for the exhibition *Cities on the Move*, curated by Hans Ulrich Obrist and Hou Hanru in 1997. When I bought a printed tourist map, I realized that the barrels barricades were missing from the tourist map printed by the Government. I added the word "Barrelism" to the tourist map and located where the actual barrel barricades were and marked them on the map. Around the map was a decoration of tiny camouflage barrels.[13]

In 1999 I made a replica of my barrel monument for innocent victims to install in Raizen Park in Fukuoka, Japan. It consisted of a pillar of seven barrels on top of each other and around sixty other barrels, all painted in camouflage—the whole installation was made with seventy barrels while I was in residence at Fukuoka Asian Art Museum. The monuments of war are to memorialize and remind people what happened during the war, to remind people not to repeat the same mistakes. "By reproducing the barrel to represent the truth I questioned the very notion of security. Security is necessary. But the question is, security for whom? Is security for the people, or those in power? Who is being protected, and from whom?"[14]

---

13. Hou Hanru and Hans Ulrich Obrist, *Cities on the Move* (Ostfildern-Ruit, Germany: Verlag Gord Ilatje, 1997).
14. Chandraguptha Thenuwara, "Barrelism: A Response to the Militarization of Urban Space," paper presented at Gendering Urban Space in the Middle East and South Asia Workshop, co-organized by the Institute for Gender and Women's Studies at the American University in Cairo and the Shehr Network, February 2005, Cairo, https://www.academia.edu/32044204/Barrelism_A_response_to_the_Militarization_of_Urban_Space.doc.

A new form of barricades appeared across the country—painted yellow barricades that accompanied the painted camouflaged barrels—and I coined the term "Neo-Barrelism." My Neo-Barrelism exhibitions started after 2006 and continued till July 2008. As the war escalated and Buddhist monks stridently supported it, I criticized this phenomenon through three selected verses from the "Dhammapada." I titled the last phase of Barrelism "Post-Barrelism." It started after the end of the ethnic war in 2009. Post-Barrelism tried to erase the mentality of camouflage and sought hope for a better future.

In 2009 the ruling government exerted military force resulting in high casualties to end the war. The extent of the war crimes from this final chapter is yet to be accounted for. Sri Lanka's brutal ethnic war had continued for nearly twenty-seven years. Although the war was forcefully ended by the military defeat of the LTTE, the ethnic conflict was not resolved. Issues such as the devolution of power to the Northern and Eastern Provinces, war crimes, racial tensions, and the disappearances of journalists and human rights defenders persist. By the time the LTTE was crushed in 2009, more than 80,000 had been killed; 11,656 Tamil Tigers either were arrested or surrendered; and even in just the final phase of the conflict, 294,000 people were internally displaced.[15] This amount of death and displacement can be shown only through symbolic images, which explain it better than words. Countless people died in these conflicts. It's difficult to understand the extent of it.

But even after the war ended, the government had to create another enemy in order to survive. Three years after the end of the war, it found that new enemy in Islam and Sri Lanka's Muslim minority. Hate against the Muslim community was an undercurrent of opposition politics led by Mahinda Rajapaksa—agitation against Muslims was the opposition's only hope for winning the next elections. Islamophobia was politically instigated and began to spread throughout the country; with it came the June 2014 anti-Muslim riots. My work *Meta-Physique* was an artistic response to the 2014 riots orchestrated by the Rajapaksa regime in Darga Town in Aluthgama, a southern coastal city in Sri Lanka, against its Muslim population. These riots occurred almost exactly one hundred years after the anti-Muslim riots of 1915.

I produced the sculpture *Meta-Physique* based on my personal experience of goons targeting a protest in which I participated. The police at the demonstration were carrying batons and shields, and the goons were visible hiding behind them. This scene triggered me to create an image of the mob hiding behind a military-type figure. I did this to make it clear that the goons were supported and shielded by the government of Mahinda Rajapaksa (2005–2014). Before that incident, the police would talk to us like normal human beings, telling us about the areas they were going to block and how to behave there. They would also be critical of the political situation. But suddenly there was an order

15. I. H. M. N. N. Herath, "Role of Military in Post-Conflict Reconstruction in Sri Lanka" (master's thesis, Naval Postgraduate School, Monterey, CA, 2012), https://apps.dtic.mil/dtic/tr/fulltext/u2/a561910.pdf.

from above, and immediately those innocent-seeming figures would transform into something like robots. My image for *Meta-Physique* was conceived after seeing them. The figure of the soldier in the piece is large and looks like a protector, dressed in a helmet and military attire. But this entity has no inside. Anyone can enter the jacket, boots, and helmet or structure. Within this attire, anyone can become a monster or a protector.

In January 2015 Mahinda Rajapaksa was defeated in the presidential election, and the "common opposition" candidate Maithripala Sirisena was elected. I thought regime change would bring about a better demo-cratic ethos in the country, with more freedom from fear of abduction or killing. Most activists and most people expected a new era would begin. Under Sirisena's presidency, ultranationalist Sinhala groups such as the Bodu Bala Sena (BBS) lost some of their impunity.[16] Even though organized national hate campaigns have become less visible, religious discrimination, intolerance, and violence have persisted. Attacks against the Muslim community continued under the new regime, though without the involvement of the regime as in previous times.

But the seeds of hatred already planted began to take root. In February and March 2018, there was a series of riots targeting Muslims in the Ampara and Kandy districts. The Ampara riots of February 26, 2018, spread to the Kandy district by March 2 and continued until March 10, 2018. My piece *MOB* was a response to the May 13, 2019, riots, which occurred in the Western and North Western Province of Sri Lanka. After mobs attacked mosques, homes, and properties of Muslims, the Sri Lankan government declared a countrywide emergency to control the violence and also intermittently blocked social media to avoid the spread of misinformation. The riots against the Muslims happened three weeks after the Easter Sunday bombings (for which the Islamic State claimed responsibility) and killed more than 250 people. In the anti-Muslim mayhem that followed, more than 500 Muslim-owned homes, prop-erties, and mosques were destroyed. I coined the word "MOB" as an abbreviation of "Maliciously Organized Bastards" because most of the riots after the end of the ethnic war were instigated by power-hungry politicians, Buddhist monks, individuals, and organizations rooted in so-called Buddhist ideology.

The hope we felt after the 2015 elections was never realized. Within the very short period of five years, the Rajapaksa juggernaut was able to sweep back into power. The Sirisena/Wickremesinghe government was riven with differences and lacked the media outreach to counter the Rajapaksa propaganda. This, combined with the Easter Sunday bombings and their fallout, adversely affected the United National Front government. Sinhala-Buddhist nationalism and anti-Muslim pro-paganda strengthened the hand of Mahinda Rajapaksa and enabled his brother to win the presidency in 2019 through the newly minted Sri

16. Gehan Gunatillake, *The Chronic and the Acute: Post-War Religious Violence in Sri Lanka* (Colombo: International Centre for Ethnic Studies & Equitas, 2015), 45–46.

Lanka People's Party, riding to victory on a populist ethnonationalist political platform powered by Islamophobia. The new president immediately moved to institute a strong military presence in key civilian institutions. Many critical positions of power are now held by active or retired military personnel.

The Sri Lankan experience proves a thesis put forward by Weiss, Newman, and Abraham that,

> most often the state is the most significant source of political violence in both South Asia and Southeast Asia. And also, where the roots of political violence are structural, geopolitical, and linked to international norms, natural solutions for amelioration are implausible. The roots of political violence are tied to local political cultures and moral economies, change is possible and has occurred.[17]

The continuation and strengthening of democracy will be crucial for Sri Lanka to go forward without "political violence." Therefore it is essential that, as David Bloomfield shows, "universal human rights become increasingly accepted as the core principles of governance," and democracy is the "most effective way of implementing those principles— equality, representation, participation, accountability." Of course, every democracy is unique, but the core principles remain constant:

> Democracy is a system for managing difference without recourse to violence. Differences (of opinion, belief, ideology, culture) are a natural part of every society. Furthermore, conflict arises from such differences. Rather than eradicating or removing differences, or excluding some groups who differ within society, democracy functions as a process through which differences are brought out, acknowledged and dealt with in a way that permits them to exist without threatening the whole system.[18]

Riots have to some extent shaped Sri Lanka's political history and its path from independence to the present. Most of the riots have been either ethnic based (against the Tamils) or based on religion (against the Muslims). My work has sought to express and to critique this reality, to speak against it politically, and to provoke thinking and solutions to end both ethnic and religious-based violence and discrimination.

17. Weiss, Newman, and Abraham, "Politics of Violence," 22.
18. David Bloomfield, "Reconciliation: An Introduction," in *Reconciliation after Violent Conflict: A Handbook*, ed. David Bloomfield (Stockholm: International Institute for Democracy and Electoral Assistance, 2003), 10.

Black Side of the Hidden Moon

Unthreading Thoughts on the Riot in My Head

Satch Hoyt

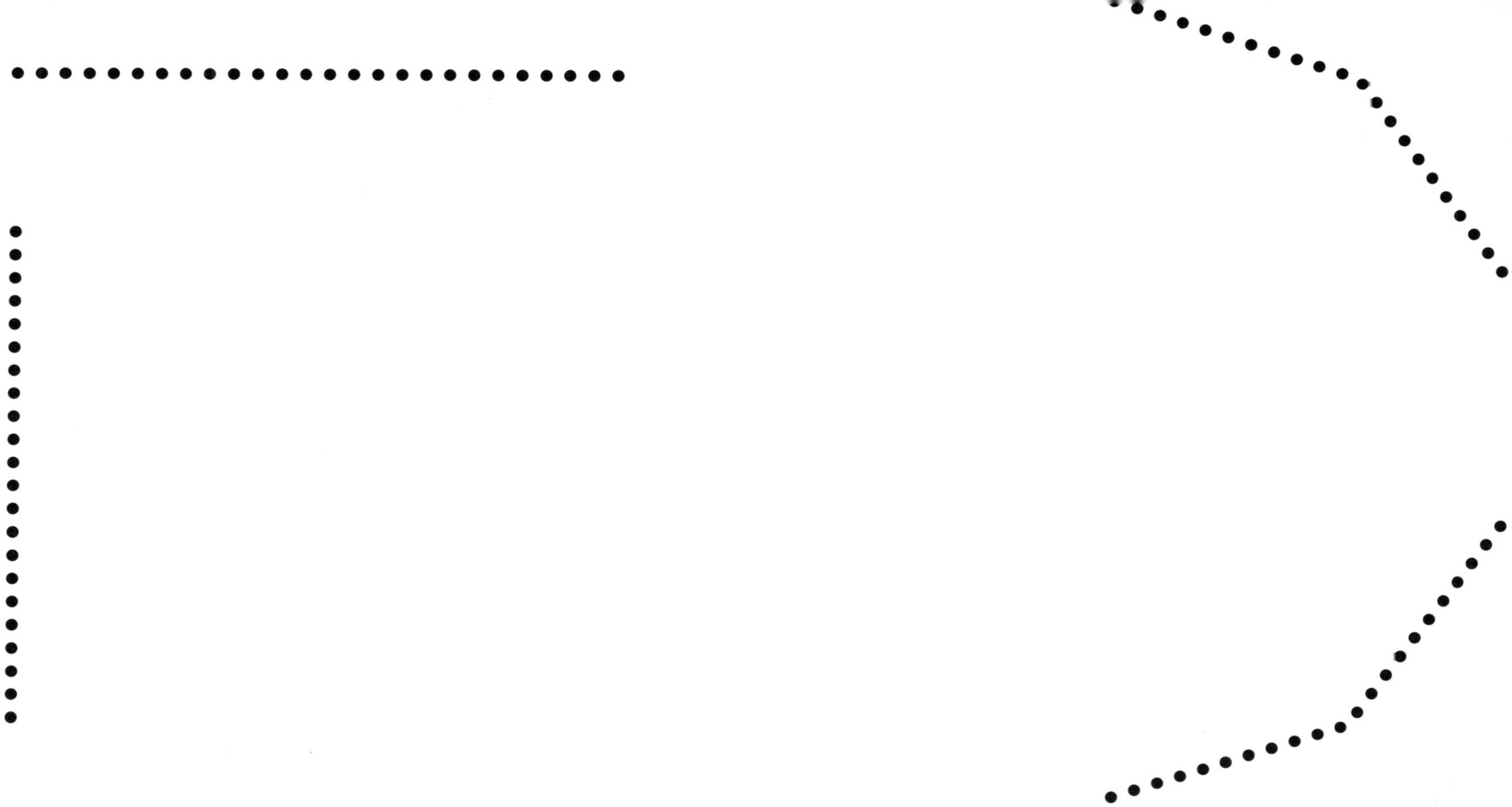

"Black Side of the Hidden Moon"

There ain't no mountain high enough to ward off the trauma that
  incubates inside the souls of the transited bodies,
Souls that trundle paths that lead to yet another bogus nowhere land.
  Denials are often spluttered from the guilty masters who offer no
  comfort or remorse, in fact no smooth arrangement exists when
  one excavates curtained centuries of fallacies seeped in taught
  implosive cycles of encrusted amnesia. The winner's version is
  under critical attack and will be written from the Black side of the
  hidden moon.

Satch Hoyt, *Portcullis*, 2007. Photograph by Trevor Lloyd Morgan.

To evolve in unfettered zones of inclusivity is the goal of liberation.
You, I, We are destined to dwell and gaze on vistas of multi-phonic,
    un-gated bliss space.
After all, isn't love what this revolution is all about?
We're not about, not about to carousel ride into repetition.
Those white halos worn by the dubious saints have melted, let's say
    morphed, into a shelf-life musty yellow.
The nowadays charlatan Al Judas will wriggle in his selfie tweet
    bubble, to be held cyber accountable for the travesties committed.
Technology has made fugitivity a limited endgame.
Yes, this is the time to believe in a new tomorrow, as we watch
    crumbling horizons implode out of view.
We know incalculable blood-blemished paths have soaked up the
    sorrows of uncountable feet.
Shoeless, forced to absorb then repel the ghosts of volcanic hate.
4, 3, 2, 1, March, yes, we Marched on Washington, then we marched
    in London, we marched in Kingston, marched in Jo-burg, marched
    in Accra, in Lagos. And, and we're still marching,
To give voice to the muted, to resurrect long buried narratives.
No more being squeezed into Sci-Fi margins.
Burn those books with the over-populated footnotes.
No more being allocated to some sort of wasteland Hollywood blind
    spot.
The seething crowd swells like multiple Nina Simone crescendos.
Screeching megaphoned chants float and flicker thru shards of
    visceral feedback.

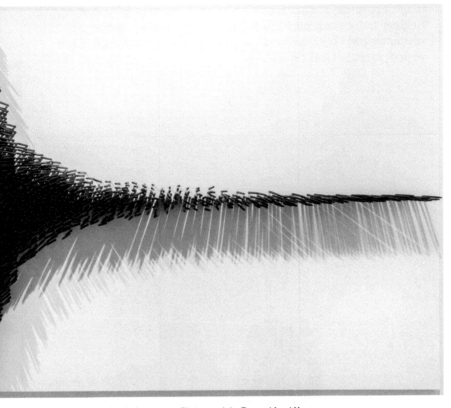

Satch Hoyt, *Afro-Sonic Snarewave*. Photograph by Trevor Lloyd Morgan.

Nzinga, she's the sister with the almond-shaped eyes, sweats a
  manifesto.
Salty tears slide down her cheeks, her furrowed brow resembles a
  music manuscript, a score so minimal, notes barely exist. She
  whispers the oratorio, her high notes screech like finger nails on a
  chalk board, the middle register notes climb up an invisible ladder
  to hit the rafters of her resilient skull. It's a riot chant, an ode to a
  world that twofold limps and lies, but begs to be revitalized.

Nostalgic conversations like tags sprayed on the walls of billions of brilliant brains are brought to the fore, which in turn reinstate the revolution back onto the frontline grid. Yeah, didn't you know it's an actual place, not just a metaphor.

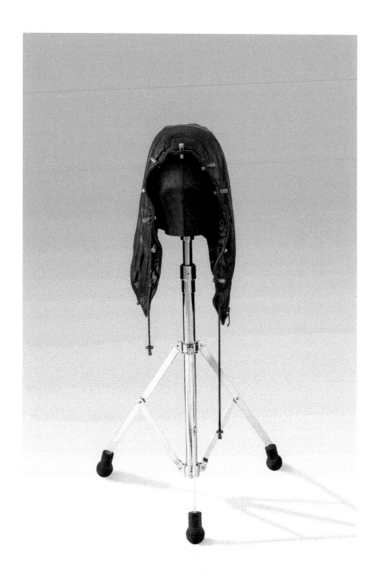

Satch Hoyt, *Hoodwinked*, 2019. Photograph by Trevor Lloyd Morgan.

Satch Hoyt, *Hair Combing Cycle 1530*. Photograph by Trevor Lloyd Morgan.

We're all out here, looking all out there, for those rare utopian moments,
  but hey, when we gonna realize they are very much here. They pump and
  pulse, pulsate from deep, deep, deep within.
Enchanting parables in live stream time zones, wave float you out to
  unchartered trans-cen-dental shores.
Whilst holding court to recount tales you kind of nearly dreamt of, but never
  really imagined could exist.
It's at times like this that you profoundly realize.
All the freedoms that you picture, all the happy endings that you've read,
  are undeniably so realizable.
They all begin as dreams inside your head.

"Unthreading Thoughts on The Riot in My Head"

Treason, uprisings, riots, and revolts.
Manifestation *mais oui* yes walk *la manif* on your bare hands of reason
the creeds on the banners, and the slogans all flutter
the chants ricochet off the buildings and collide with the cold biting
  northern wind
Not incognito, We, we traverse terrains *très* un-still with
the old detonated landmines of some near forgotten coup d'état.
Those cosmopolitan Babylon City pavements are tremendously loaded
Loaded with the daily trundle of footsteps swathed in some Brand or
  fake brand
the masses that flocked to the capital to seek their fortune
only to find unemployment at the shrine of the Job Centre
and those that fly in, in private jets to exploit those at that very same
  shrine.
You're not encouraged to, but you might want to Ne-go-sho-ate,
Negotiate with what? with who? negotiate to unravel a crowded future
  loaded with fossilized burdens
Yet we all witness the full moon, we all swim the oceans, we all make
  love,
we all have the propensity to love and be loved.
When the patriarchal stalagmite crumbles into dust and the yin and
  yang unite
then we might begin to see the light at the end of the long winding
  tunnel.

SAHMAT: Cultures of Dissent and Collective Memory

Assembled by Natasha Ginwala from Sahmat Resources

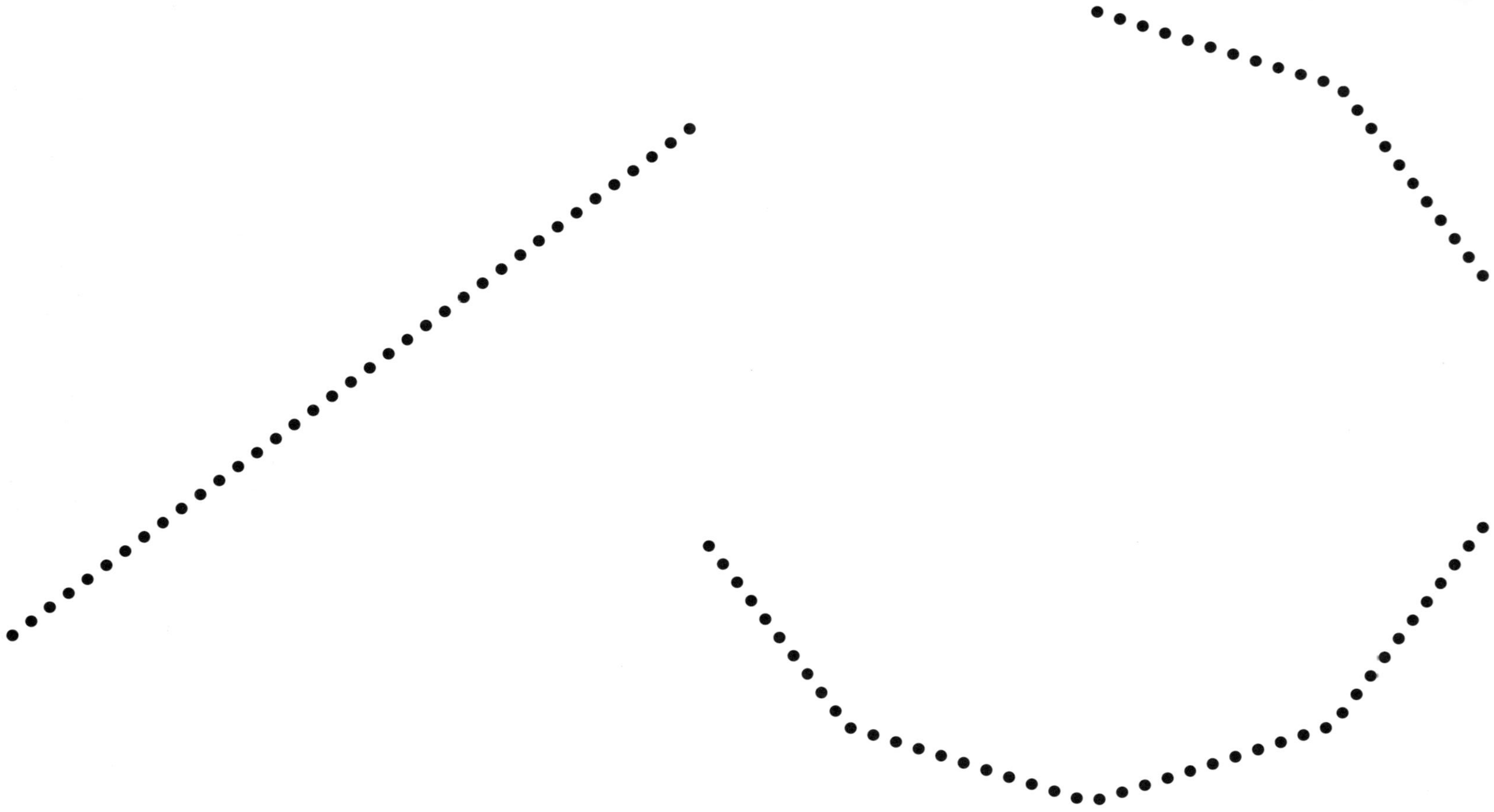

ASSEMBLED BY NATASHA GINWALA FROM SAHMAT RESOURCES

T

A fatal attack by political thugs on the political activist, actor, playwright, and poet, Safdar Hashmi, during a street performance in January 1989 led to the formation of SAHMAT—the name is both an acronym for the Safdar Hashmi Memorial Trust and the Hindi word for "in agreement."[1] In the posters, publications, concerts, and exhibitions organized by the Delhi-based SAHMAT collective, we find aesthetic and sociopolitical strategies that rose against the forces of religious extremism to defend artistic freedom, secular traditions, and plurality in history-telling. This visual folio highlights key interventions made by SAHMAT members, including visual artists, musicians, documentary filmmakers, architects, writers, and theatermakers from across India. The exhibition *Riots: Slow Cancellation of the Future* at ifa Gallery (Berlin and Stuttgart) included a display from the organization's archive and materials showing their cultural gatherings, publications, and regular collective actions. SAHMAT rapidly responded to the demolition of the nearly 500-year-old Babri Masjid (Babur's Mosque) on December 6, 1992 by Hindu nationalist groups and right-wing mobs, to the Bombay riots (1992–1993), and to the Gujarat riots (2002), among other dark chapters in Indian history that have threatened the country's communal harmony and collective memories of a secular India.

Particular highlights include artist Vivan Sundaram's *Memorial* (1993), a significant installation shown as part of the exhibition *Ways of Resisting* (2002–2003), curated by the artist, who is a founding member and trustee of SAHMAT. Critic and curator Geeta Kapur notes, "His sculptural installation *Memorial*, based on the newspaper photograph taken in the midst of the communal riots by the Bombay photographer, Hoshi Jal, positions the dead man on the street as an icon of political shame. In an elegiac act the artist gives the man a mantle of nails, places the iron coffin on a gun carriage, buries him on behalf of the State. The act tries to retrieve a political ethic through an acknowledgement of public death."[2]

The exhibition *Ways of Resisting* marked a decade (1992–2002) of mounting communal segregation, the erosion of democratic values, and anti-Muslim violence—from the demolition of the Babri Masjid to state oppression in Kashmir to massacres and rioting in Gujarat—that were part of a sweeping Hindutva mandate consolidating efforts of right-wing forces in the country. Practices of syncretic Sufi-Bhakti traditions, fluid identity lines formed through heterodox ancestries and social backgrounds, oral histories, and a public culture of vibrant debate gave way to tides of communalism not only in the political milieu but also within state-led education curricula, mainstream media, and civic life. *Ways of Resisting* cultivated a closer relationship between politically conscious installation art, performance, and documentary photography.

1. See *SAHMAT, 20 Years, 1989–2009: A Document of Activities and Statements* (New Delhi: Safdar Hashmi Memorial Trust, 2009).
2. Jessica Moss and Ram Rahman, eds., *The Sahmat Collective: Art and Activism in India since 1989* (Chicago: Smart Museum of Art, University of Chicago, 2013), 162.

The historic effort of this exhibition, bringing together thirty-five artists, three artist groups, and several documentary filmmakers to chronicle resistance strategies, acts of commemoration, and mourning and to offer counter-narratives, is vital to recall today. These works bring to light the erasures brought on by the fundamentalist reign and authoritarian rule of the Bharatiya Janata Party between 1998 and 2004 and in the current Narendra Modi government.[3]

The work *Burial* (2001) by Veer Munshi shows an inverted boat and self-portrait of the artist in an allusion to a funeral pyre. Munshi's installation addresses how the boat becomes a space of refuge but also of mourning, instead of simply floating along the reflective waters of Dal Lake. This installation also confronts the trials of misidentification, the military presence in the Kashmir valley, and the daily terror for communities caught up in the circuit of violence, disappearance, and displacement across a contested territory prone to geopolitical tensions between India and Pakistan.[4] Sheba Chhachhi and Sonia Jabber's photo-text installation *"When the Gun Is Raised, Dialogue Stops...": Kashmiri Women Speak* (2000) and Inder Salim's poster installation *Indersalim@indiatimes.com* (2002) deeply engage with the torment of Kashmiris through decades of state violence, with Kashmiri identity in exile, with testimonial production—especially of widows, martyrs, and missing persons—and with the unrequited pursuit of a peaceful homeland.

Sudhir Patwardhan's *Riot* (1996) uses his distinctive style of narrative realism to chronicle the working class, subaltern lives, and the social history of Bombay (now Mumbai). In this painting, the metropolis faces the dramatic consequences of a ruptured social fabric, growing animosity, and communal trauma in the aftermath of the 1992 Bombay Riots.

Parthiv Shah, another founding member of SAHMAT, designed several posters and pamphlets for cultural gatherings and protests alike. He composed this series of monochromatic photographs, *Jan Gan Man*, taken in Ahmedabad after the 2002 riots, to memorialize community strife and economic losses as well as the destruction of innate kinship and cultural affinity. This image was published in *Working in the Mill No More* co-authored with Jan Bremen.[5]

3. Geeta Kapur, "Secular Artist, Citizen Artist," in Moss and Rahman, *The Sahmat Collective*, 271–275.
4. *Ways of Resisting*, exhibition note by Veer Munshi, shared by Vivan Sundaram over email correspondence, SAHMAT archive, 2002–2003.
5. Parthiv Shah and Jan Bremen, *Working in the Mill No More* (Amsterdam; Oxford: Amsterdam University Press and Oxford University Press, 2004).

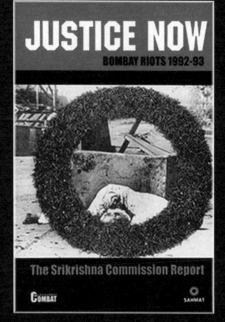

"Justice Now Bombay Riots—The Srikrishna Commission Report," August 2007. Cover image, Vivian Sundaram, *Burial II.*, from the series *Fallen Mortal*, 1993. Courtesy of SAHMAT.

Nilima Sheikh. Courtesy of SAHMAT.

Orjit Sen, *One May Seek Him in Mekka, One May Search for Him in Kashi... I have Found my Beloved, Should I Not Embrace Him?*, Ifa Gallery Berlin. Courtesy of the artist and SAHMAT.

What then are our invocations?

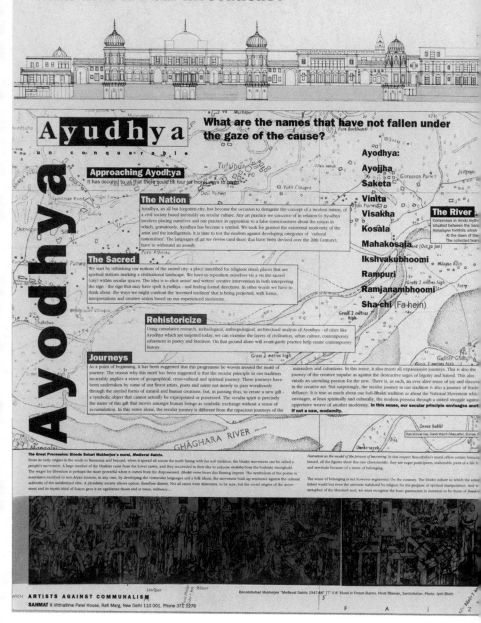

Ayudhya
un·con·quer·able

What are the names that have not fallen under the gaze of the cause?

Approaching Ayodhya
It has occured to us that there could be four (or more) ways to begin:

The Nation
Ayodhya, an all but forgotten city, has become the occasion to denigrate the concept of a modern nation, of a civil society based inevitably on secular culture. Any art practice we conceive of in relation to Ayodhya involves placing ourselves and our practice in opposition to a false consciousness about the nation in which, gratuitously, Ayodhya has become a symbol. We took for granted the existential modernity of the artist and the intelligentsia. It is time to test the modern against developing categories of 'cultural nationalism'. The languages of art we devise (and those that have been devised over the 20th Century), have to withstand an assault.

The Sacred
We start by rethinking our notions of the sacred city: a place sanctified for religious ritual; places that are spiritual stations marking a civilisational landscape. We have to reposition ourselves vis a vis the sacred (city) within secular spaces. The idea is to elicit artists' and writers' creative intervention in both interpreting the sign - the sign that may have spelt Ayodhya - and finding formal directions. In other words we have to think about the ways we might confront the 'invented tradition' that is being projected, with forms, interpretations and creative action based on our experienced modernity.

Rehistoricize
Using cumulative research, archaeological, anthropological, architectural analysis of Ayodhya - of cities like Ayodhya which are targeted today, we can examine the layers of civilisation, urban culture, contemporary references in poetry and literature. On that ground alone will avant-garde practice help create contemporary history.

Journeys
As a point of beginning, it has been suggested that this programme be woven around the motif of journey. The reason why this motif has been suggested is that the secular principle in our tradition invariably implies a sense of geographical, cross-cultural and spiritual journey. These journeys have been undertaken by some of our finest artists, poets and saints not merely to pass wondrously through the myriad forms of natural and human creations, but, in passing thus, to create a new gift - a symbolic object that cannot actually be expropriated or possessed. The secular spirit is precisely the name of this gift that moves amongst human beings as symbolic exchange without a sense of accumulation. In this sense alone, the secular journey is different from the rapacious journeys of the marauders and colonizers. In this sense, it also resists all expansionist journeys. This is also the journey of the creative impulse as against the destructive urges of bigotry and hatred. This also entails an unending passion for the new. There is, as such, an ever alive sense of joy and discovery in the creative act. Not surprisingly, the secular journey in our tradition is also a journey of fearless defiance. It is true as much about our Sufi-Bhakti tradition as about the National Movement which envisages, at least spiritually and culturally, the modern persona through a united struggle against oppressive weave of another modernity. **In this sense, our secular principle envisages another, if not a new, modernity.**

The River
Consensus in Hindu myth... situated between the San... Himalayan foothills which... At the dawn of the... The collected tears...

Ayodhya:
Ayojjha
Saketa
Vinita
Visakha
Kosala
Mahakosala
Ikshvakubhoomi
Rampuri
Ramjanambhoomi
Sha-chi (Fa-hein)

GHAGHARA RIVER

The Great Procession: Binode Behari Mukherjee's mural, Medieval Saints.

From its early origins in the south to Ramanuja and beyond, when it spread all across the north fusing with the sufi tradition, the bhakti movement can be called a people's movement. A large number of the bhaktas came from the lower castes, and they succeeded in their day to unloose moksha from the brahmin stronghold. The wager for liberation is perhaps the more powerful when it comes from the dispossessed. Bhakti verse bears this flaming imprint. The symbolism of the poetry is sometimes ascribed to non-Aryan sources; in any case, by developing the vernacular languages and a folk idiom, the movement built up resistance against the cultural authority of the sanskritized elite. A pluralistic society allows option, therefore dissent. Not all saints were dissenters, to be sure, but the social origins of the movement and its mystic ideal of fusion gave it an egalitarian thrust and at times, militancy...

Narration as the model of the process of becoming. In this respect Benodbehari's mural offers certain formula... ... larized, all the figures share this one characteristic: they are eager participants, inalienable parts of a life for... and servitude because of a sense of belonging.

The sense of belonging is not however regimental. On the contrary. The bhakti culture to which the artist ... linked would but even the universe stabilised by religion for the purpose of spiritual manipulation. And w... metaphor of the liberated soul, we must recognise the basic parameters in narration to be those of freedom...

ARTISTS AGAINST COMMUNALISM
SAHMAT 8 Vitthalbhai Patel House, Rafi Marg, New Delhi 110 001. Phone 371 1276

Ayodhya: What then are our invocations?, poster, 24 × 38 in, May 1993. Design by Ram Rahman; Texts by Charles Correa, Geeta Kapur, Madan Gopal Singh, and Ram Rahman, with contributions from Rajendra Prasad; Architectural drawings by Ravindra Bhan. Courtesy of SAHMAT.

Vivan Sundaram, *Burial*, iron nails, black-and-white photograph, 19 × 24 × 12 in, 1993.
Courtesy of the artist.

Vivian Sundaram, from the *Fallen Mortal* series, black-and-white photograph with nails, 1993.
Courtesy of the artist.

In response to the events of the riots in Bombay (today Mumbai), sparked by a violent conflict between Hindu and Muslim groups in 1992–1993, artist Vivan Sundaram produced a series of works based on a newspaper photograph taken by photojournalist Hoshi Lal. The room-filling installation *Memorial: An Installation with Photographs and Sculpture* was first shown in 1993 in New Delhi and consists of various sculptures and photographs centering around the newspaper image of an anonymous riot victim.

Vivian Sundaram, *Gun Carriage*, acrylic sheet, steel, black-and-white photograph.
Installation view of *Memorial: A Installation with Photographs and Sculpture*, from the
exhibition *Century City: Art and Culture in the Modern Metropolis*, Tate Modern, London, 2001.

जन गण
जन–गण
जन–गण
जन–गण

Photograph by Parthiv Shah from the SAHMAT collection. Courtesy of Parthiv Shah.

Veer Munshi, *Burial*, 2001, photographs, boat, cart, plastic flowers.

'89

चौराहा

September
Chauraha
All India Street Theatre Festival,
Delhi

सफदर समारोह

Janotsav Mangolpuri, Delhi.

April 12–16
National Street Theatre Day
Safdar Samaroh
Artists Alert

April 12
National Street Theatre Day

Safdar was
fatally attacked
on January 1 in
Sahibabad

SAHMAT was
formed in
February 1989

January 1

Homage to Safdar

'90

College Road,
Mandi House,
Delhi, renamed
Safdar Hashmi Marg

January 1

Artists Against Communalism

Popular
Intervention
for Communal Harmony

'92

अनहद गर्जे

January 1

February–April
Anhad Garje Tour
Bombay • Ahmedabad
Valod • Baroda • Surat
Lucknow

August 9

चौराहा '91

October
Chauraha
All India Street Theatre Festival,
Delhi

December 7–13
Protest at demolition
of Babri Masjid New Delhi

April 12

Images
and
Words
Delhi
Travels to 30 cities
August 1991 to
March 1992

April 12
National
Street
Theatre Day

August
Film Festival, Delhi

March
Artists Against Communalism, Bombay

'93

November

मुक्तनाद

August 14–15

10 Years सहमत 10 साल

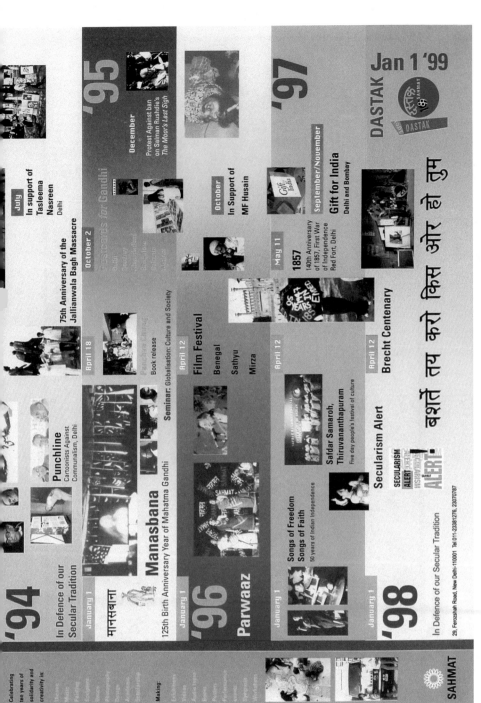

10 Years SAHMAT, 1989–1999, 1999, poster. Courtesy of SAHMAT.

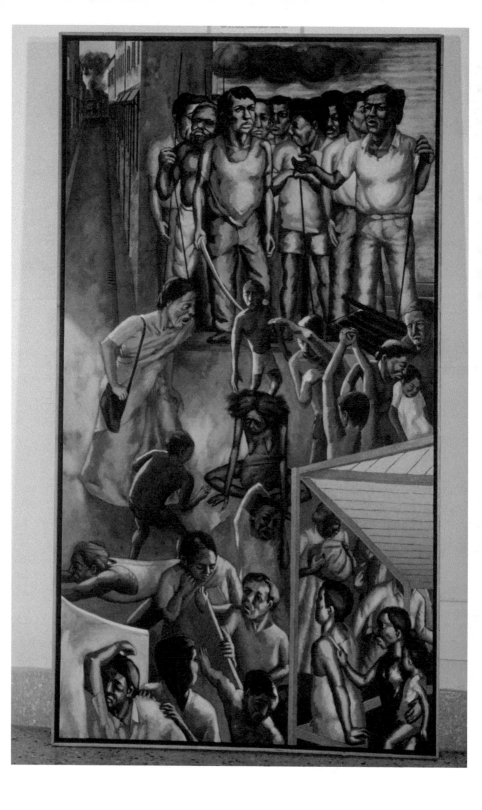

Sudhir Patwardhan, *Riot*, 1996, acrylic on canvas. Courtesy of National Gallery of Modern Art, Delhi.

The Time Is Still, Always, Now!

Josh Kun

T

In 1965, Robert F. Williams gave Santiago Álvarez a recording by Lena Horne. Williams, the civil rights leader and Black radical writer, was at the end of his four-year stay in exile in Havana. Álvarez, a founding member of the Instituto Cubano del Arte e Industria Cinematográficos (ICAIC) and the director of its companion Noticiero Latinoamericano, was already known as the Cuban Revolution's newsreel wizard and most innovative documentarian. The recording by Horne—the celebrated Broadway and Hollywood star—that passed between their hands was "Now!," a punchy Broadway-spun protest song that decried US racism and called for resistance and mass action by African Americans, written for her by Jewish American stage and screen songwriting veterans Jule Styne, Adolph Green, and Betty Comden.

For Álvarez, the song was a trigger. Its lyrics called up memories of segregation and anti-Black racism in the United States, where he had worked as a coal miner and a dishwasher in the 1930s. "After listening to it multiple times," he said, "it occurred to me to make a documentary in time with this song." The song's lyrics, penned by Comden and Green, became the script—or, as Álvarez put it, "As you follow the song, you write the script." In the closing shot, he spells out the title in bullet holes.[1]

Now! (the film) lasts as long as "Now!" (the song), and Álvarez paired the lyrics with a rhythmic barrage of quick-cut images that he pulled from whatever sources he could get his hands on: newsreels, the pages of *Life* magazine, and photos from books and newspapers published in the United States. Álvarez and his editor, Norma Torrado, zoomed in and out over still and moving images of police beatings of African Americans, the 1965 Watts Rebellion, street protests, the KKK, Nazi Germany, a meeting between Dr. Martin Luther King Jr. and President Lyndon B. Johnson, an edited beheading and reheading of the Lincoln Memorial, and a collage of portraits of Horne herself. In other words, a year before Michael Lindsay-Hogg famously cut moving images together to accompany the Beatles' "Paperback Writer," Álvarez made a music video for a Lena Horne song. He made a film using a song as both script and score.

This improvisatory approach to cutting and mixing both sound and image was Álvarez's sweet spot. He was an archivist at heart, an image collector and digger, whose métier was working with found media ("handling millions of feet of

● 1. This essay would be impossible without the intellectual collaborations of my colleague and friend Michael Renov, who first introduced me to the work of Santiago Álvarez. My thinking about this film has been shaped every step of the way by his expertise on documentary cinema. My thoughts here are just a small part of our ongoing and forthcoming collective work together on the film's history and impact. See Santiago Álvarez, "With Santiago Álvarez, Chronicler of the Third World," interview by Luciano Castillo and Manuel M. Hadad, *ReVista* 8, no. 3 (Fall 2009/Winter 2010): 54–57. I draw much of my background information on Álvarez from this interview and from Michael Chanan's scholarship on Álvarez in Michael Chanan, comp., *Santiago Álvarez: BFI Dossier, No. 2* (London: British Film Institute, 1980).

film," as he liked to say) and combining and recombining it in the editing process to invent new forms and tell new stories. It was an aesthetic practice born of the limits of working in an embargoed Cuba. "The reason for much of this inventiveness is necessity," Álvarez said. "The Americans blockade us, forcing us to improvise. For instance, the greatest inspiration in the photo-collages of American magazines in my films is the American government who has prevented me getting hold of live materials."[2] Thus, *Now!* became a prototype of what we might call a blockade aesthetic, a practice at the heart of Álvarez's riot filmmaking—a riotous method of audiovisuality that matches the radical political riot of the revolution.

Álvarez's blockade aesthetic, his craft of limits and media rations, was not limited to found images but extended to found sounds, songs, and music as well. Before the revolution, he worked as a music archivist for Cuban television and radio stations, "sorting music" that had been bought for on-air programming. As a result, he developed what he once described as "a kind of musical temperament," and he learned "to use music for given moments of an aesthetic operation."[3] *Now!* crystallized Álvarez's pirated song-meets-purloined-image approach to riot filmmaking. John Mraz has called Álvarez's technique "the militant art of image-recycling," but it was really a militant art of audiovisual recycling.[4] Álvarez was a proud inheritor of the tradition of filmic montage and its emphasis on making meaning through creative combination: the belief that, as montage pioneer Sergei Eisenstein wrote, "two film pieces of any kind, placed together, inevitably combine into a new concept, a new quality, arising out of that juxtaposition." Eisenstein famously called this new concept and quality "the third something."[5]

As an archivist and filmmaker working for and within the Cuban Revolution, Álvarez employed montage as a political aesthetic where a politics of form was inseparable from a politics of content. The combinations and juxtapositions that are seen and heard in *Now!* were part of a larger revolutionary project to combine and juxtapose different and disparate movements for freedom across the world. If, for Álvarez, "the meaning of any shot is determined by the set of relations... in which it is placed," as Mraz has argued, *Now!* must also be read as representing its own position in a Cuba linked to Cold War struggles across the Americas, Africa, and Asia.[6] It engages a lexicon of radical resistance that was echoing across global networks of insurrection at the very moment of its production.

2. Miguel Orodea, "Álvarez and Vertov," in *Santiago Álvarez*, comp. Chanan, 25.
3. Álvarez, "With Santiago Álvarez."
4. John Mraz, "Santiago Álvarez: From Dramatic Form to Direct Cinema," in *The Social Documentary in Latin America*, ed. Julianne Burton (Pittsburgh: University of Pittsburgh Press, 1990).
5. Sergei Eisenstein, *The Film Sense*, ed. and trans. Jay Leyda (New York: Meridian, 1957), 4.
6. Mraz, "Santiago Álvarez."

Following the 1966 Tricontinental Conference in Havana—a historic gathering of anti-imperialist solidarity and liberationist strategizing that drew over 500 delegates from eighty-two countries—the city became the launching pad for OSPAAAL, the Organization of Solidarity with the People of Asia, Africa, and Latin America. Álvarez linked images and sounds across this political geography to create networks of media and film as a corollary to the "networked political imaginaries" of the Tricontinental movement.[7] The "third something" of *Now!*'s montage was also a Third World something—a Third World cinema, a Third World song. Álvarez once said that his goal as a filmmaker was to "join things up in such a way that they pass before the spectator as a complete entity, with a single line of argument."[8] *Now!*'s joints and its single line of argument were a test case for Álvarez's belief that film was not merely an "extension of revolutionary action" but was, in fact, "revolutionary action itself."[9] The technique of cinematic montage was a technique of political montage, of joining together allied struggles against imperialism and global racism—the juxtaposition of image and sound as a juxtaposition of social movements, as a montage of shared struggle.

Before facilitating the juxtapositions of *Now!*, Horne's song—written two years earlier in 1963—contained juxtapositions of its own. Though Charlie Parker, on the A-side of a Savoy single, had declared "Now's the Time" back in 1945 (when it became clear that freedom abroad would not translate into freedom at home), by 1963 now really was the time. There was the March on Washington for Jobs and Freedom, the murder of President John F. Kennedy, the KKK bombing of the 16th Street Church in Alabama that buried four young African American girls beneath the dynamite rubble of hate, and the murder of civil rights leader Medgar Evers. Just days before Evers's death, Horne was with him on a tour of the US South, singing at his demonstrations. She was also there in DC, marching on Washington with Dr. King, all of it a culmination of her previous civil rights work, which included early support of communist organizations (which got her blacklisted), membership in the NAACP, active support of Progressive Citizens of America, and consistent attacks on systemic segregation.

By 1963, Horne—whose radical politics had rarely made it into the MGM-approved content of her work—knew that everything had changed, for her and for everyone. She said that she could no longer "sing the same old song." "How can I go on singing about a penthouse way up in the sky when, with housing restrictions the way they are now, I would not be

7. For a detailed study of Álvarez's connection to the Tricontinental movement, see Anne Garland Mahler, *From the Tricontinental to the Global South: Race, Radicalism, and Transnational Solidarity* (Durham, NC: Duke University Press, 2018).
8. Michael Chanan, "Introduction (In the Style of Santiago Álvarez)," in *Santiago Álvarez*, 6.
9. Orodea, "Álvarez and Vertov."

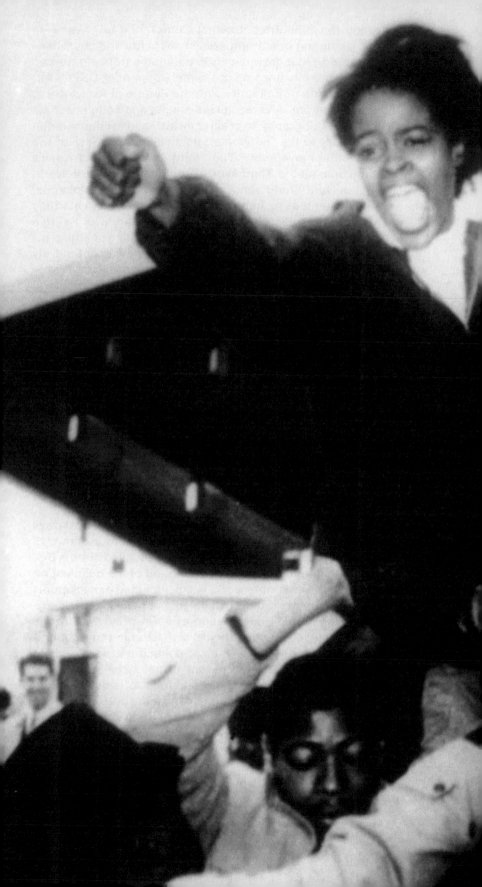

REMEMBER
MEDGAR
EVERS
A REAL AMERICAN
HERO!

GREATER NY COORDINATING
COMMITTEE FOR EQUAL
OPPORTUNITY

allowed to rent that place? I can't get up in a nightclub in a thousand-dollar dress and start singing 'Let My People Go'... I never had the right. I didn't choose it to be that way but it was the illusion that Hollywood gave me."[10]

In preparation for a planned 1963 Carnegie Hall benefit to support the Gandhi Society for Human Rights, where Horne would be introduced by Dr. King, she put the word out among her peers: now was the time for a new repertoire of songs. Harold Arlen and Yip Harburg came through with "Silent Spring," which converted Rachel Carson's call for environmental revolution into a call for civil rights revolution. And the aforementioned Broadway and Hollywood legends Comden, Green, and Styne—known for their work on shows like *Singin' in the Rain*, *Gypsy*, *Do Re Mi*, and so many others—gave Horne "Now!," with lyrics that went from pat calls for harmony ("everyone should love his brother") to strident calls for Black radical action ("the message of this song's not subtle, no discussion, no rebuttal, we want more than just a promise, say goodbye to Uncle Thomas").

Styne set these words to the tune of "Hava Nagila," the wordless nineteenth-century Hasidic *nigun* turned early twentieth-century Zionist folk song. Given lyrics inspired by the Psalms in 1918, "Hava Nagila" called for rejoicing and singing because, according to the Balfour Declaration of a year earlier, a "national home for the Jewish people" in Palestine was now possible. "Hava Nagila" became a Zionist anthem in Israel—featured in children's songbooks, popularized alongside its own dance (the hora)—but by the 1950s its celebratory Zionism was slightly defanged. It became a staple of the New York folk scene and was soon a global pop hit. Afro-Cuban bandleader Machito had reimagined it as his "Holiday Mambo" in 1931, and "Hava Nagila" went on to be covered by everyone from Cuban salsa queen Celia Cruz to Lebanese American surf guitar innovator Dick Dale. In 1959 Harry Belafonte, one of Horne's closest collaborators, inserted it into the African American civil rights songbook when he performed it live at Carnegie Hall. Soon numerous Black artists—many of them at the time more influenced by Jewish freedom struggles than Palestinian freedom struggles (a tendency that would change after the Six-Day War of 1967)—all made versions of "Hava Nagila." It even made an appearance in the 1961 film version of Lorraine Hansberry's *A Raisin in the Sun*. Horne herself was also no stranger to Israel. She visited in 1952, the same year she first played Havana, and she drew connections not between African Americans and Palestinians but between the plight of African Americans and Yemenite Jews, calling them "terribly oppressed people of color, people just emerging from the kind of bondage Negroes have been struggling so long to emerge from."[11]

10. James Gavin, *Stormy Weather: The Life of Lena Horne* (New York: Atria, 2009), 334.
11. Lena Horne and Richard Schickel, *Lena* (New York: Doubleday, 1965), 183.

So when Styne set lyrics about police terror and Black resistance to "Hava Nagila"—which Álvarez bills in *Now!*'s opening credits as a "canción hebrea," a Hebrew song—the juxtaposition was not as surprising as it may seem now. Horne sang her new song at Carnegie Hall for the 1963 benefit, and by all accounts it was the evening's smash hit. According to *Variety*, "Horne trimmed her normal output of sex and sin" and sang "of new worlds to come." She was urged to record it, which she quickly did with Ray Ellis for the 20th Century Fox label, using images of her Carnegie Hall performance to market the recording and sheet music. It was shipped nationwide, and Horne planned to donate the proceeds to the NAACP, but the song's promise was quickly foiled: one of its verses—her snide phrasing of "no one wants to grab your sister," a reference to stock racist white phobias of mythical Black male sexual preda-tion—got it banned from US radio. It never went above no. 92 on the Billboard charts, and as Comden said, "it never became what we wanted it to be." Horne dropped the song from her show, and it vanished.

That is, until Robert F. Williams passed it to Álvarez. By the time of the Cuban Revolution, African American music already had a long history in Cuban culture and entertainment—from early US jazz to the 1950s, when artists like Nat King Cole, Dorothy Dandridge, and Horne were regulars in Cuban night-clubs. Its presence remained after the Cuban Revolution in places like Williams's free-form weekly radio show, *Radio Free Dixie*. His Friday night cut-up mixtapes spliced rhythm and blues songs with instrumental jazz and excerpts of speeches, news footage, and protests. Williams was one of many Black US intellectuals, artists, and activists who supported the Cuban Revolution, visited Cuba in the early 1960s, and used African American art and music as a platform for transnational solidar-ity between the Black American freedom struggle, the Cuban Revolution, and decolonial uprisings in Asia, Africa, and Latin America. Horne's song was just one more contribution to an already rich archive of cultural production of the global, deco-lonial 1960s—a transnational "soul power" network of diasporic public spheres connecting Black America to the Black Americas, Black Africa, and global struggles against US imperialism.[12]

Nearly a decade before dub engineering arose in Jamaica and hip-hop took off in the South Bronx, these networks helped Álvarez be both DJ and VJ, mixing, sampling, and col-laging preexisting materials to create new ideas and political solidarities through thoughtful and strategic juxtaposition.

His prophetic cut-and-mix method would also go on to in-fluence filmmakers like John Akomfrah, of the Black Audio Film Collective in London, whose 1986 mix of sound sources, newsreel footage, and still photos about Black uprisings and

12. Cynthia A. Young, *Soul Power: Culture, Radicalism, and the Making of a US Third World Left* (Durham, NC: Duke University Press, 2006).

anti-Black police violence, *Handsworth Songs*, was an homage to Álvarez. More recently, Álvarez haunts Arthur Jafa's 2017 *Love Is the Message, the Message Is Death*, which, like *Now!*, is only as long as the song in it—in this case, Kanye West's "Ultralight Beam," which plays as Jafa cuts together purloined, watermarked photos with political speeches, tennis matches, and cell phone videos to re-member Black bodies dis-membered by racist violence. Like Álvarez, Jafa uses new assemblages of music and film, new juxtapositions and new joints, new media kinships, to repair what has been fractured, to connect broken histories, and to name the injured and the dead. Because now is always still the time.

The images that accompany this piece are all stills from *Now!*, directed by Santiago Álvarez (1965).

Biographies

Asef Bayat is the Catherine and Bruce Bastian Professor of Global and Transnational Studies and a professor of sociology at the University of Illinois, Urbana-Champaign. His latest books include *Post-Islamism: The Changing Faces of Political Islam* (Oxford University Press, 2013), *Life as Politics: How Ordinary People Change the Middle East* (Stanford University Press, 2013), *Revolution without Revolutionaries: Making Sense of the Arab Spring* (Stanford University Press, 2017), and *Global Middle East: Into the Twenty-First Century* (coedited with Linda Herrera; University of California Press, forthcoming 2021).

Joshua Clover is the author of seven books, including *Roadrunner* (Duke University Press, forthcoming 2021) as well as *Riot. Strike. Riot: The New Era of Uprisings* (Verso, 2016), a commentary on the political economy of social movements. A former journalist with the *Village Voice*, the *Nation*, and other publications, he is currently a professor of English and comparative literature at the University of California, Davis, as well as affiliated professor of literature and modern culture at the University of Copenhagen.

Vaginal Davis is an artist, musician, and performer in Los Angeles known for her "multiracial, maxigendered" bands and her influential zines and video work. From 1985 to 2002, she taught at the University of California, Los Angeles; California Institute of the Arts; Art Center School of Design; Otis Parsons School of Design; and New York University. She performs widely and teaches at HEAD University of Art and Design Geneva. Her paintings and video works are exhibited internationally. She is represented by Adams&Ollman, Portland; New Discretions, New York; and Galerie Isabella Bortolozzi, Berlin.

Keller Easterling is a designer, writer, and professor at Yale University. Her books include *Medium Design* (Verso, 2021), *Extrastatecraft: The Power of Infrastructure Space* (Verso, 2014), *Subtraction* (Sternberg, 2014), *Enduring Innocence: Global Architecture and Its Political Masquerades* (MIT Press, 2005), and *Organization Space: Landscapes, Highways, and Houses in America* (MIT Press, 1999).

Zena Edwards is a poet, mentor, and cultural producer, as well as the creative strategist for Verse In Dialog—a socially conscious arts enterprise championing "arts that serve." Edwards is internationally acclaimed as a writer and a vocalist and was the winner of the Hidden Creatives award in 2012.

Dilip Parameshwar Gaonkar is professor in rhetoric and public culture and the director of the Center for Global Culture and Communication at Northwestern University. He is also the director of the Center for Transcultural Studies and was the executive editor (2000–2009) and editor (2009–2011) of *Public Culture*. Gaonkar has edited a series of books on global cultural politics: *Globalizing American Studies* (with Brian Edwards, University of Chicago Press, 2010), *Alternative Modernities* (Duke University Press, 2001), and *Disciplinarity and Dissent in Cultural Studies* (Routledge, 1995).

Gauri Gill is a New Delhi-based photographer and visual artist. She has exhibited internationally at venues including the Venice Biennale; Museum Tinguely, Basel; MoMA PS1, New York; documenta 14, Athens and Kassel; the Kochi Biennale; and the Whitechapel Gallery, London. Her work is in the collections of the Museum of Modern Art, New York; the Tate Museum, London; and the Fotomuseum Winterthur, Switzerland, among other institutions.

Natascha Sadr Haghighian is a choreographer, performer, filmmaker, and producer. She studied film and media art at the Academy of Media Arts Cologne with Valie Export and at the School of the Art Institute of Chicago with Lin Hixson as part of a DAAD scholarship. She cofounded the Berlin drama and performance group machina eX and is a founding member of Fernwärme, a performance program of the project space Ausland, Berlin.

Louis Henderson is a filmmaker whose work addresses the ways our current global condition is defined by racial capitalism and ever-present histories of European colonialism. Developing an archaeological method in cinema, his films explore the sonic space of images, listening to the echoes and spirals of the stratigraphic. Since 2017 Henderson has been working within the artist group The Living and the Dead Ensemble. His work is distributed by LUX, Video Data Bank, and Phantom, and is produced by Spectre. He lives and works in Paris.

Satch Hoyt, of British and African-Jamaican ancestry, lives and works in Berlin. His sculpture, painting, and performances focus on the role of sound and music in the Transnational African Diaspora. His *Afro-Sonic Mapping* project, in its various manifestations, occupies his current practice.

Hamid Khan is the campaign coordinator for the Stop LAPD Spying Coalition, an alliance working to dismantle all surveillance and profiling practices used by the Los Angeles Police Department. He also founded the South Asian Network and is active in several other networks and grassroots initiatives for immigrant and refugee rights.

Gal Kirn has a PhD from the University of Nova Gorica in Slovenia. He has since worked, among other places, at the Berlin Institute for Cultural Inquiry, Humboldt University in Berlin, GWZO in Leipzig, and the Akademie Schloss Solitude. He is currently a research fellow at TU Dresden, where he researches the Soviet avant-garde and partisan memory. His book *Partisan Ruptures* was published by Pluto Press (2019), and *The Partisan Counter-Archive* is forthcoming from De Gruyter.

Josh Kun is chair in Cross-Cultural Communication and professor at the University of Southern California. His recent books include *The Tide Was Always High: The Music of Latin America in Los Angeles* (University of California Press, 2018), *Double Vision: The Photography of George Rodriguez* (Hat & Beard, 2018), and *The Autograph Book of LA: Improvements on the Page of the City* (Angel City Press, 2019). As a curator and artist, he has worked with SFMOMA, the Getty Foundation, the Grammy Museum, the California African American Museum, and the Vincent Price Art Museum, among others.

Léopold Lambert is the founding editor of the *Funambulist*. He is a trained architect, as well as the author of three books that examine the inherent violence of architecture on bodies, and the political instrumentalization of architecture at various scales and in various geographical contexts (Palestine, Paris *banlieues*, etc.). His forthcoming book examines the spatial history of the French states of emergency and colonial continuum.

Margit Mayer is a professor of comparative and North American politics at Freie Universität Berlin; since 2014 she has also been a senior fellow at the Center for Metropolitan Studies at Technical University Berlin. She coauthored *Nonprofits in the Transformation of Employment Policies* (2004) and has coedited books including *Urban Movements in a Globalising World* (Routledge, 2000), *Cities for People Not for Profit* (Routledge, 2012), *Neoliberal Urbanism and Its Contestations* (Palgrave Macmillan, 2012), and *Urban Uprisings: Challenging the Neoliberal City in Europe* (Palgrave Macmillan, 2016).

Vivek Narayanan was born in India and raised in Zambia. He was a fellow at the Radcliffe Institute at Harvard University (2013–2014) and a Cullman Fellow at the New York Public Library (2015–2016) while working on a book of poems about the ancient Indian epic poem *Ramayana*. His books of poems include *Universal Beach* (Harbour Line Press, 2006/In Girum Books, 2011) and *Life and Times of Mr S* (HarperCollins India, 2012). He is coeditor of *Almost Island*, and his writing has appeared in *Agni*, *Granta*, the *Village Voice*, *Harvard Review*, and *Caravan*, as well as several poetry anthologies.

Ai Ogawa (1947–2010) is the author of eight books of poetry, including the National Book Award–winning *Vice*. In 2009 she was named a United States Artist Ford Fellow. She was a professor at Oklahoma State University.

Oana Pârvan is a Romanian researcher with a PhD in cultural studies from Goldsmiths, University of London, where she is currently an assistant lecturer. She is also a member of the research and practice network Sound System Outernational, and she takes an interest in popular music cultures. Her work has been published in *Anglistica AION: An Interdisciplinary Journal*, *darkmatter: in the ruins of imperial culture*, and *MetaMute*. Her first monograph, *The Arab Spring between Transformation and Capture: Autonomy, Media and Mobility in Tunisia* will be published by Rowman and Littlefield.

Elizabeth A. Povinelli is an anthropologist and filmmaker. She is the Franz Boas Professor of Anthropology at Columbia University, New York; corresponding fellow of the Australian Academy for the Humanities; and one of the founding members of the Karrabing Film Collective. Recent publications include *Geontologies: A Requiem to Late Liberalism* (Duke University Press, 2016). Povinelli lives and works in New York and Darwin, Australia

Thomas Seibert is a philosopher and an activist based in Frankfurt. His most recent books include *Zur Ökologie der Existenz: Freiheit, Gleichheit, Umwelt* (Laika Verlag, 2017) and *Kritik und Aktualität der Revolution* (Mandelbaum, 2017), which he coedited with Martin Birkner.

Niloufar Tajeri is an architect, an activist, and a writer. She teaches in the department of history and theory of architecture and city at the TU Braunschweig, where she is pursuing a PhD. She coedited *Small Interventions: New Ways of Living in Post-War Modernism* (Birkhäuser, 2016) and *Kabul: Secure City Public City* (Archis, 2008). She has taught at the Institute of Architectural Design, Art, and Theory at the Karlsruhe Institute of Technology and has worked as an editor for *ARCH+* and *Volume*.

Dariouche Tehrani is a student in Paris. He follows movements against police violence in Paris *banlieues*. He is interested in the link between secularism, colonialism, and Christianity and the way in which this link frames state institutions.

Chandraguptha Thenuwara is an artist and a senior lecturer at the University of the Visual and Performing Arts Colombo. He is also the director of the Vibhavi Academy of Fine Arts, which he founded in 1993. He acquired his education in visual arts at the Institute of Aesthetic Studies, University of Kelaniya, Sri Lanka, and Surikov State Art Institute, Moscow, Russia. Thenuwara has exhibited widely in Sri Lanka and abroad.

Ala Younis is an artist based in Amman. Her work has been shown at the 56th Venice Biennale, the New Museum (2014), Home Works 5 (2010), the Istanbul Biennial (2011), and the Gwangju Biennial (2012), among other venues. She curated Kuwait's first national pavilion at the 55th Venice Biennale (2013), and in 2012 she cofounded the publishing initiative Kayfa ta. She is a member of the Advisory Board of Berlinale's Forum Expanded, as well as the Akademie of the Arts of the World in Cologne.

Acknowledgments

This book is a product of years of work consisting of multiple collaborations and ongoing conversations between editors, contributors, activists, artists, and publics across diverse institutional settings and social events. We would first like to express deep gratitude to the Graham Foundation for Advanced Studies in the Fine Arts for financially supporting this project. We would also like to thank ifa Gallery Berlin, Alya Sebti, ifa Gallery Stuttgart, Iris Lenz, as well as Akademie Schloss Solitude, Jean-Baptiste Joly, and Elke aus dem Moore, for granting us the space and resources to produce and exhibit our work on riots. Needless to say, we are incredibly grateful to Columbia Books on Architecture and the City for supporting this project and bearing with us throughout the process as we expanded the scope of contributions and worked amidst the challenging times of the pandemic. We would like to express our gratitude to a handful of wonderful individuals who have in their own ways contributed to this book and without whom this book would not be possible. Major thanks goes to Krisztina Hunya and Jesse Connuck for their assistance all along with the editing of the book, and to Isabelle Kirkham-Lewitt and Joanna Joseph for their editing and proofreading work at the final stages of production. We would also like to thank Remco van Bladel and Kimberley ter Heerdt for their design work that aims to reflect the topic through its varied design formats; and Eyal Weizman and Jodi Dean for their support at the start of the project.

To the long list of authors who contributed and allowed us to reproduce their artworks and images—Satch Hoyt, Dilip Parameshwar Gaonkar, Thomas Seibert, Vaginal Davis, Joshua Clover, Elizabeth A. Povinelli, Ai Ogawa, Ala Younis, Margit Mayer, Natascha Sadr Haghighian, Zena Edwards, Nadine El-Enany, Léopold Lambert, Dariouche Tehrani, Asef Bayat, Gauri Gill, Vivek Narayanan, Oana Pârvan, Louis Henderson, Chandraguptha Thenuwara, SAHMAT, and Josh Kun—we warmly thank you. The project grew out of Gal Kirn and Niloufar Tajeri's residency at the Akademie Schloss Solitude in 2015–2016 and the public program "Riots: Dissent and Specters, Control, and Ruptures" at ACUD Macht Neu, Berlin, in 2018, with further contributions by Benedict Seymour and screenings by Alex Johnston and Daniel Tutt. The program accompanied the group exhibition *Riots: Slow Cancellation of the Future* at ifa Gallery Berlin and Stuttgart, curated by Natasha Ginwala and assistant curator Krisztina Hunya. For further information, we invite you to visit: http://untietotie.org/en/phase-1/#exhibition/chapter-4.

We hope that readers enjoy this interdisciplinary and collaborative journey into a subject that will continue to redefine our times and "shake the ground" in the words of Keller Easterling, who was kind enough to write a thoughtful foreword for this book.

Columbia Books on Architecture and the City
An imprint of the Graduate School of
Architecture, Planning, and Preservation

Columbia University
1172 Amsterdam Ave
407 Avery Hall
New York, NY 10027

arch.columbia.edu/books

Distributed by Columbia University Press
cup.columbia.edu

Nights of the Dispossessed: Riots Unbound

Editors: Natasha Ginwala, Gal Kirn,
and Niloufar Tajeri
Editorial Assistant: Krisztina Hunya
Contributors: Asef Bayat, Joshua Clover,
Vaginal Davis, Zena Edwards, Nadine El-Enany,
Dilip Parameshwar Gaonkar, Gauri Gill, Natasha
Ginwala, Natascha Sadr Haghighian, Louis
Henderson, Satch Hoyt, Gal Kirn, Josh Kun,
Léopold Lambert, Margit Mayer, Vivek Narayanan,
Ai Ogawa, Oana Pârvan, Elizabeth A. Povinelli,
SAHMAT, Thomas Seibert, Niloufar Tajeri,
Chandraguptha Thenuwara, Dariouche Tehrani,
and Ala Younis.

ISBN: 978-1-941332-63-4
LCCN: 2020925243

Director of Publications: Isabelle Kirkham-
Lewitt
Associate Editor: Joanna Joseph

Project Editor: Jesse Connuck
Copyeditor: Erica Olsen
Graphic Designer: Studio Remco van Bladel
Printer: Raddraaier SSP, Amsterdam
Paper: Munken Lynx, Crush Kiwi
Typefaces: Monument Grotesk

This book has been produced through the Office
of the Dean, Amale Andraos, and the Office of
Publications at Columbia University GSAPP.

This project was supported by a generous grant
from The Graham Foundation for Advanced Studies
in the Fine Arts.

Graham
Foundation

The publication was initiated with the public
program "Riots: Dissent and Spectres, Control
and Ruptures" organized by Natasha Ginwala,
Gal Kirn, and Niloufar Tajeri, at Acud Macht Neu,
January 26–27, 2018, supported by ifa Gallery
Berlin.